The Designation of Marine Protected Areas

Anna von Rebay

The Designation of Marine Protected Areas

A Legal Obligation

Springer

Anna von Rebay
Munich, Germany

ISBN 978-3-031-29174-6 ISBN 978-3-031-29175-3 (eBook)
https://doi.org/10.1007/978-3-031-29175-3

This Springer imprint is published by the registered company Springer Nature Switzerland AG
The registered company address is: Gewerbestrasse 11, 6330 Cham, Switzerland

Two families so dear,
always far and always near,
One in the northern and one in the southern
hemisphere.
When we see the lights in the stars so
luminous,
That reflect on the skin of the octopus,
The realization of oneness enlightens us:
Never far, even when not here,
my dear Marcus.

Acknowledgement

'We must save the oceans if we are to save ourselves' was the famous declaration of the First Lady of the Ocean, Elisabeth Mann Borgese, a marine biologist and one of the early women in the law of the sea, who vigorously dedicated her life to the protection of the marine environment. Like her, this treatise was born in Munich, Bavaria and gratefully took the author on journeys around the world to investigate the actual questions impeding effective marine protection in the remotest islands of Indonesia, across scholarly debates in Australia and to the judicial centre for the law of the sea in Hamburg. It is thus in the spirit of the words of the Mother of the Oceans that this investigation set out to prove that States are obliged to protect and preserve the marine environment—an obligation that is legally binding.

This dissertation was submitted to the faculty of law of the University of Potsdam, Germany in the summer term of 2022 and was awarded the academic title "*Dr. jur.*". The investigations consider publications until October 2021. The composition of this preface allows for the opportunity to humbly thank many people for the support I have received.

My special thanks, first and foremost, goes to my doctoral supervisor, Prof. Dr. M. Schladebach. Not only did he provide me with the freedom to choose a topic which is the expression of my passion for the world's ocean as well as litigation, but also contributed significantly to the success of this thesis with his trust and encouragement. I am grateful to Prof. Dr. N. Weiß for the speedy revision and provision of the second assessment of my work.

A considerable contribution to the awakening of my interest in the law of the sea was due to the Summer Academy at the International Tribunal for the Law of the Sea, then organised by the honourable J. König, who motivated and provided inspiration to every single participant. I am grateful for the opportunity to have met the judges of the Tribunal and the successor of the organisation of the Summer Academy, Prof. Dr. A. Proelss, whose works are a major source of reference for this book. On my journeys through the world, I was lucky enough to meet Prof. Dr. T. Stephens, who not only offered his valuable time to discuss topics in the law of the sea but also provided me the exceptional opportunity to deliver a guest lecture at the University of Sydney, an opportunity that showed me the importance of education and passion to this end.

This dissertation was nominated for the *Better World Award* by the University of Potsdam and Land Brandenburg Lotto GmbH, which deserves my heartfelt gratitude.

The sincerest appreciations and thankfulness go to my families in the northern and in the southern hemisphere—it wasn't without their support that this journey departed, was pursued and concluded, all in the name of saving the oceans. It is one person, though, whose light shines through the lines of every single page of this book: with my deepest gratitude, this work is dedicated to my partner in adventure and life, Marcus.

Contents

List of Abbreviations

ABNJ	Areas Beyond National Jurisdiction
Antarctic Treaty	1959 Antarctic Treaty with its 1991 Protocol on Environmental Protection to the Antarctic Treaty and Annexes
ARS	2001 Articles on the Responsibility of States for Internationally Wrongful Acts (UNGA A/56/49(Vol. I)/Corr.4)
AUNJ	Areas Under National Jurisdiction
Barcelona Convention	1995 Convention for the Protection of Marine Environment and the Coastal Region of the Mediterranean
BBNJ	(upcoming) International legally binding instrument under the United Nations Convention on the Law of the Sea on the conservation and sustainable use of marine biological diversity of areas beyond national jurisdiction
BGBl.	Bundesgesetzblatt
Bonn Convention	1997 Bonn Convention on the Conservation of Migratory Species
BWM Convention	2004 International Convention for the Control and Management of Ships' Ballast Water and Sediments
Cartagena Convention	1983 Convention for the Protection and Development of the Marine Environment of the Wider Caribbean Region
CBD	1992 United Nations Convention on Biological Diversity
CCAMLR	1980 Convention for the Conservation of Antarctic Marine Living Resources
CCS	1958 Geneva Convention on the Continental Shelf
CFCLR	1958 Geneva Convention on Fishing and Conservation of the Living Resources of the High Seas
CHS	1958 Geneva Convention on the High Seas

CITES	1975 Convention on International Trade in Endangered Species of Wild Fauna and Flora
CTSCZ	1958 Geneva Convention on the Territorial Sea and the Contiguous Zone
Draft-BBNJ	2019 Revised draft text of an agreement under the United Nations Convention on the Law of the Sea on the conservation and sustainable use of marine biological diversity of areas beyond national jurisdiction, United Nations General Assembly, UNGA A/CONF.232/2020/3
ECHR	1950 European Convention on Human Rights
ECtHR	European Court of Human Rights
EEZ	Exclusive Economic Zone
EU	European Union
FAO	United Nations Food and Agriculture Organization
German Basic Law	1949 Basic Law for the Federal Republic of Germany
ICJ	International Court of Justice
ICJ Statute	1945 Statute of the International Court of Justice
ICTY.	International Criminal Tribunal for the former Yugoslavia
ILC	International Law Conference
IMO	International Maritime Organization
ISA	International Seabed Authority
ITLOS	International Tribunal for the Law of the Sea
IUCN	International Union for Conservation of Nature
IWC	1946 Convention for the Regulation of Whaling
Kuwait Convention	1978 Kuwait Regional Convention for Co-operation on the Protection of the Marine Environment from Pollution
LAT	Lowest Astronomical Tide
London Convention	1972 Convention on the Prevention of Marine Pollution by Dumping of Wastes and Other Matter
Marine Strategy Directive	2008 Marine Strategy Framework Directive 2008/56/EC
MARPOL	1973/78 International Convention for the Prevention of Marine Pollution from Ships
Montreal Guidelines	1985 Montreal Guidelines for the Protection of the Marine Environment against Pollution from Land-based Sources
MPA	Marine Protected Area
Natura 2000 Directives	1979 Birds Directive 2009/147/EC and 1992 Habitats Directive 92/43/EEC
NEAFC	North-East Atlantic Fisheries Commission
Oil Spills Protocol	1983 Protocol Concerning Co-operation in Combating Oil Spills in the Wider Caribbean Region
Oslo Convention	1972 Convention for the Prevention of Marine Pollution by Dumping from Ships and Aircraft

OSPAR	1992 Convention for the Protection of the Marine Environment of the North-East Atlantic
PCA	Permanent Court of Arbitration
PCIJ	Permanent Court of International Justice
Ramsar Convention	1971 Convention on Wetlands of International Importance especially as Waterfowl Habitat
Rio Declaration	1992 Rio Declaration on Environment and Development, UNGA A/CONF.151/26 (Vol. I)
SOLAS	1974 International Convention for the Safety of Life at Sea
SPAW Protocol	1990 Protocol Concerning Specially Protected Areas and Wildlife
Stockholm Declaration	1972 Declaration of the United Nations Conference on the Human Environment, adopted at Stockholm, UN Doc A/CONF/48/14
TFEU	2007 Treaty on the Functioning of the European Union
TSS	Traffic Separation Schemes
UN	United Nations
UN-Charter	1945 Charter of the United Nations
UNCLOS	1982 United Nations Convention on the Law of the Sea
UNCLOS I	First United Nations Conferences on the Law of the Sea, 1958 in Geneva
UNCLOS III	Third United Nations Conference of the Law of the Sea, from 1973 to 1982
UNEP	United Nations Environment Programme
UNFSA	1995 United Nations Agreement for the Implementation of the Provisions of the UNCLOS relating to the Conservation and Management of Straddling Fish Stocks and Highly Migratory Fish Stocks
UNTS	United Nations Treaty Series
VCLT	1969 Vienna Convention on the Law of Treaties
World Heritage Convention	1972 Convention for the Protection of the World Cultural and Natural Heritage

Chapter 1
Introduction

1.1 Problem and Resulting Research Question

> Hail! Hail! Anew! How happy I feel, too,
> Pierced by the Beautiful and True.... All things came from the watery view!
> All things are sustained by water! Ocean, grant us your realm forever.
> (Thales of Miletus, in Johann Wolfgang von Goethe's drama Faust II)[1]

We are living on a blue planet. More than two-thirds of planet Earth's surface consist of water.[2] And yet, not even the grandness of the ocean is immune against the deteriorating effects of human activities.[3] Plastic debris in the ocean will outweigh fish by 2050 unless people cease to use single-use plastic items.[4] According to the 2018 SOFIA-Report by the United Nations Food and Agriculture Organization (FAO), almost 90% of the world's marine fish stock is fully fished or overfished.[5] The bottom of the deep sea, one of the last pristine areas of the world, untouched by humankind, is about to be excavated by deep seabed mining with unknown consequences. [6] In the light of these facts, is mankind of the twenty-first century still eligible to call upon the ocean like Goethe's dramatic figure Thales of Miletus to grant us its realm forever?[7]

---

[1]Goethe (1832), V. 8432–8437–1832 (translated by author).

[2]https://www.itlos.org/fileadmin/itlos/documents/statements_of_president/wolfrum/uebersee_club_270208_eng.pdf, p. 6.

[3]Molenaar (2007), p. 625.

[4]https://www.ellenmacarthurfoundation.org/assets/downloads/publications/NPEC-Hybrid_English_22-11-17_Digital.pdf, pp. 12, 22; https://news.un.org/en/story/2017/04/556132-feature-uns-mission-keep-plastics-out-oceans-and-marine-life.

[5]FAO (2018), pp. 39 f.

[6]Schladebach and Esau (2012), p. 142.

[7]The Greek mathematician, astronomer and philosopher Thales of Miletus was regarded by many, most notably Aristotle, as the first philosopher in the Greek Tradition. His most famous philosophical position about the nature of all matter is delivered through a passage from Aristotle's

A. von Rebay, *The Designation of Marine Protected Areas*,
https://doi.org/10.1007/978-3-031-29175-3_1

30 by 30 is the official target goal of the members of the International Union for Conservation of Nature (IUCN).[8] The aim is to designate 30% of the ocean as Marine Protected Areas (MPAs) and other effective area-based conservation measures by 2030. Scientific research shows that this percentage is the minimum required to save the seas and that it can only be achieved by creating a planet-wide network of ocean sanctuaries.[9] Nonetheless, by December 2020, no State had even realized the 10% by 2020 goal, as agreed upon by 193 States at the Conference of Parties of the Convention on Biological Diversity in Japan in 2010.[10] Not even 7.72% of the oceans and only 1.18% of the High Seas are protected by the beginning of the year 2023.[11] What is impeding the progressive designation of MPAs?

Effective marine protection depends on the interplay of many branches: scientific findings, economic and ecological concerns, socio-ecological needs, political evaluations, technological developments, to name a few. Areas in which navigation and fishing are regulated, for instance, ought to interfere with the interests of strong naval forces. No take or no trawl areas affect the fisheries sector, an industry in which 59.6 million people were employed in 2016 and that produced 171 million tonnes of fish with an export value of USD 143 billion. Naval and fishing lobbies are equivalently strong.[12] It is not surprising that States are disinclined to accept regulations that do not reflect their economic benefits.[13] In coastal areas, the involvement of the local communities is a decisive factor for the establishment of effective protected areas. The interests of indigenous people and local fishermen need to be taken into account so that the establishment of MPAs does not deprive them of their livelihoods.[14] On top of this, the practical enforcement of conservation measures is a Herculean task in an area that covers more than 361 million square kilometres.[15] New technologies, such as satellite remote sensing for illegal fishing, devices for recoding coral reef data and other maritime surveillances are paramount to ensure effective marine

Metaphysics: 'That of which all things that are consist, the first from which they come to be, the last into which they are resolved (the substance remaining, but changing in its modifications), this they say is the element and this the principle of things, and therefore they think nothing is either generated or destroyed, since this sort of entity is always conserved, [...] nothing else comes to be or ceases to be; for there must be some entity—either one or more than one—from which all other things come to be, it being conserved. [...] Thales, the founder of this type of philosophy, says the principle is water [...]' (Ross, http://www.classicallibrary.org/aristotle/metaphysics/book01.htm).

[8] ICUN WCC-2016-RES-050.

[9] O'Leary et al. (2016), p. 401.

[10] https://www.greenpeace.org/static/planet4-international-stateless/2019/04/4475b2c2-updatedgreenpeace_30x30_blueprint_report_web.pdf, p. 9; https://www.cbd.int/doc/press/2017/pr-2017-06-05-mpa-pub-en.pdf; Grafton et al. (2011), p. 478.

[11] https://www.protectedplanet.net/en/thematic-areas/marine-protected-areas.

[12] FAO (2018), p. 6; Tanaka (2008), p. 204.

[13] Tanaka (2008), p. 204.

[14] https://geographical.co.uk/nature/oceans/item/3482-do-marine-protected-areas-harm-local-communities (19.02.2021).

[15] https://www.ngdc.noaa.gov/mgg/global/etopo1_ocean_volumes.html.

protection.[16] At the same time, new technologies allow for the exploitation of hitherto unknown terrains, such as the unexplored, deepest parts of the seabed. Simultaneously, the human craving to exploit natural resources has advanced to long unreachable grounds, even leaving behind terrestrial boundaries of planet Earth and advancing to the deepest trenches of the sea, the Moon and Mars.

Law is only one piece in this versatile mosaic. A legal structure can provide a solid scaffold to equilibrate interests and legal security through binding regulations. As the failure to designate 10% of the ocean as MPAs by 2020 shows, voluntary pledges are not sufficient to meet global and national goals to reduce anthropogenic influence on marine and terrestrial environment.[17] The effective protection of the (marine) environment necessitates legal obligations of the States that are binding. The establishment of MPAs is one tool to this end. Mindful that effective protection and preservation of the environment concerns scientific, economic, socio-economic, political and ecological interests, this treatise sets out to prove that the existing law of the sea already provides a universal, legally binding obligation of all States to establish MPAs in all zones of the sea—an area whose depths are more alien to humans than the Moon.[18]

1.2 State of Research

The extant relevant literature only scratches the surface of this research inquiry. MPAs are mainly dealt with concerning the *right* of States to establish MPAs in the various zones of the Sea. The other side, however, the *obligation* of States to do so is discussed scarcely. This surprises in the light of the expressed intention of States to designate 10% of the oceans as MPAs by 2020 and 30% by 2030, respectively.

It is especially being discussed that an impediment to the progressive designation of MPAs is the hubbub of regulations concerning the protection of the marine environment. Secluded provisions float in the law of the sea like isolated islands with gaps and overlaps without a unifying ecosystem.[19] The regulations either do not provide a legal basis of claim for the designation of MPAs or require further actions from the State parties to be effective.[20] Indeed, today, more than 1000 instruments either regulate the environment and its protection or contain environmental

---

[16] https://news.mongabay.com/2021/03/how-technology-can-help-us-achieve-at-least-30-ocean-protection-commentary/.

[17] https://unfccc.int/news/climate-commitments-not-on-track-to-meet-paris-agreement-goals-as-ndc-synthesis-report-is-published.

[18] Only in 2020, the 12th person ever has visited the Marianna Trench, the deepest known point in the ocean, which finally equals the number of the 12 astronauts that have visited the Moon in 1969 (https://www.bbc.com/news/science-environment-53112621).

[19] Proelss (2017), Art. 194, mn. 34; Franke (2007); Molenaar (2007), p. 680; Rothwell et al. (2015), p. 487.

[20] Franke (2007); Hossain (2016).

regulations.[21] These instruments and problems are mainly dealt with fragmentarily concerning specific areas, such as the Arctic or the South China Sea, or concerning certain marine activities, such as fisheries or navigation.[22] This book closes this gap and provides evidence that, in fact, the existing law of the sea regime already possesses a comprehensive obligation, which binds all States to protect the marine environment: the obligation to protect and preserve the marine environment under Art. 192 of the 1982 United Nations Convention on the Law of the Sea (UNCLOS).[23] It will be demonstrated that this umbrella obligation not only provides a unifying ecosystem for the numerous single protection instruments but moreover binds the whole State community to establish MPAs in all zones of the sea.

MPAs manage and regulate activities in the sea; naturally, they ought to collide with sovereign rights of the States and the freedoms of the High Seas. The conflict of the zones of the sea and respective sovereign rights is well established in the extant literature and can be traced back beyond Hugo Grotius' famous dissertation '*Mare Liberum*' in 1609.[24] While the zonal distribution of the sea, thus, is discussed broadly, the sovereign rights to protect and preserve the marine environment are discussed scarcely. The literature points out that the lack of sovereign rights and of a comprehensive legal mandate of States to establish MPAs in Areas Beyond National Jurisdiction (ABNJ) imposes severe obstacles for their designation, let alone the designation of a comprehensive network of MPAs across the whole ocean.[25]

This book will prove that States do have the sovereign power to establish MPAs in all zones of the sea because the freedoms of the High Sea are subordinated under the obligation to protect and preserve the marine environment. The *erga omnes* effect of Art. 192 UNCLOS binds all States regardless of jurisdictional zones. Although Art. 192 UNCLOS is formulated as an 'obligation' rather than a 'duty' such as, i.e. Art. 193 UNCLOS, the interpretation will prove that its objective and purpose is not only an expression of a political objective of States but the codification of a legally binding tie.[26] Furthermore, while the extant literature seems to accept the customary status of the Art. 192 UNCLOS unanimously, its status as a rule of customary international law has not been proven empirically. It will therefore be evidenced that the obligation as embodied under Art. 192 UNCLOS is not only a universal rule of customary international law but has emerged into *jus cogens* that *erga omnes* binds the whole State community.

---

[21] Matz (2005), p. 53.

[22] Vöneky (2008), pp. 165–197; Dang (2014); Oral (2013); Weidemann (2014); Fitzmaurice (2016), pp. 33–77.

[23] United Nations Treaty Series (UNTS), Vol. 1833, No. I-31363; Bundesgesetzblatt (BGBl.) II 1994, p. 1799.

[24] Deman Magoffin (2001); Treves (2015), p. 1; Treves (2015), p. 2; Nordquist et al. (2012), p. 885; Rothwell and Stephens (2016), p. 7.

[25] Tanaka (2019), pp. 288 f; Tanaka (2008), p. 204; Gjerde and Rulska-Domino (2012), p, 370; https://portals.iucn.org/library/sites/library/files/resrecrepattach/ELC%20MPA%20Framework%20Sept%204%20%282%29.pdf, p. 7.

[26] Proelss (2017), Art. 192, mn. 18 f.; McConnell and Gold (1991), p. 89.

It is furthermore being argued that the obligation under Art. 192 UNCLOS is too general to be applicable in practice, and because MPAs are not expressly mentioned in the UNCLOS, it is argued that there is no legal basis of claim to establish MPAs at all.[27] To this end, the literature points out that the 'General Obligation' under Art. 192 UNCLOS is expressly designed as an umbrella regulation, the content of which needs to be filled with more specific legislations.[28] This is not only dictated by the legal principles of *lex generalis* and *lex specialis* but codified explicitly in Art. 237 UNCLOS, which provides that the provisions of Part XII UNCLOS are without prejudice to the specific obligations assumed by States under special agreements. Accordingly, the Permanent Court of Arbitration (PCA) established in its *South China Sea Arbitration* that the 'content of the general obligation in Article 192 is further detailed in the subsequent provisions of Part XII, including Article 194, as well as by reference to specific obligations set out in other international agreements, as envisaged in Article 237 of the Convention.'[29] An extensive investigation of the substantive scope of Art. 192 UNCLOS will prove that firstly, Art. 192 UNCLOS entails the obligation of States to take 'active measures', and secondly, the interpretation of active measures to protect and preserve the marine environment means the adoption of legislation for this purpose. The adoption of legislation for the protection and preservation of the marine environment constitutes the designation of MPAs if it connotes geographically defined areas. Because of this spatial scope, the hitherto most acknowledged basis to establish MPAs in the literature is Art. 194 (5) UNCLOS.[30]

Lastly, the United Nations (UN) are currently convening an intergovernmental conference to establish an international legally binding instrument under the UNCLOS on the conservation and sustainable use of marine biological diversity of areas beyond national jurisdiction (BBNJ).[31] The objective of the BBNJ is to ensure the conservation and sustainable use of marine biodiversity, including area-based management tools such as MPAs.[32] The BBNJ is one of the most widely discussed issues in the contemporary law of the sea. It is touted as a potential milestone in the establishment of ocean governance and effective measures for marine protection in ABNJ—yet its adoption will face the known obstacles of international treaties in ABNJ, which only bind the State parties. Because this book establishes a legally binding obligation of all States to adopt national laws

[27] Guo (2020), p. 1; Proelss (2017), Art. 194, mn. 34; Druel (2011), p. 8.

[28] PCA, *South China Sea Arbitration*, The Republic of the Philippines v. The People's Republic of China (in the following: Philippines v. China), (Award), p. 373, para. 941; UNGA A/44/461, 18, p. 5; Tanaka (2019), p. 333; Freestone (2009), p. 45; McConnell and Gold (1991), p. 85.

[29] PCA, *South China Sea Arbitration*, Philippines v. China (Award), p. 373, para. 942; Tanaka (2019), p. 333; Freestone (2009), p. 45; Proelss (2017), Art. 192, mn. 8.

[30] PCA, *Chagos Marine Protected Area Arbitration*, Mauritius v. UK (Award) 2015, p. 211, para. 538 and p. 128 f., para. 320; Proelss (2017), Art. 194, mn. 35; Oude Elferink (2018), p. 445.

[31] UNGA A/RES/60/292, Preamble; UNGA A/RES/72/249.

[32] https://www.un.org/depts/los/biodiversity/prepcom_files/Chairs_streamlined_non-paper_to_delegations.pdf; https://www.un.org/bbnj/content/background.

and regulations and international treaties for the protection of the marine environment, its findings provide important leverage to enhance the adoption of the BBNJ in the light of its final session in 2022.

The focus of this monograph will be on filling the gaps in the literature to comprehensively prove that Art. 192 UNCLOS provides a legally binding, *erga omnes* obligation of all States to establish MPAs in the existing law of the sea.

1.3 Course of Examination and Limitation

The following course of examination will corroborate this conclusion: Firstly, the scene will be set in Chap. 2, by providing the foundations for the research question of the legal obligation of States to designate MPAs. To this end, MPAs will initially be put in the context of their historical development and their policy framework of Ocean Governance. General principles which partially still prevail in the law of the sea date back more than 400 years. These principles will be outlined, starting with the zonal division of the sea, which has its roots in Hugo Grotius' dissertation '*Mare Liberum*', published in 1609.[33] It establishes the sovereign rights in the different zones of the sea and is therefore decisive for the rights and obligations of the States concerning the designation of MPAs in the relevant terrain. This is followed by an introduction of further pertinent principles of public international law: the sources of public international law determine which legal instruments of the protection and preservation of the marine environment are binding. They are, therefore, a crucial prerequisite for the investigation of a legally binding obligation of States to establish MPAs. The book focuses on the obligation of States to establish MPAs under the law of the sea as a primary legal obligation and does not reflect upon the responsibility and liability as a secondary legal obligation of States that follows from the breach of the primary obligation to establish MPAs.

The outcome of legal claims depends on fulfilling precise legal requirements as constituted in the relevant legal provision. There is no legally binding definition of MPAs in the law of the sea.[34] A comprehensive cross-section of existing definitions of MPAs shows that they consist of three elements: a geographical area in the sea, which is designated by legislation and pursues a protection and conservation objective.[35]

National, regional and international policies and regulations deal with marine protection issues and MPAs in a secluded manner, which will be outlined in an overview before investigating the *erga omnes* obligations under Art. 192 UNCLOS

[33] Deman Magoffin (2001).

[34] Tanaka (2019), p. 418; Tanaka (2008), p. 161; Kellerher (1999), pp. xviii f.

[35] IUCN GA Rec. 17.38 (1988); Proelss (2017), Art. 194, mn. 34, fn. 99; Jakobsen (2016), p. 7; https://www.cbd.int/doc/publications/cbd-ts-13.pdf, p. 7; Wolf (2012), p. 1057, para. 2.

in detail.[36] The UNCLOS, the so-called Constitution for the Ocean, is the broadest framework of the international law of the sea.[37] Part XII UNCLOS is dedicated to the protection and preservation of the marine environment. Its opening regulation, Art. 192 UNCLOS is specifically designed as an umbrella regulation that obliges all States to protect and preserve the marine environment in all zones of the sea. To this end, this monograph will investigate the legally binding effect of the 'obligation' under Art. 192 UNCLOS in three regards: Firstly, Chap. 3 will establish the legally binding effect of Art. 192 UNCLOS, which is not only a political statement. Secondly, Chap. 4 provides a comprehensive investigation of the discourse and conduct of States to empirically evidence that the obligation as embodied in Art. 192 UNCLOS has not only grown into a rule of customary international law but—due to its universal acceptance and fundamental value of humankind—evolved into a *jus cogens* regulation that *erga omnes* binds the whole States community. Thirdly, Chap. 5 demonstrates that the geographical scope of the obligation as embodied under Art. 192 UNCLOS applies to all marine spaces in the UNCLOS. Even more, the interpretation of the relevant regulations shows, that the protection of the marine environment includes estuaries and direct or indirect influences from land and the atmosphere.

The substantive scope of the obligation to protect and preserve the marine environment will be investigated in Chap. 6. An interpretation of the obligation to protect and preserve the marine environment will show that it entails the obligation of States to take 'active measures' to protect the marine environment from future damages and preserve the present condition by maintaining or improving it from all threats (Chap. 6, Sect. 6.1).[38] A comprehensive analysis of the meaning of 'active measures' by States, including the interpretation of national, regional and 'international' administrative law, concludes that active measures by States are the adoption of legislation (Chap. 6, Sect. 6.3). National legislation is the adoption of laws and regulations, while 'international' legislation will be defined as the adoption of international treaties. National and 'international' legislation for the protection and preservation of the marine environment, as per their definition, are MPAs if they connote a geographically defined marine area. The obligation to protect and preserve the marine environment, therefore, does entail the obligation to take active measures in the form of the establishment of MPAs.

The obligation to adopt legislation varies according to the sovereign rights in the sea, which will be investigated subsequently (Chap. 6, Sect. 6.5). While the States have exclusive sovereignty, jurisdiction and single sovereign rights to this end in the Territorial Sea, the Exclusive Economic Zone (EEZ) and on the Continental Shelf, the High Sea and the Area are generally governed by the freedoms of the High Sea. The freedoms of the High Sea, however, are not granted limitless, as can be seen

---

[36] Tanaka (2019), p. 47; Rothwell and Stephens (2016), p. 1; Treves (2015), p. 11.

[37] https://www.un.org/Depts/los/convention_agreements/texts/koh_english.pdf; Mann Borgese (1978), p. 371; https://ioc.unesco.org/topics/law-sea; UNGA A/74/PV.42, p. 12.

[38] PCA, *South China Sea Arbitration*, Philippines v. China (Award), p. 373, para. 941.

under Art. 87 (1) (Second Sentence) UNCLOS and have to respect other provisions of the UNCLOS and international law. The adoption of international treaties for the protection and preservation of the marine environment is therefore compatible with the freedoms of the High Sea.

The determination of the minimum and maximum scope of the obligation to protect and preserve the marine environment will provide for the definition of its specific content (Chap. 6, Sect. 6.6). *Prima facie*, the establishment of MPAs seems to collide with the exercise of other activities in the sea. As *jus cogens* regulation, the obligation to protect and preserve the marine environment may not be derogated and only be modified by subsequent norms having the same character. Due to its cogent status, derivative regulations that collide with this obligation are void. The harmonious interpretation of the specific content of the obligation to protect and preserve the marine environment as well as the rights that provide for activities in the sea, however, reveals that no relevant normative conflict exists. An exemplary application of these findings illustrates that States are obliged to establish MPAs to regulate large-scale fishing in all zones of the sea. The obligation to protect and preserve the marine environment does not necessarily require the absolute ban of all activities in the sea. The interpretation of its content in the light of the freedom of fishing shows that low impact fishing techniques are still permissible. The interpretation in the context of deep seabed mining shows that the regulatory regime of the UNCLOS stipulates a sequence of exploring an area before exploiting it. The ISA will need to keep this obligatory sequence in mind when granting permissions, especially in light of the recent application of Nauru to commence deep seabed mining.[39]

The last part of the main inquiry will investigate other potential *erga omnes* regulations that provide for the establishment of MPAs in Chap. 7, namely Art. 194 (5) UNCLOS and the BBNJ. Due to its spatial scope, Art. 194 (5) UNCLOS is the most commonly acknowledged basis for the establishment of MPAs. The universally accepted unjustifiable interference regulations, as stipulated in Art. 194 (4) UNCLOS, however, necessitates that measures necessary to protect and preserve rare or fragile ecosystems as well as the habitat of depleted, threatened or endangered species and other forms of marine life are balanced with other activities in the sea. Relevant balancing evaluations are the extent of the interference, the availability of alternatives and the importance of the rights at issue. The evolution of society from the age of discovery, through industrialisation, to the recognition of the fundamental value of the (marine) environment for the well-being of humankind, decreases the value of the freedoms of the High Sea in the light of the obligation to protect and preserve the marine environment in the twenty-first century. Furthermore, the interpretation of the wording of Art. 194 (4) UNCLOS implies that measures for the protection and preservation of rare and fragile ecosystems that interfere with activities in the sea are generally justified. This places the burden of

[39] https://www.reuters.com/business/environment/exclusive-deep-sea-mining-rules-be-fast-tracked-push-nauru-source-2021-06-25/.

proof on the State exercising activities in the sea, who needs to invoke and evidence that measures under Art. 194 (5) UNCLOS unjustifiably interfere with its activities.

The BBNJ aims to develop an international legally binding instrument under the UNCLOS on the conservation and sustainable use of marine biological diversity of areas beyond national jurisdiction, including MPAs. The influence of the findings of this book on the BBNJ will be outlined before summarizing all results in theses in the last Chap. 8.

Laws and regulations are tools to manage the life of people amongst each other and as a part of society. In order to remain valid for an ever-evolving civilisation, laws and regulations require adaptation. Regulations that served the discovery of the seas in the sixteenth century, in which awareness of marine pollution did not exist, cannot apply unaltered to the societal needs in the twenty-first century, which are dominated by climate catastrophes and the extinction of species. The adaptation of law to the needs of mankind is dragging; it is motivated and accelerated by political and scientific discourse. The exchange of blows of scholars such as Grotius, Selden, Bynkershoek and other 'fathers' of international law has shown that the evolution of law requires the exchange of pioneering thoughts. This is the starting point from which the journey to establish the *erga omnes* obligation of all States to designate MPAs in all zones of the sea embarks.

References

Dang VH (2014) Marine protected areas network in the South China Sea, charting a course for future cooperation. In: Legal aspects of sustainable development, vol 18. Martinus Nijhoff Publishers, Leiden

Deman Magoffin R (2001) The freedom of the seas or the right which belongs to the Dutch to take part in the East Indian Trade. A dissertation by Hugo Grotius, New Jersey

Druel E (2011) Marine protected areas in areas beyond national jurisdiction: the State of play. Institut du Développement Durable et des relations Internationales (IDDRI) Working Paper Number 7/11, Paris

Fitzmaurice M (2016) The International Convention for the Prevention of Pollution from Ships (MARPOL). In: Attard DJ, Malgosia F, Guitérrez M, Norman A, Hamza R (eds) The IMLI manual on international maritime law, Volume VIII: Marine environmental law and maritime security law. Oxford University Press, Oxford, pp 33–77

Food and Agriculture Organization of the United Nations (FAO) (2018) SOFIA Report 2016, The state of world fisheries and aquaculture 2016 – Contributing to food security and nutrition for all. FAO, Rome

Franke V, The European Community and Marine Environmental Protection in the International Law of the Sea - implementing global obligations at the regional level, Publications on ocean development, Volume 58 (Brill, Leiden, 2007).

Freestone D (2009) Modern principles of high seas governance – the legal underpinnings. Env Policy Law 39(1):44–49

Gjerde KM, Rulska-Domino A (2012) Marine protected areas beyond national jurisdiction: some practical perspectives for moving ahead. Int J Mar Coast Law 27(2):351–374

Goethe JW (1832) Faust. Der Tragödie zweiter Teil. Deutsche Grammophon, Stuttgart

Grafton RQ, Akter S, Kompas T (2011) A policy-enabling framework for the ex-ante evaluation of marine protected areas. Ocean Coast Manag 54(6):478–487

Guo J (2020) The developments of marine environmental protection obligation in article 192 of UNCLOS and the operational impact on China's marine policy – A south China sea fisheries perspective. Mar Policy 120(104140):1–7
Hossain K (2016) Arctic marine biodiversity in areas beyond national jurisdiction - framing a le-gally binding MPA regime? Am Soc Int Law Insights 20(14)
Jakobsen IU (2016) Marine protected areas in international law – an arctic perspective. In: Fitzmaurice M, Okowa P, Singer S (eds) Queen Mary Studies in International Law, vol 25. Brill, Leiden
Kellerher G (1999) Guideline for marine protected areas. World Commission on Protected Areas of IUCN – The World Conservation Union, Gland
Mann Borgese E (1978) A constitution for the oceans: comments and suggestions regarding part XI of the informal composite negotiating text. San Diego Law Rev 15:371–408
Matz N (2005) Wege zur Koordinierung völkerrechtlicher Verträge – Völkervertragsrechtliche und institutionelle Ansätze. In: Max-Planck-Institut für ausländisches öffentliches Recht und Völkerrecht - Beiträge zum ausländischen öffentlichen Recht und Völkerrecht, vol 175. Springer, Heidelberg
McConnell ML, Gold E (1991) The modern law of the sea: framework for the protection and preservation of the marine environment. Case West Res J Int Law 23(1):83–106
Molenaar EJ (2007) Managing Biodiversity in Areas Beyond National Jurisdiction. In: Nordquist MH, Long R, Heidar TH, Moore JN (eds) Law, science & ocean management. Brill, Leiden, pp 625–681
Nordquist MH, Nandan SN, Kraska J (2012) UNCLOS 1982 commentary – supplementary documents. Center for Oceans Law and Policy, Leiden
O'Leary BC, Winther-Janson M, Bainbridge JM, Aitken J, Hawkins JP, Roberts CM (2016) Effective coverage targets for ocean protection. Conserv Lett 9(6):398–404
Oral N (2013) Regional co-operation and protection of the marine environment under international law – the Black Sea. In: Freestone D (ed) Legal aspects of sustainable development, vol 16. Brill, Leiden
Oude Elferink AG (2018) Coastal states and MPAs in ABNJ: ensuring consistency with the LOSC. Int J Mar Coast Law 33:437–466
Proelss A (2017) United Nations Convention on the Law of the Sea – a commentary. C.H. Beck, Munich
Rothwell DR, Stephens T (2016) The international law of the sea, 2nd edn. Oxford University Press, Oxford
Rothwell DR, Oude Elferink AG, Scott KN, Stephens T (2015) Charting the future for the law of the sea. In: Rothwell D, Oude Elferink AG, Scott KN, Stephens T (eds) The Oxford handbook of the law of the sea. Oxford, pp 888–912
Schladebach M, Esau C (2012) Aktuelle Herausforderungen im Seerecht. Deutsches Verwaltungsblatt (DVBl), Köln, pp 475–483
Tanaka Y (2008) A dual approach to ocean governance - the cases of zonal and integrated management in international law of the sea. Routledge, Surrey
Tanaka Y (2019) The international law of the sea, 3rd edn. Cambridge University Press, Cambridge
Treves T (2015) Historical development of the law of the sea. In: Rothwell D, Oude Elferink AG, Scott K, Stephans T (eds) The Oxford handbook of the law of the sea, pp 1–23
Vöneky S (2008) The liability annex to the protocol on environmental protection to the Antarctic Treaty. In: König D, Stoll P-T, Röben V, Matz-Lück N (eds) International Law Today - new challenges and the need for reform? Beiträge zum ausländischen öffentlichen Recht und Völkerrecht, vol 193. Springer, Heidelberg, pp 165–197
Weidemann L (2014) International governance of the arctic marine environment – with particular emphasis on high seas fisheries. In: Hamburg studies on marine affairs, vol 27. Springer, Hamburg
Wolf S (2012) Marine protected areas. In: Wolfrum R (ed) Max Planck Encyclopedia of Public International Law (MPEPIL), vol VI. Oxford University Press, Oxford, pp 1056–1063

Chapter 2
Setting the Scene

2.1 Context

The embedding of MPAs in their historical context shows that the designation of MPAs addresses one of the most traditional conflicts in the history of the law of the sea: the spatial distribution of marine jurisdiction.[1] While the High Sea is generally free (*mare liberum*), MPAs are closed areas in which activities are regulated (*mare clausum*).

2.1.1 Historical Development

It seems to breed in the nature of humankind that the possibility to assert sovereign rights by one party reciprocally evokes a feeling of scarcity and disadvantage in others. This is not surprising, as the positive right to assert exclusive sovereignty also includes the negative right to exclude others from doing so; the assertion of common areas of mankind to one's terrain, therefore, automatically limits the range of free movement of others. Moreover, it seems that the attainment of sovereign rights and territorial expansion does not saturate but appeases an insatiable hunger to gain more, or, as the President of the Third UN Conference on the Law of the Sea Tommy Koh put it, 'men like animals, seem to be driven by a territorial imperative [. . .].'[2] With the conquering of the sea, the hunger to extend territorial sovereign rights exceeded the land borders and spilled over to the ocean. Thus, the law of the sea is one of the oldest fields of international law.[3]

---

[1] O'Connell (1982), p. 1; Proelss (2017), Art. 89, mn. 4.

[2] Koh (1989), p. 15; Mensah (2006), p. 143.

[3] Treves (2010), p. 11.

A. von Rebay, *The Designation of Marine Protected Areas*,
https://doi.org/10.1007/978-3-031-29175-3_2

2.1.1.1 Mare Liberum vs Mare Clausum

Up until the twentieth century, the law of the sea was mainly governed by European practices. The development of maritime technology allowed people to explore the Earth by sea. The dominion of marine trading routes in the sea opened valuable sources for trade and commerce, and the control and regulation of activities in the sea evolved into a determining factor for the domination of enemies.[4] In the aftermath of Columbus' voyages across the Atlantic Ocean, the two papal bulls *Inter Caetera* of 1493 by Pope Alexander VI delimited the territories in the Atlantic Ocean between Spain and Portugal by drawing an imaginary line from pole to pole and appointed all territories west of it to Spain and east of it to Portugal. One year later, this delimitation was reapproved with slight alterations in the Treaty of Tordesillas.[5]

With further opening of maritime trade routes in the Age of Discovery in the fifteenth to seventeenth century, this delimitation was attacked by a theoretical exchange of blows by scholars: The Dutch, who experienced their 'Golden Age' by gaining independence in European waters and establishing shipping lanes, trade and colonies in many parts of the world, had a great interest in proclaiming that the sea is fully navigable and free of access to common humankind. In this light, Hugo Grotius published his famous dissertation '*Mare Liberum, seu de jure, quod Batvis ad Indica commercial*' in 1609, arguing that the High Sea shall be free and not be purported to sovereign rights of any state.[6] The Portuguese, however, had already put in place a great dominion over the High Seas and tried to defend 'The Just Portuguese Asian Empire' by claiming a closed sea.[7] The Anglophones picked up this notion, who, likewise, wanted to secure their marine ways. In 1635, John Selden's *Mare Clausum* contested Grotius' *Mare Liberum* by debating that the sea was in practice virtually as capable of appropriation as terrestrial territory and therefore belongs to the coastal State.[8] Only in 1709, the dispute of the freedom of the sea and the establishment of sovereign rights came to a halt with Cornelius van Bynkershoek's famous cannon-shot rule: because the '[t]he power of the land properly ends where the force of arm ends. Therefore, the sea can be considered subject as far as the range of cannon extends[. . .]', which, in this time, was three nautical miles off the coast.[9]

---

[4]Rothwell and Stephens (2016), p. 3.

[5]Treves (2015), p. 2; Nordquist et al. (2012), p. 885; Rothwell and Stephens (2016), p. 3.

[6]Deman Magoffin (2001); Rothwell and Stephens (2016), p. 7; Tomuschat (2019), p. 588.

[7]Freitas (1625).

[8]Selden (1635), p. 3; Rothwell and Stephens (2016), p. 3; Cottier (2015), p. 63.

[9]Deman Magoffin (1923), p. 44; Proelss (2017), Art. 3, mn. 3.

2.1.1.2 The Codification of the Law of the Sea and Its Functions

First Function of the UNCLOS: Spatial Distribution of State

In 1945, economic considerations contested the established sea borders once again, when U.S. President Truman was advised that after the war, most of the resources on land had been exploited and more were to be found in the High Seas and its seabed.[10] In an attempt to change the existing law in order to exploit resources beyond the three NM border of the Territorial Sea, Truman declared that the resources on the Continental Shelf that were contiguous to the United States belonged to the United States and hoped that other States would follow in order to establish a new rule of customary international law (Truman Proclamation). Once again, this shows that the economic imperative was the actual leading factor in the formation of the law.[11]

Up until the mid-twentieth century, the law of the sea was mainly governed by customary international law.[12] A rising collective attempt of States to codify the existing rules of law in one all-encompassing agreement progressed through three UN Conferences on the Law of the Sea starting in 1958 in Geneva, which was attended by 86 States. The codification of the regime of the High Seas and the Territorial Sea was still one of the main issues in Geneva. In order to at least conclude some of the highly disputed matters concerning the law of the sea, the idea of one unifying treaty was abandoned in favour of four Conventions concerning issues of the law of the sea: the 1958 Geneva Convention on the Territorial Sea and the Contiguous Zone (CTSCZ),[13] the 1958 Geneva Convention on the High Seas (CHS),[14] the 1958 Geneva Convention on Fishing and Conservation of the Living Resources of the High Seas (CFCLR)[15] and the 1958 Geneva Convention on the Continental Shelf (CCS)[16] along with the Optional Protocol of Signature concerning the Compulsory Settlement of Disputes.[17] For the first time Art. 3, 4 CFCLR introduced an obligation to conserve marine living resources at the global level, which obliged States to apply conservation measures to their nationals.[18]

The hoped-for unity of the law of the sea was ultimately reached at the final stages of the Third United Nations Conference of the Law of the Sea (UNCLOS III) from 1973 to 1982, with the codification of the UNCLOS in Montego Bay on

[10] Scharf (2012), p. 107.

[11] Crawford (2012), p. 23.

[12] Treves (2015), p. 2.

[13] UNTS, Vol. 516, No. I-7477.

[14] UNTS, Vol. 450, No. I-6465.

[15] UNTS, Vol. 559, No. I-8164.

[16] UNTS, Vol. 499, No. I-7302.

[17] UNTS, Vol. 450, No. I-6466; UN Doc. A/CONF.13/L.58, p. 147.

[18] Tanaka (2019), p. 282.

10 December 1982.[19] This 'Constitution for the Ocean' stipulates general procedural as well as material principles in the international law of the sea. Its first function, however, still is the spatial distribution of the jurisdiction of the States.[20] Accordingly, the UNCLOS divides the water of the ocean into five zones, Internal Waters, Territorial Sea, Archipelagic Waters, EEZ and the High Seas, with separate regulations on the seabed, namely the Continental Shelf and the Area. Although the traditional, strict dualism of the marine spaces of an open or closed sea had been abandoned in favour of a multilateral distribution, its idea is still maintained: While the Territorial Sea, Archipelagic Waters and Internal Waters are marine Areas *Under* National Jurisdiction (AUNJ), the High Sea is a Marine Area *Beyond* National Jurisdiction (ABNJ). Because of the interest of States to exploit resources, the fixation of the 12 NM Territorial Sea could only be reached by 'institutionalising a new resource-oriented zone under the coastal State's jurisdiction: the 200-mile EEZ.'[21] Today, it is once again in question if those rigid sea borders are still feasible considering the new challenges of the twenty-first century.

Second Function of the UNCLOS: Cooperation to Manage the Ocean

The delimitation of sea borders on paper is an important means to manifest the reach of the jurisdiction of States. The reality shows, however, that migratory fish stock or ocean currents that spread microorganisms and pollution throughout the entire ocean do not obey human-made borders drawn on a map.[22] The awareness that not only States' interests need to be equilibrated but that the ocean must be administered by the international community as a whole rose in the negotiation process of the UNCLOS III at the beginning of 1972. The preamble of the UNCLOS, therefore, interludes the text of the treaty by stating the consciousness 'that the problems of ocean spaces are closely interrelated and need to be considered as a whole'. The second function of the modern law of the sea, thus, is to nurture international cooperation and coordination between States in order to provide for the management of the ocean as one unit in a physical sense.[23] Simultaneous to the UNCLOS III Conference, major oil tanker accidents started to contaminate the hitherto prevailing conviction that the bounty of the marine environment was immeasurably rich and its resources inexhaustible.[24] The *Torrey Canyon Disaster* in 1967, for instance, made

---

[19] Tanaka (2019), pp. 3, 47; Treves (2015), pp. 14 ff.; Rothwell and Stephens (2016), p. 6; https://legal.un.org/avl/ha/gclos/gclos.html.

[20] https://www.un.org/Depts/los/convention_agreements/texts/koh_english.pdf; Mann Borgese (1978), p. 371; https://ioc.unesco.org/topics/law-sea; UNGA A/74/PV.42, p. 12; Tanaka (2019), p. 3; Rothwell and Stephens (2016), p. 1.

[21] Tanaka (2008), pp. 5 f.; Tanaka (2019), pp. 38 f.

[22] Tanaka (2019), p. 3.

[23] Wolfrum (1990), p. 322; Tanaka (2019), pp. 3, 46; Rothwell and Stephens (2016), p. 506.

[24] Hafner (2006), p. 355, mn. 1; Tomuschat (2019), p. 510.

the harmful human impact on the marine environment very visible by causing the spread of 31 million gallons of oil in the sea in front of the British south coast.[25] According to marine biologist Dr Sylvia Earl, '[i]f humankind were given a mandate to do everything in our power to undermine the Earth's functioning, we could hardly do a better job than we have in the past 30 years on the world's oceans, both by what we are putting into it—millions of tons of trash and toxic materials—and by what we are taking out of it—millions of tons of wildlife. Yet only recently have we begun to understand the scale of those impacts.'[26]

The first international treaty for the protection of the marine environment from oil pollution was the 1954 International Convention for the Prevention of Pollution of the Sea by Oil,[27] which opened the gate to numerous protection regulations and policies concerning specific issues and activities in the sea, such as the 1973/1978 International Convention for the Prevention of Marine Pollution from Ships in 1973 (MARPOL),[28] the 1991 Protocol on Environmental Protection to the Antarctic Treaty,[29] the 1992 Convention for the Protection of the Marine Environment of the North-East Atlantic (OSPAR)[30] and Part XII UNCLOS. Today more than 300 instruments either regulate the marine environment and its protection or contain some marine environmental regulations.[31] Treaties, rules of customary international law, general principles, policies on national, regional and global levels make the law of the sea one of the widest fields of international law today.[32]

2.1.2 Ocean Governance

> '*Conscious* that the problems of ocean space are closely interrelated and need to be considered as a whole,' [. . .] the State Parties have agreed to the United Nations Convention of the Law of the Sea—(Preamble of UNCLOS)

Modern ocean threats concern the ocean as a whole. Marine pollution and ocean debris is spread across the ocean by currents, where it forms garbage patches such as the Great Western and Eastern Pacific Garbage Patches.[33] Migratory fish stock, such as humpback whales, travel 5000 km from their feeding grounds in the polar regions to their breeding grounds in warmer tropical waters and back, a journey on which

---

[25] Tanaka (2019), pp. 3, 46; Hafner (2006), p. 356, mn. 3; Rothwell and Stephens (2016), p. 506; Adede (1995), p. 33; König (2001), para. 3.

[26] Glover et al. (2004), backcover.

[27] UNTS, Vol. 327, No. I-4714.

[28] UNTS, Vol. 1340, p. 184; UNTS, Vol. 1340, No. I-22484.

[29] UNTS, Vol. 2941, No. A-5778.

[30] UNTS, Vol. 2354, No. I-42279.

[31] Matz (2005), p. 53.

[32] Tanaka (2019), pp. 3, 47; Rothwell and Stephens (2016), p. 1.

[33] https://marinedebris.noaa.gov/movement/great-pacific-garbage-patch.

they frequently get caught in fishing gear or shark nets.[34] Overfishing in one territory leads to scarcity of fish in adjacent ocean terrains, such as in the Mediterranean Sea, where traditional Tunisian charfia-fishermen struggle with declining catches and income due to commercial large-scale fishing techniques, such as bottom trawling.[35] The decline of one marine organism, such as corals, leads to the decline of co-dependent organisms, such as fish stock that feed on them. Vice versa, the depletion of key reef species can have a rippling effect on the coral reef ecosystem.[36] The Ocean is one ecosystem as a whole, which can only be protected by dealing with the effects of human activities on marine life through an integrated ocean management system. This is reflected in the second function of the UNCLOS, to safeguard international cooperation between States for the proper management of the ocean, which is one single unit in a physical sense.[37]

In this sense, Ocean Governance promotes the shift from a sovereign-rights perspective to integrated ocean management, taking the transboundary nature of most ocean issues into account.[38] Ocean Governance is an attempt to manage and structure all treaties, regulations, policies, principles, institutions and political measures concerning the ocean as a whole in one comprehensive architecture.[39] The lack of a unifying governance system, however, undermines possibilities for a cooperative, coherent and effective protection of the marine environment.[40] Unlike national law, international law does not provide for one centralized authority mandated to adopt and enforce laws. Governance, therefore, connotes a process of close cooperation and coordination between the States and other actors in order to achieve desired objectives concerning the sea.[41] Ocean Governance can be described as concepts, formal and informal rules, arrangements and institutions that aim to structure the use of sea space regarding permissible activities in the sea, sanctioning and responding to non-compliance and the monitoring and assessment of ocean problems. Tools of Ocean Governance include but are not limited to the ecosystem approach, which pays due regard to the interaction of human activities and the ecosystem as a whole or area-based management tools, which aim to regulate activities in certain areas through marine spatial planning or the designation of MPAs.[42] Contextually MPAs are one area in the whole ecosystem of Ocean Governance.

---

[34] https://www.environment.nsw.gov.au/topics/animals-and-plants/native-animals/native-animal-facts/whales/humpback-whale#:~:text=Threats,the%20Biodiversity%20Conservation%20Act%202016; https://www.environment.gov.au/marine/marine-species/cetaceans/entanglements.

[35] https://www.un.org/depts/los/UNCLOSinAction.mp4.

[36] Jones et al. (2004), p. 8251; https://oceanservice.noaa.gov/facts/coral-overfishing.html.

[37] Tanaka (2019), pp. 3, 46; Rothwell and Stephens (2016), p. 506.

[38] Tanaka (2019), pp. 6, 252; Gidel (1981), p. 40.

[39] Mondré and Kuhn (2017), p. 4.

[40] Gjerde et al. (2019), p. 4; Sands (2012), p. 395.

[41] Rothwell and Stephens (2016), p. 507.

[42] https://www.un.org/Depts/los/ecosystemapproaches/ecosystemapproaches.htm; Rothwell and Stephens (2016), p. 507.

2.2 Relevant Principles of Public International Law

Before delving into the legal framework that ought to oblige States to establish MPAs, it may be appropriate to provide some background on general legal principles of public international law that influence this scientific inquiry. As such, it is a prerequisite to establish the different zones of the sea as determined by the UNCLOS, which designate different jurisdictional rights and obligations of the State in each zone of the sea and therefore influence the obligation to establish MPAs. Furthermore, in order to establish the obligation to protect and preserve the marine environment through the establishment of MPAs, it is relevant to establish which rules of international law are binding for their addressee and to define MPAs in their legal context. This will culminate in an overview of the legal framework for the designation of MPAs before investigating the specific provisions in the following chapter.

2.2.1 Zonal Division of Marine Spaces Under the UNCLOS

> The sea has always been lashed by two major contrary winds:
> the wind from the high seas towards the land is the wind of freedom;
> the wind from the land toward the high seas is the bearer of sovereignties.
> The law of the sea has always been in the middle between these conflicting forces.[43]

The UNCLOS divides the sea into jurisdictional zones with varying rights and obligations of the States. In AUNJ, the coastal State has exclusive sovereignty or single sovereign rights, respectively; ABNJ are free to all States, no State may validly purport to subject any part of it to their sovereignty (Art. 89 UNCLOS).[44] While the BBNJ, for example, in its legal ambit is limited to ABNJ, the provisions of the Rio Convention with regard to the conservation of biological diversity only apply to AUNJ.[45] In order to establish obligations of the States in the sea, it is a prerequisite to establish and understand the principles of the zonal division of the sea. States show that they accept the division of sea spaces as law and delimit their borders accordingly, so that the zonal division of sea spaces has (at least partly) grown into customary international law.[46]

[43]Dupuy and Vignes (1991), p. 247.

[44]Tanaka (2019), p. 3; Rothwell and Stephens (2016), p. 1.

[45]Tanaka (2019), p. 417.

[46]The breadth of the Territorial Seas of the States varies so that it is argued that only the existence of marine spaces but not their breadth emanated in Customary International Law.

2.2.1.1 Areas Under National Jurisdiction: Exclusive Sovereignty

'[M]aritime territory is an essential appurtenance of land territory [...].'[47] The exclusive sovereignty of the coastal State thus stretches from the land territory to an adjacent sea-belt of up to 12 NM off the relevant baseline on the coast, described as the Territorial Sea of a State pursuant to Art. 2 (1) UNCLOS. The coastal State has exclusive sovereignty in these areas. The Territorial Sea includes the Internal Waters, the Archipelagic Waters and a belt of the sea of up to 12 NM off the relevant baseline on the coast, including the seabed and its resources (Art. 2 (1), (2), 3 UNCLOS). The management of activities in the sea, including the establishment of MPAs, is therefore determined by the national law of the coastal State.[48] This sovereignty, however, is not granted unrestrictedly and finds its limitations in other rules of international law pursuant to Art. 2 (3) UNCLOS. Obligations, such as to protect and preserve the marine environment as embodied in Art. 192 UNCLOS, are therefore applicable in the Territorial Sea and must be respected.

2.2.1.2 Areas Under National Jurisdiction: Single Sovereign Rights

The EEZ, Continental Shelf and Contiguous Zone

The EEZ is a resource-orientated hybrid zone beyond and adjacent to the Territorial Sea (Art. 55 UNCLOS), which can be designated up to 200 NM off the relevant baseline (Art. 57 UNCLOS). The EEZ was introduced to balance the strict limit of 12 NM of the Territorial Sea and the States' interests to exploit resources beyond these limits.[49] In the EEZ, the States generally enjoy the freedoms of the High Sea by virtue of Art. 58 (1), 87 and 58 (2), 89 UNCLOS; however, the coastal State has single Sovereign rights, such as jurisdiction for the protection and preservation of the marine environment under Art. 56 (1) (b) (iii) UNCLOS. The rights in the EEZ concerning the seabed and subsoil shall be exercised with respect to the regulations on the Continental Shelf under Art. 56 (3), 76 ff. UNCLOS.

The Continental Shelf of a coastal State comprises the seabed and subsoil of the submarine areas that extend beyond its Territorial Sea throughout the natural prolongation of its land territory to the outer edge of the continental margin or to a distance of 200 nautical miles from the baselines from which the breadth of the Territorial Sea is measured where the outer edge of the continental margin does not extend up to that distance (Art. 76 (1) UNCLOS). Hence the Continental Shelf is either limited by the outer edge of the continental margin, which can be beyond 200 NM of the baselines, or, where it does not extend up to this breadth, ends

[47] PCA, *Grisbådarna Case*, Norway v. Sweden (Award), Unofficial English Translation, p. 4; Tanaka (2019), p. 103.

[48] Harrison (2017), p. 21.

[49] Tanaka (2019), pp. 38 f.; Tanaka (2008), p. 1.

200 NM off the relevant baseline. The water column above the Continental Shelf can therefore be the EEZ (where and to the extent established) or the High Sea. Other than the EEZ that has to be established, the Continental Shelf exists *de facto*. Like the EEZ, the provisions on the Continental Shelf were established to serve the States' demands for exploitation and exploration rights beyond their 12 NM Territorial Sea border. The *ratio legis* of the EEZ and the Continental Shelf is resource-oriented and involves management and conservation of marine resources.[50]

Divergently, the Contiguous Zone is a zone up to 24 NM from the relevant baseline contiguous to the Territorial Sea, which was established to prevent (Art. 33 (1) (a) UNCLOS) and to punish (Art. 33 (1) (b) UNCLOS) the infringement of customs, fiscal, immigration or sanity law of a coastal State. The Contiguous Zone is contiguous and therefore distinguishable from the Territorial Sea but becomes part of the EEZ where established and grants single sovereign Rights to the State for the stated purposes. The Contiguous Zone likewise is an AUNJ with Sovereign Rights.[51]

The Legal Status of the EEZ

The legal status of the EEZ was one of the highly disputed issues during the UNCLOS III Conferences. Representatives who focused on the economic interests of the coastal States favoured approximating the legal status of the EEZ to the one of the Territorial Sea, granting the coastal State comprehensive jurisdiction and administrative rights. Opposingly, in particular shipping nations and the group of landlocked and geographically disadvantaged States took the view that the EEZ should continue to be considered as part of the High Seas, in which the freedoms of the High Sea prevail and only certain legal rights to use the resources of the zone are granted to the coastal State or declare the EEZ as an entirely new zone *sui generis*.[52] This fundamental antagonism of the concepts, to assert the legal nature of the EEZ primarily to the High Sea or primarily to the sovereignty of the coastal State, has far-reaching consequences for the interpretation of the rights of the coastal State on the one hand and the rights of the other States on the other hand. The legal classification of the EEZ to the Territorial Sea or the High Sea concerns not only the delimitation of exploitation rights itself but also the hierarchy between those rights, should they conflict with each other and the residual rights.[53]

Although the representative of the coastal States jurisdiction in the EEZ was strong in the first phase of the conferences, the notion of approximating the status of the EEZ to the one of the Territorial Sea could not supersede and did not make its way in the UNCLOS, as can evidently be seen in the today's regulatory regime: Art.

[50]Tanaka (2019), p. 145; Harrison (2017), p. 21.

[51]Tanaka (2019), p. 9.

[52]Koh (2009), p. 53; Proelss (2017), Art. 55, mn. 12.

[53]Jaenicke (1978), pp. 485 f.

55 UNCLOS expressly defines the EEZ as an area *beyond* and *adjacent* to the Territorial Sea and is explicitly not a part of it. Furthermore, Art. 58 (1) and (2) UNCLOS stipulate the general applicability of the freedoms of the High Sea in the EEZ, according to which no State may validly purport any part of it to its sovereignty. The decision to make the freedom of the High Sea, which is the precise opposite of the exclusive sovereignty of the coastal State, the basic principle in the EEZ and only grant single sovereign rights to the coastal State under Art. 56 UNCLOS leads to the unambiguous conclusion that the EEZ is not part of the Territorial Sea. Thus, it remains to be resolved whether the EEZ is part of the High Sea or a zone *sui generis*.

According to the precise wording of Art. 55 UNCLOS, the EEZ is subject to the 'specific legal regime' established in Part V UNCLOS. The codification of a 'specific legal regime' clearly shows the intention of the State parties to establish a specific legal framework that only applies to the EEZ, which argues in favour of its categorisation as zone *sui generis*. This is furthermore supported by a reverse conclusion of the wording of Art. 86 UNCLOS (*argumentum e contrario*), which defines the High Sea as all parts of the Sea that are not included in the EEZ or Territorial Sea. It, therefore, evidently distinguishes between EEZ and the High Sea. The systematic distinction of Part V UNCLOS on the EEZ and Part VII UNCLOS on the High Sea, too, shows the distinction of the EEZ and the High Sea in the UNCLOS. If the EEZ were part of the High Sea, it would be codified as a subcategory of the provisions on the High Sea and not as a separate part.

Lastly, also a historic examination on the development of Part V UNCLOS on the EEZ shows the intention of the State parties to stipulate a zone *sui generis* rather than subjecting the EEZ to the High Sea. While some States at the UNCLOS III Conference indeed favoured a regulatory system, which subordinates the EEZ to the regulations on the Territorial Sea or the High Sea respectively, a working group consisting of 17 States, the Castañada Group, worked out a middle ground for the EEZ, which was adapted and is now reflected in Part V UNCLOS. A critical discussion point was the residual rights, which determine the rights and jurisdiction regarding conflicts in which the UNCLOS does not contain any regulation under Art. 56, 58 UNCLOS to attribute rights or jurisdiction to either the coastal State or the international community. The compromise of the working group is reflected in Art. 59 UNCLOS, which does not clearly assign the residual rights to the coastal State or the international community, stipulates that each conflict has to be judged on its merits based on equity and in the light of all relevant circumstances of the case.[54] Conclusively the EEZ is neither part of the High Sea or the Territorial Sea, but a zone *sui generis* to which the regulations of Part V of the UNCLOS apply.

[54] Koh (2009), pp. 53 ff; Proelss (2017), Art. 55, mn. 13; Proelss (2012), p. 88.

Conclusion: EEZ, Continental Shelf, Contiguous Zone

Concludingly, the EEZ, the Continental Shelf as well as the Contiguous Zone are zones beyond, adjacent and contiguous to the Territorial Sea and therefore not subject to the exclusive sovereignty of Art. 2 (1) UNCLOS. Nevertheless, Arts. 56, 77 and 33 UNCLOS respectively grant single sovereign rights to the coastal State in the respective zone of the Sea, so that the coastal State does have some jurisdictional rights. Hence, they are Areas *Under* National Jurisdiction (AUNJ) with single sovereign rights of the coastal State.[55] The categorisation as AUNJ, as opposed to Areas Beyond National Jurisdiction (ABNJ), is furthermore reflected in the systematic structure of the UNCLOS: Art. 1 (1) (1) UNCLOS describes the Area as the seabed and ocean floor and subsoil thereof, *beyond* the limits of national jurisdiction. The Continental Shelf describes the seabed and subsoil of the sea of an area expressly *beyond* the Territorial Sea. If this described zone of the Continental Shelf were an area *beyond* national jurisdiction as opposed to *under* national jurisdictions, this would lead to the conclusions that both provisions, the rules of the Area according to Art. 1 (1) (1) UNCLOS as well as the regulations on the Continental Shelf according to Art. 76 UNCLOS would be applicable in the same geographical scope, which would make the separate regulations on the Continental Shelf obsolete.

2.2.1.3 Areas Beyond National Jurisdiction

The ABNJ encompasses two areas with two basic principles of the law of the sea: the High Sea with the freedoms of the High Sea and the Area as the common heritage of mankind. The High Sea is defined in negative terms and, by virtue of Art. 86 UNCLOS, includes all parts of the sea which are not the EEZ, Territorial Sea, Internal Waters or Archipelagic Waters. The border of the High Sea, therefore, depends on the breadth of the Territorial Sea and—where established—the EEZ and is all parts of the sea beyond that. The Area is the seabed, ocean floor and subsoil thereof beyond the limits of national jurisdiction under Art. 1 (1) (1) UNCLOS.

The freedoms of the High Sea consist of the no-sovereignty principle in Art. 89 UNCLOS as well as the listed freedoms under Art. 87 UNCLOS. According to Art. 89 UNCLOS no State may validly purport to subject any part of the High Sea to its sovereignty. By virtue of Art. 87 (1) (first sentence) UNCLOS the High Seas are open to all States, whether coastal or land-locked. Art. 87 (1) (third sentence) UNCLOS furthermore '*inter alia*' enumerates single freedoms of the High Sea. The '*inter alia*' wording shows that those freedoms are only listed inconclusively. Furthermore, under Art. 87 (1) (second sentence) UNCLOS the freedoms of the High Sea are conditioned by the UNCLOS and other rules of international law. The freedoms of the High Sea are therefore not granted in an absolute manner but are

[55] Tanaka (2019), p. 9.

conditional.[56] International obligations such as the protection and preservation of the marine environment, therefore, must be respected even in the free High Sea.

In the Area, no State shall claim or exercise sovereignty over any parts of it or its resources, nor shall any State or natural or juridical person appropriate any part thereof under Art. 137 (1) UNCLOS. The International Seabed Authority (ISA), as the competent Authority in the Area, shall adopt appropriate rules, regulations and procedures *inter alia* for the prevention, reduction and control of pollution and the protection and conservation of the natural resources and the prevention of damage to flora and fauna of the marine environment from activities in the Area under Art. 145 UNCLOS. Activities in the Area are defined in Art. 1 (1) (3) UNCLOS and comprise the exploration for and exploitation of natural resources in the Area. Natural resources in the Area are defined in Art. 133 UNCLOS and comprise mineral resources. Therefore, the competence of the ISA to adopt rules and regulations for the protection of the marine environment in the Area is limited to the exploration for and exploitation of mineral resources on the seabed, ocean floor and its subsoil of ABNJ under Art. 145, 1 (1) (3), 133 UNCLOS. The role of the ISA in this regard is twofold: on the one hand, it is the competent authority to permit activities such as deep seabed mining; on the other hand, its mandate is to ensure the sustainable use of the ocean floor. Otherwise, the Area is free from sovereign rights and sovereignty claims of States under Art. 137 (1) UNCLOS.

2.2.1.4 Impediment for the Designation of MPAs: Zonal Division of the Sea

> Therein is the tragedy. Each man is locked into a system that compels him to increase his herd without limit – in a world that is limited. Ruin is the destination toward which all men rush, each pursuing his own best interest in a society that believes in the freedom of the commons. Freedom in a common brings ruin to all.[57]

The delimitation of sea borders determines the reach of the jurisdiction for the States; however, the reality shows that migratory fish stock or ocean pollution do not obey human-made borders drawn on a map. Marine zones are designated according to the distance of baselines on the coast, without taking the geographic and ecologic specifics of the respective marine area into account. The distribution of jurisdictions over marine spaces according to rigid zones in the sea, therefore, can cause a significant divergence between the natural conditions and the applicable law and therefore imposes severe obstacles for effective marine protection in real life.[58]

The 1893 *Bering Sea Fur Seals Arbitration*, for instance, shows the divergence of rigid jurisdictional zones and effective conservation of marine species that migrate between jurisdictional zones. In order to protect fur seals in the Bering Sea, the

---

[56] Freestone (2012), p. 201.

[57] Hardin (1968), p. 1244.

[58] Tanaka (2019), pp. 3, 288.

United States extended its national jurisdiction beyond the then ordinary three NM limit and claimed authority over the Bering Sea waters. It argued that the Bering Sea had been *mare clausum* under the former Russian sovereignty, to which the United States then had succeeded. The United Kingdom refused to recognise this claim and advocated the application of the freedom of the High Seas. In the dispute, the conservation of the fur seals had to take a blow in favour of the regime of marine zones, according to which the Bering Sea was part of the High Sea and no State had jurisdiction over it. The tribunal tried to reconcile the conservation of marine species with the interests of third States in the free use of the sea by determining regulations such as the prohibition of hunting of fur seals within a 60 NM zone around the Pribilov Islands. Today, effective marine protection is still impeded by the same issue as in the 1893 B*ering Sea Fur Seals Arbitration* of strict jurisdictional zones.[59] Effective marine protection and conservation, therefore, requires a holistic approach that takes the ocean as one ecosystem into account.

2.2.2 *Sources of International Law*

In order to establish a legally binding obligation of States to establish MPAs, it has to be established which sources of law are capable of binding the State community. In national as well as international law, legal sources are divided into formal and material sources of law. While the material sources of law connote the substantive content of specific rules, the formal sources of law provide a legal rule its validity that makes it binding. In national law, formal laws are passed by a formal legislative process of an entitled authority such as the government. The decentralised system of international law does not provide such mandated legislative machinery. Nevertheless, also in international law, formal legal sources are those that are generally applicable and legally binding for their addressees.[60] Although no regulation in international law expressly states its formal sources, Art. 38 (1) of the 1945 Statute of the International Court of Justice (ICJ Statute) stipulates the formal sources to which the International Court of Justice (ICJ) is bound in finding its decisions.[61] Since these sources are capable of binding the highest international court, it is generally accepted that these sources are the formal sources of international law with a binding effect. As the law of the sea is a branch of international law, it likewise derives its formal sources from Art. 38 (1) ICJ Statute, which states:

> The Court [. . .] shall apply:
>
> (a) international conventions, whether general or particular, establishing rules expressly recognized by the contesting States;

[59] Tanaka (2019), pp. 288 f.

[60] Sands (2012), p. 144; Vitzthum (2016), pp. mn. 113, f.; Crawford (2012), pp. 20 f.; Tanaka (2019), p. 12.

[61] BGBl. II 1973, p. 505.

(b) international custom, as evidence of a general practice accepted as law;
(c) the general principles of law recognized by civilized nations;
(d) subject to the provisions of Article 59, judicial decisions and the teachings of the most highly qualified publicists of the various nations, as subsidiary means for the determination of rules of law. [62]

Art. 38 (1) ICJ Statute enumerates three equivalent sources of law: international conventions, international customs and general principles of law.[63] Although there is no hierarchy of this enumeration, in practice, the obligations of treaty law frequently are more specific and therefore tend to prevail rules of customary international law as the relevant *lex specialis*. This, however, is a consequence of the general rules of interpretation of law, which applies to all the mentioned sources of international law. A treaty may as well be prevailed by customary international law or general principles and vice versa. [64]

2.2.2.1 Treaties

The 1969 Vienna Convention on the Law of Treaties (VCLT) governs the law of international treaties (Art. 1 VCLT). [65] According to Art. 2 (1) (a) VCLT, a treaty is an international agreement concluded between States in written form and governed by international law, whether embodied in a single instrument or in two or more related instruments and whatever its particular designation. Different terminologies of the treaty such as agreement, convention or protocol can be applied equivalently, as long as it is bilateral or multilateral. Unilateral acts by States do not fall upon this definition.

Binding Effect of Treaties

The geographical scope of the treaty depends on its content and can be regional or global. The personal scope, beyond the strict wording of Art. 2 (1) VCLT, binds not only States but also international organisations are eligible parties to international treaties.[66] States are independent actors in international law. 'International Law governs relations between independent States. The rules of law binding upon States,

---

[62] Although the judicial decisions and the teachings of publicists according to Art. 38 (1) (d) UNCLOS are 'subsidiary' means for the determination of rules of law and thus are not formal sources of international law with binding effect, they play an important role in the development of international law as they are capable of giving evidence of the law; Crawford (2012), p. 37; Vitzthum (2016), p. 56, mn. 147.

[63] Sands (2012), p. 153; Sands (2007), p. 314; Tanaka (2019), p. 12; Vitzthum (2016), p. 56, mn. 147.

[64] Crawford (2012), pp. 22 f.; Vitzthum (2016), p. 58, mn. 154.

[65] UNTS, Vol. 1155, No. I-18232.

[66] Tanaka (2019), p. 15.

therefore, emanate from their own free will as expressed in conventions [. . .].'[67] Therefore, according to Art. 34 VCLT, treaties do not create either obligations or rights for a third State without its consent (*pacta tertiis non nocet*).[68] However, a treaty rule can at the same time declare, crystalize or generate a rule of customary international law and have a binding effect on non-parties by means of custom.[69]

Impediment for the Establishment of MPAs: Limited Binding Effect of Treaties

The limited binding effect of treaties to its parties is a further impediment to effective marine protection. The principle of consent is an expression of the independence of the States. At the same time, it is a major impediment for the creation of a unifying regime for the law of the sea in general and marine conservation in particular, for it also imposes the freedom not to conclude treaties if they are, for instance, perceived to be limiting the economic freedoms of the State. The UNCLOS has been signed and ratified by 168 States. The USA, for instance, did not ratify the UNCLOS because of Part XI UNCLOS, which regulates deep seabed mining and 'does not meet the United States objectives.'[70] It shows that like the Truman Proclamation 70 years ago, the economic imperative still takes the lead in forming law today, despite the knowledge of the disastrous impact of human activities on the environment.

MPAs are zones of *mare clausum* in which activities are managed and regulated in an otherwise free High Sea and therefore collide with the basic principle of the freedom of the High Sea. This collision could be solved by a respective treaty between the States for the establishment of MPAs in a certain region. However, due to the *pacta tertiis non nocet* principle, only the State parties to such a treaty would be bound by its regulations; it cannot impose rights and duties to a third State.[71] While the State-parties would have to obey conservation guidelines, such as no trawl-fishing in one area, all other States that did not sign and ratify such an agreement could unimpededly conduct any fishing activity in a relatively competition-free terrain.[72] Therefore, if not concluded by the whole State community, the designation of MPAs that only bind a part of the State community poses the danger of elevated activities of non-State parties, which would reverse the conservation effect. Only where a treaty regulation reflects or matures into customary international law or *jus cogens*, the *inter partes* effect of treaties would transform

[67] PCIJ, *Lotus Case*, PCIJ Pub. Series A.-No. 10 (1927), pp. 2, 18.

[68] Tanaka (2019), p. 16.

[69] Vitzthum (2016), pp. 43 f., mn. 115; Crawford (2012), p. 15.

[70] https://www.reaganlibrary.gov/research/speeches/70982b; Tanaka (2019), p. 35; Harrison (2011), p. 2; https://www.itlos.org/en/main/the-tribunal/states-parties/.

[71] Billé et al. (2011), p. 3; Wolfrum (1990), pp. 324 f.

[72] Tanaka (2008), p. 204.

into an *erga omnes* obligation that binds the whole international community. The establishment of MPAs under the cogent obligation to protect and preserve the marine environment as embodied in Art. 192 UNCLOS is therefore vital for the effective protection of the marine environment.

2.2.2.2 Customary International Law

The Relationship of Treaties and Customary International Law

Historically, customary international law has been the primary source of International Law.[73] Rules of customary international law can be particularly important in legal branches such as the law of the sea, in which no treaty exists to which all States have consented. Other than the *inter partes* effect of treaties, rules of customary international law generally bind the whole State Community (with exception to persistent objectors and local customary international law). Rules of general customary international law 'by their very nature, must have equal force for all members of the international community and cannot therefore be the subject of any right of unilateral exclusion exercisable at will by any one of them in its own favour.'[74] Thus, the rules of general customary international law can have a wider binding effect than the rules of treaties.

If a treaty and a rule of customary international law are identical, the treaty can have a declaratory, crystalizing or generating effect. When a treaty only casts into writing what has been established as a rule of customary international law before, such as the freedom of the High Sea in Art. 89 UNCLOS, the treaty merely has a declaratory effect of an already existing customary international law.[75] Also, the VCLT is generally applicable, as it merely codifies what has already existed before as customary international law.[76] Furthermore, a treaty can have a crystalizing effect of an emerging rule of customary international law, as the ICJ, for instance, held for Arts. 1–3 CCS on the definition and sovereign rights of the Continental Shelf, as 'these three Articles being the ones which, it is clear, were then regarded as reflecting or as crystallizing, received or at least emergent rules of customary international law relative to the Continental Shelf [...].'[77] Lastly, treaties not only crystalize and confirm an already existing rule of customary international law but, together with an according States' practice, the treaty itself can have sufficient impact to create a rule of customary international law when it expresses its acceptance as law. Treaties, therefore, have a generating effect. 'There is no doubt that this process is a perfectly

[73] Tanaka (2019), p. 12.

[74] ICJ, *North Sea Continental Shelf*, Judgment, ICJ Reports 1969, pp. 3, 38 f., para. 63; Vitzthum (2016), p. 45, mn. 120, p. 49, fn. 308.

[75] Tanaka (2019), p. 17.

[76] Schladebach (2020), pp. 25 f., mn. 3.

[77] ICJ, *North Sea Continental Shelf*, Judgment, ICJ Reports 1969, pp. 3, 39, para. 63.

possible one and does from time to time occur: it constitutes indeed one of the recognized methods by which rules of customary international law may be formed.'[78] Therefore, even a State that is not party to a law-making treaty can be bound by the norms contained in the treaty by means of international customs.[79] In these cases of identical customary and treaty regulation, the rule of 'customary international law continues to exist and to apply, separately from international treaty law, even where the two categories of law have an identical content.'[80] Therefore, even if a treaty for some reason ceases to apply between the parties, the States are still bound by the identical customary law provision, which continues to apply between them. Although the great majority of the State community has signed and ratified the UNCLOS, important States such as the USA, to date, still are not members of the UNCLOS. The assessment of the customary status of the regulations of the UNCLOS, therefore, are of particular importance for the establishment of a general and universal obligation of all States to designate MPAs under the law of the sea.

The Creation of Customary International Law

Art. 38 (1) (b) ICJ Statute requires two constituting conditions for the creation of a rule of customary international law: the act of States that amounts to a settled general States' practice as an objective element and the acceptance as law of this practice on the subjective side. The acceptance as law can be evident through the States' conviction that it renders the practice as obligatory due to a corresponding rule of customary international law; *vice versa*, this opinion of law or necessity has to be confirmed by the corresponding States' practice.[81]

General Practice of States

General States' practice is a repeated, established or regular, consistent States' practice. Not the kind of the act itself, but the uniformity of the practice is decisive.[82] While it is not required that all States have to be involved universally, especially if only a limited number of the States are interested, the absence of 'important' or

---

[78] ICJ, *North Sea Continental Shelf*, Judgment, ICJ Reports 1969, pp. 3, 41, para. 71; Tanaka (2019), pp. 15, 17; Sands (2012), p. 145.

[79] ICJ, *North Sea Continental Shelf*, Judgment, ICJ Reports 1969, pp. 3, 41, para. 70; Crawford (2012), pp. 144 ff.; UNGA A/73/10, pp. 140 f.

[80] ICJ, *Military and Paramilitary Activities in and against Nicaragua*, Nicaragua v. USA, Judgment (Merits), ICJ Reports 1986, pp. 14, 96, para. 179, p. 94, para. 176.

[81] ICJ, *Military and Paramilitary Activities in and against Nicaragua*, Nicaragua v. USA, Judgment (Merits), ICJ Reports 1986, pp. 14, 98, para. 184; ICJ, *North Sea Continental Shelf*, Judgment, ICJ Reports 1969, pp. 3, 43, para. 74, p. 44, para. 77; UNGA A/73/10, p. 129; Vitzthum (2016), p. 51, mn. 131 f., fn. 321; Tanaka (2019), p. 12.

[82] Schieder (1984), p. 63.

particularly affected States may deprive the practice of being representative and qualified to show a general practice. Moreover, acts of only single States or only a fraction of the international community are not sufficient to constitute general customary international law. It may, however, cause a binding effect between the States involved by ways of special customary international law. The strong opposition from a vast number of States can exclude the formation of customary international law in general or at least exclude its applicability to the objecting State.[83] As to the element of time, a particularly short period 'is not necessarily, or of itself, a bar to the formation of a new rule of customary international law' as long as the 'State practice, including that of the States whose interests are specially affected, should have been both extensive and virtually uniform in the sense of the provision invoked—and should moreover have occurred in such a way as to show a general recognition that a rule of law or legal obligation is involved.'[84]

The evidence of a general States' practice can be evident through various manifestations of States' behaviour which cannot be enumerated exhaustively. Relevant acts include but are not limited to the participation in the negotiation process of multilateral conventions or the signature and ratification thereof; votes, pronouncements and other acts in international organisations or collections of diplomatic materials or drafts produced by the International Law Commission (ILC). Furthermore, national and international legislation and jurisdiction or pleadings of States in national and international courts can be evidence of a practice of governments and with a preponderance of similar behaviour can lead to the creation of customary international law. Policy statements, parliamentary debates, public statements and proclamations by States, i.e. through claims to ocean areas or protests to such claims, provide further evidence to State practice and are relevant to identify customary international law.[85]

Acceptance as Law

The subjective element of a customary international law requires the evidence that a State acted in a particular way because it thought it was obliged to do so by a rule of customary international law.[86] In the *North Sea Continental Shelf* Case, the ICJ held that Art. 6 CCS on the delimitation of the Continental Shelf according to the equidistance principle did not reflect a rule of customary international law, because even if the 'States concerned agreed to draw or did draw the boundaries concerned

[83] Vitzthum (2016), p. 52, mn. 133.; Schieder (1984), p. 63; Tanaka (2019), p. 13.

[84] ICJ, *North Sea Continental Shelf*, Judgment, ICJ Reports 1969, pp. 3, 43, para. 74; Crawford (2012), p. 24.

[85] ILC, A/CN. 4/SER.A/1950/ADD. 1, p. 368, para. 31; Sands (2012), p. 144; Schieder (1984), p. 63; Vitzthum (2016), pp. 51 f., mn. 131 ff.; Tanaka (2019), p. 13; ICJ, *Military and Paramilitary Activities in and against Nicaragua*, Nicaragua v. USA, Judgment (Merits), ICJ Reports 1986, pp. 14, 97, para. 183; ICJ, *Continental Shelf*, Libyan Arab Jamahiriya/Malta, Judgment, ICJ Reports 1985, pp. 13, 29 f., para. 27.

[86] Sands (2012), p. 146.

according to the principle of equidistance. There is no evidence that they so acted because they felt legally compelled to draw them in this way by reason of a rule of customary law obliging them to do so–especially considering that they might have been motivated by other obvious factors.'[87]

The element of *opinio juris sive necessitatis* has been disputed extensively because of a paradox in its formation. Before the rule comes into existence the States cannot believe that they are obliged to act in a certain way because of the rule. In the beginning, it is therefore sufficient that the States regard their general practice as obeying a rule that would be desirable or useful and therefore should exist. Since a rule of customary international law develops gradually over a period of time (short it may be), it may well be argued that the conviction of the legal obligation matures progressively within this process.[88]

In practice, the evidence of the *opinio juris sive necessitatis* can be difficult since it requires the consideration of underlying motives of States' actions. Means of evidence may take a wide range.[89] The general State practice itself, for instance, can already raise a presumption that a State rendered the act as obligatory by a corresponding rule of international law.[90] The clearest indications that a State has avoided or undertaken a respective practice out of a sense of a legal obligation is shown by express public statements made on behalf of a State that a given practice is permitted, prohibited or mandated under customary international law. Such Statements could include but are not limited to debates in multilateral settings; assertions when introducing draft legislation; written and oral pleadings before courts and tribunals as well as court decisions; protests that characterise the conduct of other States as unlawful, such as concerning the South China Sea; governmental legal opinions; diplomatic correspondence or statements by representatives of States. Furthermore, the conclusion of a treaty itself can be evidence that a State renders a specific practice obligatory under law.[91] Overall, in assessing evidence to ascertain whether the necessary *opinio juris sive necessitatis* supports a general State practice, the nature of the rule, the general context and the particular circumstances in which the *opinio* was expressed are determining factors.[92]

If the *opinio juris sive necessitatis* is not articulated or shown in an active act but is constituted passively through omission or silence, the evidence of the acceptance as law of a general State practice as the subjective element can be especially difficult. The absence of an expression of a State's opinion can mean both, either a simple lack of interests or a tacit agreement showing that the State believes the law does not

---

[87] ICJ, *North Sea Continental Shelf, Judgment*, ICJ Reports 1969, pp. 3, 44, para. 78.

[88] ICJ, *North Sea Continental Shelf, Judgment*, ICJ Reports 1969, pp. 3, 44, para. 77; ICJ, *Military and Paramilitary Activities in and against Nicaragua*, Nicaragua v. USA, Judgment (Merits), ICJ Reports 1986, pp. 14, 108 f, para. 207; Tanaka (2019), p. 13; Sands (2012), p. 146.

[89] UNGA A/73/10, pp. 140 f.

[90] Crawford (2012), p. 27.

[91] Tanaka (2019), p. 13.

[92] UNGA A/73/10, p. 117, Conclusion 3.

exist.[93] Acquiescence is the counter element of actively creating laws by assent or protest and proposes that a binding effect can result from passivity or inaction. According to the ICJ, if the abstention is based on a conscious act because the State is under the impression that it is obliged to act, it is sufficient to constitute an international custom, for a different interpretation of the silence is not possible in good faith.[94] The failure to act or silence does therefore not necessarily prevent States from becoming bound by a rule despite their passivity.

Relativity of Customary International Law

Although customary international law generally binds the whole State community, it is not absolute in its character. It can be open to exceptions for single States (persistent objectors) or only applicable in certain terrains (special customary international law).

Persistent Objector

A State can prevent being bound by a rule of general customary international law by persistently objecting to it during its formation and for so long as it upholds its objection.[95] The possibility to object to a single rule of customary international law and to prevent to be bound by it for a specific State is to be distinguished from the situation in which a significant number of States objects to the emergence of the rule of law, which prevents the formation of the rule in general due to a lack of general State practice. Furthermore, it does not stop the binding effect of peremptory norms of general international law. A rule can only be objected to before the State is bound by it, hence before the rule has emerged into existence. Furthermore, the objection has to be maintained persistently and clearly expressed, made known to other States. Whereas there are no requirements concerning the form of the objection, the evidence of objection must be clear, for as soon as the State abandons the objection, it becomes bound by the rule. As an exception to the general binding effect of customary international law, it is on the objecting State to establish the right to benefit from the status as a persistent objector, and its invocation is subject to stringent conditions.[96] Generally, mere delinquency with a rule of customary

[93] Kellerher (1999), p. 5.

[94] PCIJ, *Lotus Case*, PCIJ Pub. Series A.-No. 10 (1927), pp. 2, 28; ICJ, *Fisheries Case*, Judgement, ICJ Reports 1951, pp. 116, 139; Vitzthum (2016), p. 52, mn. 133.

[95] UNGA A/73/10, p. 152, Conclusion 15; Crawford (2012), p. 28; Vitzthum (2016), pp. 51 f., mn. 133; Tanaka (2019), p. 14.

[96] UNGA A/73/10, p. 152, Conclusion 15.

international law by a State cannot blatantly be interpreted as its nonrecognition rather than misconduct with the rule.[97]

Special Customary International Law

Customary international law can also exist only between a certain number of States or in a certain region. As opposed to general customary international law, rules of special customary international law create rights or obligations only for the States concerned.[98] This allows accommodating differing values of interests which are particular only in some regions or between only a few States (as few as two States).[99] In fields of law such as environmental protection and marine protection in particular, in which global regimes are rare or do not exist at all, this is of particular importance. In regions such as the Caribbean or the North Sea, borders of marine ecosystems often cross the borders of adjacent States.[100] The effectiveness of marine conservation is, therefore, majorly determined by the cooperation of the States concerned. A regional approach allows the creation of flexible rules that are customised to the particularities, needs, habits and capacities of certain regions.[101] In Fiji, for instance, Tabu (taboo) areas were traditionally created for a certain period of time, in which no fishing is allowed. After fish catch has dropped in modern Fijian times, Tabu areas have been reintroduced by local communities and are now further implemented under the support of the government and non-governmental organisations. The Fiji Locally Managed area network provides for one or more Tabu areas in each of the traditional fishing grounds of the participating villages.[102] The requirements for the emergence of a rule of General customary international law apply *mutatis mutandi* to the formation of rules of Special customary international law. Thus, the emergence of a rule of Special customary international law requires evidence of general State practice among the States concerned that is accepted this practice as law.[103]

[97] ICJ, *Military and Paramilitary Activities in and against Nicaragua*, Nicaragua v. USA, Judgment (Merits), ICJ Reports 1986, pp. 14, 98, para. 186.

[98] UNGA A/73/10, pp. 154 f., Conclusion 16; Crawford (2012), p. 12.

[99] ICJ, *Case concerning Right of Passage over Indian Territory*, Judgement (Merits), ICJ Reports 1960, pp. 6, 39; UNGA A/73/10, pp. 154 f., Conclusion 16; Crawford (2012), p. 12.

[100] Kellerher (1999), p. 2.

[101] Sands (2012), p. 149; Wolfrum (1990), p. 318.

[102] https://nebula.wsimg.com/0ae527a313a892dd6d9e8134b2e3886e?AccessKeyId=536E0831567821C953C4&disposition=0&alloworigin=1; https://www.fijimarinas.com/flmma-fiji-locally-managed-marine-protected-area-network/; Kellerher (1999), pp. xviii f.

[103] ICJ, *Colombian-Peruvian Asylum Case*, Judgment, ICJ Reports 1950, pp. 266, 276; UNGA A/73/10, p. 156, Conclusion 16; Crawford (2012), p. 30.

Jus Cogens

Pursuant to Art. 53 (second sentence) VCLT peremptory norms of general international law are norms that are accepted and recognised by the international community of States as a whole as norms from which no derogation is permitted and which can be modified only by a subsequent norm of general international law having the same character. The emergence of a rule into *jus cogens,* thus, requires that the norm is a general rule of international law, which is universally accepted as well as the consensus that no derogation from this norm is permitted.[104]

Additionally, in 1951, even before the 1966 Draft Articles on the Law of Treaties and the 1969 Vienna Convention, the ICJ linked the prohibition of genocide, one of the most widely accepted and recognised *jus cogens* regulations, with fundamental values of humankind because genocide is '"a crime under international law" involving a denial of the right of existence of entire human groups, a denial which shocks the conscience of mankind and results in great losses to humanity and which is contrary to moral law and to the spirit and aims of the United Nations [...].'[105] In 2007, again, the court stated in the *Case Concerning the Application of the Convention on the Prevention and Punishment of the Crime of Genocide* that obligations under peremptory norms are 'obligations which protect essential humanitarian values and which may be owed *erga omnes*.'[106] The connection between the peremptory character of a norm and fundamental values of the international community has also been made clear by other international courts and tribunals.[107] In the *Furundzija Case*, for instance, the International Criminal Tribunal for the former Yugoslavia (ICTY) substantiated the status of the prohibition of torture as *jus cogens* because of the 'importance of the value it protects [...]. Clearly, the *jus cogens* nature of the prohibition against torture articulates the notion that the prohibition has now become one of the most fundamental standards of the international community.'[108] This judgment was quoted with approval by the European Court of Human Rights (ECtHR) in its *Al-Adsani v. the UK Case*, in which the ECtHR further stated that the prohibition of torture is one of the fundamental values of a democratic society.[109] The most widely accepted *jus cogens* regulations are the prohibition of aggression, genocide, crimes against humanity, racial discrimination and apartheid,

---

[104] Vitzthum (2016), p. 49, mn. 126.

[105] ICJ, *Reservations to the Convention on the Prevention and Punishment of the Crime of Genocide*, Advisory Opinion, ICJ Reports 1951, pp. 15, 23; UNGA A/RES/96(I), pp. 188 f.; UNGA A/74/10, p. 151.

[106] ICJ, *Case Concerning the Application of the Convention on the Prevention and Punishment of the Crime of Genocide*, Bosnia and Herzegovina v. Serbia and Montenegro, Judgment, I.C.J. Reports 2007, pp. 43, 104, para. 147.

[107] UNGA A/74/10, p. 151.

[108] ICTY, *Prosecutor v. Furundžija*, Judgement (1998), Case No.: IT-95-17/1-T, pp. 58 f., paras. 153 f.

[109] ECtHR, Case of Al-Adsani V. The United Kingdom (No. 35763/97), Judgement (2001), pp. 9 f., para. 30, p. 18, para. 59, p. 19, para. 60.

slavery, torture and self-determination and the basic rules of international humanitarian law.[110] To be considered *jus cogens*, the norm, thus, has to be of such fundamental value to the whole international community that no derogation, neither by consent nor by treaty, is permitted, such as the prohibition of the use of force.[111] Concludingly, *jus cogens* regulations are norms of general international law that reflect and protect fundamental values of the international community that are universally accepted and from which no derogation or modification is permitted, except for subsequent norms of the same character.[112]

For the law of the sea, the content of some provisions of the UNCLOS shows the incorporation of the notion of *jus cogens* in its provisions, such as the prohibition of slavery and piracy under Arts. 99, 100 UNCLOS.[113] This book will evidence that the obligation to protect and preserve the marine environment, from which the obligation to establish MPAs will be derived, has achieved the status of a peremptory norm of international law.

2.2.2.3 Inter Partes and Erga Omnes Effect of Rules of International Law

Rules and obligations in international law have different effects. While treaties due to the *pacta tertiis non nocet* rule in Art. 34 VCLT have *inter partes* effect and only bind the member States, other rules are owed by a State towards the international community as a whole, 'they are obligations *erga omnes*'.[114] The *erga omnes* effect requires a common interest of the international community as a whole.[115] Because of the persistent objector rule and special customary international law, not all rules of general customary international law have *erga omnes* effect. Peremptory rules of general international law, however, are non-derogatory and may only be modified by a peremptory norm having the same status. Therefore, while customary rules can have *erga omnes* effect, the status as a cogent rule necessarily requires the *erga omnes* effect of a rule.[116]

---

[110]UNGA A/74/10, p. 147; Crawford (2012), p. 595; Vitzthum (2016), p. 49, mn. 126.

[111]Helmersen (2014), p. 167.

[112]UNGA A/74/10, p. 142.

[113]Proelss (2004), p. 74, fn. 7.

[114]ICJ, *Barcelona Traction*, Light and Power Company, Limited (Second Phase), Judgment, ICJ Reports 1970, pp. 3, 32, para. 33.

[115]König (2001), para. 8; Proelss (2004), p. 78.

[116]ICJ, *Barcelona Traction*, Light and Power Company, Limited (Second Phase), Judgment, ICJ Reports 1970, pp. 3, 32, para. 34.

2.2.2.4 General Principles

General principles have been introduced as formal sources of law in Art. 38 (1) (c) ICJ in order to authorise the ICJ to apply municipal jurisprudence. Whereas the ICJ has rarely relied solely on general principles in finding a decision, they can play an important role in assisting to do so by filing regulation gaps and preventing *non liquet* decisions.[117] In the law of the sea, the ecosystem approach and sustainable development are acknowledged principles in the law of the sea, which may be used to guide the interpretation of the UNCLOS.[118] Principles that safeguard the functioning of legal systems such as good faith, equity, estoppel and *pacta sund servanda* are frequently regarded as general principles.[119] In its *Nuclear Test Case,* for instance, the ICJ held that although unilateral declarations by States generally do not create legal obligations and rights, a unilateral declaration made by a French government officer did create an environmental obligation on France because other States may have good faith in the binding character of declarations by States and put confidence in them.[120]

2.2.2.5 Soft Law

Soft law can be declarations, statements or other non-binding acts by States often made at international conferences or acts by international organisations such as resolutions by the UN General Assembly.[121] Soft law connotes agreements, principles and declarations that themselves are not legally binding but have legal significance in particular in the formation of international law. Soft law can confirm existing rules of customary international law, contribute to the development of new laws and by providing guidance on the interpretation of treaty texts.[122] In the law of the sea and marine protection, the declarations adopted at the United Nations Conference on Environment and Development in Stockholm in 1972 and Rio de Janeiro in 1992 are particularly important.[123] Agenda 21, which was adopted in Rio 1992, for instance, supports the interpretation that the obligation to protect and preserve the marine environment under Art. 192 UNCLOS is a rule of customary international law.

---

117 Sands (2012), p. 150; Crawford (2012), pp. 34 ff.

118 Harrison (2017), pp. 25 f.

119 Vitzthum (2016), p. 54, mn. 142.

120 ICJ, *Nuclear Tests* (Australia v. France), Judgement, ICJ Reports 1974, pp. 253, 268, para. 46; Sands (2012), p. 151.

121 Schieder (1984), p. 62; Sands (2012), p. 140.

122 Tanaka (2019), p. 19.

123 UN A/CONF.48/14/Rev.1, pp. 3 ff.; UN A/CONF.151/26/Rev.1 (Vol. I), p. 3 ff.; UN A/CONF.151/26/Rev.1 (Vol. I), pp. 9 ff.

2.2.2.6 The UN General Assembly and Security Council and the Formation of Law

International organisations play an important role in the formation of international law. Although only a few international organisations have formal legislative powers, such as the EU, they can provide an important forum where States come together to create traditional sources of international law, such as treaties and customary international law.[124] The United Nations General Assembly is an important actor in the formation of international treaties, as can be seen by the gradual evolution of the 1982 UNCLOS through three United Nations Law of the Sea Conferences and recently through the BBNJ. Although resolutions of the General Assembly themselves are not legally binding and only recommendary in nature (Arts. 10, 14 of the 1945 Charter of the United Nations (UN-Charter)), they can grow into formal sources of law by means of international customs.[125] Furthermore, because all States have an equal vote and voice, the UN General Assembly is an important platform for the States to express a concurring or objecting *opinio juris sive necessitates* and 'provide evidence important for establishing the existence of a rule or the emergence of an *opinio juris*.'[126] A resolution 'may be understood as an acceptance of the validity of the rule or set of rules declared by the resolution by themselves' and is hence eligible to confirm an *opinion juris*.[127] Furthermore, 'a series of resolutions may show the gradual evolution of the *opinio juris* required for the establishment of a new rule'.[128]

Decisions adopted by the UN Security Council under Art. 25 of the UN-Charter, by contrary, are binding for the States. Under Art. 24 (1) UN-Charter, the Security Council is responsible for the maintenance of international peace and security. If it can be argued that the protection of the marine environment through the establishment of MPAs is a matter of international security and peace, the Security Council may be mandated to adopt binding decisions for this purpose.[129]

2.2.2.7 Relationship of National and Public International Law

The interplay of national and international law plays an important role in stipulating an international, legally binding obligation that binds all States to establish MPAs,

[124] Harrison (2011), p. 3.

[125] BGBl. II 1973, p. 431.

[126] ICJ, *Legality of the Threat or Use of Nuclear Weapons* (in the following: Nuclear Weapons), Advisory Opinion, ICJ Reports 1996, p. 226, 254 f., para. 70; Tanaka (2019), p. 45.

[127] ICJ, *Military and Paramilitary Activities in and against Nicaragua*, Nicaragua v. USA, Judgment (Merits), ICJ Reports 1986, pp. 14, 100, para. 188.

[128] ICJ, *Nuclear Weapons*, Advisory Opinion, ICJ Reports 1996, pp. 226, 254 f. para. 70.

[129] Crawford (2012), p. 24; Alvarez (2018), pp. 84 f.; Vitzthum (2016), p. 51, fn. 323, p. 1, 53, mn. 137.

also in AUNJ. The issue is dealt with theoretically, either with the monist or dualist approach. Monists acknowledge that national and international law are one single legal order, with the effect that international law is directly applicable in the national legal system. Dualists argue that both legal systems are independent and international rules must be implemented in national law.[130] International law itself does not contain regulations concerning the application and implication of international law in national law. Only in the law of treaties, Art. 27 VCLT stipulates that no State may invoke the provisions of its internal law for the failure to perform with an international treaty. States thus may not escape their obligations under international law by referring to their domestic legal order, including constitutional law.[131]

In practice, the variety of international laws and the difference in national legal systems impede a unitary theoretical approach to regulate the relationship between international and national law conclusively. Rather than establishing a rigid theory, the result of the application of an international legal provision to national law must be achieved. Generally, it is acknowledged that national law may not dispense obligations under international law and that States have leeway in creating a national legal structure that provides for compliance with obligations under international law. An obligation under international law can either be transformed through the adoption of a national law with the same content (transformation); it can be made directly applicable through the incorporation, adoption or absorption by a national law (incorporation) or simply be applied by the national judicial branch. It is the result that is important rather than the way to achieve it. If a State lacks sufficient implementation of international law, it breaches international law. Other State parties have a primary claim against the State in breach to fulfil the international obligation. Furthermore, the lack of implementation of international law can also have secondary effects, such as liability or tortious claims, i.e. claims for damages, if the lack of implementation has caused damage to another subject of international law. This monograph will demonstrate that all States are under a primary obligation to establish MPAs in the law of the sea. If a State fails to do so, even in its AUNJ, it breaches international law. Other States have a primary claim against this State to comply with its obligation to establish MPAs in its AUNJ.

2.3 Definition of MPAs

In order to investigate the legally binding obligation of States, MPAS have to be defined legally. Parallel to the gap of an international, legally binding framework for the designation of MPAs, the law of the sea also lacks a unifying, international, legally binding definition of MPAs.[132]

130 Crawford (2012), p. 48; Kunig (2016), p. 77, mn. 30 f.

131 Will (2015), p. 1165.

132 Tanaka (2019), p. 418; Tanaka (2008), p. 161; Druel (2011), p. 6.

2.3.1 Requirements to a Suitable Legal Definition of MPAs

Definitions play a fundamental role in law. Hardly any other scientific discipline engulfs definitions as much as legal science does.[133] Definitions allow the accuracy of interpretation and determination of the ambit of a norm so that facts of a case can be subsumed without any doubt. The more precise a regulation is articulated, the less doubt there is in its application. Even more, the practice has shown that the clarity of a definition of an MPA directly influences its functionality. When the formulation of regulations is simple and straightforward, competent institutions and the community can understand and accept their protective scope, and they are more likely to be obeyed.[134]

At the same time, a strict and rigid definition limits the applicability of a legal norm to a variety of cases and can hinder the synchronous evolution of law with modern issues.[135] The development of new technologies, for instance, necessitates an adaptation of legal regulations from time to time. Activities such as carbon sinking in the ocean to reduce the level of greenhouse gases in the air, for instance, have not been foreseen in the times of the development of the UNCLOS. The effects of drawing CO2 in the marine ecosystem, however, are prone to disrupt the oceanic flora and fauna significantly by becoming toxic for marine organisms.[136] From a legal perspective, carbon sinking could potentially be categorised as marine pollution under Art. 1 (1) (4) UNCLOS, exploration and exploitation of the marine environment under Art. 56 (1), (3) UNCLOS in conjunction with Art. 77 (1), (4) UNCLOS or drilling and tunnelling on the Continental Shelf under Arts. 60, 80, 81 and 85 UNCLOS.[137] This shows that the regulations of the UNCLOS are flexible enough to cover activities that did not yet exist at the time of its creation. In order for a legal rule to maintain its validity over a period of time, the regulation thus needs to be flexible and adapt to modern usages of the sea. Furthermore, a definition that clearly defines and regulates any usage of and activity in the sea and tries to target all problems at once may create a complex management system that could jeopardise its practical feasibility and functionality. The key for the designation of functioning MPAs, therefore, is to simplify regulations in a way that they are easily understandable for the community and Institutions and allow a flexible application of the norm to a variety of cases while still being precise in its scope.[138]

---

[133] Proelss (2017), Art. 194, mn. 34, fn. 99; Druel (2011), p. 6.

[134] Kellerher (1999), p. 2.

[135] Vitzthum (2016), p. 60, mn. 158; Tanaka (2019), p. 40.

[136] https://www.sydney.edu.au/environment-institute/opinion/international-law-and-the-anthropocene/.

[137] Proelss (2017), Art. 81, 13 and Art. 56, mn. 35.

[138] Kellerher (1999), pp. 2, 12.

2.3.2 Definitions of MPAs in Policies and Legal Frameworks

The most commonly referred to, however, not legally binding definition of MPAs was established by the IUCN in 1988. According to it, an MPA is

> [a]ny area of intertidal or subtidal terrain, together with its overlying waters and associated flora, fauna, historical and cultural features, which has been reserved by legislation to protect part or all of the enclosed environment.[139]

The definition shows three elements: a geographically defined area as expressed by 'any area of intertidal or subtidal terrain, together with its overlying waters and associated flora, fauna, historical and cultural features'; 'which has been reserved by legislation' as a legislative element and 'to protect part or all of the enclosed environment' as conservation purpose or objective. A comparison of the most common definitions of MPAs reveals that all contain those three elements. According to the latest definition by the IUCN an MPA is

> [a] clearly defined geographical space, recognised, dedicated and managed, through legal or other effective means, to achieve the long-term conservation of nature with associated ecosystem services and cultural values.[140]

The 1992 Convention on Biological Diversity (CBD), one of the rare international, legally binding instruments on the conservation and sustainable use of biological diversity, does not explicitly define MPAs but 'protected areas' in general.[141] As the geographical scope of the CBD also includes marine spaces, the definition of protected areas under Art. 2 CBD also applies for MPAs and states:

> "Protected area" means a geographically defined area which is designated or regulated and managed to achieve specific conservation objectives.

This definition has been redefined by the CBD Ad Hoc Technical Expert Group on Marine and Coastal Protected Areas and endorsed by the Conference of the Parties to the CBD in 2004 and now builds upon the IUCN definition:

> "Marine and Coastal Protected Area "means any defined area within or adjacent to the marine environment, together with its overlying waters and associated flora, fauna, and historical and cultural features, which has been reserved by legislation or other effective means, including custom, with the effect that its marine and coastal biodiversity enjoys a higher level of protection than its surroundings.[142]

The OSPAR Commission, which was established to protect and conserve the North-East Atlantic, defined MPA in its OSPAR Recommendation 2003/3 as follows:

> "[M]arine protected area" means an area within the maritime area for which protective, conservation, restorative or precautionary measures, consistent with international law have

---

139 IUCN GA Rec. 17.38 (1988); Proelss (2017), Art. 194, mn. 34, fn. 99; Jakobsen (2016), p. 7.

140 https://www.iucn.org/content/when-a-marine-protected-area-really-a-marine-protected-area.

141 UNTS, Vol. 1760, No. I-30619.

142 SCBD, Technical Series 13 (2004), p. 7; UNEP/CBD/COP/DEC/VII/5, p. 2, fn. 1.

> been instituted for the purpose of protecting and conserving species, habitats, ecosystems or ecological processes of the marine environment.[143]

The definition of MPAs in the Draft-BBNJ defines MPAs in Art. 1 (10) Draft-BBNJ defines:

> "Marine Protected Areas" means a geographically defined marine area that is designated and managed to achieve specific [long-term biodiversity] conservation and sustainable use objectives [and that affords higher protection than the surrounding areas].[144]

In order to provide a universal definition for MPAs, the three common elements of MPAs, geographically defined area, designated by legislation and protection or conservation objective, will be analysed in the following.

2.3.3 Geographically Defined Marine Area

According to the prevailing definitions, an MPA must be a geographically defined area, commonly referred to as within the 'maritime' (OSPAR) or 'marine area' (Draft-BBNJ), 'within or adjacent to the marine environment' (CBD Ad Hoc Technical Expert Group) and of 'intertidal or subtidal terrain, together with its overlying waters and associated flora, fauna, historical and cultural features' (IUCN). Accordingly, an MPA can be designated in any zone of the Sea, including the seabed as well as the water column, together with the flora, fauna, historical and cultural features. MPAs are thus not only relevant for the protection of natural but also cultural features such as shipwrecks, jetties or lighthouses.[145] Furthermore, the definitions show that MPAs do not only include the subtidal terrain, which is the region below the level of low tide that is always underwater, but also the intertidal terrain, which is the area that is above water level at low tide and underwater at high tide. According to those definitions, MPAs can also comprise the shoreline and parts of the coastal land, which shows the interconnectedness of marine and terrestrial protection.

Marine and terrestrial ecosystems are closely interrelated, which can illustratively be seen with the effects of land-based pollution on the marine environment. Land-based pollution refers to pollution that enters the sea from land, such as fertilizers, nutrients or sewerage. The increased load of nutrients in the water can lead to harmful algal blooms resulting in hypoxia, commonly referred to as 'dead zones'. Hypoxic zones show a reduced level of oxygen in the water, which makes it inhabitable for many marine organisms that need oxygen to live.[146] It shows that

[143] OSPAR 03/17/1, Annex 9.

[144] UNGA A/CONF.232/2020/3, p. 5, Art. 1 (1).

[145] Kellerher (1999), pp. xviii f.

[146] https://oceanservice.noaa.gov/facts/deadzone.html; https://www.nationalgeographic.org/encyclopedia/dead-zone/#:~:text=Because%20most%20organisms%20need%20oxygen,such%20as%20phosphorus%20and%20nitrogen.

effective marine protection can, in fact, only be granted if the sea and land areas are dealt with in one integrated system.[147] Rather than *Ocean Governance* through the designation of a network of MPAs, effective protection of the ocean needs a *Global Governance* through the integrated designation of Protected Areas on land and in the sea. The geographical limit to marine areas, therefore, marks one of the limits of MPAs. As to the size of MPAs in the ocean, there is no limit. While there are studies that suggest that the geographic size of the area impacts the conservation outcome, from a legal perspective, MPAs can range from small marine sanctuaries to large scale MPAs.[148]

2.3.4 Designated by Legislation

Under the prevailing definitions, an MPA must be designated and managed (Art. 1 (10) Draft-BBNJ), instituted by measures consistent with international law (OSPAR Recommendation), reserved by legislation or other effective means (CBD Ad Hoc Technical Expert Group), designated or regulated and managed (Art. 2 CBD) or reserved by legislation (IUCN). The establishment of an MPA thus requires an act or measure of the relevant international body to designate, manage, regulate, institute or reserve by legislation a geographical area for a protection or conservation objective.

The objective of this monograph is to establish the legally binding obligation of States to establish MPAs. This requires not only a legally binding obligation of States to establish MPAs but also that the established MPAs are legally binding. In national law, 'legislation' refers to the creation of a legally binding law through a formal law-making process. Legislation, therefore, entails both the outcome of legally binding laws and their adoption through a formal process by a law-making body.[149] As the ICTY pointed out in its *Tadić Case* in 1995, there is 'no legislature, in the technical sense of the term, in the United Nations system and, more generally, no Parliament in the world community. That is to say, there exists no corporate organ formally empowered to enact laws directly binding on international legal subjects.'[150]

Nonetheless, irrefutably, there are legally binding international laws. Sources of international law, according to Art. 38 (1) ICJ Statute are treaties, rules of customary international law and general principles. While rules of customary international law come into existence through a consistent State practice that is accepted as law, international treaties are adopted by international bodies. The closest process of

[147] Kellerher (1999), p. 1.

[148] Toonen et al. (2013), p. 7.

[149] Hudson et al. (1931), p. xiii.

[150] ICTY, *Prosecutor v. Dusko Tadić a/k/a 'Dule'*, Decision on the Defence Motion for Interlocutory Appeal on Jurisdiction (2 October 1995), para. 43.

legislation in international law, therefore, is the adoption of legally binding treaties by states or competent international bodies. For this reason, one notion in the literature excludes customary international law and only accepts the adoption of treaties as 'international legislation'.[151] However, it is thinkable that an MPA comes into life through a consistent State practice that is accepted as law if States, for instance, refrain from certain activities in a specific marine area because they believe they are required to do so by law. The 'tabu' areas in Fiji, for instance, have evolved through traditional fishing practices. Thus, as there is no competent authority in international law, which is mandated to adopt legally binding laws in a formal procedure, 'international legislation' is condensed to the product of any source of legally binding law, in lieu of the procedure and comprises international treaties and rules of customary international law. For the further course of this monograph, 'legislation' is a generic term and comprises both national and 'international' legislation.

2.3.5 Protection, Preservation or Conservation Objective

MPAs can pursue one or multiple purposes. Existing legal treaties for the protection and preservation of the marine environment vary from slightly managed tourism areas to entire marine reserves, in which no human activity is allowed.[152] MPA is, therefore, an umbrella term for specific marine areas that have been designated for a wide range of protection, preservation and conservation objectives with varying levels of protection.[153]

2.3.5.1 Level of Protection and Categories

The level of protection of an MPA varies according to its conservation purpose from slightly to fully protected areas. MPAs can have one specific purpose, such as no-trawl or no-fishing zones, or multiple purposes, in which any human interference is excluded. Fully Protected Areas provide the highest form of protection, in which no destructive or extractive activities are allowed at all. Studies have shown that the designation of fully protected areas is vital for the efficacy of area-based management tools. The GEOMAR Helmholtz Institute investigated MPAs in the North-East Atlantic, which do not exclude commercial fishing. This monograph has shown that as a result, trawling activities within the MPAs were 38% higher compared to unprotected marine areas, which renders the conservation purposes absurd.[154] This

[151] Brunée (n.d.), para. 1.

[152] Druel (2011), p. 6.

[153] Jakobsen (2016), p. 1057, para. 2.

[154] Dureuil (2018), p. 1403.

is not due to a potentially limited impact of MPAs as such. On the contrary, no take or no trawl areas evidently show an increase in biodiversity and biomass in other studies. However, 59% of the studied MPAs by GEOMAR are fished industrially, which undermines their overall conservation outcome.[155]

A further categorization system has been introduced by the IUCN, which is recognised by the United Nations as well as several national governments. Its objective is to classify MPAs according to their management objective to provide global standards for defining and recording protected areas. The classification system introduces six categories varying from areas for the sustainable management of resources to nature reserves, in which no human activities are allowed.[156] There are currently 1533 Category Ia MPAs, which is the highest category of protection, in which human activities are strictly controlled and managed.[157]

2.3.5.2 Stages of Establishment

The establishment of MPAs is a process, which evolves in stages. The categorisation of the stages of MPAs from their proposal to their designation, implementation and active management helps to define global standards and to record and keep track of the progress of the States' commitments to establish MPAs.[158] The process of the establishment of MPAs is usually set in motion when a government or authorised body expresses its intention to establish an MPA publicly, followed by the designation of the MPA through its codification by legally recognised means. The MPA now exists on paper. The next stage, the implementation, is a critical step to transform MPAs from 'paper parks' to becoming operational on water. The designation of protected areas often gets stuck at this stage. For this reason, some studies even suggest that States should refrain from designating new protected areas and instead invest funds in managing existing protected areas, for without their implementation, the whole world could be a protected area on paper without any conservation outcome in practice.[159] The MPA reaches its final stage when the conservation objectives show outcomes, the conservation regulations are being enforced through means, such as monitoring, and it is actively managed.[160]

---

155 http://www.fao.org/fishery/mpas/en; Dureuil (2018), p. 1403.

156 https://www.iucn.org/theme/protected-areas/about/protected-area-categories; Dudley (2008), p. 6; Jakobsen (2016), pp. 8 f.

157 https://www.iucn.org/theme/protected-areas/about/protected-area-categories; https://www.protectedplanet.net/en/search-areas?filters%5Bdb_type%5D%5B%5D=wdpa&filters%5Bis_type%5D%5B%5D=marine&filters%5Biucn_category%5D%5B%5D=Ia.

158 https://old.mpatlas.org/.

159 https://www.scientificamerican.com/article/heres-why-expanding-protected-areas-isnt-saving-nature/; https://old.mpatlas.org/; Rothwell et al. (2015), p. 899; Maron et al. (2018), p. 1994.

160 https://old.mpatlas.org/.

2.3.6 Conclusion: Definition of MPAs

The concept of MPA is a generic term that encompasses a wide range of maritime zones which have been established for various protection, preservation and conservation purposes. The conservation objective, the geographic area of small ocean sanctuaries to large scale MPAs as well as national, regional and international legislation for the establishment of MPAs vary significantly.[161] In general, a marine area is protected when human activities are regulated and managed in order to fulfil any kind of protection, preservation or conservation outcome. While the most effective MPAs are fully protected areas in which no human activity is allowed, also reserves that regulate single activities, such as fishing, provide protection, preservation and conservation. Despite the varying effectiveness of minimally or fully protected areas, all categories fall within the MPAs for the purpose of this monograph. Concludingly, an MPA can generally be defined as a specific geographic marine area that has been designated by legislation for protection purposes.

2.4 Overview of the International Legal Framework of MPAs

> *The States Parties to this Convention*, [. . .] *Recognizing* the desirability of establishing through this Convention, with due regard for the sovereignty of all States, a legal order for the seas and oceans which will facilitate international communication, and will promote the peaceful uses of the seas and oceans, the equitable and efficient utilization of their resources, the conservation of their living resources, and the study, protection and preservation of the marine environment, [. . .] Have agreed as follows [. . .].—(Preamble UNCLOS).

Treaties for the protection and preservation of the (marine) environment developed thematically and pose significant gaps and overlaps.[162] More than 1000 instruments regulate international environmental law today, of which some 300 treaties interplay with the international law of the sea. The number of regulations in the law of the sea with reference to MPAs is accordingly broad. Binding and non-binding instruments exist on a national, regional and global level with varying protection objectives.[163] Concepts concerning the obligation to protect and preserve the marine environment can also be derived outside the traditional canon of the law of the sea, such as Human Rights Law, which will be introduced at the end of this chapter. To structure the regulations, the objective of MPAs can be divided into three main categories concerning the protection and regulation of species, activities and regions.

---

161 Jakobsen (2016), p. 1057.

162 Proelss (2017), Art. 194, mn. 34; Franke (2007); Molenaar (2007), p. 680; Rothwell et al. (2015), pp. 463, 487.

163 Matz (2005), pp. 53 f.; Tanaka (2019), pp. 282, 429; Mondré and Kuhn (2017), p. 8; Sands (2012), p. 169.

2.4.1 Global and General Regulations

2.4.1.1 Art. 192, 194 (5) UNCLOS and BBNJ

The broadest obligation to protect and preserve the marine environment in the law of the sea is Art. 192 UNCLOS. Art. 192 UNCLOS is an umbrella regulation, which is further detailed in the following provisions of the UNCLOS as well as other international agreements (Art. 237 UNCLOS). This monograph will prove that Art. 192 UNCLOS is a transzonal obligation, which *erga omnes* binds the whole States community and that entails the obligation of States to adopt active measures to protect the marine environment, namely, to establish MPAs. As the obligation as embodied under Art. 192 UNCLOS is the broadest obligation to protect and preserve the marine environment, this obligation will be the focus of this monograph. The concept of MPAs is furthermore entailed in Art. 194 (5) UNCLOS, which stipulates that measures taken in accordance with Part XII UNCLOS shall include those necessary to protect and preserve rare or fragile ecosystems as well as the habitat of depleted, threatened or endangered species and other forms of marine life. The extant literature, as well as the jurisprudence, accept Art 194 (5) UNCLOS as a legal basis to establish MPAs. The concept of MPAs furthermore builds part of the area-based management tools under the new BBNJ. Both Art. 194 (5) UNCLOS and the BBNJ will therefore be analysed at the end of the monograph.

2.4.1.2 Other Global and General Obligations

Further global and general regulations for MPAs are contained in various provisions, such as Art. 8 (a) CBD. However, it is debated whether the CBD applies to all areas in the sea or only to those that are under national jurisdiction. The global Convention on Wetlands of International Importance Especially as Waterfowl Habitat adopted in Ramsar in 1971 (Ramsar Convention), provides under Art. 2 (1) Ramsar Convention that each party shall designate suitable wetlands, however, only within its territory.[164] Biosphere reserves designated under the 1971 UNESCO's Man and the Biosphere Programme, which serve to contribute to the objectives of the CBD and other pertinent conventions and instruments according to Art. 2 (2) Statutory Framework of the World Network of Biosphere Reserves, similarly remain under the sovereign jurisdiction of the States (Art. 2 (3) Art. 2 (2) Statutory Framework of the World Network of Biosphere Reserves). Also rules of customary international law potentially provide a basis for the establishment of MPAs, however, limited to a specific issue. The prohibition of transfrontier damage, for instance, prohibits States to use or permit the use of their territories in such a manner as to injure the territory of

[164] UNTS, Vol. 996, No. I.14583.

another State (*sic utere tuo ut alienum non laedas*) and is therefore limited to marine pollution.[165]

2.4.2 Specific Regulations

Specific regulations with regard to the establishment of MPAs can be divided into species-, activity- and region-specific regulations. Because all of the specific instruments are limited with regard to their objective, they do not provide a general obligation of all States to establish MPAs in all zones of the sea, such as Art. 192 UNCLOS.[166] The following outline, therefore, serves to provide an overview and structure of the numerous respective legal instruments with specific conservation objectives, before delving into the specific investigation of the general obligation to establish MPAs under Art. 192 UNCLOS in the subsequent chapter.

2.4.2.1 Species Specific Regulations

There are two categories of treaties with the objective of the conservation of species: treaties with the primary objective to protect and preserve species and fisheries conventions, which manage fish as a resource in order to maintain the maximum stable productivity and that's conservation objective therefore is only secondary.

Species Specific Treaties with Primary Conservation Objective

One of the first global species-specific regulations that entails the concept of MPAs is the 1946 Convention for the Regulation of Whaling (IWC).[167] The IWC is one of the pioneer treaties with regard to the protection of the marine environment with a mandate for the International Whaling Commission to adopt 'regulations with respect to the conservation and utilisation of whale resources, fixing [...] open and closed waters, including the designation of sanctuary areas' under Art. V (1) IWC. The IWC is not limited to a specific region but aims to provide effective and proper conservation and development of whale stocks globally.[168] Two sanctuaries in which commercial whaling is prohibited have been designated under the IWC, one in the Indian Ocean south of 55°S in 1979 and one in the Southern Ocean and Antarctica in 1994.[169]

---

165 Tanaka (2019), p. 329.

166 Scovazzi (2004), p. 10.

167 UNTS, Vol. 161, No. 2124.

168 Tanaka (2008), p. 164; Druel (2011), p. 6.

169 https://iwc.int/sanctuaries; Scovazzi (2004), p. 8; Tanaka (2008), p. 164; Druel (2011), p. 6.

Today, the variety of treaties that entail the concept of MPAs with the primary objective of the conservation of specific species in specific regions is very broad and include but are not limited to instruments adopted under the 1997 Bonn Convention on the Conservation of Migratory Species (Bonn Convention), which is a framework convention under which groups of governments make action plans, agreements and memoranda of understanding to conserve specific migratory species worldwide.[170] Agreements with regard to the concept of MPAs concluded under the Bonn Convention are the 1991 Agreement on the Protection of Seals in the Wadden Sea with Special Areas under Art. VII,[171] the 1991 Agreement on the Conservation of Small Cetaceans of the Baltic, North-East Atlantic, Irish and North Seas[172] and the 1996 Agreement on the Conservation of Cetaceans of the Black Sea, Mediterranean Sea and Contiguous Atlantic Area with specially protected areas for cetaceans under Annex 2, para. 3.[173] An example outside the Bonn Convention are marine sanctuaries under Art. 2 of the 1999 Agreement Concerning the Creation of a Marine Mammal Sanctuary in the Mediterranean (Mediterranean Sanctuary Agreement).[174]

Fisheries Convention with Secondary Conservation Objective

Fisheries is an important sector of the economy of many States. The regulation and management of fish stock, such as through the determination of allowable catch and protected areas, has become an important means to secure the food supply as well as the livelihood of citizens in countries.[175] Ecological conservation is only a secondary effect that automatically follows the economic conservation of the maximum level of fish stock. The UNCLOS contains regulations for the conservation of species under Arts. 61 ff., 116 ff. UNCLOS. Further examples of treaties in this category include but are not limited to the 1958 CFCLR or the 1995 United Nations Agreement for the Implementation of the Provisions of the UNCLOS relating to the Conservation and Management of Straddling Fish Stocks and Highly Migratory Fish Stocks (UNFSA).[176] The regulations of the UNFSA provide that States shall take active measures to protect and conserve the relevant fish and fish stock and take into account the area of application and potentially give rise to an obligation to designate

---

[170] UNTS, Vol. 1651, No. I-28395; Kellerher (1999) p. 6.

[171] UNTS, Vol. 2719, No. I-48123.

[172] UNTS, Vol. 1772, No. I-30865.

[173] UNTS, Vol. 2183, No. I-38466.

[174] UNTS, Vol. 2176, No. I-38306; https://www.cms.int/en/legalinstrument/cms; Qureshi (2018), p. 866; Kellerher (1999), p. 6.

[175] FAO (2018), pp. 5 f.

[176] UNTS, Vol. 2167, No. I-37924; https://www.un.org/depts/los/convention_agreements/reviewconf/FishStocks_EN_B.pdf.

MPAs for the conservation of highly migratory and straddling fish stocks. The personal scope of the UNFSA is limited to its 91 member-States.[177]

The FAO

A special role with regard to fisheries play agreements in connection with the FAO. The FAO is a specialised agency of the UN with the objective to achieve food security and to defeat hunger that also comprises fisheries policies.[178] Although one of its primary objectives is to regulate illegal, unreported and unregulated fishing, compliance agreements have been adopted under the auspices of the FAO, which require flag states to supervise the activities of their fishing vessels on the High Sea, such as the 1995 FAO Code of Conduct for Responsible Fisheries. In 2008 the FAO released the FAO International Guidelines for the Management of Deep-sea Fisheries in the High Seas with guidelines to identify vulnerable marine ecosystems (VME) in para. 42 ff. The Guidelines assist States to define VMEs according to an internationally agreed upon set of criteria and to identify which actions must be taken for the long-term conservation and sustainable use of marine living resources in the deep sea. While the Guidelines can give assistance to identify VME, the FAO Guidelines are voluntary and are therefore not capable to stipulate a legal obligation for States to designate MPAs.[179]

2.4.2.2 Activity Specific Regulations

Activity- or issue-specific legislation comprise a large variety of rules and regulations, mainly concerning pollution.

Section 5 of Part XII UNCLOS

Section 5 of Part XII UNCLOS sets out international rules and national legislation to prevent, reduce and control pollution of the marine environment from various sources. Arts. 207 ff. UNCLOS are specific expressions of the general obligation to protect and preserve the marine environment that has already been codified at the beginning of Part XII, in Art. 192 UNCLOS. As *lex specialis* of the general obligation, Arts. 207 ff. UNCLOS will not be investigated separately, however, the regulations serve as an important tool to interpret the obligation under Art.

[177] https://treaties.un.org/Pages/ViewDetails.aspx?src=IND&mtdsg_no=XXI-7&chapter=21&clang=_en.

[178] http://www.fao.org/about/en/.

[179] http://www.fao.org/fishery/topic/166303/en; http://www.fao.org/3/a-i7774e.pdf; http://www.fao.org/3/i0816t/i0816t.pdf, pp. 9 ff., paras. 42 ff.

192 UNCLOS, as they entail the obligation to adopt national laws and regulations and to endeavour to conclude international agreements to prevent, reduce and control pollution of the marine environment.

Land-Based Pollution

Land-based pollution is estimated to cause 70–80% of marine pollution.[180] Plastic debris is known to be the cause for the death of a vast number of marine lives that mistake plastic for food or absorb it as microplastic. Ocean currents spread debris across the sea where it forms islands such as the Great Pacific Garbage Patch.[181] Fertilizer and waste are washed in the sea from land, where it causes ocean acidification and eutrophication. In the Gulf of Mexico, for instance, a 20,000 km^2 hypoxic 'dead zone' forms each summer due to the fertilizers and waste that enter the sea from the Mississippi River, in which oxygen levels are so low that almost no life exists beneath the surface of the water.[182]

The 1985 Montreal Guidelines for the Protection of the Marine Environment against Pollution from Land-based Sources (Montreal Guidelines), for instance, entails concepts of specially protected areas for the protection of the marine environment from land-based pollution.[183] The status of the Montreal Guidelines, however, is debated, which causes uncertainty in determining its legally binding status.[184] The 1972 Convention on the Prevention of Marine Pollution by Dumping of Wastes and Other Matter (London Convention) addresses vessel-source as well as land-based marine pollution.[185] However, the degree to which States have accepted and even implemented those regulations varies considerably and makes the determination of international guidelines for dumping difficult.[186]

Pollution from Dumping

Communities around the world have used the ocean as a place to dispose of waste for decades. The US alone has dumped 55,000 tons of radioactive waste in the Pacific and 34,000 tons in the Atlantic Ocean between 1946 and 1970, as estimated by the

---

[180] UN A/CONF.151/26 (Vol. II), para 17.18; Billé et al. (2011), p. 36; Proelss (2017), Art. 211, mn. 2.

[181] https://www.nationalgeographic.org/encyclopedia/great-pacific-garbage-patch/.

[182] https://www.nationalgeographic.org/encyclopedia/dead-zone/; https://www.boell.de/sites/default/files/web_170607_ocean_atlas_vektor_us_v102.pdf, p. 14.

[183] UNEP/WG. 120/3 (Part IV), printed in: UNEP (1985), p. 77.

[184] McConnell and Gold (1991), p. 100; Tanaka (2019), pp. 419 f.

[185] UNTS, Vol. 1046, No. I-15749.

[186] McConnell and Gold (1991), p. 101.

US Environmental Protection Agency.[187] In 2020, Japan announced its plan to dump more than 1 million tons of contaminated water from the Fukushima nuclear power plant into the ocean.[188] Examples of treaties to regulate dumping are the 1972 Convention for the Prevention of Marine Pollution by Dumping from Ships and Aircraft (Oslo Convention) or the mentioned 1972 London Convention.[189] The personal scope, however, is limited, as not all of the member States of the London Convention are parties to the London Protocol, which counts only 53 member States.[190]

Pollution from Vessels

The International Maritime Organization (IMO) is the competent UN specialized organisation, which is responsible for the safety and security of ships and marine pollution by ships.[191] The 1973/1978 MARPOL Convention was adopted under its auspices. The 1973/1978 MARPOL Convention is the main international instrument concerning the pollution from ships and provides for the designation of 'Special Areas' in its Annexes.[192] MARPOL Special Areas exist *inter alia* in the Mediterranean Sea, the Baltic Sea, the Red Sea, the Black Sea, the Antarctica Area or the North Sea.[193] The IMO is furthermore mandated to identify Particularly Sensitive Sea Areas under the IMO Guidelines, to protect vulnerable areas that need special protection because of ecological, socio-ecological or scientific reasons.[194] Furthermore, Art. 234 UNCLOS specifically regulates vessel source pollution in ice-covered areas in the EEZ of a coastal State.

2.4.2.3 Region Specific Regulations

Some of the most significant regional regulations which oblige States to protect and preserve the marine environment and that entail potential obligations to establish MPAs have been adopted under the Regional Seas Programme of the United Nations

[187] https://www.epa.gov/ocean-dumping/learn-about-ocean-dumping#:~:text=Following%20decades%20of%20uncontrolled%20dumping,levels%20in%20some%20ocean%20waters.

[188] https://theconversation.com/japan-plans-to-dump-a-million-tonnes-of-radioactive-water-into-the-pacific-but-australia-has-nuclear-waste-problems-too-148337.

[189] UNTS, Vol. 932, No. I-13269.

[190] https://www.imo.org/en/OurWork/Environment/Pages/London-Convention-Protocol.aspx.

[191] https://www.imo.org/en.

[192] Tanaka (2019), pp. 419 f.; Tanaka (2008), p. 174; http://www.imo.org/en/About/Conventions/ListOfConventions/Pages/International-Convention-for-the-Prevention-of-Pollution-from-Ships-(MARPOL).aspx.

[193] https://www.imo.org/en/OurWork/Environment/Pages/Special-Areas-Marpol.aspx.

[194] IMO A 24/Res. 982; https://www.imo.org/en/OurWork/Environment/Pages/PSSAs.aspx; Kellerher (1999), p. 8.

Environment Programme (UNEP). The Programme led to the adoption of non-binding action plans as well as binding Conventions with regard to the conservation of the marine environment. Examples of binding Conventions adopted under the UNEP include but are not limited to the 1980 Convention for the Conservation of Antarctic Marine Living Resources (CCAMLR),[195] the 1992 OSPAR and the 1995 Convention for the Protection of Marine Environment and the Coastal Region of the Mediterranean (Barcelona Convention).[196]

In the Antarctic, MPAs, which are entirely located in the Antarctic High Sea, have been designated under the 1959 Antarctic Treaty with its 1991 Protocol on Environmental Protection to the Antarctic Treaty and Annexes (Antarctic Treaty)[197] and the CCAMLR. The Antarctic Treaty provides for the designation of Antarctic Specially Protected Areas or Antarctic Specially Managed Areas for the regulation of mining and establishment of environmental controls. The CCAMLR MPAs are the 94,000 km^2 South Orkney Islands MPA, which was designated in 2009 and the 1.55 million km^2 Ross Sea MPA in 2016.[198] Cross-sections exist with the whale sanctuaries designated in the Southern Ocean under the IWC.[199]

In the North-East Atlantic, MPAs have been established by the OSPAR and the North-East Atlantic Fisheries Commission (NEAFC). Between 2010 and 2012 seven MPAs have been designated on the High Sea under the OSPAR's Regulatory Regime.[200] The Memorandum of understanding between the OSPAR Commission and NEAFC is an example, of how coordination between overlapping OSPAR and NEAFC areas can effectively be sought and enhance a geographical linkage between the OSPAR and NEAFC areas.[201]

In the European Union (EU) the Natura 2000 Network is the largest network of terrestrial and marine protected areas in the world, stretching over 18% of the EU's terrestrial terrain and more than 8% of its marine territory.[202] It consists of the 1979 Birds Directive and the 1992 Habitat Directive (Natura 2000 Directives) for the protection of vulnerable natural habitats and wild fauna and flora.[203] While a coherent approach concerning the protection of seabirds, turtles and marine mammals has been achieved through Natura 2000 sites, the protection of fish, invertebrate species and marine habitats was incomprehensive. The 2008 Marine Strategy

[195] UNTS, Vol. 1329, No. I-22301.

[196] UNTS, Vol. 1102, No. I-16908; Adede (1995), pp. 33, 36 ff.; Tanaka (2008), pp. 202 ff.

[197] UNTS, Vol. 402, No. I-5778; UNTS, Vol. 2941, No. A-5778.

[198] https://www.ccamlr.org/en/science/marine-protected-areas-mpas; Tanaka (2019), p. 425; https://www.ccamlr.org/en/science/marine-protected-areas-mpas; https://www.ccamlr.org/en/organisation/members; Scovazzi (2004), p. 9.

[199] Kellerher (1999), p. 3.

[200] https://www.ospar.org/work-areas/bdc/marine-protected-areas/mpas-in-areas-beyond-national-jurisdiction; Tanaka (2019), p. 425.

[201] Tanaka (2019), p. 427.

[202] https://ec.europa.eu/environment/nature/natura2000/indexen.htm.

[203] Birds Directive 2009/147/EC; Habitats Directive 92/43/EEC; https://ec.europa.eu/environment/nature/natura2000/index_en.htm.

Framework Directive and the 2014 Marine Spatial Planning Directive have been adopted in response to this shortcoming.[204]

Furthermore, in some areas traditional fishing rights are accepted as customary law, such as 'Tabu' Areas and Fiji Locally Managed Marine Protected Area Network in Fiji.[205]

As treaties are only binding for the States parties, in the relevant terrain with regard to their objective, the scope of all mentioned treaties is limited. The number of specific treaties that include the basis to establish MPAs in specific terrains or with regard to specific activities is very large.

2.4.3 *Relevant Rules of Customary International Law and General Principles*

As this monograph focuses on the *erga omnes* obligation to establish MPAs, short reference may be had to exemplary, relevant rules of customary international law and general principles, from which an obligation to establish MPAs may be derived. Although customary rules of international law possess the potential to bind all State parties (with exception to persistent objectors), they are limited with regard to their substantive scope.

One of the earliest and universally accepted rule of customary international law in this regard, is the prohibition of transboundary damage, which is also codified in several binding and non-binding international regulations such as Art. 194 (2) UNCLOS, Principle 2 of the 1992 Rio Declaration on Environment and Development (Rio Declaration) and Principle 21 of the 1972 Declaration of the United Nations Conference on the Human Environment, adopted at Stockholm (Stockholm Declaration).[206] This prohibition was first acknowledged in the *Trail Smelter Arbitration* in 1941 and restated in the consistent jurisprudence of international courts and tribunals ever since. It puts the State under a due diligence obligation to 'ensure that activities within their jurisdiction and control respect the environment of other States or of areas beyond national control.'[207]

---

[204] Marine Strategy Framework Directive 2008/56/EC; Marine Spatial Planning Directive 2014/89/EU; EEA Report 3/2016, p. 12.

[205] https://nebula.wsimg.com/0ae527a313a892dd6d9e8134b2e3886e?AccessKeyId=536E0831567821C953C4&disposition=0&alloworigin=1; https://www.fijimarinas.com/flmma-fiji-locallymanaged-marine-protected-area-network/; Kellerher (1999), pp. xviii f.

[206] UN A/CONF.151/26 (Vol. I); UN A/CONF.48/14/Rev.1, pp. 3 ff.

[207] PCA, *South China Sea Arbitration*, Philippines v. China (Award), p. 374, para. 941; ICJ, *Nuclear Weapons*, Advisory Opinion, ICJ Reports 1996, pp. 226, 241 f., para. 29; *Trail Smelter Case*, Reports of International Arbitral Awards (1938 and 1941), Volume III, pp. 1905, 1938; ICJ, *Corfu Channel Case*, Judgment, ICJ Reports 1949, pp. 4, 22; ICJ, *Pulp Mills on the River* Uruguay (Argentina v. Uruguay), Judgment, ICJ Reports 2010, pp. 14, 78, para. 193; Kojima (2015), p. 171; Roach (2014), p. 250; Sands (2012), p. 241.

The obligation of States to cooperate, as envisaged in Art. 197 UNCLOS, is expression of the 'good-neighbourlyness' principle and has been accepted as general principle and rule of customary international law.[208] The precautionary principle puts States under the duty to take preventive measures and perform due diligence assessments in case in which there is scientific uncertainty as to the effects of activities on the (marine) environment. Its core is described in Principle 15 of the Rio Declaration, which states that where there are threats of serious or irreversible damage, lack of full scientific certainty shall not be used as a reason for postponing cost-effective measures to prevent environmental degradation. The precautionary principle is accepted as rule of customary international law and incorporated in universal and regional instruments and the consistent jurisprudence.[209] It is accepted in a widespread range of subject areas, such as Art. 2 (2) (a) OSPAR Convention for the law of the sea.[210]

The ecosystem approach aims to manage human activities to support the conservation, sustainable use and integrated management of land, water and living resources.[211] MPAs can therefore be regarded as tools to implement the ecosystem approach.[212] However, there is no universally established definition of an ecosystem approach.[213] Elements of it are mentioned in Principle 2 of the Stockholm Declaration and are reflected in a broad number of conventions for the conservation of the marine environment such as Art. II CCAMLR.[214] Its normative content however is not yet clear.[215]

Environmental impact assessment are procedures to determine the beneficial and adverse consequences of decisions, policies, programmes or projects on the environment, including socio-economic, cultural and human-health impacts.[216] The obligation to conduct an environmental impact assessment is embodied in

[208] ITLOS, *MOX Plant*, Ireland v. United Kingdom, Provisional Measures (3 December 2001), ITLOS Reports 2001, pp. 95, 110, para. 82; Sands (2012), p. 249; ITLOS, *MOX Plant*, Ireland v. United Kingdom, Provisional Measures (3 December 2001), ITLOS Reports 2001, pp. 95, 110, para. 82; Proelss (2017), Art. 197, mn. 10 f.

[209] ITLOS, *MOX Plant*, Ireland v. United Kingdom, Provisional Measures (3 December 2001), sep. op. Judge Wolfrum, ITLOS Reports 2001, p. 133; ITLOS, *Responsibilities and Obligations of States Sponsoring Persons and Entities with Respect to Activities in the Area*, Advisory Opinion, ITLOS Reports 2011, pp. 10, 47, para. 135; dissenting: ITLOS, *Southern Bluefin Tuna Cases*, New Zealand v. Japan; Australia v. Japan, Provisional Measures, diss. op. Judge Laing, p. ITLOS Reports 1999, p. 311, fn. 6; Roach (2014), p. 241.

[210] Sands (2012), p. 272; ITLOS, *Responsibilities and Obligations of States Sponsoring Persons and Entities with Respect to Activities in the Area*, Advisory Opinion, ITLOS Reports 2011, pp. 47, 135.

[211] https://www.cbd.int/ecosystem/; Ryan Enright and Boteler (2020), p. 333.

[212] Proelss (2017), Art. 194, mn. 34.

[213] UNGA A/61/156, p. 2, para. 6; Ryan Enright and Boteler (2020), p. 335.

[214] Ryan Enright and Boteler (2020), p. 338.

[215] Ryan Enright and Boteler (2020), p. 334.

[216] https://www.cbd.int/impact/whatis.shtml; https://ec.europa.eu/environment/eia/index_en.htm.

international Conventions such as Art. 206 UNCLOS and recognised as a general obligation under customary law.[217]

The ICJ established in its *Legality of the Threat or Use of Nuclear Weapons* that 'the environment is not an abstraction but represents the living space, the quality of life and the very health of human beings, including generations unborn'.[218] This obligation toward younger generations is furthermore expressly or implicitly entailed in many environmental agreements, such as the preamble of the 1946 IWC, Art. 4 of the 1972 Convention for the Protection of the World Cultural and Natural Heritage (World Heritage Convention)[219] or the preambles of the 1978 Kuwait Regional Convention for Co-operation on the Protection of the Marine Environment from Pollution (Kuwait Convention)[220] and the 1983 Convention for the Protection and Development of the Marine Environment of the Wider Caribbean Region (Cartagena Convention)[221] with specific regard to the marine environment.[222] In a recent lawsuit in Australia, a group of 'Younger People' applied to the Federal Court of Australia to hold that the environment minister has a duty of care to younger people which obliges it not to act in a way that causes harm from climate change to younger people. The obligation was confirmed by the court.[223]

States are under the customary obligation to ensure that their resources are exploited, developed and used sustainably under the principle of sustainable development.[224] Especially fishery conservation treaties, that's first objective is the maintenance of optimum sustainable yield or maximum and optimum utilisation of fish stocks are referred to in this regard.[225]

In the *Case concerning the Gabčíkovo-Nagymaros Project,* the ICJ connected the sustainable development principle with the obligation toward younger generations in a way that shows the necessity of the evolution of law in the light of new challenges, which will become relevant for the establishment of a legally binding obligation to establish MPAs later in this monograph. The ICJ stated that '[t]he Court is mindful that, in the field of environmental protection, vigilance and prevention are required

---

[217] ITLOS, *Responsibilities and Obligations of States Sponsoring Persons and Entities with Respect to Activities in the Area, Advisory Opinion*, ITLOS Reports 2011, pp. 10, 75 and 50, para. 145; ICJ, *Pulp Mills on the River Uruguay* (Argentina v. Uruguay), Judgment, ICJ Reports 2010, pp. 14, 83, para. 204; Roach (2014), pp. 241 and 250.

[218] ICJ, *Nuclear Weapons*, Advisory Opinion, ICJ Reports 1996, pp. 226, 241, para. 29; Sands (2012), p. 249.

[219] UNTS, Vol. 1037, No. I-15511.

[220] UNTS, Vol. 1140, No. I-17898.

[221] UNTS, Vol. 1506, No. I-25974.

[222] Sands (2012), p. 256.

[223] https://theconversation.com/in-a-landmark-judgment-the-federal-court-found-the-environment-minister-has-a-duty-of-care-to-young-people-161650.

[224] ICJ, *Case concerning the Gabčíkovo-Nagymaros Project*, Judgement (Merits), ICJ Reports 1997, pp. 7, 78, para. 140; PCA, *Iron Rhine Arbitration*, Belgium v. Netherlands (Award) 2005, pp. 28 f. para. 59; Sands (2012), p. 241.

[225] Sands (2012), p. 258.

on account of the often irreversible character of damage to the environment and of the limitations inherent in the very mechanism of reparation of this type of damage. Throughout the ages, mankind has, for economic and other reasons, constantly interfered with nature. In the past, this was often done without consideration of the effects upon the environment. Owing to new scientific insights and to a growing awareness of the risks for mankind—for present and future generations—of pursuit of such interventions at an unconsidered and unabated pace, new norms and standards have been developed, set forth in a great number of instruments during the last two decades. Such new norms have to be taken into consideration and such new standards given proper weight, not only when States contemplate new activities but also when continuing with activities begun in the past. This need to reconcile economic development with protection of the environment is aptly expressed in the concept of sustainable development.'[226]

2.4.4 *Other Branches of Public International Law*

Lastly, concepts concerning the obligation to protect and preserve the marine environment can be derived from other branches of public international law, such as Human Rights Law, Non-Human Rights Law, climate change or cultural heritage.

2.4.4.1 Human Right to Environment

Human activities in the sea, such as deep seabed mining or navigation are not free from risk. The interaction between considerations of humanity and the law of the sea can play an important role when managing human activities in the sea.[227]

Traditionally this question is dealt with from the view of the law of the sea and investigates the application of Human Rights in this field. In this light it is established, that States' obligations can arise from 'certain general and well-recognized principles, namely: elementary considerations of humanity [. . .].'[228] 'Considerations of humanity must apply in the law of the sea, as they do in other areas of international law.'[229] They can either be taken into account through specific treaty regulations that embody Human Rights considerations themselves, such as Art. 146 UNCLOS which states that humanitarian considerations have to be taken into account for activities with respect to activities in the Area. Or, otherwise, they

[226] ICJ, *Case concerning the Gabčíkovo-Nagymaros Project*, Judgement (Merits), ICJ Reports 1997, pp. 7, 77 f, para. 140.

[227] Tanaka (2019), p. 20.

[228] ICJ, *Corfu Channel Case, Judgement* (1949), ICJ Reports 1949, pp. 4, 22.

[229] ITLOS, *M/V "Saiga"* (No. 2) Case, Saint Vincent and the Grenadines v. Guinea, Judgment, ITLOS Reports 1999, pp. 10, 62, para. 155.

can be made applicable to the whole treaty through general opening clauses such as Art. 293 UNCLOS.[230] Moreover, Art. 31 (3) (c) VCLT opens the applicability of Human Rights to international treaties in general by providing the applicability of any relevant rule of international law in the relations between the parties.[231]

The interplay is not unilaterally limited to the influence of considerations of humanity on the law of the sea. Reciprocally, concerns of the law of the sea and marine pollution, in particular, can influence considerations of humanity. In a case, in which the ECtHR was to decide about the amount required by way of bail for environmental damage caused due to marine pollution by Spain, the ECtHR held that 'the growing and legitimate concern both in Europe and internationally in relation to environmental offences' had to be taken into consideration in interpreting Human Rights.[232] This is of particular interest considering the mandate of the UN Security Council to adopt legally binding decisions under Art. 25, 24 (1) UN-Charter for the maintenance of Human Rights. The developments in international and national jurisprudence as outlined later in this monograph, indicate the emergence of a Human Right to Environment to this end.

2.4.4.2 Non-Human Right of Nature

Not only the question of a Human Right to Environment but also a Right of Nature itself and its legal standing in a lawsuit has gained momentum in international law. In 1948 the Universal Declaration of Human Rights was adopted and stipulated the right to life for humans.[233] This anthropogenic legal system left out the indigenous visions of life on earth, which included that all the living species have equal rights, including forests, mountains, rivers and the Earth itself. UK barrister Monica Feria-Tinta asks: 'Did we get it wrong? Has a system of law that only respects the right to life of human beings (legally speaking) missed the true protection of *life*?'[234] One of the first countries to recognise the Rights of Nature in its Constitution was Ecuador. Art. 71 of the Ecuadorian Constitution provides that nature, or Pacha Mama, where life is reproduced and occurs, has the right to integral respect for its existence and for the maintenance and regeneration of its life cycles, structure, functions and evolutionary processes.[235]

---

[230] Treves (2010), pp. 5 f.

[231] Tanaka (2019), pp. 20 f.

[232] ECtHR, *Case of Mangouras v. Spain* (Application no. 12050/04), Judgment (2010), p. 28, para. 86; Treves (2010), pp. 2 and 12.

[233] UNGA 217 A (III), p. 71.

[234] https://www.counselmagazine.co.uk/articles/does-nature-have-rights-.

[235] 'La naturaleza o Pacha Mama, donde se reproduce y realiza la vida, tiene derecho a que se respete integralmente su existencia y el mantenimiento y regeneración de sus ciclos vitales, estructura, funciones y procesos evolutivos', Art. 71 Constitución Política de la República del Ecuador, Published in the Official Register No. 449 on 20.10.2008.

The concept of legal personhood of nature or environmental personhood was introduced by Christopher S. Stone in its article in 1975. It consists of three rights, the legal standing of nature in court, the possibility to enter into contracts and to take legal actions to protect itself. It raises the question, furthermore, if legal personhood of nature only comprises rights of nature or necessarily bears the counter element of its liability, i.e. in the case of natural disaster.[236] Stone argues that it is not to say that nature should not have rights, because it cannot speak on its own. 'Corporations cannot speak either; nor can states, estates, infants, incompetents, municipalities or universities. Lawyers speak for them [. . .]. One ought, I think, to handle the legal problems of natural objects as one does the problems of legal incompetents—human beings who have become vegetable.'[237] Legal questions connected to environmental personhood, therefore, are not insurmountable. Like corporate law, which includes the legal standing and liability of companies, the right to nature and its legal standing would have to be codified or recognised in legal systems. Legal personhood of certain rivers has been recognised in national law in New Zealand, Australia, India, Colombia and for all rivers in Bangladesh.[238] Non-human personhood can be an important step for animal rights such as suggested for dolphins or whales. Legal personhood of the Moon could potentially protect its resources from exploitation plans of private companies and States.[239] Recognition in international law and jurisprudence to this end has not yet occurred. In the light of increasing environmental and climate litigation, however, further developments in this direction are to be expected.

2.4.4.3 Cultural Heritage

A few of the widest known marine reserves have been established under the auspices of the 1972 World Heritage Convention. World Heritage Sites with large marine components are the Belize Barrier Reef, the Great Barrier Reef and Shark Bay in Australia, the Tubbataha Reef in the Philippines, the Ujong Kulong in Indonesia, the Galapagos Islands in Ecuador, Glacier Bay in Canada, the Banc d'Arguin ín Mauritania or the Sunderbans in Bangladesh.[240]

---

[236] https://law.unimelb.edu.au/news/MLS/should-rivers-have-legal-rights.

[237] Stone (1972), p. 464.

[238] https://www.jurist.org/commentary/2020/04/sanket-khandelwal-environment-person/; https://law.unimelb.edu.au/news/MLS/should-rivers-have-legal-rights.

[239] https://wearesonar.org/dolphin-and-whale-nonhuman-personhood/.

[240] Tanaka (2008), p. 165.

2.5 Conclusion: Universal Obligation Art. 192 UNCLOS

There are numerous legal regulations that potentially provide for the establishment of MPAs in the law of the sea and other fields of international law. The ambit of specific regulations, however, is limited either with regard to their personal, substantive or geographical scope. The only global, *erga omnes* and unlimited substantive regulations is the obligation to protect and preserve the marine environment under Art. 192, 194 (5) UNCLOS. The following investigation will therefore focus on evidencing that the obligation of States to establish MPAs is entailed in this regulations.

References

Adede AO (1995) The treaty system from Stockholm (1972) to Rio de Janeiro (1992). Pace Environ Law Rev 13(1):33–48

Alvarez JE (2018) Legal perspectives. In: Weiss TG, Daws S (eds) The Oxford handbook on the United Nations, 2nd edn. Oxford University Press, Oxford, pp 79–103

Billé R, Druel E, Rochette J (2011) Advancing the Oceans agenda at Rio+20: where we must go. Institut du Développement Durable et des Relations Internationals (IDDRI), Policy Brief, No 5/11, November 2011 (Biodiversity)

Brunée J (n.d.) International legislation. In: Max Planck Encyclopedia of Public International Law (MPEPIL), p 1429

Cottier T (2015) Equitable principles of maritime boundary delimitation – the quest for distributive justice in international law. Cambridge University Press, Cambridge

Crawford JR (2012) Brownlie's principles of public international law, 8th edn. Oxford University Press, Oxford

Deman Magoffin R (1923) De Dominio Maris Dissertatio by Cornelius van Bynkershoek. Oxford University Press, New York

Deman Magoffin R (2001) The freedom of the seas or the right which belongs to the Dutch to take part in the East Indian Trade, A Dissertation by Hugo Grotius. New Jersey

Druel E (2011) Marine protected areas in areas beyond national jurisdiction: the state of play, Institut du Développement Durable et des relations Internationales (IDDRI) Working Paper Number 7/11, Paris

Dudley N, Stolton S, Shadie P (2008) Guidelines for applying protected area management categories, IUCN WCPA best practice guidance on recognising protected areas and assigning management categories and governance types. Best practice protected area guidelines series no. 21. International Union for the Conservation of Nature, Gland

Dupuy R-J, Vignes D (1991) A handbook on the law of the sea, vol 1. Martinus Nijhoff Publishers, Leiden

Dureuil M, Boerder K, Burnett KA, Froese R, Worm B (2018) Elevated trawling inside protected areas undermines conservation outcomes in a global fishing hot spot. Science 362(6421): 1403–1407

Food and Agriculture Organization of the United Nations (FAO) (2018) SOFIA Report 2016, The State of World Fisheries and Aquaculture 2016 - contributing to food security and nutrition for all. Rome

Franke V (2007) The European Community and Marine Environmental Protection in the International Law of the Sea - Implementing Global Obligations at the Regional Level, Publications on Ocean Development, vol 58. Leiden

Freestone D (2012) International governance, responsibility and management of areas beyond national jurisdiction. Int J Mar Coast Law 27(2):191–204
Freitas S (1625) De Iusto Imperio Lusitanorum Asiatico. Hieronymus Morillo, Madrid
Gidel G (1981) Le droit international public de la mer: le temps de paix, vol 1. Librairie Edouard Duchemin, Paris
Gjerde KM, Clark NA, Harden-Davies HR (2019) Building a platform for the future - the relationship of the expected new agreement for marine biodiversity in areas beyond National Jurisdiction and the UN Convention on the Law of the Sea. In: Chircop A, Coffen-Smout S, McConnel ML (eds) Ocean yearbook online, vol 33(1), pp 1–44
Glover LK, Earle S, Kelleher G (2004) Defying oceans end – an agenda for action. Island Press, Washington
Hafner G (2006) Schutz der Meeresumwelt. In: Vitzthum W (ed) Handbuch des Seerechts. C. H. Beck, Munich, pp 355–421
Hardin G (1968) The tragedy of the commons. Science 162(3859):1243–1248
Harrison J (2011) Making the law of the sea - a study in the development of international law. Cambridge University Press, Cambridge
Harrison J (2017) Saving the oceans through law – the international legal framework for the protection of the marine environment. Oxford University Press, Oxford
Helmersen ST (2014) The prohibition of the use of force as jus cogens: explaining apparent derogations. Neth Int Law Rev 61(2):167–193
Hudson MO, Bacon RE, Sohn LB (1931) International legislation: a collection of the texts of multipartite international instruments of general interest - beginning with the Covenant of the League of Nations, vol 1. Carnegie Endowment for International Peace, Washington, pp 1919–1921
Jaenicke G (1978) Die Dritte Seerechtskonferenz. Zeitschrift für ausländisches öffentliches Recht und Völkerrecht 38:437–511
Jakobsen IU (2016) Marine protected areas in international law – an Arctic perspective. In: Fitzmaurice M, Okowa P, Singer S (eds) Queen Mary studies in international law, vol 25. Brill, Leiden
Jones GP, McCormick MI, Srinivasan M, Eagle JV (2004) Coral decline threatens fish biodiversity in marine reserves. Proc Natl Acad Sci 101(21):8251–8253
Kellerher G (1999) Guideline for marine protected areas. World Commission on Protected Areas of IUCN – The World Conservation Union, Gland
Koh TTB (1989) Extended maritime jurisdiction – a global approach. In: Craven JP, Schneider J, Stimson C (eds) The international implications of extended maritime jurisdiction in the pacific: proceedings of the 21st annual conference of the law of the sea institute. Hawaii University, Honolulu, pp 13–17
Koh TTB (2009) Remarks on the legal status of the exclusive economic zone. In: Nordquist MH, Koh TTB, Norton Moore J (eds) Freedom of seas, passage rights and the 1982 law of the sea convention. Center for Oceans Law and Policy, Leiden, pp 53–56
Kojima C (2015) South China Sea arbitration and the protection of the marine environment: evolution of UNCLOS part XII through interpretation and the duty to cooperate. Asian Yearb Int Law 21:166–180
König D (2001) Marine environment, international protection. In: Max Planck Encyclopedia of International Law. Oxford University Press, Oxford, p 1594
Kunig P (2016) Völkerrecht und staatliches Recht. In: Vitzthum W, Proelss A (eds) Völkerrecht, 7th edn. De Gruyter, Berlin, pp 61–132
Mann Borgese E (1978) A constitution for the oceans: comments and suggestions regarding part XI of the informal composite negotiating text. San Diego Law Rev 15:371–408
Maron M, Simmonds JS, Watson JEM (2018) Bold nature retention targets are essential for the global environment agenda. Nat Ecol Evol 2:1194–1195
Matz N (2005) Wege zur Koordinierung völkerrechtlicher Verträge – Völkervertragsrechtliche und institutionelle Ansätze. In: Max-Planck-Institut für ausländisches öffentliches Recht und

Völkerrecht - Beiträge zum ausländischen öffentlichen Recht und Völkerrecht, vol 175. Springer, Heidelberg

McConnell ML, Gold E (1991) The Modern Law of the Sea: framework for the protection and preservation of the marine environment. Case Westrn Res J Int Law 23(1):83–106

Mensah TA (2006) Joint development zones as an alternative dispute settlement approach in maritime boundary delimitation. In: Lagoni R, Vignes D (eds) Maritime delimitation, publications of ocean development, vol 53. Brill, Leiden, pp 143–152

Molenaar EJ (2007) Managing biodiversity in areas beyond national jurisdiction. In: Nordquist MH, Long R, Heidar TH, Norton Moore J (eds) Law, science & ocean management. Brill, Leiden, pp 625–681

Mondré A, Kuhn A (2017) Ocean governance, Aus Politik und Zeitgeschichte (APuZ), Meere und Ozeane, 67. Jahrgang, 51-52/2017, Bonn, pp 4–9

Nordquist MH, Nandan SN, Kraska J (2012) UNCLOS 1982 commentary – supplementary documents. Center for Oceans Law and Policy, Leiden

O'Connell DP (1982) The international law of the sea, vol I, 1st edn. Oxford University Press, Oxford

Proelss A (2004) Meeresschutz im Völker- und Europarecht, Das Beispiel des Nordatlantiks. In: Oppermann T (ed) Tübinger Schriften zum internationalen und europäischen Recht, vol 71. Duncker & Humblot, Berlin

Proelss A (2012) The law on the exclusive economic zone in perspective - legal status and resolution of user conflicts revisited. The law of the sea and ocean governance. In: Chircop A, Coffen-Smout S, McConnell M (eds) Ocean yearbook, vol 26, pp 87–112

Proelss A (2017) United Nations Convention on the Law of the Sea – a commentary. C.H. Beck, Munich

Qureshi WA (2018) Marine biodiversity conservation: the international legal framework and challenges. Hous J Int Law 40(3):845–936

Roach JA (2014) Today's customary international law of the sea. Ocean Dev Int Law 45(3): 239–259

Rothwell DR, Stephens T (2016) The international law of the sea, 2nd edn. Bloomsbury Publishing, Oxford

Rothwell DR, Oude Elferink AG, Scott KN, Stephens T (2015) Charting the future for the law of the sea. In: Rothwell D, Oude Elferink AG, Scott KN, Stephens T (eds) The Oxford handbook of the law of the sea. Oxford University Press, Oxford, pp 888–912

Ryan Enright S, Boteler B (2020) The ecosystem approach in international marine environmental law and governance. In: O'Higgins TG, Lago M, DeWitt TH (eds) Ecosystem-based management, Ecosystem services and aquatic biodiversity – theory, tools and applications. Springer, Cham, pp 333–352

Sands P (2007) Litigating environmental disputes: courts, tribunals and the progressive development of international environmental law. In: Ndiaye TM, Wolfrum R (eds) Law of the sea, environmental law and settlement of disputes. Brill, Leiden, pp 313–325

Sands P (2012) Principles of international environmental law, 3rd edn. Cambridge University Press, Cambridge

Scharf MP (2012) Customary international law in times of fundamental change – recognizing Grotian moments. Cambridge University Press, Cambridge

Schieder T (1984) Customary international law. In: Bernhardt R (ed) Encyclopedia of Public International Law (EPIL) 7, History of International Law, Foundations and Principles of International Law, Sources of International Law, Law of Treaties. North Holland, pp 61–66

Schladebach M (2020) Weltraumrecht. Mohr Siebeck, Tübingen

Scovazzi T (2004) Marine protected areas on the high seas: some legal and policy considerations. Int J Mar Coast Law 19(1):1–17

Selden J (1635) Mare Clausum seu de Domino Maris: of the dominion or ownership of the sea two books. The Lawbook Exchange, Ltd., London

Stone CD (1972) Should trees have standing - toward legal rights for natural objects. South Calif Law Rev 45(2):450–501

Tanaka Y (2008) A dual approach to ocean governance - the cases of zonal and integrated management in international law of the sea. Routledge, Surrey

Tanaka Y (2019) The international law of the sea, 3rd edn. Cambridge University Press, Cambridge

Tomuschat C (2019) Enforecement of international law. Zeitschrift für ausländisches öffentliches Recht und Völkerrecht 79:579–631

Toonen RJT, Wilhelm AT, Maxwell SM, Wagner D, Bowen BW, Sheppard CRC, Taei SM, Teroroko T, Moffitt R, Gaymer CF, Morgan L, Lewis N, Sheppard ALS, Parks J, Friedlander AM (2013) The big ocean think tank, one size does not fit all: the emerging frontier in large-scale marine conservation. Mar Pollut Bull 77:7–10

Treves T (2010) Human rights and the law of the sea. Berkeley J Int Law 28(1, Article 1):1–14

Treves T (2015) Historical development of the law of the sea. In: Rothwell D, Oude Elferink AG, Scott K, Stephans T (eds) The Oxford handbook of the law of the sea, pp 1–23

United Nations Environment Programme (UNEP) (1985) Environmental policy and law, 14/2/3, p 77

Vitzthum W (2016) Begriff, Geschichte und Rechtsquellen des Völkerrechts. In: Vitzthum W, Proelss A (eds) Völkerrecht, 7th edn. De Gruyter, Berlin, pp 1–60

Will M (2015) Völkerrecht und nationales Recht - Dogmatische Grundlagen und konkrete Ausgestaltung am Beispiel der deutschen Verfassungsordnung. Juristische Ausbildung 11: 1164–1176

Wolfrum R (1990) Purposes and principles of international environmental law. Ger Yearb Int Law 33:308–330

Chapter 3
Legally Binding Obligation

The legally binding obligation to establish MPAs based on of Art. 192 UNCLOS prerequires the establishment of its legally binding effect. The issue arises for two reasons, the first due to a comparison of the wording of Art. 192 UNCLOS and Art. 193 UNCLOS. While the former puts States under the ‘obligation’ to protect and preserve the marine environment, the latter codifies the States’ ‘duty’ to this end. This leads to the question if ‘obligation’ in fact refers to a legally binding obligation or rather to a mere political objective without binding effect.[1] Secondly, it is being argued, that the specific obligation of States to take measures to prevent, reduce and control pollution under Art. 194 (1) UNCLOS would be obsolete if it were already entailed in the general obligation of States to protect and preserve the marine environment under Art. 192 UNCLOS.[2]

3.1 Interpretation of the Obligation Under Art. 192 UNCLOS

The content of a rule of international law is determined through its interpretation. The UNCLOS does not entail specific regulations on the interpretation of treaties. Recourse may therefore be had to the customary regulations on the interpretation of treaties under Arts. 31–33 VCLT.[3] According to Art. 31 (1) VCLT a treaty shall be interpreted in good faith as to the ordinary meaning of the terms of the treaty itself, its context and in the light of its objective and purpose. The principle of good faith is

[1] Proelss (2017), Art. 192, mn. 18 f.

[2] Hafner (2006), p. 367, mn. 39.

[3] Schladebach (2020), pp. 25 f., mn. 3; Linderfalk (2007), p. 7; Bernhardt (1984), p. 321; PCA, *Chagos Marine Protected Area Arbitration*, Republic of Mauritius v. the United Kingdom of Great Britain and North Ireland (in the following: Mauritius v. UK), (Award) 2015, p. 197, para. 501.

A. von Rebay, *The Designation of Marine Protected Areas*,
https://doi.org/10.1007/978-3-031-29175-3_3

not a means of interpretation itself but applies to the use of the interpretation tools. The secondary means of interpretation under Art. 32 VCLT, include the preparatory work of the treaty and the circumstances of its conclusion. This historical interpretation can be applied independently but only in order to confirm the meaning resulting from the application of Art. 31 VCLT or to determine the meaning when the interpretation according to Art. 31 VCLT leaves the meaning ambiguous or obscure or leads to a result which is manifestly absurd or unreasonable.[4] Art. 33 VCLT, furthermore, applies to the interpretation of a treaty that is authenticated in multiple languages and provides to this end that, unless otherwise indicated, the text is equally authoritative in each language. The following interpretation of the obligation to protect and preserve the marine environment will demonstrate that there is no doubt in the legally binding effect of Art. 192 UNCLOS, which poses a suitable basis for the establishment of a legal obligation of States to establish MPAs.

3.2 Literal Interpretation

The canon of Art. 31 ff. VCLT commences with the most important means of interpretation of international treaties, the ordinary meaning of the text of the treaty in Art. 31 (1) VCLT.[5]

The terms 'obligation' and '(legal) duty' are often used synonymously, whereas obligation is defined as a (legal) duty and vice versa.[6] On the one hand, 'duty' is a 'legal obligation that is owed or due to another and that needs to be satisfied; an obligation for which somebody else has a corresponding right.'[7] A 'legal duty' is a 'duty arising by contract or by operation of law; an obligation the breach of which would give a legal remedy'.[8] 'Duty', thus is defined as a legally binding obligation. 'Obligation' on the other hand is a 'legal or moral duty to do or not to do something. [...] It may refer to anything that a person is bound to do or forbear from doing, whether the duty is imposed by law, contract, promise, social relations, courtesy, kindness, or morality [...] esp. a duty arising by contract.'[9] It is 'anything that a person is bound to do or forbear from doing, whether the duty is imposed by law, contract, promise, social relations, courtesy, kindness, or morality.'[10] The ordinary meanings of 'obligation' and 'duty', therefore, are synonymous, both meaning a legal tie.[11]

[4] Linderfalk (2007), p. 8; Bernhardt (1984), p. 323.

[5] Crawford (2012), p. 379; Bernhardt (1984), p. 322.

[6] Proelss (2017), Art. 192, mn. 18 f.; Martin (2003), pp. 165 and 337.

[7] Garner (2009), p. 580.

[8] Garner (2009), p. 580.

[9] Garner (2009), p. 1179.

[10] Garner (2009), p. 1179.

[11] Stewart and Burgess (2001), p. 278.

Another view regards the term 'obligation' as generic for any kind of duty or liability in international law. This is supported by the heading of Art. 192 UNCLOS, which refers to the obligation under Art. 192 UNCLOS as a 'General Obligation'. This leads to the conclusion that 'duty' is comprised in obligation, whereas obligation is not always comprised by 'duty'.[12] Correspondingly the contracting parties to the UNCLOS, could not decide on a unified use of the wording of Art. 192, Art. 193 UNCLOS, which shows that although 'obligation' and 'duty' are often used synonymously, they are used in different contexts, whereby 'obligation' is the broader term. Both, however, are legally binding for their addressees.

This interpretation is further supported by the comparison of the authentic texts of the UNCLOS under Art. 33 (4) VCLT. Pursuant to Art. 320 UNCLOS, the Arabic, Chinese, English, French, Russian and Spanish texts of the UNCLOS are equally authentic. If the authentic texts disclose a difference of meaning, which the application of Art. 31, 32 VCLT does not remove, the meaning which best reconciles the texts, having regard to the object and purpose of the treaty, shall be adopted.[13] The French and Spanish versions use the terms 'obligation' and 'obligación' respectively for both, Art. 192 as well as Art. 193 UNCLOS. This comparison shows that there is no substantive distinction between the words for the purpose of the UNCLOS. Thus, the interpretation of the ordinary meaning shows that the obligation to protect and preserve the marine environment is a legally binding obligation.

3.3 Systematic Interpretation

The interpretation of the obligation under Art. 192 UNCLOS as legally binding is consistent with its structural placement in the context of the UNCLOS.[14] The words of a treaty cannot always be understood correctly when read in isolation. According to the systematic interpretation under Art. 31 (1) VCLT the words of the treaty must be read in the context of the treaty, its annexes, protocols, any subsequent agreements or practices as well as other applicable principles of international law, which shall be taken into account under Art. 31 (2), (3) VCLT. The interpretation of Art. 192 UNCLOS in its systematic embedding in the UNCLOS proves its status as a legally binding obligation rather than a mere political objective.

Objectives and intentions of parties to treaties are typically expressed in the preamble; legally binding rights, obligations and duties in the legal regulations of the treaty itself. The State parties to the UNCLOS have expressed their intention to establish 'a legal order for the seas and oceans which will facilitate [...] the study,

[12] Proelss (2017), Art. 192, mn. 18 f.

[13] Vitzthum (2016), p. 47, mn. 123; PCA, *Chagos Marine Protected Area Arbitration*, Mauritius v. UK (Award) 2015, p. 197, para. 501.

[14] PCA, *Chagos Marine Protected Area Arbitration*, Mauritius v. UK (Award) 2015, p. 197, para. 503.

protection and preservation of the marine environment [...]' in the preamble. The State parties, however, did not limit this intention to the preamble but dedicated a whole Part XII of the UNCLOS to codify this intention in a legal obligation in the treaty text itself. The codification of the obligation to protect and preserve the marine environment under Art. 192 UNCLOS within the text of the treaty, thus, expresses the intention to establish an according legally binding obligation. If the State Parties wanted to limit their intention to a mere objective without legally binding effect, the codification of Part XII UNCLOS would have been obsolete.[15]

3.4 Teleological Interpretation

The teleological interpretation under Art. 31 (1) VCLT stipulates to interpret the treaty according to its objective and purpose given to the treaty in its entirety as well as the specific clause of the treaty. An interpretation of the treaty, that serves its objective and purpose is to be preferred. The interpretation of the preamble of the UNCLOS, as well as Art. 235 and 194 UNCLOS show that its objective is more readily achieved when viewing the obligation under Art. 192 UNCLOS as legally binding.

3.4.1 Preamble

The object and purpose of treaties are typically expressed in their preamble. In its *Chagos Marine Protected Area Arbitration*, the PCA had to consider the legally binding effect of Art. 2 (3) UNCLOS. Recalling the intention of the UNCLOS as expressly referenced in the preamble the need to consider the 'closely interrelated' problems of the ocean space 'as a whole,' and the 'desirability of establishing through this Convention, [...] a legal order for the seas and oceans [...]', the tribunal found that this objective as expressed in the preamble is more suited by viewing Art. 2 (3) UNCLOS as a source of obligation.[16] Correspondingly, the objective to establish 'a legal order for the seas and oceans which will facilitate [...] the study, protection and preservation of the marine environment [...]', is more readily achieved when viewing Art. 192 UNCLOS as a legally binding obligation.

[15]Proelss (2017), Art. 192, mn. 18 f.

[16]PCA, *Chagos Marine Protected Area Arbitration*, Mauritius v. UK (Award) 2015, p. 198, para. 504.

3.4.2 Liability and Responsibility Under Art. 235 UNCLOS

Section 9 of Part XII UNCLOS codifies the responsibility and liability of States for the breach of their obligations under Art. 192 ff. UNCLOS. According to Art. 235 (1) UNCLOS, States are responsible for the fulfilment of their international obligations concerning the protection and preservation of the marine environment. They shall be liable in accordance with international law. The responsibility and liability under Art. 235 UNCLOS is a secondary obligation that can only be invoked as the consequence of the breach of a legally binding primary obligation. If Art. 192 UNCLOS was only a political objective, it's disobedience would not be capable to cause a secondary obligation. Therefore, Art. 235 UNCLOS necessarily pre-requires that Art. 192 UNCLOS is the primary obligation with a legally binding effect.[17]

3.4.3 Obligation Entailed Under Art. 194 (1) UNCLOS

Likewise, it is arguable that if the obligation of States to take active measures to protect and preserve the marine environment was already entailed in Art. 192 UNCLOS, the obligation to take measures to prevent, reduce and control pollution under Art. 194 (1) UNCLOS would be obsolete.[18] Art. 194 UNCLOS, according to its heading, stipulates measures to prevent, reduce and control pollution of the marine environment. Art. 194 (1)–(4) UNCLOS, correspondingly, regulate 'measures aimed at the prevention, control and reduction of pollution of the marine environment' and, like Sections 5 and 6 of Part XII UNCLOS, are therefore more specific than the general obligation to protect and preserve the marine environment under Art. 192 UNCLOS. However, in its *Chagos Marine Protected Area Arbitration*, the PCA stated that due to the last paragraph of Art. 194 UNCLOS, namely Art. 194 (5) UNCLOS, which is not limited to measures aimed at pollution, Art. 194 UNCLOS in its entirety is 'not limited to measures aimed strictly at controlling pollution and extends to measures focused primarily on conservation and preservation of ecosystems.'[19]

3.4.3.1 Interpretation of Art. 194 (1)–(4) UNCLOS

This interpretation is legally not convincing. The wording of Art. 194 (1)–(4) UNCLOS as well as the heading of this provision, unambiguously stipulate

---

[17] McConnell and Gold (1991), p. 89.

[18] Hafner (2006), p. 367, mn. 39.

[19] PCA, *Chagos Marine Protected Area Arbitration*, Mauritius v. UK (Award) 2015, p. 211, para. 538 and pp. 128 f., para. 320.

measures to prevent, control and reduce pollution. If the State parties wanted to codify a general provision on the adoption of measures to conserve the marine environment in general, they would have not expressly added the limitation to pollution. There is no scope for an interpretation of the wording that opens Art. 194 (1)–(4) UNCLOS to all measures to conserve and protect the marine environment, which is *contra legem*.

3.4.3.2 Application of Art. 194 (5) UNCLOS to Art. 194 (1)–(4) UNCLOS

Art. 194 (5) UNCLOS is the only paragraph that does not contain the limitation of the measures to prevent, reduce and control pollution. Because of its systematic position as a subparagraph of Art. 194 UNCLOS, the heading of which is 'measures to protect, reduce and control pollution', it can be argued that Art. 194 (5) UNCLOS, therefore, must be limited to measures aimed at pollution as well. Otherwise, it would have been regulated in a separate provision.

However, because of the wording of Art. 194 (5) UNCLOS, which applies to 'measures taken in accordance with' Part XII UNCLOS and which is explicitly not limited to pollution, it may be argued that Art. 194 (5) UNCLOS, despite being a subparagraph of Art. 194 UNCLOS, applies to all measures to conserve and protect the marine environment. This shows that it is already debatable if Art. 194 (5) UNCLOS itself applies to all measures to conserve and protect the marine environment. The reverse argumentation, however, that because of the wording of Art. 194 (5) UNCLOS the entire provision of Art. 194 UNCLOS, despite its heading, applies to all measures to conserve and protect the marine environment is not convincing.

If Art. 194 (5) UNCLOS was the first provision of Art. 194 UNCLOS, it might be arguable that it, therefore, is the *lex generalis and* all the other provisions also must be interpreted and applied in a way that they include all measures to conserve the marine environment. But because of Art. 194 (5) UNCLOS being the last paragraph, it is not capable to give recourse to and open the entire provision of the previous paragraphs of Art. 194 UNCLOS to all measures to conserve and preserve the marine environment. The precise and unambiguous wording of the heading and the text of the other subparagraphs of Art. 194 UNCLOS and the structural codification of Art. 194 (5) UNCLOS at the end of this provision, does not allow an interpretation that eradicates the specification of measures to prevent, reduce and control pollution of Art. 194 (1)–(4) UNCLOS.

3.4.3.3 Obligation to Protect and Preserve the Marine Environment as Lex Generalis

Even if one was of the opinion that Art. 194 (1) UNCLOS indeed were not limited to pollution and applies to all issues related to the conservation and preservation of the marine environment, Art. 194 (1)–(4) UNCLOS are still more specific than the general obligation under Art. 192 UNCLOS. Art. 194 (1) UNCLOS is not obsolete, even if Art. 192 UNCLOS is a binding obligation. Art. 192 UNCLOS is addressed to all States to protect and preserve the marine environment from any threat in all zones of the sea. Art. 194 UNCLOS contains specific regulations as to the measures to be adopted. It is a well-established legal technique to codify a general *lex generalis* before more specific regulations in subsequent *lex specialis*. Even if both regulations have the same content, Art. 194 UNCLOS codifies in its following paragraphs more specific regulations. Furthermore, a certain lack of coherence and apparent duplications can be detected throughout the structure of Part XII UNCLOS in general.[20] If one was to argue that Art. 194 (1) UNCLOS was obsolete if Art. 192 UNCLOS was legally binding, many of the provisions of the UNCLOS would be obsolete. For instance, Art. 207 ff. UNCLOS contain specific regulations for the adoption of laws and regulations and the conclusion of international treaties to prevent, reduce and control pollution of the marine environment. All of the provisions of Art. 207 UNCLOS are already entailed in the more general Art. 194 UNCLOS. Therefore, the regulation of Art. 194 (1) UNCLOS does not negate the legally binding effect of Art. 192 UNCLOS. For the same reason, also Art. 207 ff. UNCLOS do not negate the legally binding quality of Art. 192 UNCLOS but are *lex specialis* of the general obligation to protect and preserve the marine environment.[21]

3.4.3.4 Objective to Formulate an Open Obligation

The UNCLOS is the so-called 'Constitution for the Ocean'.[22] While it provides a comprehensive legal framework for all maritime issues in general and environmental protection in particular, the UNCLOS 'is likely to serve as a model or a foundation on which international law on various aspects of environment will be developed.'[23] Likewise, the general obligation under Art. 192 UNCLOS as an opening provision of Part XII UNCLOS, had to be designed in an open manner in order to be adaptable to known and unknown harmful anthropogenic influences on the marine environment.[24] An overly strict interpretation of Art. 192 ff. UNCLOS does not allow the derivation of legally binding regulations for the conservation of the marine environment and cannot withstand the change of time. Law must adapt to the continuous evolution of societal needs and new techniques to keep its relevance. Rapid developments of technology in particular in the sea, such as deep seabed mining, offshore windfarms or carbon sinking, necessitate the parallel development of a legal regime,

[20] Nordquist et al. (2013), p. XII.23.

[21] Harrison (2017), p. 27.

[22] https://www.un.org/Depts/los/convention_agreements/texts/koh_english.pdf; Mann Borgese (1978), p. 371; https://ioc.unesco.org/topics/law-sea; UNGA A/74/PV.42, p. 12.

[23] UNGA A/44/461, p. 5, para. 5 and p. 7, para. 15; Gavounelli (2006), p. 205.

[24] Proelss (2017), Art. 192, mn. 13.

which is able to deal with modern issues. Accordingly, the preamble of the UNCLOS stresses the 'progressive development of the law of the sea' (Preamble UNCLOS). In this light, the codification of the UNCLOS in 1982 already marked a paradigm shift. The UNCLOS dedicates an entire part to the protection and preservation of the marine environment, making it an integral part of its regulatory framework and raised the 'discretion of States to the duty of protection by States' as a fundamental principle.[25] In order to remain applicable to new developments and technologies, it is necessary to formulate an open but legally binding obligation of States to protect and preserve the marine environment.

3.5 Historical Interpretation

A historical interpretation, including the preparatory work of the treaty and the circumstances of its conclusion, are "supplementary means of interpretation" under Art. 32 VCLT. Its application is only indicated in order to confirm the meaning resulting from the application of Art. 31 VCLT, or to determine the meaning when the previous interpretation leaves the meaning ambiguous or obscure (Art. 32 (a) VCLT) or leads to a result which is manifestly absurd or unreasonable (Art. 32 (b) VCLT). The previous interpretation has already shown that the obligation to protect and preserve the marine environment must be legally binding. The further investigation of the *travaux préparatoires*, therefore, only serves to support this result:

The issue, whether there should be one word for 'duty' and 'obligation' throughout the UNCLOS has been dealt with in the Drafting Committee at the Eight Session of the UNCLOS III Conference. The Drafting Committee recognised that a harmonised wording would be preferable and, as the issue arises in a different manner in other languages, it should be dealt with by the language group. It did not, however, elaborate on the difference of the binding effect of 'duty' or 'obligation'.[26] While harmonisation of the wording was achieved in other authentic texts, such as Spanish and French which both refer to 'obligation' and 'obligación' respectively, the different terms remained in the English version.

However, the legal nature of the obligation under Art. 192 UNCLOS as a legally binding duty becomes evident through a comparison with the 1971 Principles for the Preservation of the Marine Environment (IWGMP Principles).[27] The IWGMP Principles have been adopted by the Intergovernmental Working Group on Marine Pollution (IWGMP) on its second session in Ottawa. Art. 192 UNCLOS serves to

[25] Tanaka (2019), p. 333; Rothwell and Stephens (2016), pp. 338, 342; Proelss (2017), Art. 192, mn. 10.

[26] UNGA A/CONF.62/L.40, Section XXIV; Nordquist et al. (2013), p. 192.3.

[27] A/CONF.48/IWGMP.II/5.

express IWGMP Principles in treaty language.[28] According to Principle 1 IWGMP '[e]very State has a duty to protect and preserve the marine environment [. . .].' The historical interpretation, likewise, indicates that there is no substantial difference in the 'obligation to protect and preserve the marine environment' under Art. 192 UNCLOS and a duty to this end, which both are legally binding.

3.6 Conclusion: Legally Binding Obligation

The interpretation with regard to the multi-lingual terms of the treaty in its context and in the light of its objective together with the ordinary meaning of the word 'obligation' and its historical development leads to the result that Art. 192 UNCLOS contains a legally binding obligation. This result is consistent with the relevant jurisprudence that acknowledges the legal status of Art. 192 UNCLOS as a legal duty rather than a mere objective.[29]

References

Bernhardt R (1984) Interpretation in international law. In: Bernhardt R (ed) Encyclopedia of public international law (EPIL) 7, History of international law, foundations and principles of international law, sources of international law, law of treaties. North Holland, pp 318–327

Crawford JR (2012) Brownlie's principles of public international law, 8th edn. Oxford University Press, Oxford

Garner BA (2009) Black's law dictionary, 9th edn. Thomas Reuters Westlaw, Dallas

Gavounelli M (2006) From uniformity to fragmentation? The ability of the UN convention on the law of the sea to accommodate new uses and challenges. In: Strati A, Gavouneli M, Skourtos N (eds) Unresolved issues and new challenges to the law of the sea, time before and time after, Publications on ocean development, vol 54. Brill, Leiden, pp 205–234

Hafner G (2006) Schutz der Meeresumwelt. In: Vitzthum W (ed) Handbuch des Seerechts. C.H. Beck, Munich, pp 355–421

Harrison J (2017) Saving the oceans through law – the international legal framework for the protection of the marine environment. Oxford University Press, Oxford

Linderfalk U (2007) On the interpretation of treaties - the modern international law as expressed in the 1969 Vienna Convention on the Law of Treaties. In: Law and philosophy library, vol 83. Springer, Dordrecht

Mann Borgese E (1978) A constitution for the oceans: comments and suggestions regarding part XI of the informal composite negotiating text. San Diego Law Rev 15:371–408

Martin EA (2003) Oxford dictionary of law, 5th edn. Oxford University Press, Oxford

[28] Nordquist et al. (2013), p. 192.3.

[29] PCA, *South China Sea Arbitration*, Philippines v. China (Award), p. 373, para. 941; ITLOS, *M/V "Louisa"*, Saint Vincent and the Grenadines v. Kingdom of Spain, Provisional Measures, ITLOS Reports 2008–2010, pp. 58, 70, para. 76; ITLOS, *Delimitation of the Maritime Boundary in the Atlantic Ocean*, Ghana v. Côte d'Ivoire, Provisional Measures, ITLOS Reports 2015, pp. 146, 160, para. 69.

McConnell ML, Gold E (1991) The modern law of the sea: framework for the protection and preservation of the marine environment. Case West Res J Int Law 23(1):83–106

Nordquist MH, Nandan S, Rosenne S (2013) UN Convention on the Law of the Sea Commentary 1982 Online. Center for Oceans Law and Policy, Leiden

Proelss A (2017) United Nations Convention on the Law of the Sea – a commentary. C.H. Beck, Munich

Rothwell DR, Stephens T (2016) The international law of the sea, 2nd edn. Oxford University Press, Oxford

Schladebach M (2020) Weltraumrecht. Mohr Siebeck, Tübingen

Stewart WJ, Burgess R (2001) Collins dictionary of law, 2nd edn. Collins, Pymble

Tanaka Y (2019) The international law of the sea, 3rd edn. Cambridge University Press, Cambridge

Vitzthum W (2016) Begriff, Geschichte und Rechtsquellen des Völkerrechts. In: Vitzthum W, Proelss A (eds) Völkerrecht, 7th edn. De Gruyter, Berlin, pp 1–60

Chapter 4
Personal Scope: An Obligation Erga Omnes

Having established that Art. 192 UNCLOS is a binding rule of International Law, it is necessary to assess its personal scope in order to determine which States are bound by the obligation. According to its wording, Art. 192 UNCLOS addresses all States. This raises two interrelated, questions: Firstly, is the obligation under Art. 192 UNCLOS capable to exceed the *inter partes* effect of treaties and to *erga omnes* bind the international community as a whole? Secondly, may any State, therefore, invoke a violation of this obligation by another State, even if the State has not suffered individual harm (individual concern)? Both questions are connected, as Art. 48 (1) (b) of the 2001 Articles on the Responsibility of States for Internationally Wrongful Acts (ARS) stipulates that any State is entitled to invoke the responsibility of another State, if 'the obligation breached is owed to the international community as a whole.'[1]

4.1 Art. 192 UNCLOS as Treaty Regulation

Different than other regulations in the UNCLOS, such as Art. 311 UNCLOS which particularly addresses the 'State Parties', Art. 192 UNCLOS is addressed to all States. This might lead to the conclusion, that the wording of Art. 192 UNCLOS is intended to exceed the *inter parts* effect of treaties and aims to address the international community as a whole.[2] As part of public international law, however, the UNCLOS is subjected to the law of treaties as codified in the VCLT and is therefore not exempted from the general rule of *pacta tertiis non nocet* under

[1] UNGA A/56/49(Vol. I)/Corr.4.

[2] PCA, *South China Sea Arbitration*, Philippines v. China (Jurisdiction), p. 102, para. 284; PCA, *South China Sea Arbitration*, Philippines v. China (Award), p. 373, para. 940; König (2001), para. 8.

A. von Rebay, *The Designation of Marine Protected Areas*,
https://doi.org/10.1007/978-3-031-29175-3_4

Art. 34 VCLT, according to which every treaty only creates rights and obligations for its contracting parties. As a treaty obligation, Art. 192 UNCLOS, therefore, only binds the parties to the Convention.[3]

4.2 Art. 192 UNCLOS as Customary International Law

The obligation of Art. 192 UNCLOS exceeds the *inter partes* effect of treaties and also bind UNCLOS non-member States if the regulation is a universally accepted rule of customary international law at the same time as a treaty regulation.

4.2.1 No General Customary Status of the UNCLOS

There is a broad consensus in the relevant law of the sea literature, that most of the rules of the UNCLOS, with the major exception of Part XI UNCLOS on the Area, are rules of customary international law, as it does not stipulate new regulations but is a comprehensive codification of the already existing regime of the law of the sea.[4] It, therefore, merely casts into writing what has already been established by means of customary international law before (declaratory effect of treaties). The statement, however, that the UNCLOS generally reflects customary international law, with the only exception of Part XI UNCLOS on the Area, can legally not be supported and is incorrect. While the UNCLOS undoubtedly contains existing rules of customary international law, such as the freedom of the High Sea, it does also stipulate entirely new provisions such as the regime of transit passage through straits used for international navigation, the regime of archipelagic sea lane passage or the breadth of the Continental Shelf.[5] In order to derive the customary status of regulations of the UNCLOS in a legally convincing way, the status has to be established for each relevant regulation. According to Art. 38 (1) (c) VCLT, the assessment of the customary status of Art. 192 UNCLOS requires two constituent elements, a general State practice, which is acknowledged as law.

[3]Proelss (2017), Art. 192, mn. 16.

[4]Scovazzi (2004), pp. 5 and 17; Matz-Lück (2017), p. 411, mn. 38; McConnell and Gold (1991), p. 89; Proelss (2017), Art. 192, mn. 10, 21; Roach (2014), p. 241; Sands (2012), p. 396; Crawford (2012), pp. 31 f.; Birnie et al. (2009), p. 387; Oude Elferink and Rothwell (2004), p. 167; Lagoni (1992), p. 145.

[5]https://www.un.org/Depts/los/convention_agreements/texts/koh_english.pdf, p. xxxiv.

4.2.2 General States' Practice to Protect and Preserve the Marine Environment

General State practice is a consistent State practice, which can be evident through numerous manifestations of States' behaviours. While it does not have to be universal, the absence of important States can affect the creation of customary international law. Evidence of general State practice can include but is not limited to international law and municipal court decisions, the practice of the executive branches, diplomatic practices, government comments, publications of international organisations and NGOs, as well as treaty practice.[6] Hence, the accumulation of a treaty practice, even of bilateral treaties, 'could combine to corroborate the evidence of the existence of a general practice of States [...].'[7] The following assessment will demonstrate the general States' practice to protect and preserve the marine environment as evident through an extensive practice to adopt global and specific instruments to this end, as well as through the practice of States to protect and preserve the marine environment through the establishment of MPAs.

4.2.2.1 States' Practice to Adopt International Treaties

The general practice of States to protect and preserve the marine environment is evident through the adoption of a broad number of general as well as specific instruments for this purpose.

States' Practice to Adopt General and Global Instruments

The practice to protect and preserve the marine environment is reflected in the adoption of global treaties such as the 1982 UNCLOS with 168 State parties, as well as the almost universal 1992 CBD, which has been signed by all UN member States, except for the USA.[8] Further global instruments with regard to the protection and preservation of the marine environment are entailed in the 1971 Ramsar Convention for the protection of rare or unique wetlands with 170 State parties, the 1971 UNESCO's Man and the Biosphere Programme with 193 members and 11 associate members and the 2001 UNESCO Underwater Cultural Heritage Convention with 59 State Parties.[9] Especially the UNCLOS, CBD, Ramsar Convention and the UNESCO's Man and the Biosphere Programme have been adopted by the

[6]UN Doc. A/CN.4/459, p. 152.

[7]UN Doc. A/CN.4/459, p. 152; ILC, A/CN.4/SER.A/1991/ADD.L (PART 2), p. 39, para. 20.

[8]https://www.itlos.org/en/main/the-tribunal/states-parties/; https://www.cbd.int/information/parties.shtml.

[9]UNTS, Vol. 2562, No. I-45694; https://www.ramsar.org/country-profiles; https://en.unesco.org/countries.

great majority of all States and show an almost universal State practice. As evident through the 1971 Ramsar Convention and the 1971 UNESCO's Man and the Biosphere Programme, this States' practice already existed before the UNCLOS, has been manifested through the 1982 UNCLOS and was reinforced by the 1992 CBD and 2001 UNESCO Underwater Cultural Heritage Convention.

Universal States' Practice to Protect and Preserve the Marine Environment

The non-ratification of the UNCLOS by 15 States such as the USA does not impede the emergence of Art. 192 UNCLOS as a rule of customary international law for two reasons: first, the emergence of a rule into customary international law requires a uniform but not universal States' practice. Second, although the absence of important States, as might be said for the USA, may be capable to hinder the creation of a rule of customary international law, the USA have expressly stated, that the only reason for their non-ratification of the UNCLOS is Part XI UNCLOS on the Area.[10] Moreover, the following investigation will show that all UNCLOS non-members, including the USA, have demonstrated their practice to protect and preserve the marine environment i.e. by being party to numerous similar conservation treaties, such as the CCAMLR, which gave rise to the South Orkney Islands southern shelf MPA and the Ross Sea Region MPA, which are the first MPAs entirely located in the High Sea, or the almost universal CBD.

Participation of Important States

Furthermore, if the non-participation of an important State can harm the creation of a rule of customary international law, it is *e contrario* conclusive that the practice of important States to protect and preserve the marine environment weighs in favour of the creation of such a customary rule. The EU which represents 27 member States, for instance, is not only a party to the UNCLOS but adopted the Marine Strategy Framework Directive which is legally binding for its member States as to the result to be achieved under Art. 288 of the 2007 Treaty on the Functioning of the European Union (TFEU) and is specifically aimed at the protection of the marine environment.[11] The majority of the States of all other continents, too, are parties to the UNCLOS. The UNCLOS has been signed and ratified by 168 UN member States, including Australia, all States of Central and South America, except for El Salvador and Colombia (signed but not ratified) as well as Peru and Venezuela (neither signed nor ratified); all States of the African Continent except for the Central African Republic, Burundi, Ethiopia, Libya and Rwanda (signed but not ratified) as well as Eritrea and South Sudan (neither signed nor ratified); all States of the Asian continent except for Afghanistan, Bhutan, Cambodia, Iran, North Korea and the

[10] https://www.reaganlibrary.gov/research/speeches/70982b; Tanaka (2019), p. 35; Harrison (2011), p. 2.

[11] Official Journal of the European Union, C 202, 07.06.2016.

United Arab Emirates (signed but not ratified) as well as Israel, Kazakhstan, Kirgizstan, Syria, Tajikistan, Turkmenistan and Uzbekistan (neither signed nor ratified); and all States of the European continent except for Liechtenstein (signed but not ratified) as well as Andorra, San Marino, Turkey and the Holy See (neither signed nor ratified).[12] Thus, the major parts of all continents participate in a consistent practice to protect and preserve the marine environment, which is reflected in their member status to the UNCLOS. Furthermore, all States except for the USA, are parties to the CBD which is addressed to conserve the (marine) biodiversity.

Particularly Affected States

For the evaluation of the States' practice for the creation of a rule of customary international law, the participation of particularly affected States is especially important.[13] In the law of the sea, this is typically the case for coastal States which have an elevated interest over landlocked States in matters such as the delimitation of sea borders between States.[14] However, the obligation to protect and preserve the marine environment is not limited to coastal areas but applies to the High Sea and the Area. Landlocked and geographically disadvantaged States that do not have a broad coastline may even have an elevated interest in activities in the High Sea and the Area, as they are free to all States and grant economically high valued access i.e. to offshore resources such as through seabed mining.[15] The protection and preservation of these areas, i.e. from overfishing, overexploitation or pollution, therefore, does also affect the interest of landlocked States. Nonetheless, the interest of landlocked States is limited to the High Sea and the Area. Coastal States, however, do also have an elevated interest in the protection and preservation with regard to particular issues in their Territorial Sea and EEZ such as overfishing in adjacent waters or transboundary pollution. In its video 'UNCLOS in Action', for instance, the UN aims to demonstrate and create awareness for the struggles of traditional fishermen in Libya due to overfishing in the Mediterranean Sea.[16] Ultimately, the State practice of coastal States, therefore, does weigh more than the one of landlocked States in the evaluation of the States' practice to create a rule of customary international law.

Out of the 15 UN members that have signed but not ratified the UNCLOS seven States are landlocked (Afghanistan, Bhutan, Burundi, Central African Republic, Ethiopia, Liechtenstein, Rwanda) while eight members have a coastline (Cambodia, Colombia, El Salvador, Iran, North Korea, Libya, United Arab Emirates and the

[12] Kazakhstan and Turkey are transcontinental countries, straddling Europe as well as Asia; https://treaties.un.org/pages/ViewDetailsIII.aspx?src=TREATY&mtdsg_no=XXI-6&chapter=21&Temp=mtdsg3&clang=_en.

[13] Vitzthum (2016), p. 52, mn. 133; Schieder (1984), p. 63; Tanaka (2019), p. 13.

[14] ICJ, *North Sea Continental Shelf*, Judgment, ICJ Reports 1969, pp. 3, 42, para. 70.

[15] https://www.un.org/en/chronicle/article/international-seabed-authority-and-deep-seabed-mining.

[16] https://www.un.org/depts/los/UNCLOSinAction.mp4.

United States of America); out of the 15 UN members that have neither signed nor ratified the UNCLOS, further seven members are landlocked (Andorra, Kyrgyzstan, San Marino, South Sudan, Tajikistan, Uzbekistan and the Holy See) while eight members (Eritrea, Israel, Kazakhstan, Peru, Syria, Turkey, Turkmenistan, Venezuela) have a coastline.[17] The total number of coastal States, which have not signed or ratified the UNCLOS, therefore, is reduced to only 16 members of the UN. Moreover, the reason for the non-participation in the UNCLOS by these States is not due to the protection and preservation of the marine environment but has other reasons. The USA, as mentioned, only refrained from ratifying the UNCLOS because of the regulations on the deep seabed regime. Turkey did not sign the UNCLOS due to the Aegean dispute over sovereignty and pertinent rights in the Aegean Sea between Greece and Turkey.[18] Lastly, as has been pointed out, the almost universal practice to protect and preserve the marine environment of all of these States is further expressed in other instruments such as the 1992 CBD, 1971 Ramsar Convention, 1971 UNESCO Man and Biosphere Programme or the 2001 UNESCO Underwater Cultural Heritage Convention, in which the States demonstrate their practice to protect and preserve the marine environment.

States' Practice to Adopt Specific Treaties

Threats to the marine environment can take many forms, such as pollution from various sources, harmful fishing techniques or mining activities on the seabed. Concurrently, the protection and preservation of the marine environment can take many forms. Besides treaties with regard to the protection and preservation of the marine environment in general, there is a widespread practice to adopt treaties concerning the protection and preservation of elements of the marine environment from specific threats, both before and after the UNCLOS. The number today amounts to over 300 instruments for the protection and preservation of the marine environment in specific regions, for specific species or concerning specific threats.

Treaties for the Protection of Specific Regions and Ecosystems

Treaties to protect and preserve specific marine regions or ecosystems include but are not limited to the 1959 Antarctic Treaty, 1976 Convention on Conservation of

[17] Kazakhstan and Turkmenistan only share a coastline with the Caspian Sea, which is the world's largest inland, saline body. It is suspected that it holds the world's largest undiscovered deposit of oil and natural gas. However, it does not have access to the sea, which is why its status as sea or lake is disputed; Vinogradov and Wouters (1995), p. 605; Kembayev (2008), pp. 1028 and 1035 f.; Nakatani (2002), p. 1106.

[18] https://www.reaganlibrary.gov/research/speeches/70982b; Tanaka (2019), p. 35; Siousiouras and Chrysochou (2014), p. 13; https://www.institutmontaigne.org/en/blog/whose-sea-turkish-international-law-perspective-greek-turkish-disputes.

Nature in the South Pacific,[19] the 1980 CCAMLR, the 1981 Convention for Co-operation in the Protection and Development of the Marine and Coastal Environment of the West and Central African Region,[20] the 1982 Protocol Concerning Mediterranean Specially Protected Areas,[21] the 1985 Convention for the Protection, Management and Development of the Marine and Coastal Environment of the Eastern African Region,[22] the 1985 ASEAN Agreement on the Conservation of Nature and Natural Resources,[23] the 1989 Protocol for the Conservation and Management of Protected Marine and Coastal Areas of the South-East Pacific,[24] the 1990 Protocol Concerning Specially Protected Areas and Wildlife in the Wider Caribbean Region,[25] the 1991 Protocol on Environmental Protection to the Antarctic Treaty,[26] the 1992 OSPAR Convention or the 1992 Convention on the Protection of the Marine Environment of the Baltic Sea Area.[27] While first treaties with regard to the protection of specific marine regions have occasionally been adopted since the beginning of the second half of the twentieth century, the adoption of treaties in in this category especially emerged in 1980 and later. The UNCLOS contains a region-specific protection provision in Art. 234 UNCLOS for the protection of ice-covered areas within the EEZ from pollution from vessels.

Treaties for the Protection of Species

Examples of treaties for the protection and preservation of specific treaties include but are not limited to the 1946 IWC, 1958 CFCLR, the 1975 Convention on International Trade in Endangered Species of Wild Fauna and Flora (CITES),[28] the 1991 Agreement for the Protections of Seals in the Wadden Sea,[29] the 1991 Agreement on the Conservation of Small Cetaceans of the Baltic, North East Atlantic, Irish and North Seas,[30] the 1995 UNFSA, the 1996 Inter-American Convention for the Protection and Conservation of Sea Turtles,[31] the 1996 Agreement on the Conservation of Cetaceans of the Black Sea, Mediterranean Sea and Contiguous Atlantic Area,[32] the 1997 Bonn Convention, the 1999 Agreement Concerning the

[19] ECOLEX, IUCN ID: TRE-000540.
[20] ECOLEX, IUCN ID: TRE-000547.
[21] UNTS, Vol. 1425, No. I-24079.
[22] ECOLEX, IUCN ID: TRE-000823.
[23] ECOLEX, IUCN ID: TRE-000820.
[24] ECOLEX, IUCN ID: TRE-001085.
[25] UNTS, Vol. 2180, No. A-25974.
[26] UNTS, Vol. 2941, No. A-5778.
[27] UNTS, Vol. 1507, No. I-25986.
[28] UNTS, Vol. 993, No. I-14537.
[29] UNTS, Vol. 2719, No. I-48123.
[30] UNTS, Vol. 1772, No. I-30865.
[31] UNTS, Vol. 2164, No. I-37791.
[32] UNTS, Vol. 2183, No. I-38466.

Creation of a Marine Mammal Sanctuary in the Mediterranean,[33] the 2001 Stockholm Convention on Persistent Organic Pollutants[34] and the 2009 and 2012 Convention on the Conservation and Management of High Seas Fishery Resources in the South Pacific Ocean.[35] Like region-specific treaties, first treaties in this category were occasionally adopted before the UNCLOS, an enhanced and consistent treaty practice for the protection and preservation of specific marine species is evident since 1991. The UNCLOS entails several species-specific conservation and protection provisos, such as Art. 61 ff. or Section 2 of Part VII UNCLOS.

Treaties for the Protection of the Marine Environment from Pollution

Furthermore, there is a widespread State practice with regard to treaties concerning marine pollution in international law and national legislations.[36] Examples of legalisations concerning the protection of the marine environment from pollution in the international law of the sea include but are not limited to the 1958 CHS, the 1972 London Convention, the 1972 Oslo Convention, the 1973/78 MARPOL Convention and Annexes, the 1974 Convention for the Prevention of Marine Pollution from Land-Based Sources,[37] the 1976 Barcelona Convention, the 1978 Kuwait Convention, the 1981 Agreement for the Protection of the Marine Environment and Coastal Areas of the South-East Pacific,[38] the 1983 Cartagena Convention with its three Protocols (1983 Protocol Concerning Co-operation in Combating Oil Spills in the Wider Caribbean Region (Oil Spills Protocol),[39] the 1990 Protocol Concerning Specially Protected Areas and Wildlife (SPAW Protocol)[40] and the 1999 Protocol Concerning Pollution from Land-Based Sources and Activities),[41] the 1985 Montreal Guidelines, the 1990 International Convention on Oil Pollution Preparedness, Response and Co-operation[42] and the 2000 Protocol on Preparedness, Response and Co-operation to Pollution Incidents by Hazardous and Noxious Substances.[43] As the overview shows, instruments for the protection and preservation of the marine environment from specific activities and issues such as pollution were adopted before and after the UNCLOS. The UNCLOS itself contains numerous provision on this issue, such as Section 5 and 6 of Part XII UNCLOS.

[33] UNTS, Vol. 2176, No. I-3806.

[34] UNTS, Vol. 2256, No. I-40214.

[35] UNTS, Vol. 2899, No. I-50553.

[36] Sands (2012), p. 396.

[37] UNTS, Vol. 1546, No. I-26842.

[38] UNTS, Vol. 1648, No. I-28325.

[39] UNTS, Vol. 1506, No. I-25974.

[40] UNTS, Vol. 2180, No. I-26974.

[41] ECOLEX, IUCN, ID: TRE-001331.

[42] UNTS, Vol. 1891, No. I-32194.

[43] UNTS, Vol. n.a., No. I-56797; Adede (1995), pp. 33 and 36 ff.; Tanaka (2008), pp. 202 ff.

Evaluation of Instruments

The assessment of the existing legal framework shows that there is a vast practice of the States to adopt instruments for the protection and preservation of the marine environment. General instruments to this end have already been adopted before the UNCLOS and were manifested through it. Especially the 1992 CBD reinforced this obligation with an almost universal acknowledgement. Region- and species-specific conservation treaties especially took off after the adoption of the UNCLOS in 1982, while treaties for the protection and preservation of the marine environment form pollution have been adopted before 1982 and after. The majority of the 300 instruments with regard to the protection and preservation of the marine environment was adopted after 1982.

4.2.2.2 States' Practice to Establish MPAs

The States' practice to protect and preserve the marine environment is furthermore expressed in the actual establishment of MPAs. The following investigation will show that the establishment of MPAs is a generally adopted tool by the State community to fulfil their obligation to protect and preserve the marine environment. This is evident through declarations of Governments as well as the actual States' practice to designate MPAs, which rapidly increased over the last 20 years on a national and international level.

Government Declarations to Establish MPAs

The States' practice to protect and preserve the marine environment through the establishment of MPAs is evident through frequent expressions of States on international conferences. At the Conference of Parties of the CBD in Japan 2010, 193 States agreed to designate 10% of the whole ocean as MPA by 2020. The number of participating States even exceeds the State parties to the UNCLOS.[44] In 2016, 129 States and government agencies of the IUCN voted in favour to designate 30% of the ocean as MPAs by 2030.[45] Also the USA, as one of the most prominent non-State parties to the UNCLOS declared in an 'Executive Order on Tackling the

[44] https://www.greenpeace.org/static/planet4-international-stateless/2019/04/4475b2c2-updatedgreenpeace_30x30_blueprint_report_web.pdf, p. 9; https://newint.org/features/2019/08/14/big-story-oceans-who-owns-sea; https://www.cbd.int/kb/record/pressRelease/113159?RecordType=pressRelease; Grafton et al. (2011), p. 478.

[45] https://mpanews.openchannels.org/news/mpa-news/iucn-members-approve-30-2030-goal-mpas-most-ambitious-target-so-far-mpa-coverage.

Climate Crisis at Home and Abroad' their goal 'of conserving at least 30% of our lands and waters by 2030.'[46]

Enhanced States' Practice to Establish MPAs

These intentions are reiterated through an increasing States' practice to establish MPAs in ABNJ as well as AUNJ. Since 2000, the coverage of MPAs has grown from approximately 2,000,000 km^2 (0.7% of the ocean) to more than 27,800,000 km^2 (7.65% of the ocean) today, which reflects a more than ninefold increase of MPAs on a global level in the past 20 years.[47] Due to the known impediments of the lack of sovereign rights as well as the collision with other freedoms of the High Sea, the percentage of MPAs in the AUNJ is much higher than in the ABNJ. 39% of the oceans are AUNJ, of which 17.78% are protected, while only 1.18% of the 61% of the ocean that makes up ABNJ are designated as MPAs. The massive increase of MPAs therefore can mainly be tracked by the national legislations of the States.

National States' Practice to Establish MPAs

The biggest growth of MPAs is in the Polar region with 44.78% growth since 2000.[48] The statistics furthermore show that the States' practice to establish MPAs is not limited to the member States of the UNCLOS or CBD. The coverage of MPAs in the AUNJ of the USA increased by 25.95% since 2000 with 37.4% of their waters now being protected today.[49] The European Commission expressly stated the EU's determination to protect Europe's marine environment more effectively and to this end, has proposed a marine thematic strategy on the protection and conservation of the marine environment which led to the adoption of the Marine Strategy Framework Directive in June 2008 to protect the marine environment across Europe more effectively.[50] Correspondingly, the United General Assembly acknowledges in its resolution A/68/71/Add. 1 that the '[e]fforts are continuing in all regions of the world to establish marine protected areas, ranging from areas with full protection to areas where activities are allowed and regulated.'[51] Out of the 18,408 Marine Protected Areas included in the World Database on Protected Areas, a joint database between the UNEP and the IUCN, managed by the UNEP World Conservation

[46] https://www.whitehouse.gov/briefing-room/presidential-actions/2021/01/27/executive-order-on-tackling-the-climate-crisis-at-home-and-abroad/.

[47] https://www.protectedplanet.net/en/thematic-areas/marine-protected-areas.

[48] https://www.protectedplanet.net/en/thematic-areas/marine-protected-areas.

[49] https://www.protectedplanet.net/en/thematic-areas/marine-protected-areas.

[50] https://ec.europa.eu/environment/pubs/pdf/factsheets/marine.pdf; https://ec.europa.eu/environment/marine/eu-coast-and-marine-policy/marine-strategy-framework-directive/index_en.htm.

[51] UNGA A/68/71/Add.1, p. 25, para. 105.

Monitoring Centre, 664 are in Africa, 3498 in Asia and the Pacific, 10,762 in Europe, 1273 in Latin America and the Caribbean, 2115 in North America, 19 in the Polar Region and 77 in West Asia.[52]

International States' Practice to Establish MPAs

Although the biggest increase in MPAs coverage can be traced in AUNJ, there is notable growth in MPA coverage also in ABNJ. This is of particular importance, considering the impediments to establish MPAs in AUNJ because of the *inter partes* effect of treaties and the zonal division of the sea. International MPAs in ABNJ have been specially established to comply with the obligation under the OSPAR Convention in the North-East Atlantic and the CCAMLR Convention in the Antarctic region.

Under Art. 2 (1) (a) OSPAR Convention, the contracting Parties are obliged to take all possible steps to prevent and eliminate pollution and to take the necessary measures to protect the maritime area against the adverse effects of human activities so as to safeguard human health, to conserve marine ecosystems and to restore marine areas which have been adversely affected. The OSPAR Convention is OSPAR maritime areas comprise extensive areas in the High Sea in the Wider Atlantic and the Arctic Waters. Seven MPAs have been established in the OSPAR-ABNJ between 2010 and 2012.[53]

The objective of the CCAMLR is the conservation of the Antarctic marine environment. Conservation measures are divided into four groups, compliance, general fishery matters, fishery regulations and protected areas.[54] The according States' practice to protect and preserve the marine environment in this region is manifested through the designation of the South Orkney Islands Southern Shelf MPA and the Ross Sea region MPA, which are both located entirely in the Arctic ABNJ. The Ross Sea Region MPA is the largest MPA, covering 1.55 million km^2.[55] The OSPAR Convention counts 16 members and the CCAMLR 26, both including the EU.[56] The States' practice to protect and preserve the marine environment is thus not only expressed through an extensive treaty practice to this end but moreover, through the establishment of MPAs, such as under the OSPAR and CCAMLR Conventions in practice.

[52] https://www.iucn.org/theme/protected-areas/our-work/world-database-protected-areas; https://www.protectedplanet.net/c/world-database-on-protected-areas.

[53] https://www.ospar.org/work-areas/bdc/marine-protected-areas/mpas-in-areas-beyond-national-jurisdiction.

[54] https://www.ccamlr.org/en/conservation-and-management/conservation-and-managment.

[55] https://www.ccamlr.org/en/science/marine-protected-areas-mpas; Scovazzi (2004), p. 9; Tanaka (2008), p. 425.

[56] https://www.ospar.org/organisation/contracting-parties; https://www.ccamlr.org/en/organisation/members.

4.2.2.3 Conclusion: General States' Practice

Thus, it has been demonstrated that there is extensive States' practice with regard to the protection and preservation of the marine environment. The practice to protect and preserve the marine environment is evident through a vast array of treaties. The evaluation of the treaty practice with regard to the obligation to protect and preserve the marine environment has shown that although single instruments have already been adopted before the UNCLOS, such as the 1971 Ramsar Convention and several instruments for the prevention of pollution, the majority of protection treaties and instruments to this end were adopted after 1982. In particular, the 1992 CBD manifested the practice to this end. The practice to protect and preserve the marine environment is further demonstrated through active acts, such as the establishment of MPAs, which accelerated since 2000. Within 20 years, the coverage of protected areas increased more than ninefold. The States' practice to protect and preserve the marine environment is further reiterated by repeated government statements to significantly enhance the designation of MPAs, such as on the COP of the CBD in 2010 or the IUCN in 2016. In particular, it has been demonstrated that also non-State parties of the UNCLOS, such as the USA, show an extensive State practice with regard to the protection and preservation of the marine environment, which is evident through the designation of large MPAs in its national waters as well as the participation i.e. in the CCAMLR. In total, this evidences a repeated, established, consistent, longlisting and uniform States' practice to protect and preserve the marine environment.

4.2.3 *Opinio Juris Sive Necessitatis*

The subjective element of international customs requires that the States render the practice as obligatory due to a belief of a corresponding rule of law (*opinio juris sive necessitatis*). In the case of Art. 192 UNCLOS, the demonstrated States' practice to protect and preserve the marine environment, therefore, had to be carried out in a manner that denotes the States believe that they are obliged to do so, not only because of Art. 192 UNCLOS, but because of a rule of customary international law.[57] The evidence of acceptance as law is difficult, as it refers to the subjective, underlying motives of States; however, it can be evident through various expressions: the general States' practice itself already implies a respective conviction of the States that they rendered their behaviour as obligatory. The adoption of respective treaties is another strong indicator of a respective acceptance as law. The *opinio juris* can furthermore be evident through expressions such as public statements, debates in multilateral settings, pleadings before courts and tribunals, protests against other

[57] Churchill and Lowe (1999), p. 6; Proelss (2017), Art. 192, mn. 21.

States behaviour or statements by States' representatives.[58] The *opinio juris* of States concerning the obligation to protect and preserve the marine environment is evident through the States' practice to protect and preserve the marine environment, the adoption of according treaties for this purpose, statement of States, non-binding instruments, statements of international organisations and the relevant jurisprudence.

4.2.3.1 Opinio Juris Expressed Through the States' Practice

The consistent and universal practice of States to protect and preserve the marine environment has been demonstrated broadly. This practice has not only emerged because of the UNCLOS but was manifested through it and is performed by parties and non-parties to the UNCLOS alike. This extensive State practice itself already indicates a corresponding *opinio juris* of the States, that they render the protection and preservation of the marine environment as obligatory.[59]

4.2.3.2 Opinio Juris Expressed Through Treaties

The adoption of treaties can be a confirmation that States render a certain behaviour obligatory by law and indicates a corresponding *opinio juris*. In the case of a similar treaty provision and rules of customary international law, this requires that the States did not only sign and ratify the treaty in order to create new binding law through the treaty itself but because they believe that they are either bound by an existing or wanted to develop a new rule of customary international law. With regard to Art. 192 UNCLOS, a great number of global and regional, general and specific regulations for the protection and preservation of the marine environment were adopted before, during and after the negotiations of the UNCLOS from 1973–1982. In 1992 already, the UN General Assembly counted about 20 conventions of a general character, which include eight regional conventions for the protection and preservation of the marine environment.[60] Today the number of treaties reflecting general or particular aspects of the protection and preservation of the marine environment exceeds 300 such instruments.

Opinio Juris Before and Subsequent to the UNCLOS

The review of treaties to assess the general States' practice has shown that many concepts with regard to the protection and preservation of the marine environment have already been entailed in conservation treaties before the UNCLOS. This

[58] ILC, A/71/10, p. 99.

[59] Crawford (2012), p. 27.

[60] UNGA A/47/512, p. 15, para. 62.

indicates that at the time of the adoption of the UNCLOS, the State community already possessed an *opinio juris* regarding the obligation to protect and preserve the marine environment, which has been repeated through the adoption of corresponding treaties after 1982. The protection of the marine environment from pollution, for instance, was included in the 1958 CHS, which obliges States under Art. 24, 25 CHS to adopt measures to prevent pollution from vessels and pipelines and dumping of radioactive waste and to cooperate to this end. The CHS was signed and ratified by 63 parties, including the USA. Although the UNCLOS is wider in its protective scope as it protects from all sources of marine pollution, it repeats and develops principles that are already entailed in treaties such as the CHS.[61] The appreciation of the need to protect and preserve the marine environment started rising in the second half of the twentieth century—and with it an according awareness of a legal obligation to this end. The adoption of treaties for the protection of the marine environment indicates that a concurring *opinio juris* may have already existed before and was manifested and deepened through the adoption of the UNCLOS.

Opinio Juris in the UNCLOS: The UNCLOS III Conference

The opening of the UNCLOS for signature was held on the 10th December 1982 in Montego Bay, Jamaica and attracted an unprecedented record of 119 signatures on the first day.[62] The signature and ratification of the UNCLOS by 168 States today, already shows that the great majority of States accept the obligation to protect and preserve the marine environment as law. However, for the assessment of the customary status of Art. 192 UNCLOS, it is necessary to prove that the State parties do not (only) believe that they are obliged by this rule because of the treaty, but (also) because of its status as a rule of customary international law. This can be evident, *inter alia*, if the States expressed that they want to adopt Art. 192 UNCLOS because it is a rule of customary international law during its negotiations.

The review of all records and documents of the UNCLOS III Conference from 1973 to 1982 only confirms the States' belief that the UNCLOS generally reflects or creates rules of customary international law, however, is inconclusive with regard to the customary status of the specific obligation as envisaged under Art. 192 UNCLOS.[63] Greece, for instance, points out that the whole UNCLOS, with exception of Part XI, reflects already existing rules of customary international law.[64] Other States such as Finland and Cameroon acknowledge the importance of the UNCLOS as a historic event because it 'creates a new international regime which

61 Birnie et al. (2009), p. 388; Lee (2006), p. 409.

62 https://www.isa.org.jm/news/isa-and-government-jamaica-commemorates-30th-anniversary-unclos.

63 https://legal.un.org/diplomaticconferences/1973_los/.

64 UN A/CONF.62/SR.191, p. 110, para. 13.

did not exist in contemporary customary international law' without specifying, however, if this 'new international régime' is conventional solely or also contributes to the development of new rules of customary international law.[65] The latter is expressly stressed by a further group of States such as Spain, Cape Verde, Kenya and Bahrain, who stress that the UNCLOS plays an important role not only in the codification of existing but also for the development of new rules of customary international law, such as the common heritage of mankind principle.[66] Although no direct Statement as to the customary status of the specific obligation to protect and preserve the marine environment can be derived from these statements, Sudan points out that for the first time, the UNCLOS 'has managed to establish within the framework of international law a regime for the protection and preservation of the marine environment,' and assigns it the status of a general principle, which is in harmony with the other 'principles of freedom of navigation, innocent passage and transit passage [. . .].'[67]

Whether State parties signed and ratified the UNCLOS believing that they merely cast into writing what already existed as a rule of customary international law before or in order to create a new international legally binding rule of customary international law, the review of the negotiation documents shows that they were convinced that the UNCLOS generally reflects customary international law, except for where the contrary is expressly stated, such as for Part XI UNCLOS. This is further stressed by the level of participation in the UNCLOS negotiations, which is an almost universal expression of the acceptance of the obligation to protect and preserve the marine environment as a legally binding obligation under public international law.[68] This view, too, is taught in the virtual training and research centre of the United Nations themselves. In the UN Audio-visual Library of International Law, Judge of the International Tribunal for the Law of the Sea (ITLOS) Tullio Treves honours the substantial impact of the UNCLOS on the formation of customary international law by suggesting, that instead of corroborating that the provisions of the UNCLOS reflect customary international law, the great number of States bound by it as well as its practical influence, rather allows the presumption that its (non-institutional provisions) are rules of customary international law unless the contrary is proven.[69]

[65] UN A/CONF.62/SR.190, p. 87, para. 64; UN A/CONF.62/WS/36, p. 233; UN A/CONF.62/SR.187, p. 42, para. 61.

[66] UN A/CONF.62/SR.190, p. 87, para. 65; UN A/CONF.62/SR.187, p. 47, para. 130; UN A/CONF.62/SR.188, p. 62, para. 120; UN A/CONF.62/SR.190, p. 87, para. 100.

[67] UN A/CONF.62/SR.191, p. 115, para. 192.

[68] Boyle (2005), p. 571.

[69] https://legal.un.org/avl/ha/uncls/uncls.html.

Opinio Juris Expressed in Other Agreements

The *opinio juris* of the protection and preservation of the marine environment is furthermore expressed in other agreements. The 16 parties of the OSPAR Convention expressly recall in the preamble that Part XII UNCLOS reflects already existing rules of customary international law.[70] Art. 16 of the 2004 International Convention for the Control and Management of Ships' Ballast Water and Sediments (BWM Convention),[71] as well as Art. 16 of the 2013 Agreement on Cooperation on Marine Oil Pollution, Preparedness and Response in the Arctic (MOSPA Agreement)[72] both state that nothing in the respective Conventions shall be construed as altering the rights or obligations of any Party under other relevant international agreements or customary international law as reflected in the UNCLOS. Although the State parties do not specify which of the provisions of the UNCLOS are regarded as customary international law both agreements include the protection and preservation of the marine environment from different threats. The BWM Convention is signed and ratified by 79 States including non-UNCLOS State parties such as Iran, Peru, Syria, Turkey and the United Arab Emirates and the MOSPA Agreement is a regional treaty that is signed and ratified by Canada, Finland, Iceland, Kingdom of Denmark, Norway, the Russian Federation, Sweden and the non-UNCLOS member USA.[73] This shows that also important coastal States such as Iran, Peru, Syria, Turkey, the United Arab Emirates and the USA, which are not members of the UNCLOS, acknowledge, that the UNCLOS indeed does generally contain rules of customary international law.

4.2.3.3 Opinio Juris Through States' Statements

An *opinio juris sive necessitatis* can furthermore be deduced from any official statement of States. The following analysis demonstrates the *opinio juris* of States regarding the obligation to protect and preserve the marine environment through statements in the UN General Assembly regarding the customary status of the UNCLOS in general as well as the obligation to protect and preserve the marine environment specifically, pleadings of States in courts and tribunals and official statements of States, including non-member States to the UNCLOS. It will be demonstrated to this end that although there are persistent objectors to the customary

[70] https://www.ospar.org/organisation/contracting-parties.

[71] UNTS, Vol. n.a., No. 55544.

[72] ECOLEX, IUCN (ID: TRE-160032).

[73] https://treaties.un.org/Pages/showDetails.aspx?objid=080000028053b465; https://oaarchive.arctic-council.org/bitstream/handle/11374/1748/EDOCS-3258-v2A-ACSAOUS202_Fairbanks_2016_InfoDoc2_Update_on_Arctic_Council_Agreements_Ratification_Depositary.pdf?sequence=5&isAllowed=y.

status of parts of the UNCLOS, there are no persistent objectors to the obligation to protect and preserve the marine environment.

General Statements of States in the UN General Assembly

The opinion of States concerning the customary status of the general customary status of the UNCLOS in general as well as the obligation to protect and preserve the marine environment specifically is evident through the official records of the Plenary Meetings of the UN General Assembly relating to debates under the agenda item 'Oceans and Law of the Sea' from 1993 until 2020.[74] The comprehensive review of all the documents reveals that all States and organisations that comment acknowledge the customary status of the UNCLOS with variations only to its extent. While some States and organisations accept the customary status of the UNCLOS in general (Argentina, Cyprus, El Salvador, EU, Federated States of Micronesia, the Rio Group consisting of 19 States (Argentina, Bolivia, Brazil, Chile, Colombia, Costa Rica, Dominican Republic, Ecuador, El Salvador, Guatemala, Guyana, Honduras, Mexico, Nicaragua, Panama, Paraguay, Peru, Uruguay, Venezuela), Sierra Leone, Sri Lanka; Ukraine)[75] other States and Organisations accept that the UNCLOS at least in parts reflects or has grown into customary international law (Australia, Austria, Brazil, Canada, Denmark, Fiji, Finland, General Assembly of the United Nations, Georgia, Iceland, Indonesia, ICJ, ISA, Mexico, Morocco, New Zealand, Nicaragua, Norway, Republic of Korea; Singapore, South Africa, Sweden, United States of America, Uruguay, Vietnam).[76] This makes a total of 43 States and four international organisations that expressly acknowledge the customary status of the UNCLOS entirely or in parts, including the EU which represents 27 States and non-parties to the UNCLOS, such as the USA.

The analysis of these statements requires three remarks: Firstly, the comments are not answers to specific questions on the customary status of the UNCLOS. The omission of statements by other States are therefore not tacit declarations against the customary status. Rather, the statements are self-initiated by the States, so that

---

[74] https://www.un.org/Depts/los/general_assembly/general_assembly_records.htm.

[75] UNGA A/69/PV.64, p. 20, UNGA A/69/PV.66, p. 19; UNGA A/67/PV.50, p. 7, UNGA A/69/PV.66, p. 22, and UNGA A/47/PV.83, p. 62; UNGA A/67/PV.51, p. 1; UNGA A/69/PV.66, p. 4; UNGA A/67/PV.49, p. 26; UNGA A/58/PV.63, p. 4; UNGA A/57/PV.74, p. 22; UNGA A/64/PV.56, p. 26; UNGA A/72/PV.64, p. 3.

[76] UNGA A/62/PV.46, p. 28; UNGA A/48/PV.100, p. 8 and UNGA A/48/PV.72, p. 6; UNGA A/60/PV.54, p. 2; UNGA A/47/PV.84, p. 78; UNGA A/57/PV.71, p. 8; UNGA A/59/PV.55, p. 9; UNGA A/48/PV.101, p. 16; UNGA A/57/PV.70, p. 1; UNGA A/67/PV.49, p. 9; UNGA A/57/PV.71, p. 16; UNGA A/48/PV.73, p. 5; UNGA A/57/PV.70, p. 18; UNGA A/67/PV.49, p. 13; UNGA A/48/PV.101, p. 2; UNGA A/57/PV.74, p. 11; UNGA A/47/PV.83, p. 104; UNGA A/67/PV.51, p. 3; UNGA A/61/PV.69, p. 23; UNGA A/67/PV.49, p. 8; UNGA A/69/PV.67, p. 7; UNGA A/65/PV.59, p. 16; UNGA A/67/PV.50, p. 24, UNGA A/48/PV.72, p. 17 and UNGA A/47/PV.83, p. 93; UNGA A/59/PV.54, p. 25, UNGA A/49/PV.77, p. 5, UNGA A/47/PV.83, p. 62 and UNGA A/67/PV.49, p. 12; UNGA A/47/PV.83, p. 111; UNGA A/57/PV.71, p. 14.

the lack to comment by the rest of the States does not mean that they do not recognize the UNCLOS as customary international law, but only that they did not give any statement to that effect.

Secondly, although the representative for the Rio Group, of which Venezuela is a party, generally accepted the UNCLOS as customary international law, Venezuela and Colombia are the only States that expressly oppose being bound by the UNCLOS by means of custom or treaty.[77] The opposition of single States does not hamper the creation of a rule of customary international law, it may, however, exempt these States to be bound by this rule as Persistent Objectors, which will be discussed in the following.

Thirdly, the statements of the States are general remarks concerning the customary status of the UNCLOS and do not specifically address any part of it, such as Part XII UNCLOS on the protection and preservation of the marine environment. However, as the statements contain affirmative expression regarding the customary status of the UNCLOS in general even by non-State parties to the UNCLOS, the review strongly indicates that the regulations of the UNCLOS generally have evolved into rules of customary international law, except where the contrary is expressed. Specific Statements of the States with regard to the obligation to protect and preserve the marine environment will be addressed in the following.

Specific Statements of States in the UN General Assembly

The records of the Plenary Meetings of the UN General Assembly furthermore evidence the affirmative expressions of various UNCLOS member States as to the customary status of the obligation to protect and preserve the marine environment specifically. Norway, for instance, states that 'States have a general responsibility to protect and preserve the marine environment and living resources in all ocean areas'.[78] Kenya points out the 'critical importance' of the protection of the coastal and marine environment, which it protects on a national and regional level.[79] Egypt expresses its conviction 'that maritime environmental protection is the responsibility of the international community as a whole'.[80] 'Belize is committed to the sustainable development of its marine environment and of the oceans and the seas as a whole.[81] Mexico expressly acknowledges the 'overall obligation to conserve and protect the marine environment'.[82] Korea stresses the 'great importance to the protection and conservation of the marine environment'.[83] Grenada points out that 'we, as an

[77] For Venezuela see i.e. UNGA A/74/PV.43, pp. 23 f.; for Colombia UNGA, A/69/PV.77, p. 4.

[78] UNGA A/59/PV.54, p. 6.

[79] UNGA A/59/PV.54, p. 14.

[80] UNGA A/59/PV.54, p. 17.

[81] UNGA A/58/PV.64, p. 20.

[82] UNGA A/58/PV.63, p. 24.

[83] UNGA A/58/PV.63, p. 28.

international community, must do more to ensure the protection of our global environment',[84] while the Bahamas 'is committed to safe sea transport and to the need for environmental protection'.[85] This inconclusive list shows single examples of States' acknowledgements of the obligation to protect and preserve the marine environment and the responsibility of the whole international community to this end.

States' Pleadings Before Courts and Tribunals

Statements of States evidencing an existing *opinio juris,* can further be derived from oral or written pleadings before courts and tribunals.

Request for an Advisory Opinion Submitted by the SRFC

In the oral proceedings before the ITLOS concerning the *Request for an Advisory Opinion Submitted by the Sub-Regional Fisheries Commission (SRFC)* on 4 September 2014, New Zealand expressly affirmed the status of Art. 192 UNCLOS as a general principle of environmental protection.[86] In the same proceedings, on the same day, also Micronesia noted 'States Parties to UNCLOS, as well as non-States Parties that are nevertheless bound by the customary nature of the provisions of UNCLOS, therefore owe a legal obligation to the international community as a whole to safeguard the world's fragile Ocean for the benefit of all mankind.'[87] In the same proceeding the following day, the Caribbean Regional Fisheries Mechanism acknowledged the *erga omnes* obligation relating to the preservation of the environment of the High Seas.[88]

MOX Plant

In the public sitting of the *MOX Plant Case* at the ITLOS, Ireland stated that the 'protection of the environment has emerged as a central foundation of the international legal order and part of the corpus of customary law'.[89]

---

[84] UNGA A/74/PV.42, p. 6.

[85] UNGA A/58/PV.63, p. 29.

[86] ITLOS, *Request for an Advisory Opinion Submitted by the Sub-Regional Fisheries Commission* (in the following: SRFC), Oral Proceedings on 04 September 2014 (Verbatim Record), ITLOS/PV.14/C21/3/Rev.1, p. 15, l. 2–3.

[87] ITLOS, *SRFC*, Oral Proceedings on 04 September 2014 (Verbatim Record), ITLOS/PV.14/C21/3/Rev.1, p. 7, l. 29–32.

[88] ITLOS, *SRFC*, Oral Proceedings on 5 September 2014 (Verbatim Record), ITLOS/PV.14/C21/4/Rev.1, p. 8, l. 26–33.

[89] ITLOS, *MOX Plant* (Ireland v. United Kingdom), Public Sitting on 19 November 2001 (Verbatim Record), ITLOS/PV.01/06, p. 33, l. 26–28.

South China Sea Arbitration (Philippines v. China)

In the *South China Sea Arbitration*, the PCA, acting as arbitral tribunal under the UNCLOS in a dispute between the Philippines and China, *inter alia* had to decide about the lawfulness of Chinese fishing and construction activities in the South China Sea under Art. 192 ff. UNCLOS.[90] On day four of the hearing in the merits, the Philippines expressly stated that Art. 192 UNCLOS 'is to be treated as declarators of customary international law.'[91] Moreover, according to the Philippines, the 'view that the normative provisions of UNCLOS as a whole are today to be treated as customary international law is too widely held by states parties and non-parties alike to require further iteration.'[92] The Philippines furthermore laid down, that the regional seas agreements adopted by the Philippines reflect the notion of the customary status of the principle embodied in Art. 192 UNCLOS and other provisions of Part XII UNCLOS, even before the UNCLOS entered into force, which makes it evident that Art. 192 UNCLOS and Part XII UNCLOS 'can reasonably be regarded today as declaratory of customary international law on the marine environment.'[93]

Official Statements by Ministers (China)

China, in its defence, has not stated its position regarding the assertion of the Philippines. In order to ascertain China's position, the tribunal reviewed statements by its Foreign Ministry officials that indicate that China considers the protection and preservation of the marine environment as a binding obligation as well.[94] In a statement given on 09 April 2015, the Foreign Ministry Spokesman of China emphasised China's intention to better perform its international responsibility and obligation to environmental protection. According to the Minister, China's contested construction projects around the disputed islands and reefs in the South China Sea had gone through scientific assessments and rigorous tests putting 'equal emphasis on construction and protection by following a high standard of environmental protection and taking into full consideration the protection of ecological environment and fishing resources.'[95]

---

[90] Dipla (2006), p. 246.

[91] PCA, *South China Sea Arbitration*, Philippines v. China, Final Transcript Day 4—Merits Hearing, 30 November 2015, p. 170, l. 21, 22; PCA, *South China Sea Arbitration*, Philippines v. China (Award), p. 360, para. 907.

[92] PCA, *South China Sea Arbitration*, Philippines v. China, Final Transcript Day 4—Merits Hearing, 30 November 2015, p. 173, l. 15–18.

[93] PCA, *South China Sea Arbitration*, Philippines v. China, Final Transcript Day 4—Merits Hearing, 30 November 2015, p. 173, l. 25-p. 174, l. 2.

[94] PCA, *South China Sea Arbitration*, Philippines v. China (Award), pp. 363 f., para. 912, 916.

[95] https://www.fmprc.gov.cn/mfa_eng/xwfw_665399/s2510_665401/t1253488.shtml; PCA, *South China Sea Arbitration*, Philippines v. China (Award), p. 365, para. 917.

Statements of Non-members of the UNCLOS

As evident by statements of UNCLOS non-parties, the reason for the non-signature or non-ratification of the treaty is not related to the obligation to protect and preserve the marine environment.

The USA

One of the most prominent non-members of the UNCLOS are the USA. In a statement of 9 July 1982, the former president Ronald Reagan laid down the reason for the refusal to ratify the UNCLOS by the USA despite its participation in the long negotiation process for 9 years. Accordingly Reagan stated that the deep seabed represented an important source of strategic and other minerals and that the aim of the USA in this regard had been to establish with other nations an order that would allow exploration and development of the same. Because 'the deep seabed mining part of the convention does not meet United States objectives' the USA did not ratify the UNCLOS.[96] In the same statement Reagan recognised how critical the oceans are to mankind and how important an international treaty is to the use of the ocean, however, without further commenting on the customary status of any of the rules of the UNCLOS.

In 1989, however, the USA expressly recognised in a joint statement with the Soviet Union that the 'Governments are guided by the provisions of the 1982 United Nations Convention on the Law of the Sea, which, with respect to traditional uses of the oceans, generally constitute international law and practice and balance fairly the interest of all States. They recognize the need of all States to harmonize their internal laws, regulations and practices with those provisions.'[97] Furthermore, as evident by a letter from the Co-Chairpersons of the Consultative Process addressed to the President of the General Assembly, dated 20 May 2002, the representative of the USA, despite not being part of the UNCLOS, expressly 'accepted the Convention's provisions on traditional uses of the oceans as reflecting existing customary international law and practice and that the current Administration supported United States accession to the instrument.'[98] It remains questionable, whether the USA considers the obligations as embodied in Art. 192 UNCLOS as such 'traditional use of the oceans', which generally constitutes international law. Nonetheless, it is evident that the USA consider itself bound by the UNCLOS with exception to Part XI UNCLOS, which generally confirms the status of the other provisions as customary international law.

Congruently, in the Plenary Meetings of the UN General Assembly, the USA repeatedly pointed out that the USA does not have any opposition to the UNCLOS

[96] https://www.reaganlibrary.gov/research/speeches/70982b; Tanaka (2019), p. 35; Harrison (2011), p. 2.

[97] United Nations (1989), p. 12.

[98] UNGA A/57/80, p. 15, para. 28.

anymore and is interested in joining the Convention and in doing so 'hopes that this will achieve the goal of establishing a legal order to promote freedom of the High Seas, peaceful use of the oceans and the study, protection and preservation of the marine environment.'[99] The USA recurrently stated that the 'Convention both codifies pre-existing customary international law and has contributed to the acceptance of many of its provisions as customary international law' and that many countries, including the USA 'have been acting in accordance with these principles for some time' and benefit greatly from its existence.[100]

Lastly, the acceptance of the protection and preservation of the marine environment as a binding rule of international law by the USA is also reflected in its national legislation. Even permits for mining activities in the deep seabed under the U.S. Deep Seabed Hard Mineral Resources Act of 1980, may only be issued 'with due regard for the conservation and protection of the environment' under 30 U.S.C. §1401, (a) Applications, (2) (E) (i) and (ii) (I), 30 U.S.C. §1415 (b) (1).[101] The act establishes a licensing regime that ensures the protection of the marine environment and dedicates a whole part to this end (30 U.S.C. § 1419). This shows the importance and recognition that the USA attribute to the obligation to protect and preserve the marine environment, which is even capable to influence seabed activities. The Secretary of State is expressly encouraged to successfully negotiate a comprehensive law of the sea treaty, which amongst others provides the establishment for the protection of the environment (30 U.S.C. §1402 (b) (1)). A comprehensive review of the Statements of the USA therefore shows their acceptance of the obligation to protect and preserve the marine environment as binding national and international law, which strongly indicates an according *opinio juris* of the customary status of the principle embodied in Art. 192 UNCLOS by the USA.

Turkey

Turkey did not sign the UNCLOS due to the Aegean dispute over sovereignty and pertinent rights in the Aegean Sea between Greece and Turkey. Due to the existence of a great number of Greek islands in the Aegean Sea, the application of the 12 NM Territorial Sea under Art. 3, 2 (1) UNCLOS would convert most of the respective waters into Greek territory. This would not only reduce the High Sea in this terrain by half but also diminish Turkey's EEZ and Continental Shelf significantly.[102] Turkey expressly stated that it agrees with the UNCLOS in its general intent and with most of its provisions and that it is only unable to become party to it because it does 'not provide sufficient safeguards for special geographical situations and, as a

[99] UNGA A/59/PV.54, p. 25.

[100] UNGA A/49/PV.77, p. 5; UNGA A/47/PV.83, p. 62.

[101] Deep Seabed Hard Mineral Resources Act of 1980, Pub. L. No. 96-283, 94 Stat. 553 (codified as amended principally at 30 U.S.C. §§ 1401 et. seq. (1982)).

[102] Siousiouras and Chrysochou (2014), p. 13; https://www.institutmontaigne.org/en/blog/whose-sea-turkish-international-law-perspective-greek-turkish-disputes.

consequence, does not take into consideration conflicting interests and sensitivities arising from special circumstances' and does not allow to register reservations.[103] However, it does not oppose any provisions on the protection and preservation of the marine environment and moreover expresses its commitment to the conservation, management and sustainable use of marine living resources and attaches great importance to regional cooperation to that end.[104] The general acceptance of the UNCLOS by Turkey, its commitment to conserving the marine living resources and the specification that it only opposes the strict regulations on the special distribution of sovereign rights and the prohibition to register reservations, leads to the conclusion that it generally accepts the regulations on the protection and preservation of the marine environment.

Persistent Objectors

The majority of the States are parties to the UNCLOS and only single States refuse to sign and ratify it. Most of the States, furthermore, expressly accept at least parts of the UNCLOS as customary international law. The emergence of the UNCLOS as customary international law is therefore not impeded by the opposition of single States. However, it needs to be assessed, whether the objection to accept rules of the UNCLOS as customary international law may prevent certain States from being bound by the rule as persistent objectors. This requires that the State in question opposed to the rule at its formation and upholds this position.

USA and Turkey

It has been evidenced broadly, that the USA and Turkey had specific reasons not to conclude the UNCLOS that lie outside the obligation to protect and preserve the marine environment and that they expressly limit their objections to those other reasons. On the contrary, it has been evidenced that the USA as well as Turkey both accept the UNCLOS in general, with only exceptions to the specific rules on the Area for the USA and the distribution of sovereign rights for Turkey.

Venezuela

Venezuela is one of the 15 members of the UN (14 States and the Holy See) that has neither signed nor ratified the UNCLOS and furthermore repeatedly claims that it is not bound by the regulations of the UNCLOS neither through the Convention nor by means of customary international law. It needs to be established if Venezuela has attained the status of a persistent objector to the UNCLOS.

[103] UNGA A/67/PV.52, p. 28.

[104] UNGA A/67/PV.52, p. 28.

Venezuela has not signed nor ratified the UNCLOS, which is a sign of its opposition to the treaty at its formation. Furthermore, Venezuela upholds this position as evident in its statements in the Plenary Meetings of the UN General Assembly concerning debates under the agenda item 'Oceans and Law of the Sea'. Each time the Venezuelan representative stated on any item with regard to the UNCLOS, it did express that Venezuela is not a signatory to the UNCLOS and is therefore not bound by its provisions, neither by convention nor customs, 'except for those that the Venezuelan State has expressly recognized or will recognize in the future by incorporating them into its domestic legislation.'[105] It furthermore, each time, expressly acknowledged that the 'UNCLOS codifies certain norms of customary international law that have been incorporated into the Venezuelan domestic legal system either through the ratification of the Geneva Conventions of 1958 or through domestic legislation.'[106] Thus, Venezuela upheld its objection to be bound by the UNCLOS consistently. However, the statements also show, that Venezuela does not oppose being bound by all regulations of the UNCLOS. On the contrary, Venezuela expressly acknowledges being bound by those regulations that are incorporated in its legal system either through domestic law or through the four 1958 Geneva Conventions to which Venezuela is a party. Concludingly, although Venezuela is a persistent objector to the UNCLOS, it does accept to be bound by specific regulations either if they are reflected in the Geneva Conventions or otherwise integrated into its national legal system.

Elements of the obligation to protect and preserve the marine environment are entailed in the CHS. Art. 24 CHS requires States to adopt measures to prevent pollution from the discharge of oil from ships and pipelines and from activities on the seabed and subsoil; Art. 25 (1) CHS addresses the pollution from dumping of radioactive waste and Art. 25 (2) CHS the cooperation of States to this end. Thus, while Art. 192 UNCLOS is wider in its protective scope, it repeats and develops principles that are already entailed in the CHS, such as the pollution from specific sources.[107] Furthermore, under Art. 1 (1) CFCLR the rights of States to engage in fishing on the High Sea are subject to the conservation of the living resources of the High Sea. All States have the duty to adopt and to cooperate with other States to adopt such measures for their respective nationals as may be necessary for the conservation of the living resources of the High Sea by virtue of Art. 1 (2) CFCLR. Although the conservation of marine living resources under Art. 2 CFCLR primarily serves to secure the optimum sustainable yield to secure a maximum supply of food,

---

105 UNGA A/74/PV.43, p. 23.

106 UNGA A/74/PV.43, p. 24; UNGA A/73/PV.50, p. 14; UNGA A/72/PV.76, p. 9; UNGA A/72/PV.64, p. 28; UNGA A/71/PV.68, p. 14; UNGA A/71/PV.55, pp. 17 f.; UNGA A/70/PV.82 p. 9; UNGA A/70/PV.69, p. 15; UNGA A/69/PV.96, p. 6; UNGA A/69/PV.67, p. 19; UNGA A/68/PV.63, pp. 19, 21; UNGA A/67/PV.51, p. 6; UNGA A/66/PV.93, p. 3; UNGA A/65/PV.59, p. 27; UNGA A/64/PV.58, p. 16; UNGA A/63/PV.64, p. 22; UNGA A/63/PV.63, p. 3; UNGA A/62/PV.79, p. 3; UNGA A/62/PV.77, pp. 17 f.; UNGA A/61/PV.83, p. 21; UNGA A/61/PV.71, p. 11; UNGA A/60/PV.56, pp. 1 ff.; UNGA A/59/PV.56, pp. 14 ff.

107 Birnie et al. (2009), p. 388; Lee (2006), p. 409.

the conservation of the living resources still contains an element of the preservation of specific species (secondary conservation objective).

Moreover, in the Plenary Meetings, Venezuela stresses that the 'Oceans and the Law of the Sea' is a priority in its own policies and that its compliance with 'international obligations under the law of the sea while advocating its integral development from a standpoint of equity and stressing the fact that all negotiations related to that right must reflect criteria and principles linked to the right to sustainable development of the marine environment and its resources for future generations.'[108] Furthermore, Venezuela emphasises its efforts to cooperate in the coordination on issues related to the law of the sea. Coordination and cooperation are integral parts of the protection and preservation of the marine environment.[109] Its importance is reflected in the regulations of the UNCLOS, which regulate the coordination between States prominently in Section 2 of Part XII UNCLOS, right after stipulating the general obligations. Venezuela continues by reaffirming its constructive and positive relationship with the UNCLOS and reiterates its commitment to sustainable fisheries. According to Venezuela, its national development plan is complemented by a wide set of regulations allowing it to 'rely on programmes aimed at achieving the conservation, protection and management of marine biological resources, while promoting their responsible and sustainable use, including, inter alia, the relevant biological, economic, food security, social, cultural, environmental and commercial aspects.'[110]

Concludingly, Venezuela's acceptance of the CHS and CFCLR, its express acceptance of international obligations concerning the sustainable development of the marine environment and the cooperation of States, as well as its wide set of regulations concerning the protection and management of marine biological resources in its national legislations, undoubtedly proves Venezuela's acceptance of the international obligation to protect and preserve the marine environment as a rule of customary international law.

Colombia

Colombia has signed the UNCLOS on its opening day on the 10 December 1982 but has not ratified it. In the Plenary Meeting of the UN General Assembly on 'Oceans and Law of the Sea', Colombia claims that it, therefore, is neither bound by the UNCLOS through the convention nor through customary international law, except for those regulations that Colombia has expressly recognised in its domestic legislation.[111] The status as persistent objector requires not only that the State upholds its objection but also that it objected to the rule at its formation. As Colombia signed the UNCLOS on its opening day and only later refrained from ratifying it, is

[108] UNGA A/74/PV.43, p. 24.
[109] UNGA A/74/PV.43, p. 24.
[110] UNGA A/74/PV.43, p. 23.
[111] UNGA A/69/PV.77, p. 4.

questionable, if Colombia, therefore, is initially capable to attain the position of a persistent objector.

Even if Colombia manages to establish its position as a persistent objector, it acknowledges those regulations of the UNCLOS that it has incorporated in its national legislation. Colombia shows a distinctly high level of marine protection, which it achieved through national legislation in its marine waters. MPAs cover 12% of the Colombian AUNJ. Compared to the States that it either shares a territorial or EEZ border with, this proves that Venezuela belongs to the States with the highest coverage of MPAs in its marine waters in this area. The comparatively low MPA coverage of Peru of less than 1% is followed by Jamaica with 1.2%, Costa Rica with 2.7%, the Dominican Republic with 3.6%, Haiti with 4% and Venezuela with 4.3%. Together with Panama that has an MPA coverage of 11%, Ecuador with 13% and Nicaragua leading with 18%, Colombia, therefore, belongs to the top States concerning the coverage of MPAs in its region.[112] The designation of more than 10% of marine waters as MPAs even exceeds the average on the international level.[113]

Additionally, Colombia participates in the UNEP Regional Seas Programme and is one of the 28 member States of the Wider Caribbean Region that's governments launched the 1981 Caribbean Environment Programme to protect the region's diversity and its fragile and vulnerable coastal and marine ecosystems.[114] The countries of the Caribbean Environment Programme developed an Action Plan that led to the adoption of the 1983 Cartagena Convention along with the 1983 Oil Spills Protocol and the 1990 SPAW Protocol.[115] Furthermore, Colombia (as well as Venezuela and Turkey) is a party to the CBD, which obliges its member States to establish MPAs in their marine waters under Art. 8 (a) CBD. All of the aforementioned States hence subjected themselves to the objective of the conservation of biological diversity and the sustainable use of its components as stipulated under Art. 1 CBD.

Conclusively, even if Colombia objected to be bound by the UNCLOS in the UN Plenary Meetings, it accepted specific regulations by implementing them into its domestic legislation, including the protection and preservation of the marine environment. This is evident through its extensive practice to establish MPAs in its AUNJ, the adoption of the CBD as well as the Cartagena Convention, Oil Spills Protocol and SPAW Protocol.

---

[112] https://mpatlas.org/countries/COL/map; https://mpatlas.org/countries/JAM.

[113] https://www.protectedplanet.net/en.

[114] https://www.unep.org/cep/?_ga=2.42671845.1573124132.1615949855-99619101.1615342079.

[115] https://www.unep.org/explore-topics/oceans-seas/what-we-do/working-regional-seas/regional-seas-programmes/wider.

4.2.3.4 Opinio Juris Expressed Through Other Non-binding Instruments

Non-Binding Instruments can have significance for the creation of international law, as they can confirm existing rules of customary international law, contribute to the development of new laws and provide guidance on the interpretation of treaty texts.[116] Soft law with elements of the protection and preservation of the marine environment include but are not limited to the Stockholm and the Rio Declaration, Chapter 17 of Agenda 21, Action Plans adopted under the UNEP Regional Seas Programme and resolutions by the UN General Assembly.[117]

Stockholm, Rio and Agenda 21

Two of the most important conferences that contributed to the development of international environmental rules and jurisprudence are the first and the second global environmental conferences, namely the United Nations Conference on the Human Environment held in Stockholm in 1972 and the United Nations Conference on Environment and Development in Rio de Janeiro in 1992. With Stockholm first taking stock of the human impact on the global environment, the Stockholm Declaration expresses the attempt to address the environmental policy goals and objectives to preserve and enhance the human environment, which propelled international environmental law making and awareness without stipulating detailed normative positions though. The objective of the Rio Conference was to craft an "Earth Charter" to encompass and systemize the interim results of the past 20 years since Stockholm. The resulting compromise text of the Rio Declaration and the Agenda 21 to achieve global sustainable development are landmarks in the development of environmental law and reaffirming and reinforce the normative significance of the Stockholm Declaration. Although both Declarations and Agenda 21 are formally not binding, they contain already existing and potentially precure new rules of customary international law. Principle 21 of the Stockholm Declaration and Principle 2 of the Rio Declaration, for instance, establish the States' responsibility to ensure that its activities do not cause damage to the environment of other States or ABNJ.[118] This States' duty to prevent transboundary environmental harm is a well-established rule of customary international law today and plays an important role in marine protection.[119]

---

116 Tanaka (2019), p. 19; https://www.un.org/Depts/los/biodiversityworkinggroup/webpagelegalandpolicy.pdf, p. 1, para. 4.

117 https://www.un.org/Depts/los/biodiversityworkinggroup/webpagelegalandpolicy.pdf, p. 1, para. 4.

118 https://legal.un.org/avl/ha/dunche/dunche.html; Sands (2012), p. 142.

119 UN Doc A/CONF/48/14; Sands (2012), pp. 145, f.; Wolfrum (1990), p. 310.

Agenda 21 dedicates Chapter 17 to the 'protection of the oceans, all kinds of seas, including enclosed and semi-enclosed seas, and coastal areas and the protection, rational use and development of their living resources'. It supports the understanding that the obligation to protect and preserve the marine environment is general international law, *inter alia* by stipulating that States commit themselves to prevent, reduce and control degradation of the marine environment so as to maintain and improve its life-support and productive capacities in accordance with the provisions of the UNCLOS on protection and preservation of the marine environment under Chapter 17, para. 22.[120]

UNEP Regional Seas Programme

For regional cooperation between the States, the UNEP Regional Seas Programmes is an important development for the conservation and protection of the marine environment from pollution and overexploiting, of which MPAs are an important mechanism. Most of the Regional Seas Programmes focus on legally non-binding Action Plans. In fourteen cases these Action Plans led to the adoption of legally binding Conventions that set out what governments must do in order to implement their Action Plans and how to address common environmental issues through joint coordinated activities. The first UNEP Action Plan was adopted for the Mediterranean in 1975 and led to the 1976 Barcelona Convention, the first legally binding Regional Seas Convention, which is a framework model for environmental treaties.[121] UN Environment today administers regional programs in West Africa, Caribbean, Mediterranean, Northwest Pacific, East Asian Seas, Caspian Sea and East Africa, acknowledging the importance of the protection and preservation of the marine environment.[122] The endeavours of the States to achieve the goal of the protection and preservation of the marine environment through the adoption of Action Plans, which regularly develop into legally binding Regional Seas Conventions, as well as the adoption of international Declarations such as in Stockholm, Rio and Agenda 21, underlines the opinion of the international community that the obligation to protect and preserve the marine environment is a binding international obligation, which needs to be achieved through international cooperation.

[120] Sands (2012), p. 396.

[121] https://www.unep.org/explore-topics/oceans-seas/what-we-do/working-regional-seas/regional-seas-programmes/regional-seas; https://www.unenvironment.org/explore-topics/oceans-seas/what-we-do/working-regional-seas/regional-seas-programmes.

[122] Kellerher (1999), p. 2.

Development of the BBNJ

The potential development of non-binding declarations of States into legally binding norms can be observed with the negotiations of the BBNJ. At the UN Conference on Sustainable Development 'The Future We Want' in Rio de Janeiro in 2012, the heads of States and Governments, recognising the importance of the conservation and sustainable use of marine biodiversity in ABNJ, committed themselves to address issues of the conservation and sustainable use of marine biological diversity in ABNJ, including the development of an international instrument under the UNCLOS.[123] Responding to the commitment in Rio, the General Assembly decided to develop an international legally binding instrument under the UNCLOS on the conservation and sustainable use of marine biological diversity in ABNJ. For this purpose, it established a preparatory committee to propose substantive recommendations to the General Assembly on the elements of a draft text of an international legally binding instrument under UNCLOS.[124] In the following, the UN General Assembly convened an intergovernmental conference to consider the recommendations of the preparatory committee with a view to developing the instrument as soon as possible. A draft treaty was presented after the third of four sessions in November 2019.[125] Due to the coronavirus disease 2019 (COVID-19), the fourth and last sessions is postponed, currently to the earliest possible available date in 2022.[126] The objective of the BBNJ is to ensure the conservation and sustainable use of marine biodiversity of ABNJ particularly including area-based management tools such as MPAs.[127] This development shows how commitments of States in international conferences can set in motion corresponding UN Resolutions that can lead to the creation of binding instruments under international law.

With regard to the BBNJ, it could be argued that the participation in the negotiations of the BBNJ evidences a State practice concerning the protection and preservation of the marine environment and stipulates a corresponding *opinio juris* of the States. However, in resolution A/RES/72/249 the UN General Assembly explicitly states that neither the participation in the negotiations nor their outcome shall affect the legal status of parties or non-parties to the UNCLOS or any other related agreements with regard to those instruments. Although the participation in treaty negotiations can generally evidence an *opinio juris*, in the case of the BBNJ, the participation in the treaty negotiations is not admissible as evidence of the States' practice or a respective *opinio juris* to determine the customary status of Art. 192 UNCLOS.[128]

[123] UNGA A/RES/66/288*, p. 31, para. 162.

[124] UNGA A/RES/69/292, p. 2, para. 1.

[125] UNGA A/CONF.232/2020/3.

[126] UNGA A/74/L.41* (UNGA A/RES/74/543), UNGA A/75/L.96.

[127] https://www.un.org/depts/los/biodiversity/prepcom_files/Chairs_streamlined_non-paper_to_delegations.pdf; https://www.un.org/bbnj/content/background.

[128] UNGA A/RES/72/249, p. 2, para. 10.

Resolutions of the UN General Assembly

The importance of the General Assembly with regard to the evidence of an existing *opinio juris* is twofold: firstly, the General Assembly is a forum in which States can express their concurring or objecting *opinio juris sive necessitatis*. Therefore, as shown above, the records of i.e. the Plenary Meetings can evidence the States' opinion that the obligation to protect and preserve the marine environment is a rule of customary international law. Secondly, the resolutions of the General Assembly themselves—despite their non-binding nature—can have a certain weight in the determination of the customary status of a rule, as all States have an equal vote and voice to them.[129] Accordingly, the ICJ attributes a lot of weight to an *opinio juris* reflected in the consent of a State to a resolution of the General Assembly, which 'may be understood as an acceptance of the validity of the rule or set of rules declared by the resolution by themselves.'[130] Likewise, the Secretary General of the UN pointed out that that 'process is generating patterns of consistent State practice which, in turn, is forming rules of customary international law, as well as influencing the work of international organizations and the decisions of international tribunals.'[131]

The review of the resolutions 'Oceans and the Law of the Sea' in the General Assembly of the United Nations to this end is inconclusive. The General Assembly does not expressly accept or oppose to the customary status of the obligation to protect and preserve the marine environment in any of the resolutions.[132] It does, however, acknowledge the importance of the UNCLOS for the protection of the marine environment.[133] Furthermore, in its resolution A/RES/43/18 the General Assembly, expressing deep concern at the current state of the marine environment, requested the Secretary-General to prepare for the General Assembly at its 44th session a special report on recent developments related to the protection and preservation of the marine environment in the light of the relevant provisions of the UNCLOS.[134] In its special report A/44/461, the Secretary-General emphasised that Part XII UNCLOS and other articles of the UNCLOS are 'not merely a restatement of existing conventional law or practice but are constitutional in character [. . .].'[135] 'In addition to their status as conventional obligation binding on States parties to the Convention, Articles 192 and 193 are generally regarded as statements of customary international law on the extent of the environmental

[129] ICJ, *Nuclear Weapons*, Advisory Opinion, ICJ Reports 1996, pp. 226, 254, para. 70; Tanaka (2019), pp. 14 and 45.

[130] ICJ, *Military and Paramilitary Activities in and against Nicaragua*, Nicaragua v. USA, Judgment (Merits), ICJ Reports 1986, pp. 14, 100, para. 188.

[131] UNGA, A/47/512, para. 8; UNGA A/47/PV.83, p. 41.

[132] https://www.un.org/Depts/los/general_assembly/general_assembly_resolutions.htm.

[133] UNGA A/REA/48/28, p. 2.

[134] UNGA A/RES/43/18, para. 14.

[135] UNGA A/44/461, p. 5, para. 5.

responsibility of State towards the oceans. The mandatory language used in the two provisions reflects the importance placed upon the issues by the international community: a State breaching its obligation to protect and preserve the marine environment would be in breach of international law.'[136] Although the view of the Secretary General of the United Nations on the legally binding character of Art. 192 UNCLOS and its status as customary international law could not be clearer, the report does not have the same character as a resolution by the General Assembly, because it is not an expression of the vote by all its members. Nonetheless, as the report by the Secretary-General is a source of information for the General Assembly, its opinion weighs in evidencing the emergence of an *opinio juris* of the obligation to protect and preserve the marine environment.

4.2.3.5 Opinio Juris Expressed Through International Organisations

Further statements concerning the customary status of the obligation to protect and preserve the marine environment can be derived from international organisations. This raises the question whether an international organisation is even capable of participating in the creation of customary international law through a certain practice and expression of *opinio juris*.

The Capability of International Organisations to Express an Opinio Juris

Environmental groups and the scientific community started to play an important role in international environmental law and policy. Non-State actors seek to influence and enhance the making and implementation of environmental regulations i.e. by identifying and publishing critical environmental issues that require international legal actions. Under certain requirements, non-state actors can be subjects of public international law with degrees of rights and duties that vary amongst their categories. In contrast to States, rights and obligations of these entities do not originate in public international law itself but are derived from the authorisations by the States and therefore depend upon the purpose and function of the organisation as specified i.e. in its constituent treaties. Because these subjects only possess a certain degree of rights and obligations, they are called derivative, partial or restricted subjects of public international law.[137]

An international organisation can contribute to the creation of customary international law if the States mandated it with this competence.[138] For the EU for instance, its 27 member States have designated jurisdictional powers and mandated

[136] UNGA A/44/461, p. 10, para. 29.

[137] Kau (2016), p. 142, mn. 9; ICJ, *Reparation for injuries suffered in the service of the United Nations*, Advisory Opinion, ICJ Reports 1949, pp. 174, 180.

[138] Daugirdas (2020), p. 201.

the EU to adopt legally binding regulations and directives.[139] A *maiore ad minus* it is stringent to assume the EU's capacity to contribute to the creation of customary international law through a corresponding practice and expression of *opinio juris* in the name of its member States. The *opinio juris* expressed by the EU is a reflection of the *opinio juris* of its member States due to the designated jurisdictional power and weighs as such.

For other international organisations, it depends on which rights the founding States wanted to bestow on it as i.e. evident through its constituent treaties. At the very least, however, it is clear that international organisations such as the ILC or General Assembly are information forums for States to obtain information about the existence of a rule of customary international law and in this context indirectly contribute to the establishment of a respective *opinio juris*. The purpose of the General Assembly under Art. 13 (1) (a) UN-Charter is to 'initiate studies and make recommendations for the purpose of [. . .] encouraging the progressive development of international law and its codification'. The ILC was established by the General Assembly to undertake this mandate.[140] While the ICJ has attributed certain weight to the *opinio juris* of the General Assembly for the creation of a law in its *Military and Paramilitary Activities in and against Nicaragua* case, the General Assembly derives its information *inter alia* from the ILC. Also the reports by the ILC therefore can have an anticipating effect for a rising *opinio juris*.[141]

Opinio Juris of the European Union

The EU is an important actor in the field of international law. Its *opinio juris* concerning the obligation to protect and preserve the marine environment under customary international law is of particular importance. The EU expressly and repeatedly acknowledges the status of the UNCLOS as the 'constitution for the oceans, whose provisions generally reflect customary law', as i.e. evident in official records of the Plenary Meetings of the UN General Assembly.[142] According to the EU States 'have an obligation to ensure the viability of the ocean's environment, which is deteriorating at an alarming rate due to the over-utilization of marine resources, pollution and climate change'.[143]

Furthermore, the EU's conviction for the protection and preservation of the marine environment is reflected in the EU's strict marine protection program. With the adoption of the 2008 Marine Strategy Framework Directive, a 'thematic strategy

[139] For Germany, see Art. 23 (1) (2nd sentence) 1949 Basic Law for the Federal Republic of Germany.

[140] https://legal.un.org/ilc/.

[141] ICJ, *Military and Paramilitary Activities in and against Nicaragua*, Nicaragua v. USA, Judgment (Merits), ICJ Reports 1986, pp. 14,100, para. 188.

[142] UNGA A/74/PV.42, p. 12; see also: UNGA A/73/PV.49, p. 10; UNGA A/72/PV.63, p.12.

[143] UNGA A/59/PV.54, p. 4.

for the protection and conservation of the marine environment has been developed.'[144] Thus, the EU expresses its intention to give this rule a legally binding effect and a respective *opinio juris* with regard to the obligation to protect and preserve the marine environment.

Further statements to this end can be derived i.e. in the answer of the European Parliament to the parliamentary question of 03 December 2019 on the 'Total disregard for the principles of international law on the part of Turkey and direct threat to the sovereign rights of Greece and Cyprus'. The European Parliament expressed that the EU and its member States had ratified the UNCLOS, 'which is recognised by the US as a codification of customary international law binding on all countries'.[145] Although this Statement alone does not expressly mention the EU's recognition of the customary status of the principle embodied in Art. 192 UNCLOS, nor reflect an explicit statement by the US itself, it does, nonetheless, underline the EU's position as already expressed in the preamble of the OSPAR Convention and Statements in the General Assembly and indicates a corresponding opinion of the US.

General Assembly and International Law Commission

The General Assembly expressed on its seventieth Plenary Meeting of the 57th session that the text of the UNCLOS reflects already existing customary international law and contributes to develop international law progressively.[146] The ILC expresses its view of the obligation to protect and preserve the marine environment by classifying the prohibition of massive pollution of the atmosphere and sea as an international obligation of essential importance for the safeguarding and preservation of the human environment, the breach of which stipulates an international crime under Art. 19 (3) (d) Draft Articles on State Responsibility.[147] Furthermore, according to the ILC, the international community as a whole considers the endangerment of the preservation and conservation of the human environment as an act that violates principles which are 'so deeply rooted in the conscience of mankind that they have become particularly essential rules of general international law.'[148] The *opinio juris* as expressed by the General Assembly and the ILC as information for the States can have an anticipating function for the *opinio juris* of the State community.

---

[144] EU Directive 2008/56/EC (2008), Preamble 4.

[145] https://www.europarl.europa.eu/doceo/document/E-9-2019-004174_EN.html.

[146] UNGA A/57/PV.70, p. 2.

[147] ILC, A/CN.4/SER.A/2001/ADD.1 (PART 2), p. 32.

[148] ILC, A/CN.4/SER.A/1976/ADD.L (PART 2), p. 109, para 33.

4.2.3.6 Opinio Juris Confirmed by Jurisprudence

Judicial decisions, under Art. 38 (1) (d) UNCLOS are not formal sources of law but give evidence of the law.[149] The ITLOS repeatedly affirmed the customary status of Art. 192 UNCLOS and its *erga omnes* effect in its jurisprudence. In its *Request for Advisory Opinion submitted by the Sub-Regional Fisheries Commission* Advisory Opinion the ITLOS expressed that the obligation to protect and preserve the marine environment is a fundamental principle underlined in Art. 192 UNCLOS.[150] In its *Responsibilities and Obligations of States Sponsoring Persons and Entities with Respect to Activities in the Area* Advisory Opinion it furthermore stated that each 'State Party may also be entitled to claim compensation in light of the *erga omnes* character of the obligations relating to preservation of the environment of the High Seas and in the Area.'[151] Although the Philippines claimed in the *South China Sea Arbitration*, that Art. 192 UNCLOS is s rule of customary international law, the PCA did not state to this end but affirmed the customary status of specific obligations, such as the prohibition of transfrontier damage.[152]

4.2.4 Conclusion: Customary Status of Art. 192 UNCLOS

The investigation has proven that the obligation to protect and preserve the marine environment under Art. 192 UNCLOS has evolved into a rule of customary international law. The State practice to this end is evident through the adoption of numerous national and international treaties for this purpose and the establishment of MPAs by the States. This practice is carried out by the States believing that they are obliged to do so because of a customary international law. This *opinio juris* is evident through the State practice to protect and preserve the marine environment, the adoption of treaties to this end, Statements of States in the Plenary Meetings of the UN and in international courts and tribunals, other Statements by State ministers and non-binding instruments such as Agenda 21. The general State practice and *opinio juris* that the obligation under Art. 192 UNCLOS is a rule of customary international law is not only carried by State parties to the UNCLOS but has also been established for the non-State parties such as the USA, Turkey, Venezuela and Colombia, which not only proves the customary status of Art. 192 UNCLOS but also that there are no persistent objectors to this rule.

---

[149] Crawford (2012), p. 37; Vitzthum (2016), p. 56, mn. 147.

[150] ITLOS, *SRFC*, Advisory Opinion, ITLOS Reports 2015, pp. 14, 61, para. 216.

[151] ITLOS, *Responsibilities and Obligations of States Sponsoring Persons and Entities with Respect to Activities in the Area*, Advisory Opinion, ITLOS Reports 2011, pp. 10, 59, para. 180.

[152] *Trail Smelter Case*, Reports of International Arbitral Awards (1938 and 1941), Volume III, pp. 1905, 1938.

4.3 Art. 192 UNCLOS as Jus Cogens

Jus cogens regulations are universally accepted norms of general international law from which no derogation or modification is permitted, except by subsequent norms of the same character because of their fundamental value for the international community as a whole.[153] The fundamental value of the protection and preservation of the marine environment in the twenty-first century, as well as the universal conduct and discourse of States, including UNCLOS non-member States such as the USA, Turkey or Venezuela, proves that the obligation as embodied under Art. 192 UNCLOS has emerged into *jus cogens*.

4.3.1 Fundamental Value

> Saving our ocean must remain a priority. Marine biodiversity is critical to the health of people and our planet.[154]

Only rules that reflect fundamental values of the international community are eligible to emerge into peremptory norms of international law because they are 'obligations which protect essential humanitarian values and which may be owed *erga omnes*.'[155] The evolution of regulations into *erga omnes* binding rules, therefore, requires a special common interest of the State community.[156]

The ocean regulates global systems that make the world habitable for humankind. The ocean contains 97% of the Earth's water.[157] It distributes heat around the planet and maintains the functioning of the hydrological cycle.[158] The ocean produces approximately 50–80% of the Earth's oxygen and is the world's largest carbon sink.[159] Without it, humans would run out of air to breathe. 'Marine biodiversity is critical to the health of people and our planet.'[160]

The ocean provides for the livelihoods of millions of people. 59.6 million people were engaged in the primary sector of capture fisheries and aquaculture in 2016; around 200 million people are directly or indirectly employed in the marine fisheries

---

[153] UNGA A/74/10, p. 142; Vitzthum (2016), p. 49, mn. 126.

[154] https://www.un.org/sustainabledevelopment/oceans/.

[155] ICJ, *Case Concerning the Application of the Convention on the Prevention and Punishment of the Crime of Genocide*, Bosnia and Herzegovina v. Serbia and Montenegro, Judgment, I.C.J. Reports 2007, pp. 43, 104, para. 147.

[156] Charlesworth and Chinkin (1993), p. 65; Reilly (1995–1996), p. 767; UNGA A/74/10, p. 142; Proelss (2004), p. 78.

[157] https://www.un.org/sustainabledevelopment/oceans/.

[158] https://www.un.org/Depts/los/global_reporting/WOA_RPROC/Chapter_55.pdf, p. 1.

[159] https://www.un.org/en/conferences/ocean2020/about; https://oceanservice.noaa.gov/facts/ocean-oxygen.html.

[160] https://www.un.org/sustainabledevelopment/oceans/.

sector.[161] Yet, if the human activities in the sea are not carefully managed to maintain a healthy marine ecosystem, overfishing results in damage to the marine environment and reduction or collapse of the ecosystem and food supply.[162]

Approximately 680 million people live in low-lying coastal zones.[163] Indirect issues such as global warming and resulting sea-level rise threaten to make billions of people homeless. National and international courts and committees start to acknowledge that environmental offences must be taken into consideration in interpreting Human Rights and accept claims regarding sea level rise, which are based on humanitarian reasons.[164] The Special Rapporteur for Human Rights and the Environment stated in the petition of Torres Strait Islanders against Australia to take actions against climate change that '[h]uman rights depend on a healthy environment, which includes a safe climate.[165] In another case, the Case *Teitiota v New Zealand,* Mr. Teitiota applied to the UN Human Rights Council arguing that his deportation from New Zealand to his home country Kiribati violates his right to life under Art. 6 of the 1966 International Covenant on Civil and Political Rights[166] because sea level rise renders Kiribati uninhabitable. Although the claim was not successful because there was enough time to implement other protecting measures, the Committee confirmed that harm induced by climate change can occur through sudden onsets such as flooding and storms and slow onsets processes such as sea-level rise.[167] In the *Urgenda Case*, the Dutch Supreme Court upheld the findings of the lower courts and confirmed that the risks of climate change fell within the scope of the 1950 European Convention on Human Rights (ECHR),[168] in particular Art. 2 ECHR, the right to life and Art. 8 ECHR, private and family life, finding that climate change is a human rights issue.

The obligation to protect and preserve the marine environment also resembles the categories of basic human rights that are accepted as *jus cogens* regulations. The obligation under Art. 192 UNCLOS is not limited to areas that are under the national jurisdiction of States but applies to areas that are free from any sovereignty claims. The broad scope of this obligation leads to difficulties such as in its enforcement. Similar difficulties in the enforcement also occur in the categories of those basic

---

[161] FAO (2018), p. 6; https://www.un.org/sustainabledevelopment/oceans/.

[162] https://www.un.org/Depts/los/global_reporting/WOA_RPROC/Chapter_55.pdf, p. 1.

[163] https://www.un.org/sustainabledevelopment/oceans/.

[164] ECtHR, *Case of Mangouras v. Spain* (Application no. 12050/04), Judgment (2010), p. 28, para. 86; Treves (2010), p. 12.

[165] https://www.clientearth.org/latest/press-office/press/un-experts-lend-weight-to-torres-strait-human-rights-climate-complaint/; https://nit.com.au/torres-strait-eight-backed-by-un-human-rights-experts/.

[166] UNTS, Vol. 999, No. I-14668.

[167] https://www.ohchr.org/EN/NewsEvents/Pages/DisplayNews.aspx?NewsID=25482&LangID=E.

[168] European Treaty Series (ETS) No. 005.

human rights, which are acknowledged as *jus cogens,* such as in the prohibition of genocide.[169]

The ITLOS expressly acknowledges the fundamental value of the obligation to protect and preserve the marine environment in the *Request for Advisory Opinion submitted by the Sub-Regional Fisheries Commission* Advisory Opinion.[170] Also the literature accepts the protection of the marine environment as a common interest of the international community as a whole.[171] The ILC states that the international community as a whole considers the endangerment of the preservation and conservation of the human environment as an act that violates principles which are 'so deeply rooted in the conscience of mankind that they have become particularly essential rules of general international law.'[172] The acknowledgement of the obligation to protect and preserve the marine environment as a fundamental value of humankind is furthermore indicated by the universal acceptance of the obligation by the international community as a whole. As the ambassador of the ocean Elisabeth Mann Borgese put it, 'we must save the ocean, if we are to save ourselves!'[173] Humans are inseparably linked to the well-being of the ocean. The protection and preservation of the marine environment is a fundamental value for humankind.

4.3.2 Universal Acceptance

Jus cogens regulation with *erga omnes* effect can only be those in which 'all Stats can be held to have a legal interest in their protection.'[174] The second element for a rule to advance into *jus cogens*, therefore, requires that the embodied principle is universally accepted. *Jus cogens* regulations cannot be subjected to unilateral reservations and are therefore not open to the persistent objector exception.[175] The universal practice and acceptance of the obligation to protect and preserve the marine environment by States has been evidenced widely. This is particularly demonstrated by the enhanced designation of MPAs since 2000, an extensive treaty practice to this end, statements of States in judicial proceedings or the General Assembly, the

[169] Proelss (2004), p. 79.

[170] ITLOS, *SRFC*, Advisory Opinion, ITLOS Reports 2015, pp. 14, 61, para. 216.

[171] König (2001), para. 8.

[172] ILC, A/CN.4/SER.A/1976/ADD.L (PART 2), p. 109, para 33.

[173] 'Wir müssen die Ozeane retten, wenn wir uns selbst retten wollen!' (Elisabeth Mann-Borgese, translated by author); https://www.ardaudiothek.de/lesungen/elisabeth-mann-borgese-die-meer-frau/78862666; https://www.deutscher-meerespreis.de/2006-2009_en.html.

[174] ICJ, *Barcelona Traction*, Light and Power Company, Limited (Second Phase), Judgment, ICJ Reports 1970, pp. 3, 32, para. 33.

[175] ICJ, *North Sea Continental Shelf*, Judgment, Separate Opinion Judge Padilla Nervo, ICJ Reports 1986, pp. 86, 98; Proelss (2004), p. 80; UNGA A/74/10, p. 145.

adoption of binding and non-binding instruments in international law and relevant jurisprudence.[176] As demonstrated, there are no persistent objectors to the obligation to protect and preserve the marine environment. It has been proven that even States that are not parties to the UNCLOS, such as the USA, Turkey and Venezuela, protect and preserve the marine environment and accept the obligation hereto as law. The obligation to protect and preserve the marine environment is universally accepted.

4.3.3 No Derogation and Modification Only by Other Peremptory Norms

The third element requires a consensus by the States that no derogation from this norm is permitted and that it can only be modified by other peremptory norms of international law. The obligation to protect and preserve the marine environment in the UNCLOS is part of a system to balance the States' interests to maintain their sovereign right to exploit their natural resources and their duty to protect and preserve the marine environment as expressed in Art. 193 UNCLOS.[177] As the preamble of the UNCLOS states, 'the problems of ocean space are closely interrelated and need to be considered as a whole', it 'is in this sense that the Convention as a whole has struck an important balance between the protection of the marine environment and use of the ocean and its resources [. . .].'[178] The importance of the right of States to access and exploit resources in the Sea has been one of the main issues in the negotiations of the UNCLOS. The adoption of the 12 NM Territorial Sea in Art. 2 (1), 3 UNCLOS, for instance, was only possible through the introduction of the EEZ as a resource-oriented hybrid zone, to accommodate the States interest to exploit resources beyond the 12 NM-limit. Moreover, Part XI UNCLOS to regulate the exploration for and exploitation of the resources in the Area is rendered that important that it was the reason for the non-ratification of the UNCLOS by the USA. Therefore, as favourable a sweeping acceptance of the obligation under Art. 192 UNCLOS may be for the protection and preservation of the marine environment, the evaluation as *jus cogens* requires a detailed analysis of the interests of the States. The following investigation will prove that neither the expressions of sovereign rights in the UNCLOS, such as for the exploitation of natural resources under Art. 193 UNCLOS, the exclusive sovereignty in the Territorial Sea under Art. 2 (1) UNCLOS, the freedoms of the High Sea in Art. 87 and 89 UNCLOS or the sovereign immunity of warships under Art. 236 UNCLOS are eligible to hinder the emergence of the obligation to protect and preserve the marine environment into *jus*

[176] ITLOS, *SRFC*, Advisory Opinion, ITLOS Reports 2015, pp. 14, 61, para. 216; ITLOS, *Responsibilities and Obligations of States Sponsoring Persons and Entities with Respect to Activities in the Area*, Advisory Opinion, ITLOS Reports 2011, pp. 10, 59, para. 180.

[177] Proelss (2017), Art. 193, mn. 1.

[178] UNGA A/44/461, pp. 5 f., para. 9.

cogens because the rules either do not derogate this obligation or are peremptory norms of general international law themselves.

4.3.3.1 Art. 193 UNCLOS

Art. 193 UNCLOS does not derogate the obligation to protect and preserve the marine environment. According to the wording of Art. 193 UNCLOS, States have the sovereign right to exploit their natural resources pursuant to their environmental policies and *in accordance* with their duty to protect and preserve the marine environment. The wording of Art. 193 UNCLOS shows that it does not limit the obligation to protect and preserve the marine environment but subordinates the right to exploit natural resources to the obligation to protect and preserve the marine environment.[179] The right to exploit resources is not derogated by but has to be interpreted in harmony with the obligation to protect and preserve the marine environment.

4.3.3.2 Art. 2 (1), (3) UNCLOS

The elevation of the obligation to protect and preserve the marine environment above the right to exploit resources is further stipulated in other provisions of the UNCLOS. Under Art. 2 (1) UNCLOS, States have exclusive sovereignty in their Territorial Sea, which includes the right to exploit their natural resources. The sovereignty over the Territorial Sea, however, under Art. 2 (3) UNCLOS is to be exercised subject to the UNCLOS and to other rules of international law, which include Art. 192 UNCLOS.[180] Even when exercising their exclusive sovereignty in the Territorial Sea, States must comply with the obligation to protect and preserve the marine environment. The obligation under Art. 192 UNCLOS, therefore, is prioritized over the right to exploit natural resources as evident through the regulation system of the UNCLOS and over the sovereignty of States in their Territorial Sea.[181] Corresponding to this view, the PCA held in the *South China Sea Arbitration* that the harvesting of sea turtles, giant clams and corals in the waters of Scarborough Schoal and features in the Spratly Islands by China constitutes harm to the marine environment and breaches its obligation to protect and preserve the marine environment, which applies irrespective of the question of sovereign rights over these resources, that is, even if China succeeded to establish sovereign rights in this area.[182] Concludingly, the sovereignty of States under Art. 2 (1) UNCLOS,

[179] Rothwell and Stephens (2016), p. 342.

[180] Proelss (2017), Art. 193, mn. 1.

[181] Proelss (2017), Art. 193, mn. 1.

[182] PCA, *South China Sea Arbitration*, Philippines v. China (Award), p. 372, para. 940.

including their right to exploit resources in this area, does not derogate their obligation to protect and preserve the marine environment.

4.3.3.3 Freedom of the High Sea

The protection and preservation of the marine environment obliges States to establish MPAs to regulate activities in the sea. The regulation of activities in the sea potentially interferes with the freedoms of the High Sea under Art. 89, 87 UNCLOS.[183] It therefore needs to be assessed if the freedoms of the High Seas derogate or modify the obligation under Art. 192 UNCLOS.

Art. 87 UNCLOS

The freedoms of the High Sea belong to the most traditional and broadest accepted rights in the law of the sea. Rarely, the status of the freedoms of the High Sea under Art. 87 UNCLOS as peremptory norms of international law has been mentioned.[184] The freedom of the High Seas under Art. 87 UNCLOS are not granted in an absolute manner.[185] They must be exercised under the conditions laid down by the UNCLOS and by other rules of international law according to Art. 87 (1) (second sentence) UNCLOS and with due regard for the interests of other States in their exercise of the freedom of the High Seas and with due regard for the rights under the UNCLOS with respect to activities in the Area pursuant to Art. 87 (2) UNCLOS.

This implies two relevant inferences: One, the freedoms of the High Sea under Art. 87 UNCLOS cannot be *jus cogens*. Subsequent to Art. 53 (second sentence) VCLT, peremptory norms of international law are non-derogatory and may only be modified by subsequent norms having the same character. Besides the limitation of the freedoms of the High Sea under Art. 87 (1) (second sentence) UNCLOS to the UNCLOS and other rules of general international law, the exemplary listed freedoms under Art. 87 (1) (third sentence) (d–f) UNCLOS cross-reference to specific other regulations of the UNCLOS, which are not cogent in nature. Because the freedoms of Art. 87 UNCLOS are derogatory by non-peremptory norms of international law, they cannot be *jus cogens* under Art. 53 (second sentence) VCLT.[186]

Secondly, the freedoms of the High Sea are subordinated to other rules of the UNCLOS and general international law. The wording of Art. 87 (1) (second sentence) UNCLOS states that other rules condition the freedoms. Other rules, therefore, limit the freedoms of the High Sea. The obligation to protect and preserve the marine environment is another rule of the UNCLOS as well as of general

[183] Oral (2006), p. 102.

[184] ILC, A/CN.4/SER.A/1963, p. 71, para. 53.

[185] Freestone (2012), pp. 200 f.

[186] Proelss (2017), Art. 87, mn. 3, 7.

international law. It, therefore, conditions the freedoms of the High Sea. The obligation to protect and preserve the marine environment, thus, is elevated over the freedoms under Art. 87 UNCLOS.[187] In exercising the freedoms of the High Sea under Art. 87 UNCLOS, States, therefore, must comply with their obligation to protect and preserve the marine environment. Concludingly, the freedoms of the High Sea under Art. 87 UNCLOS do not derogate the obligation to protect and preserve the marine environment. Because they are derogatory themselves, they are not *jus cogens* regulations.

Art. 89 UNCLOS

Under Art. 89 UNCLOS, no State may validly purport to subject any part of the High Sea to its sovereignty. Other than Art. 87 UNCLOS, Art. 89 UNCLOS does not cross-reference to other provisions of the UNCLOS or contain a general limitation in favour of other regulations of the UNCLOS or general international law. Like Art. 192 UNCLOS, the no-sovereignty principle under Art. 89 UNCLOS is granted limitless. It is, therefore, eligible to evolve into *jus cogens*. In this case, Art. 192 and 89 UNCLOS are eligible to modify each other under Art. 53 (second sentence) VCLT. The cogent status of Art. 89 UNCLOS requires that the principle is a universally accepted rule of customary international law of fundamental value from which no derogation is allowed and that can be modified only by a subsequent peremptory norm of general international law (Art. 53 (second sentence) VCLT). It will be assessed if Art. 89 UNCLOS is derogatory before investigating the further requirements for its cogent status.

Application of the Conditions of Art. 87 UNCLOS to Art. 89 UNCLOS

In order to assess whether Art. 89 UNCLOS is derogatory, it is needs to be assessed if the limitations of the freedom of the High Sea under Art. 87 (1) (second and third sentence), (2) UNCLOS apply to Art. 89 UNCLOS. If they do apply, Art. 89 UNCLOS is limitable by non-peremptory norms of international law and thus cannot be *jus cogens*. If they do not apply, Art. 89 UNCLOS is granted limitless and has the potential to be classified as *jus cogens*.

The question if the conditions of Art. 87 UNCLOS apply to Art. 89 UNCLOS initially depends on whether both regulations have the same substantive scope, so that Art. 87 UNCLOS is the *lex specialis* to the more general Art. 89 UNCLOS. According to Art. 89 UNCLOS, no State may purport to subject any part of the High Sea to its sovereignty, whereases Art. 87 UNCLOS stipulates that the High Seas are open to all States and exemplary codifies specific freedoms of the High Sea, such as the freedom of navigation or fishing. While Art. 89 UNCLOS, therefore, refers to sovereignty, Art. 87 UNCLOS stipulates that no State may exercise any sovereign

[187] Freestone (2013), p. 819.

rights. It needs to be assessed if there is a substantive distinction between 'sovereignty' and 'sovereign rights' in the UNCLOS or if this distinction is artificial and both mean the same.

Freedom of the High Sea in the CHS and the UNCLOS

Before the UNCLOS, the freedoms of the High Sea under Art. 87, 89 UNCLOS were stipulated in one regulation. Pursuant to Art. 2 CHS, the 'high seas being open to all nations, no State may validly purport to subject any part of them to its sovereignty. Freedom of the high seas is exercised under the conditions laid down by these articles and by the other rules of international law. It comprises, inter alia, both for coastal and non-coastal States: (1) freedom of navigation; (2) freedom of fishing; (3) freedom to lay submarine cables and pipelines; (4) freedom to fly over the high seas. These freedoms, and others which are recognized by the general principles of international law, shall be exercised by all States with reasonable regard to the interests of other States in their exercise of the freedom of the high seas.'

On the one hand, traditionally, the freedoms of the High Sea were stipulated in one provision with the no-sovereignty principle in the first sentence. This weighs in favour of the view that the limitation of the freedoms under Art. 2 (second sentence) CHS was intended to apply to the no-sovereignty principle, too. On the other hand, the obligation to protect and preserve the marine environment in its comprehensive expression as embodied in Art. 192 UNCLOS was not codified in the articles of the CHS and may not have existed as a general rule of customary international law in 1958. It is, therefore, questionable if the parties to the CHS intended to condition the freedom of the High Sea in Art. 2 CHS in a way that it is open to limitations by all existing and evolving general rules of customary international law, such as the obligation to protect and preserve the marine environment. Or, in order to eliminate this possibility, intentionally stipulated the no-sovereignty principle in the UNCLOS independently from the conditioned freedoms of the High Sea, to clarify that the principle under Art. 89 UNCLOS is not limitable.

The balance between the freedom of the High Sea and the need for a regulatory system to protect this area was the subject of discussion in the UNCLOS conferences. In 1956, in its Report on the Law of the Sea, which provided the basis for negotiations of the States at the First United Nations Conferences on the Law of the Sea (UNCLOS I) conference, the ILC commented that '[t]he principle generally accepted in international law that the High Seas are open to all nations governs the whole regulation of the subject. No State may subject any part of the High Seas to its sovereignty; hence no State may exercise jurisdiction over any stretch of water.'[188] However, already during the negotiations on UNCLOS III many delegates were concerned about the status of the High Sea in the light of overexploitation, such as overfishing. The representatives of El Salvador, for instance, argued that '[f]ishing in the High Seas must be governed by regulations that would meet the new circumstances created by current technological development, with its threat of exhausting

[188] ILC, A/CN.4/SER.A/1956/ADD.L, p. 278, Art. 27, para. 1; Warner and Kaye (2016), p. 17.

species.'[189] Delegates from western nations and fishing nations such as the Union of Soviet Socialists Republic, on the contrary, argued 'in favour of a firm regime of the High Seas which would prevent any interference with the freedom of the High Seas.'[190] However, even the States in favour of the widest possible application of the freedom of the High Sea acknowledged the need for regulation. The United Kingdom, for instance, commented that while it 'favoured the retention of as much as possible of the existing freedom of the High Seas in the area beyond the Territorial Sea, it considered that the obligations on flag States should be clarified in order to prevent abuses.'[191] The specific reasons, however, for the divided codification of Art. 2 CHS in Art. 87 and Art. 89 UNCLOS cannot be traced in the documents of UNCLOS III. The historical interpretation, therefore, does not lead to an unequivocal result.[192]

Art. 87 UNCLOS No Lex Specialis of Art. 89 UNCLOS

Art. 89 UNCLOS would be derogatory if Art. 87 UNCLOS with its limitations were its *lex specialis*. This would necessarily be the case if both regulations had the same substantive scope.

The freedoms of the High Sea in Art. 87 UNCLOS are more specific than the general no-sovereignty principle under Art. 89 UNCLOS, as *inter alia* evident through the special cross-references in Art. 87 (1) (third sentence) UNCLOS. Usually, *lex specialis* are structurally stipulated after *lex generalis*. If the freedoms of the High Sea in Art. 87 UNCLOS and Art. 89 UNCLOS would both refer to sovereign rights, but Art. 87 UNCLOS would not be the *lex specialis* of Art. 89 UNCLOS, the conditioning of the freedoms under Art. 87 (1) (second and third sentence), (2) UNCLOS would be obliterated by the provision of the unconditional freedom under Art. 89 UNCLOS. In this case, it can only be assumed that the codification of the *lex generalis* after the *lex specialis* is an editorial inaccuracy and that the conditions of Art. 87 (1) (second and third sentence), (2) UNCLOS apply to the no-sovereignty principle under Art. 89 UNCLOS. Otherwise, the conditions of the freedoms of the High Sea under Art. 87 UNCLOS would be entirely superseded by Art. 89 UNCLOS.

Therefore, if Art. 89 and 87 UNCLOS had the same substantive scope, the limitations of Art. 87 (1) (second sentence) UNCLOS thus apply to Art. 89 UNCLOS as its *lex specialis*. The freedom under Art. 89, 87 UNCLOS would both be conditioned by other rules of the UNCLOS and general international law. Art. 89 UNCLOS was not eligible to become a *jus cogens* regulation. It is, however, not convincing that the structural codification of Art. 89 UNCLOS after Art. 87 UNCLOS is an editorial inaccuracy. In fact, the following assessment will show that the better arguments weigh in favour of the view that Art. 89 and

[189] UNGA A/CONF.62/C.2/SR.31, p. 235, para. 53.

[190] UNGA A/CONF.62/C.2/SR.31, p. 237, para. 74.

[191] UNGA A/CONF.62/C.2/SR.31, p. 237, para. 69.

[192] Proelss (2017), Art. 89, mn. 6.

87 UNCLOS do not have the same substantive scope, Art. 87 UNCLOS is not the *lex specialis* of Art. 89 UNCLOS and the no-sovereignty principle under Art. 89 UNCLOS is eligible to become *jus cogens*.

Different Substantive Scope of Art. 89 UNCLOS and Art. 87 UNCLOS

The following argumentation will demonstrate that Art. 87, 89 UNCLOS do not have the same substantive scope because there is a distinction between sovereign rights and sovereignty in the UNCLOS. Art. 87 (1) (second and third sentence), (2) UNCLOS do not have to be applied to Art. 89 UNCLOS. Art. 89 UNCLOS is granted limitless, which yields its potential to be classified as *jus cogens*.

Art. 89 UNCLOS Regulates Territorial Sovereignty

The principle of 'sovereignty' over sea spaces has traditionally been reasoned with the possibility to exercise power.

Prior to the publication of the famous dissertation *Mare Liberum* by Hugo Grotius, States claimed sovereignty over vast parts of the sea. The papal bull *Inter Caetera* of Pope Alexander VI at the end of the fifteenth century, for instance, divided the Atlantic into two spheres—one under the sovereignty of Spain, the other of Portugal.[193] It is this kind of exclusive territorial sovereignty that Grotius contested with his freedom of the Sea because 'sovereignty means a particular kind of proprietorship, such in fact that it absolutely excludes like possession by any one else.'[194] The High Sea has to be free from sovereignty because 'that which cannot be occupied, or which never has been occupied, cannot be the property of any one, because all property has arisen from occupation.'[195] The cannon-shot rule of the eighteenth century, likewise, stipulated that the breadth of the Territorial Sea in which the coastal States enjoy sovereignty extends as far as cannon shots can reach because 'the sea can be considered subject as far as the range of cannon extends.'[196] Historically, Art. 89 UNCLOS, therefore, is the counterpart to the territorial sovereignty claims of States over ocean spaces.[197]

Also today, the wording of Art. 2 (1) UNCLOS declares that the State's sovereignty *extends* to a belt of sea adjacent to its land territory. The sovereignty over the Territorial Sea, therefore, is a prolongation of the sovereignty over land.[198] The sovereignty over the Territorial Sea under Art. 2 (1) UNCLOS does not differ in nature from the one over the land territory.[199] The coastal States have legislative as well as enforcement jurisdiction over all matters and all persons in this terrain. The

[193] Treves (2015), p. 2; Nordquist et al. (2012), p. 885; Rothwell and Stephens (2016), p. 3.

[194] Deman Magoffin (2001), p. 22.

[195] Deman Magoffin (2001), p. 27.

[196] Deman Magoffin (1923), p. 44.

[197] Proelss (2017), Art. 89, mn. 4.

[198] Proelss (2017), Art. 89, mn. 7.

[199] Proelss (2017), Art. 2, mn. 14.

Permanent Court of International Justice (PCIJ) clarified in this regard that 'jurisdiction is certainly territorial; it cannot be exercised by a State outside its territory except by virtue of a permissive rule derived from international custom or convention.'[200] The codification that no State may validly purport to subject any part of the High Sea to its sovereignty reinforces the principle that sovereignty is provided territorially and may not exceed the limits of the Territorial Sea. The no-sovereignty principle under Art. 89 UNCLOS, thus, refers to the territorial sovereignty of States and prohibits the unilateral assertion of any part of the High Sea to the territory of one State. Art. 87 UNCLOS, in contrast, refers to the sovereign rights of States to exercise activities in the sea, such as navigation or fishing. While sovereign rights are conditioned by other rules of international law under Art. 87 (1), (2) UNCLOS, the assertion of territorial sovereignty is prohibited without exception in Art. 89 UNCLOS.

Distinction of Sovereignty and Sovereign Claims in the UNCLOS
The distinction between sovereignty and sovereign rights is reflected in other regulations of the UNCLOS. The UNCLOS differentiates between 'sovereignty', such as in Art. 2 (1) UNCLOS for the coastal States in their Territorial Sea and single sovereign rights, such as in Art. 56 (1) UNCLOS in the EEZ. Sovereignty is the broadest form of sovereign right of the States over all matters and all persons in its Territorial Sea, resembling the sovereignty over the land. Sovereign rights as granted under Art. 56 UNCLOS, however, only grant limited rights in an otherwise free sea where and to the extent that the UNCLOS provides for it. The applicability of Art. 89 UNCLOS to the EEZ under Art. 58 (2) UNCLOS shows that States may only exercise single sovereign rights in the EEZ under Art. 56 (1) UNCLOS in the EEZ; claims of sovereignty, however, are excluded under Art. 58 (2), 89 UNCLOS and the limits of the Territorial Sea under Art. 2 (1), 3 UNCLOS.[201] The precise wording of Art. 89 UNCLOS, in particular in the light of its historical development, prohibits the unilateral assertion of sovereignty over the High Sea but does not exclude sovereign rights under Art. 87 UNCLOS. While sovereign rights only refer to the rights of States to conduct activities in the sea, sovereignty refers to the relationship of the State to its territory.[202]

Distinction of Sovereignty and Sovereign Claims in the Jurisprudence
The relevant jurisprudence distinguishes between sovereign rights and the claim of territorial sovereignty. The PCA notes that the ICJ 'has twice had the opportunity to distinguish between historic fishing rights and historic title that would bear on the entitlement to maritime zones.'[203] While 'historic fishing rights' refer to single sovereign rights under Art. 87, 'historic title' in this sense refers to the kind of

[200] PCIJ, *Lotus Case*, PCIJ Pub. Series A.-No. 10 (1927), pp. 2, 28 f.

[201] Proelss (2017), Art. 87, mn. 2.

[202] Proelss (2017), Art. 87, mn. 1, Art. 89, mn. 7.

[203] PCA, *South China Sea Arbitration*, Philippines v. China (Award), p. 95, para. 224.

sovereignty that a State has over its Territorial Sea and internal waters.[204] In the *Maritime Delimitation and Territorial Questions between Qatar and Bahrain* Case, the ICJ distinguished between the activity of pearl fishing and the assertion of territorial sovereignty. It stated that the activity of historic pearl fishing 'seems in any event never to have led to the recognition of an exclusive quasi-territorial right to the fishing grounds themselves or to the superjacent waters.'[205] Likewise, in its *Continental Shelf* Case (Tunisia/Libyan Arab Jamahiriya), the ICJ distinguished between historic Tunisian fishing rights and historic title.[206] The jurisprudence thus acknowledges a substantive distinction between sovereignty and sovereign rights.

Legal Status of the High Sea

Furthermore, although there is no consensus on the consequence of the no-sovereignty principle for the legal status of the High Sea, it is not an area free of law. Grotius noted that 'in the legal phraseology of the Law of Nations, the sea is called indifferently the property of no one (*res nullius*), or a common possession (*res communis*), or public property (*res publica*)'.[207] While it is commonly acknowledged, that the High Sea is to be free of any sovereignty of States, the regulatory system of the whole Part VII UNCLOS shows that the High Sea, by no means, is an area entirely free of law.[208] Under Art. 87 UNCLOS the freedoms of the High Seas have to be exercised according to the conditions of Art. 87 (second sentence), (2) UNCLOS and are further limited by the cross-references in Art. 87 (1) (third sentence) UNCLOS. Therefore, while claims of territorial sovereignty over the High Sea are invalid under Art. 89 UNCLOS, the regulation of activities in the High Sea is explicitly entailed in Art. 87 UNCLOS. This proves that despite the no-sovereignty principle, the High Sea is not a terrain without law but is governed by the rules of the UNCLOS and other international law. If Art. 89 UNCLOS would have the same substantive scope as Art. 87 UNCLOS and prohibit the exercise of any sovereign right in the High Sea, the regulations of the whole Part VII UNCLOS would be obsolete.

Extensive State Practice to Adopt High Sea Treaties

This interpretation is further supported by the extensive practice of States to adopt High Sea treaties.[209] The regulation of activities in the High Sea through High Sea treaties is entailed in the condition of Art. 87 (1) (second sentence) UNCLOS.

[204] PCA, *South China Sea Arbitration*, Philippines v. China (Award), p. 94, para. 221.

[205] ICJ, *Maritime Delimitation and Territorial Questions between Qatar and Bahrain*, Judgment (Merits), ICJ Reports 2001, pp. 40, 76 f., para. 228.

[206] ICJ, *Continental Shelf, Tunisia/Libyan Arab Jamahiriya*, Judgment, ICJ Reports 1982, pp. 18, 73 f., para. 100.

[207] Deman Magoffin (2001), p. 22.

[208] Proelss (2017), Art. 89, mn. 1, 3.

[209] Proelss (2017), Art. 89, mn. 1.

If one was to argue, that Art. 87 UNCLOS would be applicable to Art. 89 UNCLOS, both regulations would not be *jus cogens* regulations because of the possibility to limit the High Sea freedoms through international law. Otherwise, if one was to argue that Art. 89, 87 UNCLOS do have the same substantive scope and *both* are *jus cogens* regulations, the adoption of treaties on the High Sea that derogate the sovereign rights of States on the High Sea would not be allowed. Any international treaty that derogates or modifies the principle of Art. 87 UNCLOS would be void under Art. 53 (first sentence) VCLT. This would render all existing High Sea Treaties void. In practice, there are numerous treaties concerning the protection and preservation of the marine environment in ABNJ. The adoption of such treaties is only possible because Art. 89 UNCLOS does not have the same substantive scope as Art. 87 UNCLOS and only prohibits the assertion of territorial sovereignty; however, it does not exclude the adoption of treaties in the High Sea. Art. 89 UNCLOS, therefore, prohibits the assertion of sovereignty, however not the exercise of single sovereign rights, such through the adoption of treaties to protect and preserve the marine environment. This interpretation is clearly shared by the international community, as can evidently be seen through the numerous treaties to protect and preserve the marine environment in ABNJ.

Decision of the Dispute

The arguments that Art. 89 UNCLOS and Art. 87 UNCLOS do not have the same substantive scope are more convincing. The distinction between 'sovereignty' in an exclusive territorial way and 'single sovereign rights' is consistent throughout the whole UNCLOS. While the former refers to the exclusive territorial sovereignty of the States in a specific marine area, such as the Territorial Sea under Art. 2 (1) UNCLOS, single sovereign rights stipulate rights of a State in a terrain without purporting it to the exclusive sovereignty of one State. No-sovereignty principle means that no State may unilaterally control the activities of another State in the High Sea by purporting to subject any part of the High Sea to its territory.[210] As the limitations of Art. 87 UNCLOS show, it does not mean that States may not adopt international treaties to regulate activities in the High Sea. The status of Art. 89 UNCLOS as *jus cogens* is widely accepted.[211] This is only possible if the conditions of Art. 87 (1) (second sentence), (third sentence), (2) UNCLOS do not apply to Art. 89 UNCLOS. Art. 87 UNCLOS and Art. 89 UNCLOS, therefore, have different substantive scope.

Jus Cogens Status of Art. 89 UNCLOS

The literature points out that the status of *jus cogens* of the no-sovereignty principle under Art. 89 UNCLOS has been accepted since the origin of the concept of the

[210] Proelss (2017), Art. 87, mn. 1.

[211] Ibler (2007), pp. 757 f., fn. 29 and pp. 747, 760; Riesenfeld (1983), p. 13, fn. 13; Proelss (2017), Art. 89, mn. 1.

freedom of the High Sea in international law.[212] The history of the law of the sea is dominated by the conflict of free areas in the sea which are open to all States (*mare liberum*) and areas in the sea in which the (coastal) State may exercise sovereign rights and exclude all other States from this territory, for instance for the exploitation of resources (*mare clausum*).[213] Indeed, although the breadth of the High Sea varied throughout time, the very concept of the no-sovereignty principle existed and can easily be traced back for centuries.[214] The principle that no State may validly purport to subject any parts of the High Sea to its territory is universally accepted.[215] Furthermore the no-sovereignty principle is granted limitless. The conditions of Art. 87 UNCLOS do not apply and derogate it, as Art. 87 UNCLOS only refers to sovereign rights. Art. 89 UNCLOS, therefore, is eligible to become a peremptory norm of international law.

The final decision if Art. 89 UNCLOS is a cogent regulation of international law is not decisive for this monograph because it does not interfere with the obligation to protect and preserve the marine environment. The obligation to protect and preserve the marine environment obliges States to regulate and manage activities in the sea, which potentially collides with Art. 87 UNCLOS. The obligation to protect and preserve the marine environment, however, does not provide for the assertion of unilateral claims of territorial sovereignty of a State in ocean terrains. It therefore does not interfere with Art. 89 UNCLOS.[216] The peremptory status of Art. 89 UNCLOS with regard to the question if it modifies the obligation to protect and preserve the marine environment in the light of Art. 53 (second sentence) VCLT is therefore not relevant for the investigation if States are obliges to establish MPAs.

Conclusion: Art. 89 UNCLOS and the Cogent Status of Art. 192 UNCLOS

Both opinions lead to the same result that they do not impede the cogent status of the obligation to protect and preserve the marine environment. If one was to argue that the distinction of sovereignty and sovereign rights in Art. 89 UNCLOS and Art. 87 UNCLOS was artificial and not convincing, both regulations would have the same substantive scope. As demonstrated, the conditions of Art. 87 (1) (second sentence) UNCLOS would necessarily have to apply to Art. 89 UNCLOS, which would hinder its status as a peremptory norm of international law under Art. 53 VCLT. Art. 89, 87 UNCLOS would not derogate the obligation to protect and preserve the marine environment because the wording of Art. 87 (1) (second sentence) UNCLOS conditions the freedoms to other rules of international law,

[212] Proelss (2016), p. 401, mn. 64; Hossain (2005), p. 74, fn. 7.

[213] See Sect. 2.1.1.1.

[214] See Sect. 2.1.1.

[215] Ibler (2007), pp. 757 f, fn. 29; Riesenfeld (1983), pp. 11, 13, fn. 13; Proelss (2017), Art. 89, mn. 1.

[216] See the section 'No Modification by the No-Sovereignty Principle' in Chap. 6.

which includes the obligation as embodied under Art. 192 UNCLOS and therefore elevates the latter obligation over the freedoms of the High Sea.

If one, more convincingly, concludes that Art. 89, 87 UNCLOS do have a different substantive scope, the conditions of Art. 87 UNCLOS would not apply to Art. 89 UNCLOS. Art. 89 UNCLOS, therefore, would not be derogated by the Art. 87 (1) (second sentence), (third sentence) (d–f), (2) UNCLOS. Art. 89 UNCLOS is granted limitless. The no-sovereignty principle of Art. 89 UNCLOS, furthermore, is the codification of one of the oldest principles of the law of the sea and has potentially achieved the status of *jus cogens*. The obligation to protect and preserve the marine environment and the no-sovereignty principle can modify each other under Art. 53 (second sentence) VCLT. Concludingly, regardless of which interpretation of Art. 89, 87 UNCLOS one was to follow, the freedoms of the High Sea do not impede the cogent status of the obligation to protect and preserve the marine environment.

4.3.3.4 Art. 194 (4) UNCLOS

Under Art. 194 (4) UNCLOS, in taking measures to prevent, reduce and control pollution of the marine environment, States shall refrain from *unjustifiable interferences* with activities carried out by other States in the exercise of their rights and pursuance of their duties in conformity with the UNCLOS. It needs to be established if the limitation of Art. 194 (4) UNCLOS applies to measures taken under Art. 192 UNCLOS. The applicability of the *unjustifiable interferences*-clause to Art. 192 UNCLOS would impede its status as a peremptory norm of international law because it opens the obligation to derogations by general international law.

The wording of Art. 194 (4) UNCLOS stipulates unjustifiable interferences with *activities* of other States and not with their rights. Art. 53 (first sentence) VCLT refers to a normative collision of rights. Because Art. 194 (4) UNCLOS does not refer to rights but activities, it is doubtful if it can be subsumed under Art. 53 VCLT.

It has already been established above that an interpretation of Art. 194 UNCLOS in a way that it is open to all measures and not limited to pollution is *contra legem*.[217] While Art. 194 (5) UNCLOS addresses 'measures' and may be open for a broad interpretation, the wording in Art. 194 (1)–(4) UNCLOS is unambiguously limited to measure preventing and controlling pollution. Art. 194 (4) UNCLOS is only applicable to the special regulations under Art. 194 UNCLOS.

4.3.3.5 Sovereign Immunity of Warships Art. 236 UNCLOS

Under Art. 236 (first sentence) UNCLOS, the provisions of the UNCLOS regarding the protection and preservation of the marine environment do not apply to any

[217] See Sect. 3.4.3.

warship, naval auxiliary, other vessel or aircraft owned or operated by a State and used, for the time being, only on government non-commercial service. Under Art. 236 (second sentence) UNCLOS, however, this immunity of the respective ships in sentence one is coupled with an obligation of the States to ensure, by the adoption of appropriate measures not impairing operations or operational capabilities of such vessels or aircraft owned or operated by it, that such vessels or aircraft act in a manner consistent, so far as is reasonable and practicable, with the UNCLOS.

The wording of Art. 236 (first sentence) UNCLOS, *prima facie*, indicates that warships and the named vessels are exempt from the obligation to protect and preserve the marine environment. Because only subsequent peremptory norms of international law are capable of modifying *jus cogens* regulations and other treaties that conflict with *jus cogens* regulations are void (Art. 53 VCLT), this necessarily leads to three mutually exclusive conclusions: one, both, the immunity of warships and the obligation to protect and preserve the marine environment are *jus cogens* regulations and may modify each other under Art. 53 (second sentence) VCLT; two, the interpretation of Art. 236 UNCLOS shows that it does not collide with the obligation to protect and preserve the marine environment; or three, Art. 236 UNCLOS is void under Art. 53 (first sentence).

Art. 236 UNCLOS as Jus Cogens

Jus cogens regulations are norms of general international law that reflect and protect fundamental values of the international community that are universally accepted and from which no derogation or modification is permitted, except for subsequent norms of the same character.[218] Art. 236 UNCLOS is accepted as customary international law.[219] It needs to be assessed if the immunity of warships reflects such a fundamental interest of the whole State community, that it may achieve the status of a norm from which no derogation or modification is allowed.

Acknowledged rules with fundamental value for humankind are such that protect basic rules of international humanitarian law.[220] The sovereign immunity of warships does not reflect any humanitarian interests of the international community of fundamental value. On the contrary, it is an expression of the power of States. The *raison d'être* of *jus cogens* regulations, however, is the limitation of sovereign immunity of States for the benefit of the protection of basic humanitarian interests.

The sovereign immunity of States is expressed in the equality of all States in Art. 2 Nr. 1 UN-Charter, which *inter alia* provides for the freedom to consent or dissent to treaties. Art. 53 (first sentence) VCLT limits this freedom by stipulating

[218] UNGA A/74/10, p. 142.

[219] Art. 236, mn. 2; Roach (2014), p. 250.

[220] UNGA A/74/10, p. 147; Crawford (2012), p. 595; Vitzthum (2016), p. 49, mn. 126; Charlesworth and Chinkin (1993), p. 65; Reilly (1995–1996), p. 767; UNGA A/74/10, p. 142.

that treaties that conflict with *jus cogens* regulations are void.[221] This limitation is justified because, as the judges Rozakis, Caflisch, Wildhaber, Costa, Cabral Barreto and Vajić put it in their dissenting opinion in the *Prosecutor v. Furundžija* Case, '[...] rules on State immunity do not enjoy a higher status, since *jus cogens* rules, protecting as they do the "*ordre public*", that is the basic values of the international community, cannot be subject to unilateral or contractual forms of derogation from their imperative contents.'[222] *Jus cogens* regulations, therefore, conceptually do not protect but serve to limit State immunity. The immunity of warships under Art. 236 UNCLOS, therefore, would be a capable regulation to be limited by *jus cogens* regulations, however, it is not eligible to achieve the status as a peremptory norm of international law itself.

No Collision with Art. 236 UNCLOS

It needs to be established if Art. 236 UNCLOS collides with the obligation to protect and preserve the marine environment. Under Art. 53 (first sentence) VCLT, treaties that collide with a peremptory norm of international law at the time of their adoption are void. Two norms of international law conflict if, after the interpretation of both provisions under Art. 31 ff. VCLT, the obeying or applying of one norm necessarily or potentially violates another norm.[223] The following interpretation of Art. 236 (first sentence) UNCLOS in the light of its adoption at UNCLOS III and its balance regulation in Art. 236 (second sentence) UNCLOS shows that the immunity of warships and the protection and preservation of the marine environment do not collide.

Objective of Art. 236 (First Sentence) UNCLOS

Art. 236 UNCLOS was adopted for various reasons, amongst others, because pollution regulations may be inappropriate to the unique configuration or mission of warships and vessels named in Art. 236 UNCLOS. It was apprehended that in the exercise of sovereign rights to protect the marine environment, coastal States could acquire leverage over the passage of those ships. Furthermore, environmental policies concerning the construction of a vessel might require the release of data concerning the ship or inspections.[224]

---

[221] UNGA A/74/10, pp. 144 f.

[222] ECtHR, *Case of Al-Adsani v. The United Kingdom* (No. 35763/97), Judgement (2001), p. 30, para. 2.

[223] Vranes (2006), p. 418; Dörr and Schmalenbach (2018), p. 990, Art. 53, mn. 54; Villiger (2009), p. 674, Art. 53, mn. 20.

[224] Oxman (1984), pp. 820 f.

There was no significant opposition to Art. 236 UNCLOS at the time of its adoption.[225] One reason is that there were already similar regulations in previous agreements that could be drawn upon, such as Art. VII (4) of the 1972 London Convention or Art. 3 (3) 1973/78 MARPOL Convention.[226] Furthermore, warships were not considered a great source of marine pollution and moreover, the rules on sovereign immunity already restricted the enforcement of rules against the will of the flag State. In times of peace, warships and the vessels named in Art. 236 UNCLOS often operate far away from their home State and a high degree of self-imposed environmental diligence by flag States was expected.[227] On ratifying the UNCLOS, Malta and Bangladesh even included declarations to this end stating that the sovereign immunity envisaged in Art. 236 UNCLOS, does not exonerate a 'State from such obligation, moral or otherwise, in accepting responsibility and liability for compensation and relief in respect of damage caused by pollution of the marine environment by any warship, naval auxiliary, other vessels or aircraft owned or operated by the State and used on government non-commercial service.'[228] Such responsibility and liability as a secondary obligation can only arise if a primary obligation to this end exists.

Interpretation of Art. 236 (Second Sentence) UNCLOS

The exemption of warships from protecting and preserving the marine environment is coupled with a shift of responsibility to the flag State under Art. 236 (second sentence) UNCLOS.[229] Art. 236 (second sentence) UNCLOS clarifies that the sovereign immunity of warships respects the obligation to protect and preserve the marine environment under the UNCLOS.[230] Art. 236 UNCLOS does not free the States to protect and preserve the marine environment; it merely shifts the responsibility to do so to the flag State. Art. 236 (first sentence) UNCLOS stipulates that while the adherence of warships to the protection and preservation of the marine environment is not regulated by international treaties of all States, it must be regulated through national laws and regulations of the flag State under Art. 236 (second sentence) UNCLOS. Art. 236 UNCLOS, therefore, does not derogate the obligation of the States to protect and preserve the marine environment; it concretises this obligation on the flag State.

---

[225] Proelss (2017), Art. 236, mn. 2; Oxman (1984), p. 821.

[226] Proelss (2017), Art. 236, mn. 4.

[227] Oxman (1984), p. 821.

[228] https://treaties.un.org/pages/ViewDetailsIII.aspx?src=TREATY&mtdsg_no=XXI-6&chapter=21&Temp=mtdsg3&lang=en; Proelss (2017), Art. 236, fn. 2.

[229] Proelss (2017), Art. 236, mn. 1.

[230] Proelss (2017), Art. 236, mn. 2.

Consequence of the Collision with Jus Cogens

If one was to conclude that Art. 236 UNCLOS does derogate the obligation to protect and preserve the marine environment, two relevant questions arise: Does the conflict with a *jus cogens* regulation lead to the voidness of the whole treaty or only the relevant provision? Does Art. 53 (first sentence) VCLT also apply if the peremptory norm arises after the adoption of the treaty?

Emergence of the Peremptory Norm Before or After the Treaty

The VCLT distinguishes between cases in which a treaty conflicts with an existing peremptory norm of international law at the time of its conclusion under Art. 53 (first sentence) VCLT and cases, in which a new peremptory norm of general international arises after the conclusion of a treaty under Art. 64 VCLT.

In the first case, Art. 53 (first sentence) VCLT codifies that the treaty is void *ex tunc*. Furthermore, according to Art. 44 (5) VCLT, the void treaty provision cannot be separated and the entire treaty is void. The ILC in its 1966 Draft Articles on the Law of Treaties with commentary reasoned this absolute voidness with 'the view that rules of *jus cogens* are of so fundamental a character that, when parties conclude a treaty which conflicts in any of its clauses with an already existing rule of *jus cogens*, the treaty must be considered totally invalid.'[231] In this case, the voidness of Art. 236 UNCLOS, thus, would lead to the voidness of the whole UNCLOS.

The second case concerns treaties that already exist when a new peremptory norm of international law emerges. The separate codification of Art. 64 VCLT from Art. 53 VCLT shows that both scenarios have to be treated differently. In this case, the treaty was legally valid at the time of its conclusion but is refuted later by subsequent legal developments. This leads to the consequence that a treaty becomes void and terminates *ex nunc* under Art. 64 VCLT. In this scenario, too, the peremptory norm of international law, therefore, does not have any retroactive effect. Art. 64 VCLT is furthermore not named in Art. 44 (5) VCLT. The void regulation is separable under the conditions of Art. 44 VCLT, so that the voidness of Art. 236 UNCLOS does not affect the whole UNCLOS.[232]

Therefore, it is relevant to assess if the peremptory obligation to protect and preserve the marine environment arose before or after the stipulation of Art. 236 in the 1982 UNCLOS. The development of a general rule of international law is a process over a period of time, 'short though it might be [. . .].'[233] The exact timing of its emergence, therefore, is difficult to pin down. The introduction of Part XII UNCLOS on the protection and preservation of the marine environment in the 1982 UNCLOS demonstrates a change of preoccupation of the governments in

---

[231] ILC, A/CN.4/SER. A/1966/ADD. 1, p. 239, Art. 41 (5).

[232] Dörr and Schmalenbach (2018), p. 1201, Art. 64, mn. 1; Villiger (2009), pp. 793 f., Art. 64, mn. 4 ff.

[233] ICJ, North Sea Continental Shelf, Judgment, ICJ Reports 1969, pp. 3, 44, para. 74.

the second half of the twentieth century.[234] While the 1958 Geneva Conventions only contained single provision regarding the protection and conservation of the marine environment, such as Art. 24, 25 CHS for the prevention of pollution of the seas, or Art. 3 CTSCZ for the conservation of fish, it did not provide for a comprehensive obligation to protect and preserve the marine environment, let alone dedicate a whole Part of one of the Conventions to this end.

The period between the 1958 Geneva Conventions, which did not entail a general obligation to protect and preserve the marine environment and the adoption of the UNCLOS in 1982, marks the birth of the awareness of the international State community for the necessity of the protection and preservation of the marine environment. While the legal framework for the protection and preservation was still at its infancy at that time, it particularly matured through an increasing understanding of environmental threats after 1982 and has grown into an obligation of customary international law since.[235] The coming of age of the obligation to protect and preserve the marine environment to its full protection status as *jus cogens* rule with *erga omnes* effect is likely to have taken place after the 1992 CBD and 1992 OSPAR Convention, perhaps even after 2000 with the beginning of the enhanced States' practice to protect the marine environment through the establishment of MPAs and the recognition of this obligation in international courts and tribunals since 2010.[236] Therefore, the peremptory obligation to protect and preserve the marine environment is likely to have emerged after the adoption of the regulation of the immunity of warships under Art. 236 UNCLOS. A potential collision of both regulations falls upon the scope of Art. 64 VCLT.

Termination of Art. 236 UNCLOS, Art. 44 VCLT

Consequently, it needs to be assessed if the voidness of Art. 236 UNCLOS under Art. 64 VCLT leads to the voidness of the entire UNCLOS or if the provision may be separated under Art. 44 VCLT. Generally, a treaty provision applies in the context of the whole treaty and can therefore only be terminated in respect of the whole treaty by virtue of Art. 44 (1), (2) VCLT. Pursuant to Art. 44 (3) VCLT, if the ground for termination relates solely to particular clauses it may be exceptionally invoked only with respect to those clauses where: (a) the said clauses are separable from the remainder of the treaty with regard to their application; (b) it appears from the treaty or is otherwise established that acceptance of those clauses was not an essential basis of the consent of the other party or parties to be bound by the treaty as a whole; and (c) continued performance of the remainder of the treaty would not be unjust.

Only Art. 236 UNCLOS conflicts with the obligation to protect and preserve the marine environment. The ground for termination, therefore, only relates to Art. 236 UNCLOS. Art. 236 UNCLOS is regulated in its own Section 10 of

[234] Oxman (1984), p. 819.

[235] See the section 'Evaluation of Instruments' in this chapter.

[236] See Sects. 4.2.2.3, 4.2.4 and 4.3.2.

Part XII UNCLOS and can therefore be separated from the application of the remainder of the UNCLOS. The fundamental reasons for consent or dissent to the UNCLOS were the spatial distribution of jurisdiction, including the regulations on the Area under Part XI UNCLOS.[237] Lastly, the continued performance of the remainder of the treaty would not be unjust. One of the main reasons for the adoption of Art. 236 UNCLOS was that States may not interfere with warships and may gain leverage as to the passageways and gather information about the construction or mission of the respective ships. This is already safeguarded through other provisions of the UNCLOS. Under the non-disclosure of sensitive information under Art. 302 UNCLOS, nothing in the UNCLOS shall be deemed to require a State Party, in the fulfilment of its obligations under the UNCLOS, to supply information the disclosure of which is contrary to the essential interests of its security, which applies to the specifics of construction, equipment, manning and capabilities of warships.[238] The immunity of warships is furthermore regulated for the specific zone under Art. 32 UNCLOS for the Territorial Sea and Art. 95 UNCLOS in conjunction with Art. 58 (2) UNCLOS for the High Sea and EEZ, respectively, which grant its immunity.

Under Art. 32 UNCLOS, with such exceptions as are contained in subsection A and in Art. 30, 31 UNCLOS, nothing in the UNCLOS affects the immunities of warships and other government ships operated for non-commercial purposes. Under Art. 95 (in conjunction with Art. 58 (2)) UNCLOS, warships on the High Sea and EEZ have complete immunity from the jurisdiction of any State other than the flag State. The jurisdiction of the flag State when sailing on the High Sea is already stipulated under Art. 94 (1) UNCLOS. Because States are obliged to protect and preserve the marine environment under Art. 192 UNCLOS, the flag State is obliged to comply with this obligation with regard to its ships. Therefore, even if one was to argue that Art. 236 UNCLOS was terminated in its entirety and also Art. 236 (second sentence) UNCLOS was invalid, the flag State obligation and responsibility for the protection and preservation of the marine environment are already codified under other provisions of the UNCLOS. Art. 236 UNCLOS may therefore be separated from the other provisions of the UNCLOS under Art. 44 (3) VCLT. The termination of Art. 236 UNCLOS under Art. 64 VCLT would not lead to the voidness of the entire UNCLOS.

Conclusion: Jus Cogens Status of Art. 236 UNCLOS

To summarize, the better arguments show that an interpretation of Art. 236 UNCLOS and Art. 192 UNCLOS lead to the conclusion that Art. 236 UNCLOS, in fact, does not collide with the obligation to protect and preserve the marine environment. However, even if one was to assume that there is a collision of the derogative

[237] See Sect. 2.1.1.2.

[238] Oxman (1984), p. 822.

regulation of Art. 236 UNCLOS with the *jus cogens* regulation of Art. 192 UNCLOS, this would lead to the voidness of Art. 236 UNCLOS under Art. 64, 44 (3) VCLT, without affecting the validity of the UNCLOS in its entirety.

4.4 Conclusion: Erga Omnes Effect of Art. 192 UNCLOS

The assessment of the universal acceptance of the customary status of the obligation to protect and preserve the marine environment has shown that Art. 192 UNCLOS has emerged as a peremptory norm of international law. It, therefore, has *erga omnes* effect that binds the whole State community. *Erga omnes* regulations can arise from any universal obligation, whether it is a treaty regulation, rule of customary international law or *jus cogens*. The *erga omnes* effect, therefore, cannot indicate whether a regulation is a rule of customary international law, *jus cogens* or a treaty regulation; however, its status as universal *jus cogens* regulation necessarily yields the *erga omnes* effect of the obligation under Art. 192 UNCLOS.[239]

Even if one was to argue that the obligation under Art. 192 UNCLOS has not emerged into *jus cogens*, it undoubtedly is a rule of customary international law because the whole State community accepts this obligation and there are no persistent objectors to it. Therefore, the obligation to protect and preserve the marine environment binds the whole State community *erga omnes,* if it is a rule of customary international law or *jus cogens*.

Independently from its status as *jus cogens* or rule of customary international law, the ITLOS noted in its *Responsibilities and Obligations of States Sponsoring Persons and Entities with Respect to Activities in the Area* Advisory opinion, that '[e]ach State Party may also be entitled to claim compensation in light of the erga omnes character of the obligations relating to preservation of the environment of the High Seas [. . .].'[240] Also, the relevant literature accepts that, as a common interest of the international community as a whole, the protection and preservation of the marine environment is a binding *erga omnes* obligation.[241] Thus, the obligation to protect and preserve the marine environment as embodied under Art. 192 UNCLOS is a *jus cogens* rule of international law with *erga omnes* effect that binds the whole States community.

---

[239] Tanaka (2019), pp. 10 f.; UNGA A/74/10, p. 145.

[240] ITLOS, *Responsibilities and obligations of States Sponsoring Persons and Entities with Respect to Activities in the Area*, Advisory Opinion of 1 February 2011, ITLOS Report 2011, p. 59, para. 180.

[241] König (2001), para. 8.

4.5 Legal Standing

The *erga omnes* effect has procedural consequences on the personal admissibility of claims. In contentious cases, the applicant usually applies to an international court or tribunal in order to assert a violation of its *own* rights.[242] Former judge and president of the ITLOS Rüdiger Wolfrum pointed out the difficulties in the enforcement of the obligation to protect and preserve the marine environment in ABNJ and asked: 'Can a State, however, claim that the interests of the State community are violated and that it acts on behalf of the community?'[243]

Under Art. 48 (1) (b) ARS any State is entitled to invoke the responsibility of another State if the obligation breached is owed to the international community as a whole. Correspondingly, the PCA noted in its *South China Sea Arbitration*, in which the Philippines brought claims against China for harmful activities to the marine environment in various areas in the South China Sea, that it had jurisdiction even for acts beyond the jurisdictional zone of the Philippines (where there is no individual harm), 'because the environmental obligations in Part XII apply to States irrespective of the where the alleged harmful activities took place.'[244] In the *Antarctic Whaling Case*, the ICJ confirmed the *jus standi* of Australia for a claim against Japan, although the whaling activities by Japan happened outside the EEZ of Australia. In its *Questions relating to the Obligation to Prosecute or Extradite* Case, the ICJ confirms 'that any State party to the Convention may invoke the responsibility of another State party with a view to ascertaining the alleged failure to comply with its obligations *erga omnes partes* [. . .].'[245] Because of the *erga omnes* effect of Art. 192 UNCLOS, a State does not have to have suffered individual harm in order to assert the obligation to protect and preserve the marine environment against another State. Therefore, any State has a legal standing to invoke a violation of the obligation to protect and preserve the marine environment by another State, even if the State has not suffered individual harm.[246]

References

Adede AO (1995) The Treaty System from Stockholm (1972) to Rio de Janeiro (1992). Pace Environ Law Rev 13(1):33–48

Birnie P, Boyle A, Redgwell C (2009) International law & the environment, 3rd edn. Oxford

Boyle A (2005) Further development of the law of the sea convention: mechanisms for change. Int Comp Law Q 54(3):563–584

[242] Schröder (2016), p. 580, mn. 95.

[243] Wolfrum (1990), p. 325.

[244] PCA, *South China Sea Arbitration*, Philippines v. China (Award), p. 368, para. 927.

[245] ICJ, *Questions relating to the Obligation to Prosecute or Extradite*, Belgium v. Senegal, Judgment, ICJ Reports 2012, pp. 422, 450, para. 69.

[246] Harrison (2011), p. 25; Proelss (2004), pp. 79 f.; UNGA A/74/10, p. 145.

Charlesworth H, Chinkin C (1993) The gender of jus cogens. Hum Rights Q 15:63–76
Churchill RR, Lowe AV (1999) The law of the sea, 2nd edn. Manchester
Crawford JR (2012) Brownlie's principles of public international law, 8th edn. Oxford
Daugirdas K (2020) International organizations and the creation of customary international law. Eur J Int Law (EJIL) 31(1):201–233
Deman Magoffin R (1923) De Dominio Maris Dissertation by Cornelius van Bynkershoek. New York.
Deman Magoffin R (2001) The freedom of the seas or the right which belongs to the Dutch to take part in the East Indian Trade. A Dissertation by Hugo Grotius. New Jersey
Dipla H (2006) The role of the International Court of Justice and the International Tribunal on the Law of the Sea in the progressive development of the law of the sea. In: Strati A, Gavouneli M, Skourtos N (eds) Unresolved issues and new challenges to the law of the sea: time before and time after, publications on ocean development, vol 54, Leiden, pp 235–250
Dörr O, Schmalenbach K (2018) Vienna Convention on the Law of Treaties – a commentary, 2nd edn. Berlin
Food and Agriculture Organization of the United Nations (FAO) (2018) SOFIA Report 2016, The State of world fisheries and aquaculture 2016 - contributing to food security and nutrition for all. Rome
Freestone D (2012) International governance, responsibility and management of areas beyond national jurisdiction. Int J Mar Coastal Law (IJMCL) 27(2):191–204
Freestone D (2013) Principles applicable to modern ocean governance. In: Rothwell DR (eds) Law of the sea. Cheltenham, pp 817–823
Grafton RQ, Akter S, Kompas T (2011) A policy-enabling framework for the ex-ante evaluation of marine protected areas. Ocean Coastal Manag 54(6):478–487
Harrison J (2011) Making the law of the sea - a study in the development of international law. Cambridge
Hossain K (2005) The concept of jus cogens and the obligation under the U.N. Charter. Santa Clara J Int Law 3(1):72–98 (Article 3)
Ibler V (2007) Jus cogens and the law of the sea. In: Kohen MG (ed) Promoting justice, human rights and conflict resolution through international law – Liber Amicorum Lucius Caflisch. Graduate Institute of International Studies, Geneva, Leiden, pp 747–766
Kau M (2016) Der Staat und der Einzelne als Völkerrechtssubjekte. In: Vitzthum W, Proelss A (eds) Völkerrecht, 7. Auflage. Berlin, pp 133–246
Kellerher G (1999) Guideline for marine protected areas. World Commission on Protected Areas of IUCN – The World Conservation Union. Gland
Kembayev Z (2008) Die Rechtslage der Kaspischen Meeres. Zeitschrift für ausländisches öffentliches Recht und Völkerrecht ZaöRV. Heidelberg Journal of International Law (HJIL), Max-Planck-Insitut für ausländisches öffetnliches Recht und Völkerrecht 68:1027–1055
König D (2001) Marine environment, international protection. Max Planck Encyclopedia of International Law (MPEPIL), p 1594
Lagoni R (1992) Die Abwehr von Gefahren für die marine Umwelt. In: Dolzer R, Kreuzer K, Kunig P, Lagoni R, Lang W, Schack H (eds) Umweltrecht im Völkerrecht und Kollisionsrecht, Berichte der Deutschen Gesellschaft für Völkerrecht (DGVR), Heft 32, 22. Tagung in Trier vom 10.-13- April 1991. Heidelberg, pp 87–244
Lee ML (2006) The interrelation between the law of the sea convention and customary international law. San Diego Int Law J 7(2):405–420
Matz-Lück N (2017) Meeresschutz. In: Proelss A (ed) Internationales Umweltrecht, Berlin, pp 393–453
McConnell ML, Gold E (1991) The modern law of the sea: framework for the protection and preservation of the marine environment. Case West Reserv J Int Law 23(1):83–106
Nakatani K (2002) Oil and gas in the Caspian Sea and international law. In: Ando N, McWhinez E, Wolfrum R (eds) Liber Amicorum Judge Shigeru Oda, vol 2. The Hague, pp 1103–1114

Nordquist MH, Nandan SN, Kraska J (2012) UNCLOS 1982 Commentary – supplementary documents, Center for Oceans Law and Policy. Leiden
Oral N (2006) Protection of vulnerable marine ecosystems in areas beyond national jurisdiction: can international law meet the challenge? In: Strati A, Gavouneli M, Skourtos N (eds) Unresolved issues and new challenges to the law of the sea, time before and time after, publications on ocean development, vol 54, Leiden, pp 85–108
Oude Elferink AG, Rothwell DR (2004) Oceans management in the 21st century: institutional frameworks and responses, publications on ocean development, vol 44. Leiden
Oxman BH (1984) The regime of warships under the United Nations Convention on the law of the sea. Virginia J Int law (VJIL) 24(4):809–864
Proelss A (2004) Meeresschutz im Völker- und Europarecht, Das Beispiel des Nordatlantiks, Oppermann, Thomas, Tübinger Schriften zum internationalen und europäischen Recht, Band 71. Berlin
Proelss A (2016) Raum und Umwelt im Völkerrecht. In: Vitzthum W, Proelss A (eds) Völkerrecht, 7. Auflage, pp 361–454
Proelss A (2017) United Nations Convention on the law of the sea – a commentary. Munich
Reilly B (1995–1996) 'Clear and Present Danger': a role for the United Nations Security Council in protecting the global environment. Melbourne Univ Law Rev 20:763–804
Riesenfeld SA (1983) The third United Nations conference on the law of the sea: what was accomplished? Comment. Law Contemp Probl 46(2):11–15
Roach JA (2014) Today's customary international law of the sea. Ocean Dev Int Law 45(3): 239–259
Rothwell DR, Stephens T (2016) The international law of the sea, 2nd edn. Oxford
Sands P (2012) Principles of international environmental law, 3rd edn. Cambridge
Schieder T (1984) Customary international law. In: Bernhardt R (eds) Encyclopedia of public international law (EPIL) 7, History of international law, foundations and principles of international law, sources of international law, law of treaties. North Holland, pp 61–66
Schröder M (2016) Verantwortlichkeit, Völkerstrafrecht, Streitbeilegung und Sanktionen. In: Vitzthum W, Proelss A (eds) Völkerrecht, 7. Auflage. Berlin, pp 539–590
Scovazzi T (2004) Marine protected areas on the high seas: some legal and policy considerations. Int J Mar Coastal Law (IJMCL) 19(1):1–17
Siousiouras P, Chrysochou G (2014) The Aegean dispute in the context of contemporary judicial decisions on maritime delimitation. Laws 3(1):12–49
Tanaka Y (2008) A dual approach to ocean governance: the cases of zonal and integrated management in international law of the sea. Surrey
Tanaka Y (2019) The international law of the sea, 3rd edn. Cambridge
Treves T (2010) Human rights and the law of the sea. Berkeley J Int Law 28(1):1–14, Article 1
Treves T (2015) Historical development of the law of the sea. In: Rothwell D, Oude Elferink AG, Scott K, Stephans T (eds) The Oxford handbook of the law of the sea, pp 1–23
United Nations (1989) Joint Statement by the United States of America and the Union of Soviet Socialist Republics, Signed at Jackson Hole, Wyoming, on 23 September 1989, Law of the Sea Bulletin, Issue 14. New York.
Villiger ME (2009) Commentary on the 1969 Vienna Convention on the Law of Treaties. Leiden
Vinogradov S, Wouters P (1995) The Caspian Sea: current legal problems. Zeitschrift für ausländisches öffentliches Recht und Völkerrecht ZaöRV. Heidelberg Journal of International Law (HJIL), Max-Planck-Institut für ausländisches öffentliches Recht und Völkerrecht 55:604–623
Vitzthum W (2016) Begriff, Geschichte und Rechtsquellen des Völkerrechts. In: Vitzthum W, Proelss A (eds) Völkerrecht, 7. Auflage. pp 1–60
Vranes E (2006) The definition of 'Norm Conflict' in international law and legal theory. Eur J Int Law (EJIL) 17(2):395–418
Warner R, Kaye S (2016) Routledge handbook of maritime regulation and enforcement. London
Wolfrum R (1990) Purposes and principles of international environmental law. German Yearb Int Law (GYIL) 33:308–330

Chapter 5
Geographical Scope: Marine Environment

The obligation as embodied under Art. 192 UNCLOS obliges States to protect and preserve the 'marine environment'. For the determination of the geographical scope, it is therefore needs to be assessed, which areas are comprised by the marine environment. As legal norms regulate actual circumstances in life, the investigation will commence with a *de facto* outline of the marine environment, before defining the term *de jure*.

5.1 Marine Environment: De Facto

5.1.1 The Deep Seabed

The author and undersea explorer Arthur C. Clarke is said to have once remarked 'how inappropriate to call this planet earth, when it is quite clearly is ocean.'

The ocean provides 95 per cent of the Earth's total habitat, yet only 0.0001 per cent of these areas are explored.[1] There are better images of the surface of Mars and the Moon than of the deep seafloor.[2] The deepest known part of the ocean, the Challenger Deep in the Marianna Trench in the West Pacific, is 11 km deep and has only been visited by eight people, while 12 astronauts have walked on the Moon.[3] Despite the lack of knowledge of the deep-sea ecosystems, the pacific island Nauru has given notice to the ISA to commence deep seabed mining, triggering a two-year deadline in which the ISA is compelled to adopt a plan for commercial mining in the

[1] https://www.iucn.org/resources/issues-briefs/governing-areas-beyond-national-jurisdiction; https://ocean.si.edu/ecosystems/deep-sea/deep-sea.

[2] https://www.nasa.gov/audience/forstudents/5-8/features/oceans-the-great-unknown-58.html.

[3] https://oceanservice.noaa.gov/facts/oceandepth.html (20.04.2021); https://www.abc.net.au/news/2020-06-09/ex-nasa-astronaut-first-person-to-space-and-challenger-deep/12337374.

A. von Rebay, *The Designation of Marine Protected Areas*,
https://doi.org/10.1007/978-3-031-29175-3_5

Area.[4] In the event of exploitation, non-living resources, such as polymetallic nodules, would be retrieved by remotely operated vehicles, which use techniques such as mechanical or pressurized water drills to extract deposits from the seabed in depths of up to 6000 m and pump the potato-sized nodules to a surface vessel through a vertical riser pipe. Waste material would be discharged back into the ocean as wastewater, causing sediment plumes that potentially contain toxic elements.[5] The consequences of seabed mining on the ecosystem of the seabed and water column above are largely unknown.[6] Even profit-orientated companies such as Google, BMW, Volvo and Samsung SDI recently signed a letter initiated by the World Wildlife Fund, calling for a moratorium on deep seabed mining, until the risks are better understood, alternatives exhausted and mining can be conducted in a more sustainable manner that preserves the marine environment and biodiversity.[7]

5.1.2 *Marine Life in the Water (Pelagic Zones)*

Vertically, the water of the ocean is divided into five pelagic zones. The epipelagic zone reaches from the surface down to 200 m. Due to the availability of sunlight, this area is home to the greatest (known) biodiversity in the sea, including fish, corals and algae such as phytoplankton, which produces 50–80 per cent of the Earth's oxygen through photosynthesis and is one of the world's largest carbon sinks. [8] Because of its easy access, the offshore epipelagic zone is considered to be most vulnerable to threats, such as the extinction of species due to large scale commercial fishing, rising sea temperature and pollution.[9] The lower mesopelagic zone, the 'twilight zone', stretches from 200 m down to 1000 m and is the last point where sunlight can reach. It is inhabited by species such as the highly overfished orange roughy, pacific armourhead or the bristlemouth.[10] The species inhabiting the darker, deeper oceans are estimated to range between 500.000 to 100 million species.[11]

---

4 https://www.reuters.com/business/environment/exclusive-deep-sea-mining-rules-be-fast-tracked-push-nauru-source-2021-06-25/.

5 https://www.isa.org.jm/exploration-contracts; Miller et al. (2008), p. 9.

6 https://www.bmbf.de/bmbf/en/research/environment-and-climate/pollution-of-the-oceans/deep-sea-mining-ecological-impacts/deep-sea-mining-ecological-impacts.html; Schladebach and Esau (2012), p. 479.

7 https://www.reuters.com/article/us-mining-deepsea/google-bmw-volvo-and-samsung-sdi-sign-up-to-wwf-call-for-temporary-ban-on-deep-sea-mining-idUSKBN2BN0I6.

8 https://oceanservice.noaa.gov/facts/ocean-oxygen.html; https://oceanservice.noaa.gov/facts/phyto.html.

9 Halpern et al. (2007), pp. 1301 and 1309.

10 https://www.economist.com/science-and-technology/2017/04/15/the-mesopelagic-cinderella-of-the-oceans.

11 https://portals.iucn.org/library/sites/library/files/documents/Rep-2004-001., p. 1.

The two photic zones with light are followed by the aphotic zones where no light can reach. The dark parts of the ocean were long thought to be scarce of any life due to extreme conditions of temperatures that can fall to 2 °C and lower, complete darkness and pressure of 1000 times greater than at sea level.[12] The development of new technology started making the exploration of these remote areas possible, which showed that marine life exists in all zones. In the 1960ies, for instance, scientists started exploring the bathypelagic zone of 1000–4000, which proved its extreme richness in species, mainly consisting of small animals, such as snails, worms, clams and crustaceans but also bigger animals such as the giant squid, which is the largest known cephalopod.[13] The adjacent abyssopelagic zone in depths of 4000–6000 m is now known to be the habitat of marine life that is specialised to live in the dark, such as bioluminescent organisms.[14] Activities such as deep seabed mining, warming seawater, microplastic and pollution that sinks to the ocean floor threaten marine species and ecosystems in these terrains, which are only beginning to be explored. The deepest regions of the sea are the hadopelagic zones, which extend into the deepest trenches and are inhabited by marine life such as bristle worms.[15]

5.1.3 Marine Life and Ecosystem on the Ocean Floor

Not only the water but also the ocean floor is rich in marine flora and fauna. Especially seabed features such as hydrothermal vents, seamounts and coral reefs provide a biologically rich habitat for the formation of abundant ecosystems and marine life.[16]

Hydrothermal vents were discovered in 1977 and are similar to volcanic hot springs on land. The vents emit fluids that appear like black smoke of up to 400 °C. Hyperthermophile (heat-loving) and extremophile (extreme-loving) bacteria and organisms around the vent feed on hydrogen sulphide and methane, which they process through chemosynthesis. The minerals and bacteria have significant pharmaceutical and bio-technological value and are of great interest to scientific research because of their ability to survive in extreme environments.[17] Animals such as giant tube worms, squat lobster, crabs, bivalves, shrimps and microbes live around the vent and feed on the bacteria or build a symbiotic relationship, forming a rich and

---

[12] https://www.pmel.noaa.gov/eoi/nemo1998/education/pressure.html#:~:text=If%20you%20are%20at%20sea,the%20pressure%20at%20sea%20level; https://www.nasa.gov/audience/forstudents/5-8/features/oceans-the-great-unknown-58.html.

[13] Rogers (2019), p. 94; https://www.marinebio.org/species/giant-squid/architeuthis-dux/; https://www.marinebio.org/oceans/marine-zones/.

[14] https://www.marinebio.org/oceans/marine-zones/.

[15] https://worldoceanreview.com/en/wor-2/fisheries/deep-sea-fishing/depth-zones-of-the-ocean/.

[16] http://www.fao.org/3/y5852e/Y5852E09.htm; https://oceanservice.noaa.gov/facts/seamounts.html; Rogers (2019), p. 43.

[17] Freestone (2012), p. 193; Mossop (2007), pp. 284 f.

unusual ecosystem.[18] Archaea, for instance, are hyperthermophile microbes that were discovered around vents and appear to be the most primitive organism found to date; according to the hydrothermal genesis theory, they could even be the origin of life.[19]

Seamounts are underwater mountains that rise from the ocean floor but do not reach the surface. The water around seamounts is very rich in nutrients due to sea currents that get caught around the mountains and their steeply rising slopes, which carry nutrients from the deeper ocean to shallower parts of the mountain. Large schools of fish that feed on the nutrients, swim around the tip of the mounts like doughnuts, where they are an easy target for overexploitation by commercial trawl fishing boats.[20]

Corals are living organisms that take centuries and millennia to grow into reef structures.[21] Coral reefs provide an environment for bountiful marine biodiversity. They have been discovered in warm coastal regions and in deep and cold sea waters. While threats to the former are especially caused by global warming and consequential ocean acidification or coastal developments, the latter are especially threatened by waste disposal, pollution and heavy deep-sea fishing gear such as from bottom trawling.[22]

5.1.4 Bottom Trawling

Bottom trawling is like clearcutting an entire forest to catch a few deer.[23]

Fishing techniques such as bottom trawling have made deeper ocean regions of up to 2000 m depths accessible to commercial fishing, which greatly endangers both, marine ecosystems and marine species. A net, held apart by two steel trawl doors weighing several tonnes each, drags along the seafloor on heavy rubber rollers or rockhoppers to catch fish (bottom otter trawl), where it removes and destroys vulnerable large, fragile and long-lived sponges and corals, which are home and cover for diverse marine life.[24] The number of corals taken when trawling on

---

[18] Freestone (2012), p. 193; Rogers (2019), p. 44.

[19] Rogers (2019), p. 46.

[20] Clark et al. (2006), p. 6; https://oceanservice.noaa.gov/facts/seamounts.html; Mossop (2007), pp. 284 f.

[21] https://oceanservice.noaa.gov/education/tutorial_corals/coral04_reefs.html#:~:text=With%20growth%20rates%20of%200.3,30%2C000%2C000%20years%20to%20fully%20form.

[22] https://www.barrierreef.org/the-reef/threats; Freestone (2012), p. 193; https://news.un.org/en/story/2004/06/105672-threats-cold-water-coral-reefs-spotlighted-uns-world-environment-day.

[23] Taylor (2010–2011), p. 126.

[24] http://www.fao.org/fishery/geartype/306/en; https://www.bfn.de/en/activities/marine-nature-conservation/pressures-on-the-marine-environment/fisheries-and-fish-stocks/impacts-of-bottom-trawling.html; Clark (2010), p. 132 f.

seamounts for deep-sea species can amount to tens of tonnes in a single trawl. As a result of bottom trawling in southern Australia, it was estimated that in the first year of the recording of the activity in 1997, 1700 tonnes of coral were caught as bycatch to 4000 tonnes of orange roughy. This makes up almost one-third of the fish catch. Losses of 95–98 per cent of coral reefs on seamounts have been documented as a result of bottom trawling.[25] In the years from 2016 to 2019, 4.9 million square kilometres of ocean floor have been trawled per year. This equals 9.323 square kilometres every minute.[26] Marine sediments are the largest carbon sink in the world.[27] The impact of heavy trawling gear on the ocean floor sets free as much carbon as the aviation industry or the Federal Republic of Germany in one year.[28]

Besides the highly destructive impact on the features of the ocean floor, bottom trawling poses significant risks for marine species.[29] 'Slimehead' (*hoplostethus atlanticus*), for instance, that's original name has been changed to the more appeasing 'orange roughy', usually lives in high densities, especially around sheltering seamounts.[30] Modern echo sounders make the large schools of orange roughy easy to detect from the surface. In the first years of bottom trawling in the south of Tasmania, Australian trawlers yielded 17,000 tonnes of orange roughy in one year around a submarine feature called St Helen's Hill. It was reputed that catches reached one tonne a second with 78 fishing vessels fishing on this feature at the same time.[31] The peak year of orange roughy catch in the Eastern Zone of Australia's Commonwealth in 1990 yielded more than 35,000 tonnes.[32] The global catch of orange roughy in this year amounted to more than 91,000 tonnes.[33] Orange roughy is a long-lived species that reaches sexual maturity at the age of 20, perhaps not until they are 30–40, and female orange roughies do not spawn every year. Compared to other warm-water species, such as the Atlantic cod that lives about 25 years and matures in two to four years, the longevity, low fecundity and slow growth of marine species in deeper ocean regions that are targeted by bottom

---

[25] https://portals.iucn.org/library/sites/library/files/documents/Rep-2004-001., p. ii.

[26] To estimate the size of the trawled areas the regions are gridded. The measures are generated by measuring trawling within each grid. The estimation of the size of the trawled area varies according to the size of the applied grid resolution of 1–3 square kilometres. The smaller the resolution, the more accurate is the result. This study was conducted with a 1 square kilometre aggregated resolution; Sala et al. (2021), p. 399; Amoroso et al. (2018), E10277.

[27] Atwood et al. (2020), p. 1.

[28] Sala et al. (2021), p. 399; Atwood et al. (2020), p. 1.

[29] https://portals.iucn.org/library/sites/library/files/documents/Rep-2004-001.pdf, p. i.

[30] https://oceana.org/marine-life/ocean-fishes/orange-roughy; Rogers (2019), p. 122; Caddell (2020), p. 259.

[31] Rogers (2019), p. 123.

[32] https://www.afma.gov.au/sites/default/files/uploads/2014/03/Orange-roughy-Handout.pdf; https://www.fishfiles.com.au/Media/FISH-Magazine/FISH-Vol-25-3/Australias-rough-road-to-recovery.

[33] http://www.fao.org/fishery/species/2249/en.

trawling make those species especially vulnerable to overfishing.[34] Correspondingly, the stocks of orange roughy in New Zealand and Australia collapsed rapidly. The big trawling fleets of Japan, New Zealand, Australia and the Cook Islands had to relocate to seamounts in more remote areas, subsequently overfishing one mount after another.[35] Trawling activities have led to the depletion and extinction of species before scientists have even studied them in detail.[36] The pacific armourhead (*pseudopentaceros richardsoni*) that lives around the Hawaiian Emperor seamount chain, for instance, had been fished up to 133,000 tonnes in 1969 by Japanese and Soviet fleets. Only in 1972, it was identified as the—already then rare—pelagic armourhead and catches had dropped to 20,000–30,000 tonnes by that point and to 3500 tonnes by 1977.[37]

5.1.5 Conclusion: Undiscovered Habitat: The Ocean

Concludingly, scientific research attests that marine life and biodiversity in the ocean are abundant further than the eye can see. The long-prevailing notion that there is no life in the deeper regions of the ocean has proven to be wrong. The marine environment in deeper parts of the ocean is now known to be rich in biodiversity and endemic species. It comprises vulnerable ecosystems, such as hydrothermal vents, seamounts, coral reefs, deep-sea trenches, cold seeps, submarine canyons and gas hydrates. The marine environment is home to some of the most exploited living resources in the world, such as species of seabirds, deep-sea fish, cetaceans, sharks and other species of marine life.[38]

Parallel to the continuous discovery of marine ecosystems and marine life, the list of anthropogenic uses of the sea that threatens the marine environment is growing. Fishing, dumping and oil pollution are accompanied by the exploration and exploitation of marine non-living resources, ocean acidification and eutrophication, carbon sinking, marine debris (especially plastic), noise- and light pollution, underwater constructions and drilling.[39] The scientific discovery and understanding of the marine environment is steadily growing, which is correspondingly reflected in an increasing number of cases in national and international courts, that acknowledge these areas as vulnerable and in need of protection. The detailed conditions of a specific marine environment in a legal dispute, certainly, have to be substantiated by specialists, such as marine biologists and geologists in every individual case. This glimpse into the reality of the marine environment is a sample of marine habitats and

[34] Victorero et al. (2018), p. 1.

[35] Rogers (2019), p. 125.

[36] Freestone (2012), p. 193.

[37] Rogers (2019), p. 126.

[38] Scovazzi (2004), p. 1; UNGA, A/AC.295/8, pp. 2 f., para. 6 ff.

[39] UNGA, A/AC.295/8, pp. 2 f., para. 8.

biodiversity, which suggests that all areas of the ocean in fact are vulnerable marine ecosystems.

5.2 Marine Environment: De Jure

The obligation as embodied in Art. 192 UNCLOS protects the 'marine environment'. As the marine environment connotes a spatial component, its investigation will provide the substantive scope of the marine environment as well as the geographical scope of the obligation.

5.2.1 Transzonal Application

The obligation to protect and preserve the marine environment is stipulated in its own Part XII UNCLOS. The obligation is regulated abstractly from the zonal regulations of the UNCLOS and therefore applies to the marine environment of all zones and areas of the sea. Questions of sovereignty or jurisdictional zones are irrelevant to the applicability of Art. 192 ff. UNCLOS.[40] Nonetheless, it needs to be established which areas of the ocean are covered by 'marine environment'.

5.2.2 No Legal Definition of Marine Environment

The term 'marine environment' is not defined in the UNCLOS. Specific treaties with regard to marine protection vary in their scope and do not provide any information on the geographical or substantive scope of 'marine environment' under the UNCLOS.

The IUCN, OSPAR Convention, Draft-BBNJ or CBD define MPAs. The specific regulations on MPAs, though, do not give recourse to the general definition of marine environment under Art. 192 UNCLOS. In the UNCLOS III negotiations, the Committee on the Peaceful Uses of the Seabed and the Ocean Floor Beyond the Limits of National Jurisdiction (Malta Group), defined 'marine environment' in Art. 1 (1) of the 1972 Draft Articles on the Preservation of the Marine Environment.[41] According to this definition, marine environment comprises the surface of the sea, the air space above, the water column and the seabed beyond the high tide mark,

[40] PCA, *South China Sea Arbitration*, Philippines v. China (Award), p. 373, para. 940; Hafner (2006), pp. 380 f., mn. 91 ff. and p. 399, mn. 155.

[41] UNGA A/AC.138/SC.III/L.33.

including the biosystems therein or dependent thereon.[42] The definition, however, was not adopted in the final version of the UNCLOS.

5.2.3 *Geographical Scope of Ocean Under the UNCLOS*

The relevant literature argues that the ordinary meaning of marine environment includes the ocean as a whole.[43] Indeed, the scope of marine environment under the UNCLOS cannot exceed the geographical scope of the UNCLOS itself. The geographical limit of the sea and seabed as defined in the UNCLOS, thus, poses the broadest possible reach of marine environment under the UNCLOS.

5.2.3.1 Water Column, Seabed, Ocean Floor and Subsoil Thereof

Seawards, the UNCLOS applies to the water column, seabed, ocean floor and subsoil thereof of the sea beyond the land territory and internal waters and in the case of an archipelagic State its archipelagic waters under Art. 2 (1), 55, 57, 86 and 76 (1), (1) (1) (1) UNCLOS.

5.2.3.2 Baselines

The breadth of the Territorial Sea and its landward limit is measured and marked by the baseline under Art. 3 UNCLOS. The relevant baselines to measure the Territorial Sea are the normal baselines under Art. 5 UNCLOS, the baselines on certain fringing reefs under Art. 6 UNCLOS, straight baselines for deeply indented coasts and fringe of islands under Art. 7 UNCLOS, straight baselines across rivers and river mouths under Art. 9 UNCLOS and certain bays under Art. 10 UNCLOS, as well as archipelagic baselines under Art. 47 UNCLOS.

5.2.3.3 Low Water Line: Lowest Astronomical Tide

The line to measure the baselines is the low-water line along the coast for the normal baseline under Art. 5 UNCLOS, the seaward low-water line of the reef for Art. 6 UNCLOS, the low-water line of its banks in case of a river under Art. 9 UNCLOS, the low-water marks of the natural entrance of the bay under Art. 10 (3), (4) UNCLOS and the outermost points of the outermost islands and drying reefs for archipelagic baselines under Art. 47 (1) UNCLOS, respectively.

---

[42] UNGA A/AC.138/SC.III/L.33; Proelss (2017), Art. 192, mn. 25.

[43] Tanaka (2019), p. 333.

The UNCLOS does not further define the low-water line. According to an examination for the UN Office for Ocean Affairs and the Law of the Sea in 1989, the 'low-water line is the intersection of the plane of low water with the shore.'[44] The low water line is described by the fall of the sea level due to the gravitational pull of the Moon and the Sun, which causes the water level to rise and fall periodically twice in one lunar day (tide). The level of the rise and fall varies according to the astronomical position of the Sun and the Moon. If the Sun and the Moon are aligned, the tide will be more pronounced (spring tide). The local geography, centrifugal forces of the earth and oscillation of the bodies of water on the coast, furthermore, influences the rise and fall of the sea.[45] A technical resolution by the International Hydrographic Organization of 1919 suggested that the level used by the States to determine the low water line shall be the lowest low tide level, 'a plane so low that the tide will not frequently fall below.'[46] This resolution was amended in 1998 to explicitly recommend the Lowest Astronomical Tide (LAT) as the relevant low water line to measure the relevant baseline to determine the Territorial Sea. Accordingly, the LAT is the 'lowest tide level which can be predicted to occur under average meteorological conditions and under any combination of astronomical conditions.'[47] This LAT has been acknowledged as the relevant measure point to determine the baseline of the Territorial Sea.[48]

The low-water line is the reference point to measure the breadth of the Territorial Sea under Art. 4 UNCLOS. The level of the low-water line, therefore, directly determines the end of the Territorial Sea in 12 NM distance, which describes the limit of the exclusive sovereignty of the coastal State, i.e., to exploit valuable resources on the ocean floor. The widest possible extension of the Territorial Sea from the land, therefore, is favourable for the economic interests of the coastal State. This reasoning is precisely the opposite concerning the protection of the marine environment, in which the highest possible baseline leads to the broadest possible application of the protection regulations of the UNCLOS. Correspondingly, Art. 1 of the 1972 Draft Articles on the Preservation of the Marine Environment intended to set the limit of the marine environment in accordance with the high tide mark.[49] Although the broadest possible scope of the UNCLOS is favourable for the broadest possible scope of its protection regulations, it needs to be noted that even a low low-water line does not leave areas on land entirely unprotected. Much more, it yields the beginning of terrestrial protection regulations on land.

---

[44] United Nations (1989), p. 3, para. 9.

[45] Proelss (2017), Art. 5, mn. 8.

[46] United Nations (1989), p. 3, para. 9.

[47] IHO (1994), p. 135, para. 2936.

[48] Proelss (2017), Art. 5, mn. 13.

[49] UNGA A/AC.138/SC.III/L.33; Proelss (2017), Art. 192, mn. 25.

5.2.3.4 Airspace

Art. 2 (2) UNCLOS stipulates the applicability of the UNCLOS to the airspace over the Territorial Sea. The sovereignty over the airspace has been recognised since the 1919 Paris Convention Relating to the Regulation of Aerial Navigation[50] and the 1944 Convention on International Civil Aviation.[51] Naturally, this is limited to the terrains in which the States have sovereignty and, therefore, does not contain the airspace over the EEZ and the High Sea. Because the UNCLOS does not explicitly codify that the airspace belongs to the marine environment, it has to be concluded the airspace above the EEZ and the High Sea is generally free.[52]

5.2.3.5 Adjustment by the Regulations on Pollution of the Maine Environment

The scope of the marine environment thus is generally congruent with the scope of the UNCLOS. Art. 1 (1) (4) UNCLOS contains a special regulation with regard to the pollution of the marine environment. Accordingly, pollution of the marine environment means the introduction by man, directly or indirectly, of substances or energy into the marine environment, including estuaries, which results or is likely to result in such deleterious effects as harm to living resources and marine life, hazards to human health, hindrance to marine activities, including fishing and other legitimate uses of the sea, impairment of quality for use of seawater and reduction of amenities.

The definition of pollution of the marine environment is wide and concerns any source of pollution from any area, including land, water, estuaries or atmosphere. Therefore, even global warming and the acidification of the marine environment through anthropogenic carbon emissions are included in the pollution of the marine environment.[53] This is reflected in the specific regulations on pollution in Part XII UNCLOS. According to Art. 194 (3) (a) UNCLOS in conjunction with Art. 207 (1), 213 UNCLOS, Art. 212, 222 UNCLOS and Art. 211 (1) UNCLOS, States shall adopt and enforce laws and regulations to prevent, reduce and control pollution of the marine environment from land-based sources, including rivers and estuaries, from and through the atmosphere and pollution of the coastline from vessels.[54] This indicates that even internal waters, such as estuaries and rivers, parts of the land such as coastlines, as well as the atmosphere can be part of the marine environment.[55] The relevant criterium in order to be regarded as pollution of the marine environment,

[50] UNTS, Vol. 11, No. LoN-297.

[51] UNTS, Vol. 15, No. II-102; Proelss (2017), Art. 2, mn. 17.

[52] Schladebach (2017), p. 27, mn. 8, p. 32, mn. 22.

[53] Matz-Lück (2017), p. 417, mn. 56.

[54] Hafner (2006), p. 361, mn. 27; Harrison (2017), p. 24.

[55] Nordquist et al. (2013), 192.11(b).

therefore, is its potential to directly or indirectly influence it. The obligation to protect and preserve the marine environment thus extends to estuaries, land and atmosphere, where and if pollution from these sources influences the marine environment directly or indirectly.[56]

5.2.4 *Marine Life, Endangered Species, Marine Biodiversity, Ecosystems*

Although marine environment can connote to a spatial area, its substantive scope is not limited to the water column and natural features of the seabed and ocean floor. The interpretation of its substantive scope also includes marine life, its habitat, marine biodiversity and ecosystems.

5.2.4.1 Marine Life, Endangered Species and Their Habitats

The definition of pollution of the marine environment under Art. 1 (1) (4) UNCLOS inconclusively lists harms such as to living resources and marine life. This indicates that in the light of the UNCLOS, marine environment comprises not only the water column and the natural features of the seabed and ocean floor but also marine life. This interpretation is confirmed by the reports of the informal meetings on protection and preservation of the marine environment of the Third Committee of UNCLOS III on its 38th meeting in 1978. It has been decided on the meeting 'to recommend to the Chairman of the Third Meeting that it had been agreed that the term "marine environment" included the concept of marine life.'[57] At the seventh session of the UNCLOS III Conference in 1978, the Chairman of the Third Committee consequently reported that 'it was understood that term "marine environment" includes "marine life".'[58]

The incorporation of marine life as an element of the marine environment is furthermore supported by consistent jurisprudence. In the *Southern Bluefin Tuna Cases* as well as in the *Request for an Advisory Opinion Submitted by the SRFC*, the ITLOS expressly stated that 'the conservation of the living resources of the sea is an element in the protection and preservation of the marine environment.'[59] In the *M/V Louisa Case,* the ITLOS considered 'that, in the view of the Tribunal, the parties should in the circumstances act with prudence and caution to prevent serious harm to

[56] Proless, Art. 192, mn. 25; Hafner (2006), p. 361, mn. 26, 38; Nordquist et al. (2013), 194.10(k).

[57] UNGA A/CONF.62/C.3/SR.39, p. 158.

[58] UN A/CONF.62/RCNG/1, p. 97, Art. 1, para. 4; Nordquist et al. (2013), 192.11(a).

[59] ITLOS, *Southern Bluefin Tuna Cases*, New Zealand v. Japan; Australia v. Japan, Provisional Measures, ITLOS Reports 1999, pp. 280, 295, para. 70; ITLOS, *SRFC*, Advisory Opinion, ITLOS Reports 2015, pp. 14, 61, para. 216; Harrison (2017), p. 24.

the marine environment' and specifically referred to the paragraph in the *Southern Bluefin Tuna Cases,* in which it stated that the parties should 'act with prudence and caution to ensure that effective conservation measures are taken to prevent serious harm to the stock of southern bluefin tuna [. . .].'[60] The protection of marine life, thus, is entailed in the protection and preservation of the marine environment.

In its *South China Sea Arbitration*, the PCA had to decide on the lawfulness of activities carried out by China at Scarborough Shoal and in the Spratly Islands in the South China Sea. According to the PCA, Art. 192 UNCLOS imposes a duty on the States to prevent the harvest of endangered species, which harms the marine environment.[61] Furthermore, 'in addition to preventing the direct harvesting of species recognized internationally as being threatened with extinction, Article 192 extends to the prevention of harms that would affect depleted, threatened or endangered species indirectly through the destruction of their habitats.'[62] This shows that both, endangered species as well as their habitat fall upon the protective scope of marine environment under Art. 192 UNCLOS.

5.2.4.2 Marine Biodiversity Including Coral Reefs

In the *South China Sea* Arbitration, the PCA furthermore confirmed the obligation under Art. 192 UNCLOS to protect and preserve the marine environment and marine ecosystems because of the high level of biodiversity of species *inter alia* found in coral reefs, which are not only 'amongst the most biodiverse and socioeconomically important ecosystems, they are also fragile and degrade under human pressures.'[63] The PCA stated that 'there is a "General Obligation" under Article 192 of the Convention to protect and preserve the marine environment, which may be broadly enough worded to include the obligation to protect and preserve marine biodiversity', including coral reefs.[64] A high level of biodiversity, such as 'fishes, corals, echinoderms, mangroves, seagrasses, giant clams, and marine turtles [. . .]' falls under the obligation to protect and preserve the marine environment.[65]

---

[60] ITLOS, *M/V "Louisa"*, Saint Vincent and the Grenadines v. Kingdom of Spain, Provisional Measures, ITLOS Reports 2008–2010, pp. 58, 70, para. 77; ITLOS, *Southern Bluefin Tuna Cases*, New Zealand v. Japan; Australia v. Japan, Provisional Measures, ITLOS Reports 1999, pp. 280, 296, para. 77.

[61] PCA, *South China Sea Arbitration*, Philippines v. China (Award), p. 382, para. 960.

[62] PCA, *South China Sea Arbitration*, Philippines v. China (Award), p. 381, para. 959; Proelss (2017), Art. 192, mn. 25.

[63] PCA, *South China Sea Arbitration*, Philippines v. China (Award), p. 322, para. 824.

[64] PCA *South China Sea Arbitration*, Philippines v. China (Jurisdiction), p. 104, para. 284.

[65] PCA, *South China Sea Arbitration*, Philippines v. China (Award), p. 321, para. 823.

5.2.4.3 Connectivity Between Ecosystems

Lastly, the PCA concluded in its *South China Sea Arbitration* that 'ocean currents and the life cycles of marine species create a high degree of connectivity between the different ecosystems. This means that the impact of any environmental harm occurring at Scarborough Shoal and in the Spratly Islands may not be limited to the immediate area, but can affect the health and viability of ecosystems elsewhere in the South China Sea.'[66] The obligation to protect and preserve the marine environment spreads from the immediate area of harmful activities to a broader terrain that may be indirectly affected by the activity due to the ocean currents.[67]

5.2.5 *Conclusion: Substantiation of the Marine Environment and Large-Scale MPAs*

Concludingly, the geographical scope of marine environment under Art. 192 UNCLOS is generally aligned with the geographical scope of the ocean in the sense of the UNCLOS, namely the water column, its seabed, ocean floor and subsoil thereof.[68] Its landward limit is the low-water line, which determines the breadth of the Territorial Sea under Art. 3 UNCLOS and is measured from the LAT. Furthermore, the protection of the marine environment includes estuaries and direct or indirect influences from land and the atmosphere.[69] Marine environment under Art. 192 UNCLOS is not limited to the water column and natural features of the seabed but includes marine life, endangered species and their habitat, marine biodiversity such as coral reefs and protects ecosystems, which may be affected by harmful activities in a connected ecosystem.

The prospects of a legal claim under Art. 192 UNCLOS depends on the substantiation of the natural conditions of the marine environment in need of protection and preservation. As marine environment connotes to a geographical area, the substantiation of the need for protection of a specific marine area through the adoption of legislation meets the definition of the establishment of an MPA. Because the entire ocean can be described with geographical coordinates, large-scale MPAs across the whole ocean would meet this criterion. The crucial element in substantiating the claim would be the presentation and proof of the need to protect the marine environment in the entire terrain of the ocean. In the individual case, it is, therefore, critical that the need for the protection and preservation of the marine environment through establishing a global MPA is substantiated by expert opinions such as marine biologists and geologists. Bottom trawling, for instance, can take place in

66 PCA, *South China Sea Arbitration*, Philippines v. China (Award), p. 322, para. 825.

67 PCA, *South China Sea Arbitration*, Philippines v. China (Award), p. 321, para. 823.

68 Tanaka (2019), p. 7.

69 Proless, Art. 192, mn. 25; Hafner (2006), p. 361, mn. 26, 38.

shallow waters and depths up to 2000 m.[70] These areas are usually rich in marine life, such as fish and corals, the destruction of which influences an expansive ecosystem. Due to the detrimental effects on the marine environment, bottom trawling in international waters is only conducted anymore by a few States, including New Zealand, Japan, Cook Islands, Spain, Korea and the Faroe Islands (Denmark).[71] This study will demonstrated that the obligation to protect and preserve the marine environment requires a global ban of large scale fishing techniques, such as bottom trawling, pelagic trawling drift net fishing and longlining.[72]

References

Amoroso RO, Pitcher CR, Rijnsdorp AD, Mcconnaughey RA, Parma AM, Suuronen P, Eigaard OR, Bastardieh F, Hintzenc NT, Althausi F, Bairdj SJ, Blackk J, Buhl-Mortensenl L, Campbellm AB, Catarino R, Colliep J, Cowan JH Jr, Durholtzr D, Engstroms N, Fairweatherr TP, Fockt HO, Fordu R, Gálvezv PA, Gerritsenw H, Góngorax ME, Gonzálezv JA, Hiddinky JG, Hughesy KM, Intelmannd SS, Jenkinsz C, Jonssonaa P, Kaingebb P, Kangascc M, Kathenabb JN, Kavadasdd S, Leslier RW, Lewisee SG, Lundyff M, Makingg D, Martinhh J, Mazorb T, Gonzalez-Mirelisl G, Newmancc SJ, Papadopoulouii N, Posenjj PE, Rochesterb W, Russokk T, Salall A, Semmensmm JM, Silvann C, Tsolosoo A, Vanelslanderpp B, Wakefieldcc CB, Woodj BA, Hilborna R, Kaisery MJ, Jenningso S (2018) Bottom trawl fishing footprints on the world's continental shelves. Proc Natl Acad Sci (PNAS) 115(43):E10275–E10282

Atwood TB, Witt A, Mayorga J, Hammill E, Sala E (2020) Global patterns in marine sediment carbon stocks. Front Mar Sci 7(Article 165):1–9

Caddell R (2020) Chapter 12: deep-sea bottom fisheries and the protection of seabed ecosystems: problems, progress and prospects. In: Banet C (ed) The law of the seabed – access, uses, and protection of seabed resources, vol 90. Publications on Ocean Development, Leiden, pp 255–284

Clark MR (2010) Box 9: effects of trawling on seamounts. Oceanography 23(1):132–133

Clark MR, Tittensor D, Rogers AD, Brewin P, Schlacher T, Rowden A, Stocks K, Consalvey M (2006) Seamounts, deep-sea corals and fisheries: vulnerability of deep-sea corals to fishing on seamounts beyond areas of national jurisdiction. United Nations Environment Program World Conservation Monitoring Centre (UNEP WCMC), Cambridge

Freestone D (2012) International governance, responsibility and management of areas beyond national jurisdiction. Int J Mar Coast Law (IJMCL) 27(2):191–204

Hafner G (2006) Schutz der Meeresumwelt. In: Vitzthum W (ed) Handbuch des Seerechts. Munich, pp 355–421

Halpern BS, Selkoe KA, Micheli F, Kappel CV (2007) Evaluating and ranking the vulnerability of global marine ecosystems to anthropogenic threats. Conserv Biol 21(5):1301–1315

Harrison J (2017) Saving the oceans through law – the international legal framework for the protection of the marine environment. Oxford

International Hydrographic Organization (IHO) (1994) Hydrographic dictionary, Part I, vol 1, English, Special publication 32, 5th edn. Monaco

[70] Morgan and Chuenpagdee (2009), p. 13; https://oceana.org/sites/default/files/reports/Trawling_BZ_10may10_toAudrey.pdf, p. 1.

[71] http://www.savethehighseas.org/deep-sea-fishing/the-main-players/.

[72] See: Application to Large-Scale Fishing Techniques.

Matz-Lück N (2017) Meeresschutz. In: Proelss A (ed) Internationales Umweltrecht. Berlin, pp 393–453
Miller KA, Thompson KF, Johnston P, Santillo D (2008) An overview of seabed mining including the current state of development, environmental impacts, and knowledge gaps. Front Mar Sci 4 (Article 418):1–24
Morgan LE, Chuenpagdee R (2009) Shifting gears, addressing the collateral impacts of fishing methods in U.S. waters, PEW Science Series. Washington
Mossop J (2007) Protecting marine biodiversity on the continental shelf beyond 200 nautical miles. Ocean Dev Int Law 38(3):283–304
Nordquist MH, Nandan S, Rosenne S (2013) UN Convention on the Law of the Sea Commentary 1982 Online. Center for Oceans Law and Policy, Leiden
Proelss A (2017) United Nations Convention on the Law of the Sea – a commentary. Munich
Rogers A (2019) The deep – the hidden wonders of our oceans and how we can protect them. London
Sala E, Mayorga J, Bradley D, Cabral RB, Atwood TB, Auber A, Cheung W, Costello C, Ferretti F, Friedlander AM, Gaines SD, Garilao C, Goodell W, Halpern BS, Hinson A, Kaschner K, Kesner-Reyes K, Leprieur F, McGowan J, Morgan LE, Mouillot D, Palacios-Abrantes J, Possingham HP, Rechberger KD, Worm B, Lubchenco J (2021) Protecting the global ocean for biodiversity, food and climate. Nature 592:397–402
Schladebach M (2017) Luftrecht, 2nd edn. Tübingen
Schladebach M, Esau C (2012) Aktuelle Herausforderungen im Seerecht. Deutsches Verwaltungsblatt (DVBl), Köln, pp 475–483
Scovazzi T (2004) Marine protected areas on the high seas: some legal and policy considerations. Int J Mar Coast Law (IJMCL) 19(1):1–17
Tanaka Y (2019) The international law of the sea, 3rd edn. Cambridge
Taylor CR (2010–2011) Fishing with a bulldozer: options for unilateral action by the United States under domestic and international law to halt destructive bottom trawling practices on the high seas. Environs: Environ Law Policy J 34:121–171
United Nations Office for Ocean Affairs and the Law of the Sea (UN), The Law of the Sea, Baselines: An Examination of the Relevant Provisions of the United Nations Convention on the Law of the Sea (New York, 1989)
Victorero L, Watling L, Deng Palomares ML, Nouvian C (2018) Out of sight, but within reach: a global history of bottom-trawled deep-sea fisheries from >400 m depth. Front Mar Sci 5(Article 98):1–17

Chapter 6
Substantive Scope: Designation of MPAs

> For that which is common to the greatest number has the least care bestowed upon it. (Aristotle)[1]

After having investigated the legally binding effect of 'obligation', the personal scope of 'all States', as well as the geographical scope and content of 'marine environment', the substantive scope of the obligation to 'protect and preserve' needs to be defined in general and in particular with regard to the question if the obligation to establish MPAs can be derived therefrom. To this end, the study will demonstrate that the obligation to protect and preserve the marine environment is (Sect. 6.1) a general and primary obligation of all States, and that it (Sect. 6.2) obliges States to protect and preserve the marine environment from all threats and (Sect. 6.3) to take active measures to this end. In this regard, this study will show that active measures by States mean the adoption of national and 'international' legislation for the protection and preservation of the marine environment, which meets the definition of MPAs. Therefore, the obligation to protect and preserve the marine environment obliges States to establish MPAs. Thus, courts do not stray into law-making when obliging States to establish MPAs under this obligation (Sect. 6.4). The obligation exists independently of the sovereign rights of the States in all zones of the Sea (Sect. 6.5). The specific content of the obligation to protect and preserve the marine environment will ultimately be specified through by determining its minimum and maximum scope (Sect. 6.6).

[1] Jowett, http://classics.mit.edu/Aristotle/politics.2.two.html.

A. von Rebay, *The Designation of Marine Protected Areas*,
https://doi.org/10.1007/978-3-031-29175-3_6

6.1 Primary, General Obligation

The wording of Art. 192 UNCLOS obliges States to protect and preserve the marine environment, regardless of an occurred damage. Therefore, the obligation to protect and preserve the marine environment does not regulate the responsibility and liability as a consequence of damages but obliges the States to protect the marine environment as a primary obligation.[2] The responsibility and liability of States for the breach of their obligation to protect and preserve the marine environment (secondary obligation) is regulated in Art. 235 UNCLOS.

The literature has argued that the obligation to protect and preserve the marine environment as embodied in Art. 192 UNCLOS is too general to be applicable in practice.[3] Art. 192 UNCLOS is a general obligation, which is designed as an umbrella regulation. Its specific content is detailed by more specific legislation.[4] The PCA confirmed in its *South China Sea Arbitration* that '[a]lthough phrased in general terms, the tribunal considers it well established that Article 192 does impose a duty on States Parties, the content of which is informed by the other provisions of Part XII and other applicable rules of international law. This "general obligation" extends both to "protection" of the marine environment from future damage and "preservation" in the sense of maintaining or improving its present condition. Art. 192 thus entails the positive obligation to take active measures to protect and preserve the marine environment and by logical implication, entails the negative obligation not to degrade the marine environment.'[5] The obligation to protect and preserve the marine environment, thus, is a primary obligation that requires the States to take active measures to protect and preserve the marine environment. Furthermore, the subsequent investigation will show that the obligation to protect and preserve the marine environment is not too general and does entail a specific obligation of States to establish MPAs.

6.2 All Threats

The obligation under Art. 192 UNCLOS obliges the States to protect and preserve the marine environment from any threat. While most of the regulations of Part XII UNCLOS are expressly designed to prevent, reduce and control pollution, the interpretation of the wording of Art. 192 UNCLOS shows that 'to protect and preserve' is not limited to any threat.[6]

---

[2] Hafner (2006), p. 364, mn. 32.

[3] Guo (2020), p. 1.

[4] UNGA A/44/461, p. 5.

[5] PCA, *South China Sea Arbitration*, Philippines v. China (Award), pp. 373 f., para. 941.

[6] Proelss (2017), Art. 192, mn. 2.

The ordinary meaning of a treaty regulation is its most important means of interpretation under Art. 31 (1) VCLT. The parties to the UNCLOS have stipulated specific regulations regarding marine pollution in the subsequent regulations of Part XII UNCLOS, while expressly not incorporating this limitation in Art. 192 UNCLOS. This shows that pollution was not left out in the regulation of Art. 192 UNCLOS unintentionally but was purposefully regulated in subsequent provisions. With regard to the interpretation of obligation to protect and preserve the marine environment in its context, this regulatory system makes Art. 192 UNCLOS the *lex generalis* before stipulating more specific regulations subsequently as *lex specialis*. Moreover, as has been shown, it has been argued that if Art. 192 UNCLOS would be limited to pollution, it would be entailed entirely in the regulation of Art. 194 (1) UNCLOS and therefore be obsolete.[7] The objective of the parties to the UNCLOS was to create a living instrument with innovative and flexible regulations that remain valid also in the light of emerging challenges that were not foreseen during the time of its drafting.[8] Art. 192 UNCLOS is therefore not limited to pollution but addresses all threats of the marine environment. The view is supported by the relevant jurisprudence, which 'confirms that Part XII is "not limited to measures aimed strictly at controlling marine pollution," which, while "certainly an important aspect of environmental protection . . . is by no means the only one."'[9] Concludingly, the obligation under obliges States to protect and preserve the marine environment from any threat.

6.3 Obligation to Adopt Active Measures: Establishment of MPAs

Naturally, the most comprehensive protection of the ocean from anthropogenic damages would be the renunciation of the use of the sea by all States.[10] The use of and activities in the sea can be regulated through the designation of MPAs. MPAs are geographically defined marine areas for a protection, preservation or conservation objective that are designated by legislation.[11] The establishment of MPAs thus requires a designating act in the form of adopting national or 'international' legislation.

The literature argues that the obligation as embodied under Art. 192 UNCLOS is too general to entail specific measures by States such as the establishment of

[7]Hafner (2006), p. 367, mn. 39; see: Obligation Entailed under Art. 194 (1) UNCLOS.

[8]Boyle (2005), p. 584; Lee and Bautista (2018), p. 138; Kojima (2015), p. 170; Proelss (2017), Art. 192, mn. 22.

[9]PCA, *South China Sea Arbitration*, Philippines v. China (Award), p. 376, para. 945; PCA, *Chagos Marine Protected Area Arbitration*, Mauritius v. UK (Award) 2015, pp. 128 f., para. 320.

[10]Proelss (2017), Art. 192, mn. 24.

[11]See: Definition of MPAs.

MPAs.[12] The following assessment will show that the obligation to protect and preserve the marine environment entails the obligation of States to adopt active measures to this end and that these active measures comprise the establishment of MPAs. The assessment of whether States are obliged to establish MPAs under the obligation to protect and preserve the marine environment will follow the following steps: firstly, it will be demonstrated that the obligation to protect and preserve the marine environment requires the adoption of active measures by States. Secondly, active measures of States are regulated in administrative law. The consequence of the obligation to adopt active measures will be assessed in national law (thirdly) and European law (fourthly) in order to deduce that active measures by States in international law mean the adoption of legislation (fifthly). The adoption of legislation for the protection and preservation of the marine environment constitutes the establishment of an MPA if the obligation refers to a specific geographical area. Generally, sovereign rights in the UNCLOS are distributed spatially, which is why the obligation to adopt legislation for the protection and preservation of the marine environment generally stipulates the obligation to establish MPAs, with exception to special jurisdiction rights such as of flag States for vessels flying their flag (sixthly).

6.3.1 *Obligation to Adopt Active Measures*

The hitherto notion in the extant literature that because the text of the obligation to protect and preserve the marine environment does not stipulate the taking of active measures, it is merely a codification of a basic principle, from which no specific obligation of the States can be derived, is superseded by the interpretation of this obligation that proves that it obliges States to adopt active measures.[13]

6.3.1.1 Legal Obligation Means to Take or Omit Actions

The interpretation of the ordinary meaning reveals that the word 'obligation' is used in legal relations to codify legally binding obligations. It has substantial legal content. Obligations put the addressee under the legal duty to adopt or omit certain actions. The duty to adopt or omit active measures is the core content of an obligation. The obligation to adopt or omit active measures follows from the word obligation itself (see: Literal Interpretation).. The codification of an obligation of States to protect and preserve the marine environment thus already codifies the obligation of States to take active measures to this end and to omit measures that harm the marine environment.

---

[12] Guo (2020), p. 1.

[13] Guo (2020), p. 1; Proelss (2017), Art. 194, mn. 34; Druel (2011), p. 8; Nordquist et al. (2013), XII.13 and 192.1.

6.3.1.2 Protection and Preservation Require Active Measures

The obligation as embodied in Art. 192 UNCLOS entails both the obligation to protect as well as to preserve the marine environment. While the protection of the marine environment refers to imminent or existing dangers or harms, the word preservation connotes conserving and retaining the quality of the marine environment, which entails the concept of a long-term policy.[14] The obligation to protect and preserve the marine environment in the 1982 UNCLOS was the first all-encompassing codification of an obligation of the States that goes beyond combating damages to the marine environment from pollution after it has occurred and obliges States to take active measures to preserve it. The obligation is thus not only addressed at the protection from deterioration of the marine environment but also to preserve it from future damages by any threat and even to improve it.[15] Conformingly, the PCA asserts in its *South China Sea Arbitration* that the obligation under Art. 192 UNCLOS entails not only the obligation to protect the marine environment from future damages but also to preserve the present condition by maintaining or improving it.[16]

6.3.1.3 Adoption of MPAs as Measure

The UNCLOS is intended to be a flexible framework that is responsive to emerging issues in the context of the new usages of the sea in order to 'stand a long time'.[17] The States parties endeavoured to create a set of rules that would remain modern and applicable over time as new technologies develop, even for activities in the sea that were not known at the time of its negotiation. For this reason, it was not possible to exhaustively stipulate the obligation with regard to the adoption of specific measures, such as Sections 5 and 6, Part XII UNCLOS for the prevention, reduction and control of pollution. This would have precluded the flexible application to new activities and technologies. In those cases, however, the UNCLOS stipulates the protection and conservation from specific threats to the marine environment, such as pollution in Section 5 and 6 of Part XII UNCLOS, over-exploitation of living resources in Art. 116 ff, 61 (2) UNCLOS or the protection of specific ecosystems under Art. 194 (5) UNCLOS, it expressly stipulates the adoption of measures to do so. The legally binding general obligation of States to protect and preserve the marine environment without conclusively regulating the specific measures to do so is a central expression of the endeavour to create a flexible regulatory framework that

[14] Nordquist et al. (2013), XII.13.

[15] Nordquist et al. (2013), XII.13.

[16] PCA, *South China Sea Arbitration*, Philippines v. China (Award), p. 373, para. 941; Tanaka (2019), p. 333; Freestone (2009), p. 45; Proelss (2017), Art. 192, mn. 23.

[17] https://www.un.org/Depts/los/convention_agreements/texts/koh_english.pdf; Kojima (2015), p. 170; Dalaker Kraabel (2019), p. 168.

remains modern even in the light of the evolution of new techniques and activities in the sea.

6.3.1.4 Conclusion: Obligation to Take Active Measures

Concludingly, an interpretation to the effect that obligation only represents a basic principle without stipulating the obligation to adopt active measures to this end is not consistent with the wording 'obligation' and 'preservation' as well as to the protection purpose of Art. 192 UNCLOS, which aims to cover all known and unknown harmful effects on the marine environment. The obligation to protect and preserve the marine environment can only have legal effect if the obligation is interpreted according to its ordinary meaning, namely as an obligation to adopt or omit from doing certain acts. The interpretation that the obligation to protect and preserve the marine environment obliges States to take active measures is also supported by the relevant jurisprudence and parts of the literature.[18] Conformingly, the PCA declares in its South China Sea Arbitration that 'Article 192 does impose a duty on States Parties, [. . .]. This "general obligation" extends both to "protection" of the marine environment from future damage and "preservation" in the sense of maintaining or improving its present condition. Article 192 thus entails the positive obligation to take active measures to protect and preserve the marine environment, [. . .].'[19]

6.3.2 Active Measures of States Regulated in Administrative Law

As the investigation has shown that States are obliged to take active measures to protect and preserve the marine environment, it needs to be assessed in a second step what 'active measures' by States are. The literature points out that the preservation of the marine environment entails the obligation to take legal and administrative measures actively.[20] Activities of governments are usually regulated in administrative law. Australia defines that administrative law as the decision-making of States.[21] In Germany, it is defined that administrative law regulates the relationship between the States on the one side and subjects of private law on the other.[22] In the US legal system, administrative law governs the powers and procedures of States in relation to

[18] Nordquist et al. (2013), XII.13 and 192.9.

[19] PCA, *South China Sea Arbitration*, Philippines v. China (Award), pp. 373 f., para. 941.

[20] Nordquist et al. (2013), XII.13 and 192.9.

[21] https://www.ag.gov.au/legal-system/administrative-law.

[22] https://www.bmi.bund.de/DE/themen/moderne-verwaltung/verwaltungsrecht/verwaltungsrecht-node.html.

the public.[23] Generally, administrative law comprises the legal programmes and legal provisions of the administration and the legally relevant acts such as decisions and implementing measures.[24]

Concurrently, in its *Request for an Advisory Opinion Submitted by the SRFC*, the ITLOS expressly confirmed that the suitable means to fulfil the States obligation to protect and preserve the marine environment is the adoption of administrative measures. According to the ITLOS, 'the flag State, in fulfilment of its responsibility to exercise effective jurisdiction and control in administrative matters, must adopt the necessary administrative measures to ensure that fishing vessels flying its flag are not involved in activities which will undermine the flag State's responsibilities under the Convention in respect of the conservation and management of marine living resources.'[25] Active measures of States, thus, are regulated in administrative law.

Other than in national administrative law, the forms of acts by the States are not codified in public international law.[26] The specific form of the active measure States must adopt will therefore be deduced using a rule of three by investigating the obligation under national administrative law using the example of Germany, under regional international administrative law using the example of the EU and subsequently applying the results to public international law. Within each legal system, it will be established, which general active measures exist in the respective system; if active measures to protect and preserve the marine environment concretise on the adoption of legislation; and if States are therefore obliged to establish MPAs.

6.3.3 *The Establishment of MPAs as Measure in (German) National Law*

As national administrative law regulates active measures of States toward their addressees, it is a suitable point of departure to investigate what 'active measures' of States under the obligation to protect and preserve the marine environment are. To this end, three question will be assessed: what are active measures of the State in the German legal system? Do active measures to protect and preserve the marine environment by Germany entail the adoption of legislation? Does the obligation to adopt legislation to protect and preserve the marine environment oblige Germany to establish MPAs?

[23] https://www.llsdc.org/federal-administrative-law-a-brief-overview.

[24] Schmidt-Aßmann and Molnár-Gábor (2019) para. 4.

[25] ITLOS, *SRFC*, Advisory Opinion, ITLOS Reports 2015, pp. 14, 36, para. 119.

[26] Dahm et al. (2002), p. 512.

6.3.3.1 Preliminary Audit: Application of the UNCLOS in (German) Domestic Law

Before assessing the specific content of the obligation to protect and preserve the marine environment, the application and implication of the UNCLOS on the German legal system need to be assessed. There is no unitary theoretical approach for the application and implementation of public international law into the national legal systems. Although States have leeway to create a structure to implement international law in national law, national law may not dispense international obligations.[27]

In German law, the general rules of international law shall be an integral part of federal law by virtue of Art. 25 1949 Basic Law for the Federal Republic of Germany (German Basic Law).[28] They shall take precedence over the laws and directly create rights and duties for the inhabitants of the federal territory. The obligation to protect and preserve the marine environment is *jus cogens* or at least a universally accepted rule of customary international law. It, therefore, binds all States *erga omnes*. Furthermore, according to Art. 59 (2) German Basic Law, treaties that regulate the political relations of the German Federation or relate to subjects of federal legislation shall require the consent or participation of the bodies responsible in such a case for the enactment of federal law in the form of federal law. In the case of executive agreements, the provisions concerning the federal administration shall apply, *mutatis mutandis*. According to Art. 25, 59 (2) German Basic Law, international law, thus, must be implemented in the domestic legal order through national law. Accordingly, the Federal Constitutional Court of Germany established in its *Görgülü* Order of 14 October 2004 that the relationship between international law and national law is a relationship between two different legal spheres and that the nature of this relationship from the perspective of national law can only be determined by national law itself.[29] Therefore, the 'law of international agreements applies on the domestic level only when it has been incorporated into the domestic legal system in the proper form and conformity with substantive constitutional law.'[30] The Federal Republic of Germany signed the UNCLOS on 10 December 1982, ratified it on 14 October 1994 and implemented it into the domestic legal system through the adoption of three national laws.[31] In doing so, the federal legislature transformed the UNCLOS

[27] See: Relationship of National and Public International Law.

[28] BGBl. I 1949, p. 1.

[29] BVerfG, Order of 14 October 2004, 2 BvR 1481/04, para. 1–72.

[30] BVerfG, Order of 14 October 2004, 2 BvR 1481/04, para. 36.

[31] https://treaties.un.org/pages/ViewDetailsIII.aspx?src=TREATY&mtdsg_no=XXI-6&chapter=21&Temp=mtdsg3&clang=_en; Gesetz zu dem Seerechtsübereinkommen der Vereinten Nationen vom 10. Dezember 1982, BGBl. II 1994, p. 1799; Gesetz zur Ausführung des Seerechtsübereinkommens der Vereinten Nationen vom 10. Dezember 1982 sowie des Übereinkommens vom 28. Juli 1994 zur Durchführung des Teils XI des Seerechtsübereinkommens, BGBl. I 1995, p. 778; Übereinkommen zur Durchführung des Teiles XI des Seerechtsübereinkommens der Vereinten Nationen vom 10. Dezember 1982, BGBl. II 1994, p. 2566.

into the German legal system. It made an order on the application of the law to this effect. Within the German legal system, the UNCLOS and the Implementation Agreement, thus, have the status of a federal statute of Germany.[32]

6.3.3.2 Active Measures in (German) Administrative Law

As Germany is bound by the obligations under the UNCLOS, it needs to be assessed what 'active measures' to protect and preserve the marine environment under the obligation as embodied in Art. 192 UNCLOS are in German administrative law? In German administrative law, there are two forms of governmental acts: the adoption of abstract and general legally binding norms and the enactment of single administrative acts, which bind the individual addressee in an individual case.[33] The obligation to protect and preserve the marine environment, therefore, could be realized abstractly through the adoption of a general legally binding norm, which applies to an undefined, open group of addressees and regulates an undefined number of cases, or through the adoption of a single administrative act for each individual case. Both are active measures of States. However, while general legally binding norms are adopted in a formal law-making process and are therefore legislation, single administrative acts are executive acts by the administration. As the definition of MPAs requires the designation by legislation, only the adoption of legally binding laws are measures by the State that constitute the establishment of MPAs.

6.3.3.3 Active Measure Specified on Adoption of National Legislation

It has to be established if the obligation to take 'active measures' can be narrowed down to the obligation to adopt a general, legally binding law.

Assessment Prerogative

In the German legal system, the legislature possesses an 'assessment prerogative'.[34] The term 'prerogative' originates in Latin (*praerogativa*) and means privilege.[35] The prerogative of assessment provides a privilege to the legislature to make the ultimate binding decision on the appropriateness and necessity of a particular legal regulation to achieve a legitimate objective. It, therefore, comprises the prerogative of the

---

[32] BVerfG, Order of 14 October 2004, 2 BvR 1481/04, para. 34.

[33] § 35 Verwaltungsverfahrensgesetz, BGBl. I 1976, p. 102.

[34] BVerfG, Beschluss vom 29. September 2010 – 1 BvR 1789/10, Rn. 18.

[35] https://www.oxfordlearnersdictionaries.com/definition/english/prerogative; https://dictionary.cambridge.org/dictionary/english/prerogative.

legislature concerning 'if' and 'how' it adopts a measure to achieve a legitimate objective. The prerogative of assessment follows from the principle of separation of powers. Due to the primacy of assessment and evaluation of the legislature, a decision by the legislative body is only open to a judicial review with regard to apparent violations, that is, if the measure is objectively unsuitable or entirely inadequate.[36] Therefore, it is primarily up to the legislative branch to decide on the type and content of measures to be adopted, taking into account the substantive laws of the subject area concerned, while a judicial review is only permissible restrictedly.[37] However, where and if a State enters a legally binding obligation, it reduces its prerogative concerning 'if' it adopts a measure to zero. This means, where a State accepts a legally binding obligation, it abdicates its assessment prerogative regarding 'if' it adopts a measure and obliges itself to do so. Because the obligation to protect and preserve the marine environment *erga omnes* binds the whole States community and Germany, furthermore, signed, ratified and implemented the UNCLOS, it accepted the obligation to protect and preserve the marine environment. Therefore, its prerogative, concerning 'if' it adopts measures to fulfil its obligation under the UNCLOS, is reduced to zero. Germany is obliged to adopt measures to protect and preserve the marine environment. With regard to the content and type of the measure, Germany has a prerogative on 'how' to fulfil its obligation to protect and preserve the marine environment. A judicial examination in this regard is only permissible if the measure is obviously unsuitable or entirely inadequate to fulfil the objective.

Active Measures: National Legislation

In order to assess whether the obligation to take active measures to protect and preserve the marine environment is narrowed down to the adoption of a general, legally binding law to this end, it needs to be assessed, if the other measure, the adoption of single administrative acts, is obviously unsuitable or entirely inadequate to fulfil the obligation to protect and preserve the marine environment.

The content of the measure will be evaluated using an example of an activity in the sea, namely bottom trawling in AUNJ. If bottom trawling was an activity that violates the obligation to protect and preserve the marine environment of States, the State is obliged to adopt active measures to regulate this activity because its prerogative concerning the 'if' is reduces to zero. However, it has a prerogative on 'how' to regulate the activity, either by adopting a general legally binding law or by adopting a single administrative act.

Single administrative acts can only be adopted for individual addressees in individual cases. They become effective upon their release (§ 43 VwVfG). In the

[36] BVerfG, Beschluss vom 27. 1. 2011 – 1 BvR 3222/09, para. 40.

[37] BVerfG, Beschluss vom 27. 1. 2011 – 1 BvR 3222/09, para. 40; BVerfG, Beschluss vom 3. 4. 2001 – 1 BvL 32/97, para. 40; BVerfG, Beschluss vom 26. März 2007 – 1 BvR 2228/02, mn. 39.

case of bottom trawling, they could only be released if a vessel conducts this activity and only become effective upon their release. Because vessels may still conduct bottom trawling until the single administrative act has been released and single administrative acts can only regulate individual cases, they are objectively unsuitable to effectively realize the objective to protect and preserve the marine environment from bottom trawling. General and legally binding norms, on the contrary, can prohibit bottom trawling initially so that vessels are not allowed to conduct this activity in the first place.

Furthermore, the adoption of a general, legally binding law to this end would also alleviate the enforcement of the prohibition of bottom trawling immensely. One of the major impediments to the effective protection and preservation of the marine environment is its enforcement. Fishing regulations, for instance, are extremely hard to enforce on the large area that makes up the High Sea. Not only is the area so vast that effective control is factually impossible, but surveys have also shown that vessels found ways to effectively conduct illegal fishing on the High Seas without being discovered by, i.e., switching off their tracking systems and fishing at night, which makes it impossible to enforce fishing regulations effectively.[38] Because the adoption of a general, legally binding law would prohibit bottom trawling initially, even the carriage of bottom trawling gear could be prohibited. This would allow better enforcement of this regulation so that no vessel which carries bottom trawling gear may even set sail.

The PCA, in its *South China Sea Arbitration,* clarifies that the obligations set forth in Art. 192 UNCLOS, applies 'not only in relation to activities directly taken by States and their organs but also in relation to ensuring activities within their jurisdiction and control do not harm the marine environment.'[39] The only possibility to regulate activities in a general way, which applies to all cases and States, is the adoption of legally binding norms. Germany, therefore, is obliged to adopt legally binding norms to comply with its obligation to protect and preserve the marine environment.

The assessment prerogative of the legislature to choose the active measure to protect and preserve the marine environment, thus, is narrowed down to the adoption of a general and legally binding law to this end in lieu of single administrative acts. In German national law, therefore, the suitable 'active measure' of the State to comply with the obligation to protect and preserve the marine environment is the adoption of a general, legally binding law.

[38] https://geographical.co.uk/nature/oceans/item/4109-going-dark-fishing-vessels-are-switching-off-their-tracking-systems-to-avoid-detection.

[39] PCA, *South China Sea Arbitration*, Philippines v. China (Award), p. 375, para. 944.

6.3.3.4 Establishment of MPAs as Active Measures in German Law

This investigation has demonstrated that under the obligation to protect and preserve the marine environment, States are obliged to take active measures to protect and preserve the marine environment. In Germany, the assessment prerogative of the State to choose which measure it adopts to this end is narrowed down to the adoption of general, legally binding norms. Because MPAs are defined as specific geographic marine areas designated by legislation for a protection and preservation purpose, legally bindings regulations for the protection and preservation of the marine environment are MPAs if they apply to specific terrains. In the UNCLOS, jurisdiction is primarily distributed spatially according to the zones of the sea (*ratione loci*). The adoption of spatial protection and preservation legislation for those terrains, as per their definition, constitutes the establishment of MPAs. Exceptions exist for flag State jurisdiction under Art. 92 (1), 94 UNCLOS.[40] Concludingly, Germany is obliged to adopt legislation to protect and preserve the marine environment. If the legislation applies to a specific terrain, it designates an MPA as per its established definition.

6.3.4 The Establishment of MPAs as Measures in EU Law

The EU is an international organisation with jurisdictional competence, as its Member States designated single sovereign rights to the EU (for Germany Art. 23 (1) (2nd sentence) German Basic Law). Accordingly, the ECJ held in its *Costa v ENEL judgement* that '[b]y contrast with ordinary international treaties, the EEC Treaty has created its own legal system which, on the entry into force of the Treaty, became an integral part of the legal systems of the Member States and which their courts are bound to apply.'[41] The EU is therefore competent to adopt legal acts that are binding for its Member States. The EU signed the UNCLOS on 7 December 1984 and ratified it on 1 April 1998.[42] It is therefore obliged to adopt active measures to protect and preserve the marine environment.

It needs to be assessed if the obligation to protect and preserve the marine environment obliges the EU to adopt MPAs. The assessment structure corresponds to that of the national system and investigates three questions: what are active measures of the EU? Do active measures to protect and preserve the marine environment by the EU entail the adoption of legislation? Does the obligation to adopt legislation to protect and preserve the marine environment oblige the EU to establish MPAs?

---

[40] Tanaka (2019), p. 189; see: The Obligation of Flag State.

[41] ECJ, *Flamino Costa v ENEL* (1946), Case 6/64, European Court Reports, 585, 593.

[42] https://treaties.un.org/pages/ViewDetailsIII.aspx?src=TREATY&mtdsg_no=XXI-6&chapter=21&Temp=mtdsg3&clang=_en.

6.3.4.1 Active Measures in EU Law

The legal administrative instruments of the EU are codified in Art. 288 TFEU and comprise the adoption of regulations, directives, decisions, recommendations and opinions. Regulations have a general character, are binding in their entirety and apply *erga omnes* in all Member States. They are therefore comparable to national laws. Directives are only binding as to the result to be achieved and for the Member States addressed; they aim to harmonise the national legislation and must be implemented in national law by the Member State. A decision is binding in its entirety, either generally when addressed to all Member States or if specified, only for the addressees, while recommendations have no binding force. Regulations and directives are adopted informal legislative procedures and are legislative acts under Art. 289 TFEU.[43] Decisions are legislative acts when adopted jointly by the European Parliament and the Council under the ordinary legislative procedure, or the European Parliament with the participation of the Council or the Council with the participation of the European Parliament under the special legislative procedure. Otherwise, they are non-legislative acts.[44] Concludingly, only recommendations and directives (and decisions, if the requirements are met) are adopted informal legislative procedures and are legislative acts.

6.3.4.2 Active Measure Specified on Adoption of European Legislation

Decisions that are only binding upon their addressee are not suitable to effectively comply with this obligation. The obligation to protect and preserve the marine environment must be complied with by adopting abstract, legally binding laws that regulate a scenario for many cases and persons.[45] Suitable acts to comply with the obligation to adopt active measures for protecting and preserving the marine environment under EU law, thus, are the adoption of regulations and directives.

6.3.4.3 Establishment of MPAs as Active Measures in EU Law

Recommendations and directives are legislative acts of the EU, Art. 288, 289 TFEU and meet the criteria of 'designated by legislation' of the definition of MPAs. If the legislation applies to a defined geographic marine area, a legislative act of the EU for the protection and preservation of the marine environment meets the definition of MPAs. Because the jurisdiction in the UNCLOS is generally distributed spatially, legislation generally applies to certain areas and therefore meets this criterion.

[43] https://eur-lex.europa.eu/legal-content/EN/TXT/?uri=LEGISSUM:l14522; https://eur-lex.europa.eu/legal-content/EN/TXT/?uri=LEGISSUM:l14527.

[44] https://eur-lex.europa.eu/legal-content/EN/TXT/?uri=LEGISSUM:ai0036.

[45] See: Active Measure specified on Adoption of National Legislation.

Exceptions exist for flag State jurisdiction under Art. 92 (1), 94 UNCLOS.[46] If a regulation or directive for protecting and preserving the marine environment applies to a specific terrain, it designates an MPA as per its established definition.

6.3.5 *The Establishment of MPAs as Measures in Public International Law*

Lastly, the obligation of States to establish MPAs in public international law needs to be investigated. To anticipate the result, it will be demonstrated that international treaties are legislation in public international law; the obligation to protect and preserve the marine environment requires the adoption of international treaties as active measures to protect and preserve the marine environment by States; this leads to the conclusion that the obligation to protect and preserve the marine environment provides for the obligation to establish MPAs in international law.

6.3.5.1 Legislation as Active Measures in Public International Law

The previous investigation has shown that States are obliged to adopt legislation to protect and preserve the marine environment in national and EU law. In public international law, the forms of acts by States are not codified. Other than in national and EU law, there is generally no mandated authority that is competent to adopt legislation (except for the Security Council).[47]

The pursuit of increasing global governance, such as through concepts of Ocean Governance, has raised the idea of a Global Administrative Law.[48] Although some attempts of Ocean Governance may be understood as administration, other than national or European administrative law, Ocean Governance does not provide binding rules and regulations. It only connotes a process to structure all treaties, regulations, policies, institutions and political measures concerning the ocean rather than a government.[49] Because of the lack of a competent authority to adopt legally binding laws in a formal process in public international law, 'international legislation' is reduced to the product of legally binding laws regardless of the procedure.[50] Legally binding laws in international law are rules of customary international law and international treaties. Whereas rules of customary international law result from a consistent States' practice that is accepted as law over time, the adoption of treaties is the expression of deliberate, active measures. The closest process to resemble

[46] See: The Obligation of Flag State.

[47] Dahm et al. (2002), p. 512; see: Security Council.

[48] Kingsbury et al. (2005), p. 2.

[49] See: Ocean Governance.

[50] See: Designated by Legislation.

legislation on an international level is, therefore, the adoption of treaties.[51] Active measures by States in public international law are thus the adoption of legally binding treaties (and the emergence of rules of customary international law).[52]

6.3.5.2 Legislation as Active Measure to Protect and Preserve the Marine Environment

In German national law, the legislature has an assessment prerogative as to the 'if' and 'how' of adopting measures. Due to the assessment prerogative, the decisions of the legislature are only open to a restricted judicial review concerning evident violations, that is, if the measure is objectively unsuitable or entirely inadequate to achieve a legitimate objective.[53]

In public international law, there is no mandated authority to adopt laws. Sources of laws are treaties, rules of customary international law and general principles (Art. 38 (1) ICJ Statute). As a consequence of the principle of the sovereign equality of States under Art. 2 Nr. 1 UN-Charter, States are free to adopt or not to adopt a treaty and freely determine its content, subject to the limitations through peremptory norms of international law under Art. 53 VCLT.[54] States, therefore, also have a prerogative in assessing if and how to implement their obligation to protect and preserve the marine environment in international law.

Prerogative Concerning If to Adopt Active Measures

Because of their sovereign equality, States are free to adopt a treaty and to determine its content. However, if States did enter a treaty obligation to adopt active measures, their assessment prerogative regarding if it adopts measures is reduced to zero. The fundamental precept of *pacta sunt servanda* is also applicable in international law and is expressly stated in Art. 300 UNCLOS.[55] Under Art. 192 UNCLOS the State parties of the UNCLOS have obliged themselves to protect and preserve the marine environment. This obligation entails the obligation to adopt active measures. This obligation entails the obligation to adopt active measures. No State persistently objected to the universally accepted obligation under Art. 192 UNCLOS. Because of their universal consent to the obligation to protect and preserve the marine environment, States must accept its binding effect; the prerogative if a State adopts an active measure to comply with this obligation is reduced to zero. States must

[51] Brunée, para. 1.

[52] Brunée, para. 1.

[53] BVerfG, Beschluss vom 27. 1. 2011 – 1 BvR 3222/09, para. 40.

[54] Caflish (1992), p. 78; Wiegandt (2001), p. 72.

[55] Oude Elferink (2012), p. 214.

adopt active measures to protect and preserve the marine environment in national and international law.

Prerogative Concerning How to Adopt Active Measures

Concerning the choice of the measure, the assessment prerogative in national law limits a judicial review to the objective unsuitability or complete inadequacy of the measure. The investigation has shown that the only suitable measure to comply with the obligation to protect and preserve the marine environment under the UNCLOS is the adoption of abstract and general legislation, which binds an open-ended range of addresses over a period of time. As to the content of the obligation to protect and preserve the marine environment, the PCA States that it 'is informed by the other provisions of Part XII and other applicable rules of international law.'[56] The subsequent comprehensive examination of the UNCLOS regulations will demonstrate that the UNCLOS explicitly requires adopting national and international legislation to comply with the obligation to protect and preserve the marine environment.

Other Measures Than Legislation Stipulated in the UNCLOS

Not all measures stipulated in the UNCLOS are legislative acts. The UNCLOS also stipulates technical measures which serve to promote legislative measures, as well as implementation measures to enforce them. However, neither of these measures is suitable to fulfil the obligation to protect and preserve the marine environment on its own but either serve to promote or enforce the underlying legislative measure.

Promotion Measures Under Art. 269, 268 UNCLOS

Art. 269, 268 UNCLOS stipulate measures to promote basic objectives for the development and transfer of marine technology. Measures in the sense of Art. 269, 268 UNCLOS are technical measures but do not refer to legislative measures. It needs to be assessed if the measures as stipulated in Art. 269 UNCLOS are suitable to fulfil the obligation to protect and preserve the marine environment.

Art. 269 UNCLOS incomprehensively lists examples of measures to promote the development and transfer of marine technology, such as establishing programs for technical cooperation under Art. 269 (a) UNCLOS, the promotion of favourable conditions for the conclusion of agreements, contracts and other similar arrangements under Art. 269 (b) UNCLOS, the holding of conferences, seminars and symposia on scientific and technological subjects under Art. 269 (c) UNCLOS, the promotion of exchange of scientists and technical experts under Art. 269 (d) UNCLOS and the undertaking of projects to promote joint ventures under

[56] PCA, *South China Sea Arbitration*, Philippines v. China (Award), p. 373, para. 941.

Art. 269 (e) UNCLOS. While measures such as the promotion of favourable conditions for the conclusion of agreements, holding conferences, seminars and symposia on scientific and technological subjects or the promotion of exchange of scientists and technical experts favour the design, implementation and enforceability of the obligation to protect and preserve the marine environment, they are not capable of protecting and preserving the marine environment as such. The promotion measures under Art. 269, 268 UNCLOS can only assist and inform the necessary laws and regulations but may not replace their adoption.

MPAs, for example, need to be carefully designed in order to achieve their protection objective. MPAs can take many forms. Areas for the conservation of fish, for instance, may vary from the regulation of fishing of single species to entire 'no take' to 'no trawl' zones. Careful design of the content and enforcement are necessary for each individual MPA. Furthermore, a large number of stakeholders are potentially involved in the establishment of MPAs in certain regions, which necessitates a functioning participative design process. Challenges in operation, i.e., large-scale MPAs that comprise ecosystems spread across several jurisdictional zones, must be coordinated through cooperation. Furthermore, the restriction of, i.e., fishing in one area may lead to increased pressure on the fish stock in other areas. Evidence suggests that well-designed MPAs can produce payoffs by providing feeding and spawning grounds for marine life, protecting species and marine flora and creating socio-economic benefits for local communities.[57] Therefore, the benefits and conservation achievements are dependent on well-designed MPAs, which are achieved through 'other measures' such as technology sharing, implementation and enforcement under Art. 269, 268 UNCLOS.

These technical and promotion measures are coupled to the underlying legislative measures but cannot fulfil the obligation to protect and preserve the marine environment themselves. Without an underlying framework of rules and regulations for the protection and preservation of the marine environment, which obligates States to adopt measures for the protection and preservation of the marine environment, such as through MPAs, development and transfer of knowledge measures lack in substance. Although they regulate essential sharing of information, which is crucial, i.e., to design effective MPAs, they require the underlying obligation to establish MPAs. Technical and promotion measures under Art. 269, 268 UNCLOS, therefore, can accompany the adoption of the relevant legislation to protect and preserve the marine environment but are not active measures of States in the sense of the obligation to protect and preserve the marine environment.

Enforcement Measures Under Art. 213 ff. UNCLOS

Under Art. 213 ff. UNCLOS States shall enforce the laws and regulations adopted under Section 5, Part XII UNCLOS to prevent, reduce and control pollution of the marine environment. According to Art. 213 UNCLOS, States shall adopt laws,

[57] UNGA A/59/298, pp. 31 f., para. 129.

regulations and *other measures* necessary to implement applicable international rules and standards to this end. This wording suggests that the adoption of laws and regulations are only a subcategory of measures in the sense of the UNCLOS beside other measures.[58]

The enforcement measures in Section 6, Part XII UNCLOS give practical effect to the general obligation under Art. 192 ff. UNCLOS and are the corollary to the prescriptive jurisdictional measures for the prevention, control and reduction of pollution of the marine environment under Section 5, Part XII UNCLOS.[59] They build upon the underlying obligation of States to adopt rules and regulations for the prevention, reduction and control of marine pollution under Art. 207 ff. UNCLOS. They, therefore, cannot exist on their own but are coupled to the respective prescriptive legislative measure in Section 5, Part XII UNCLOS. Moreover, as the following assessment will show, Section 5, Part XII UNCLOS explicitly envisages the adoption of legislation as the suitable and adequate measure to fulfil their obligation to protect and preserve the marine environment from pollution.

Legislation as Measure Under the UNCLOS

The further interpretation of the UNCLOS will show that the adoption of legislation is an adequate measure to comply with the obligation to protect and preserve the marine environment in the law of the sea.

Adoption of Rules and Regulations in Part XII UNCLOS

Especially Part XII UNCLOS recurrently stipulates the adoption of legislation as the suitable measure of States to comply with their obligation to protect and preserve the marine environment.

Obligation to Cooperate Under Art. 197 UNCLOS

By virtue of Art. 197 UNCLOS States shall cooperate on a global or regional basis, directly or through competent international organisations, in formulating and elaborating international rules, standards and recommended practices and procedures consistent with the UNCLOS for the protection and preservation of the marine environment. The customary obligation of States under Art. 197 UNCLOS interludes Section 2, Part XII UNCLOS and is accepted as the second fundamental obligation under Part XII UNCLOS.[60] Under the UNCLOS, States are expressly

[58] Art. 213 UNCLOS.

[59] Proelss (2017), Art. 213, mn. 1.

[60] Preamble of the OSPAR Convention; Proelss (2017), Art. 197, mn. 1 and 10, f.; Kojima (2015), p. 173; PCA, *South China Sea Arbitration*, Philippines v. China (Award), pp. 376 f., para. 945; ITLOS, *MOX Plant*, Ireland v. United Kingdom, Provisional Measures (3 December 2001), ITLOS Reports 2001, pp. 95, 110, para. 82; McConnell and Gold (1991), p. 91.

obliged to cooperate in formulating and elaborate international rules and standards to fulfil their obligation to protect and preserve the marine environment, which particularly reiterates the obligation of the States to adopt international legislation under Art. 192 UNCLOS.[61] The obligation to cooperate is, furthermore, specifically expressed for specific zones of the sea and concerning specific issues, such as the duty of States to adopt national laws and cooperate for the conservation and management of living resources in the areas of the High Seas under Art. 118 UNCLOS, or to cooperate to ensure through proper conservation and management measures that the maintenance of the living resources in the EEZ is not endangered by over-exploitation pursuant to Art. 61 (2) UNCLOS. Further specific cooperation obligations exist for the conservation of specific fish stock and species under Art. 63 (1), (Art. 116 (b) UNCLOS in conjunction with) 63 (2), 64, 65, 66 (4), (5), 67 (3) UNCLOS and the protection, reduction and control of the pollution of the marine environment from various sources under Art. 207 (4), 208 (5), 210 (4), Art. 211 (1) and 212 (3) UNCLOS. Because the cooperation of States is furthermore expression of the States to perform their treaty obligations in good faith under the customary provision of Art. 26 VCLT, the disobedience of this regulation is contrary to the specific regulations of the UNCLOS as well as the general principle of good faith.[62]

Measures Under Art. 194 (5) UNCLOS

Under Art. 194 (5) UNCLOS, measures taken in accordance with Part XII UNCLOS shall include those necessary to protect and preserve rare or fragile ecosystems as well as the habitat of depleted, threatened or endangered species and other forms of marine life. Art. 194 (5) UNCLOS is acknowledged as a legal basis for the establishment of MPAs under the UNCLOS in the extant literature as well as in the consistent jurisprudence.[63] The interpretation that 'measure' in the sense of Art. 194 (5) UNCLOS means legislative act to designate MPAs seems to be that evident that the PCA in its *Chagos Marine Protected Area Arbitration* simply states, that 'the MPA is such a measure.'[64]

[61] ITLOS, *Land Reclamation in and around the Straits of Johor* (Malaysia v. Singapore), Provisional Measures, Order of 8 October 2003, ITLOS Reports 2003, pp. 10, 25, para. 92; ITLOS, *MOX Plant*, Ireland v. United Kingdom, Provisional Measures (3. December 2001), ITLOS Reports 2001, pp. 95, 110, para. 82; Roach (2014), pp. 240 and 250.

[62] ICJ, *Pulp Mills on the River Uruguay* (Argentina v. Uruguay), Judgment, ICJ Reports 2010, pp. 14, 67, para. 145; Tanaka (2019), p. 288.

[63] PCA, *Chagos Marine Protected Area Arbitration*, Mauritius v. UK (Award) 2015, p. 211, para. 538 and pp. 128 f., para. 320; Proelss (2017), Art. 194, mn. 35; Oude Elferink (2018), p. 445.

[64] PCA, *Chagos Marine Protected Area Arbitration*, Mauritius v. UK (Award) 2015, p. 211, para. 538.

Measures Under Art. 194 (1)-(3) UNCLOS

Under Art. 194 (1) and (2) UNCLOS, States shall take all measures consistent with the UNCLOS that are necessary to prevent, reduce and control pollution of the marine environment, harmonise their policies to this end and ensure that activities in AUNJ do not cause pollution to another State and does not spread to ABNJ. Art. 194 (3) UNCLOS lists examples of those measures, which, *inter alia,* include those designed to minimize to the fullest possible extent the release of toxic, harmful or noxious substances from land-based sources, from or through the atmosphere or by dumping, pollution from vessels, etc. Art. 194 (3) UNCLOS stipulates the material content of the measures with regard to the source of pollution and the means of reducing and preventing it.[65] It does not stipulate the legal nature of 'measures' itself.

The measures under Art. 194 UNCLOS apply on three levels. The first level is the stipulation of the measures in Art. 194 UNCLOS, the second level concerns the implementation of those measures as more specifically stipulated under Section 5, Part XII UNCLOS and their enforcement in Section 6, Part XII UNCLOS on the third level.[66] The measures under Art. 194 (1)-(3) UNCLOS therefore necessarily refer to prescriptive legislation measures, as only those can be implemented in the specific manner under Art. 208 ff. UNCLOS and enforced under Art. 213 ff. UNCLOS. Art. 194 (1)-(3) UNCLOS has to be read in conjunction with Section 5, Part XII UNCLOS, which provides that measures for the prevention, control and reduction of pollution of the marine environment is the adoption of laws, regulations and international treaties to this end.

Obligation to Adopt Measure to Prevent, Reduce and Control Pollution

The structure of the regulations of Section 5, Part XII UNCLOS shows that the adoption of national laws and regulations are measures in the sense of the UNCLOS: by virtue of Art. 207 (1) UNCLOS States shall adopt national laws and regulations to prevent, reduce and control the pollution of the marine environment from land-based sources. According to Art. 207 (2) UNCLOS, States shall moreover take 'other measures' that may be necessary to prevent, reduce and control such pollution. This structure is repeated in the following provisions concerning pollution from seabed activities subject to national jurisdiction in Art. 208 (1), (2) UNCLOS, pollution from dumping in Art. 210 (1), (2) UNCLOS and pollution from or through the atmosphere in Art. 212 (1), (2) UNCLOS. Furthermore, States, acting through the competent international organisations or diplomatic conferences, shall endeavour to establish global and regional rules, standards and recommended practices and procedures to prevent, reduce and control pollution of the marine environment from the respective source under Art. 207 (4), 208 (5), Art. 209 (1), 210 (4), 211 (1), (6),

[65] Proelss (2017), Art. 194, mn. 1.

[66] Proelss (2017), Art. 194, mn. 1.

212 (3) UNCLOS. Under Art. 234 UNCLOS, coastal States have the right to adopt and enforce non-discriminatory laws and regulations for the prevention, reduction and control of marine pollution from vessels in ice-covered areas within the limits of the EEZ.

Section 5 and Section 8 of Part XII UNCLOS are specific regulations for protecting and preserving the marine environment from pollution. Without any exception, all these regulations require States to adopt laws and regulations to fulfil their obligation to protect and preserve the marine environment from various sources of pollution on a national level and endeavour to adopt international treaties to this end on an international level. This analysis proves that the parties of the UNCLOS deliberately stipulated the adoption of national laws and regulations and international treaties as the suitable active measure to protect and preserve the marine environment. The adoption of legislation thus is the suitable measure to protect and preserve the marine environment within the understanding of the parties to the UNCLOS.

Dissenting Opinion to the Chagos Marine Protected Areas Arbitration

In their dissenting and concurring opinion to the *Chagos Marine Protected Area Arbitration* judges James Kateka and Rüdiger Wolfrum considered whether the PCA had jurisdiction with respect to an MPA established by the UK under Art. 297 (1) (c), 56 (1) (b) (iii) UNCLOS. The judges stated that 'Part XII of the Convention does not provide a general competence for coastal States to issue rules on the protection of the marine environment.'[67]

The dissenting and concurring opinion of judges Kateka and Wolfrum has been criticised in the literature. Czybulka argues that '[i]t seems that the dissenting judges in the recent Chagos Case did not recognise fully the reach of Art. 194 (5) as it has been developed in the Award itself and that they overlooked Art. 56 (1) (b) (iii), when they argued that 'Part XII of the Convention does not provide a general competence for coastal States to issue rules on the protection of the marine environment'.'[68] Indeed, in the award itself, the PCA unanimously established that Art. 194 UNCLOS was 'not limited to measures aimed strictly at controlling pollution and extends to measures focused primarily on conservation and preservation of ecosystems.'[69] Following this argumentation, in the view of the PCA, Art. 194 (1) UNCLOS must be read in a way that stipulates that States shall take, individually or jointly as appropriate, all measures consistent with the UNCLOS that are necessary for the conservation and preservation of marine ecosystems. The statement of judges Kateka and Wolfrum is, therefore, inconsistent with the findings

[67] PCA, *Chagos Marine Protected Area Arbitration*, Mauritius v. UK (2015), Dissenting and Concurring Opinion of Judges Kateka and Wolfrum, p. 14, para. 54.

[68] Proelss (2017), Art. 194, mn. 35.

[69] Proelss (2017), Art. 194, mn. 35; *PCA, Chagos Marine Protected Area Arbitration*, Mauritius v. UK (Award) 2015, p. 211, para. 538 and pp. 128 f., para. 320.

in the award itself, as, on the one hand, they approve the application of Art. 194 UNCLOS to all measures necessary for the conservation and preservation of marine ecosystems but on the other hand deny that Part XII UNCLOS provides a general competence of the coastal States to issue rules for the protection of the marine environment. The statement in the dissenting opinion has been made with respect to the jurisdiction of the PCA under Art. 297 (1) (c) UNCLOS and does not concern the merits of the case. As the statement lacks any further reasoning as to why Part XII UNCLOS does not provide for the States' competence to issue rules on the protection of the marine environment, it, therefore, cannot be further evaluated and must be dismissed in agreement with Czybulka.

Adoption of Rules and Regulations as Measures in Part XI UNCLOS

The view that the adoption of legislation is the suitable measure to comply with the obligation to protect and preserve the marine environment is reiterated outside the specific regulations of Part XII UNCLOS. Art. 145 (1st sentence) UNCLOS stipulates that necessary measures shall be adopted with respect to activities in the Area to ensure effective protection for the marine environment from harmful effects which may arise from such activities. According to Art 145 (2nd sentence) UNCLOS, the ISA shall adopt rules, regulations and procedures to this end. This shows that the parties to the UNCLOS understand the adoption of rules, regulations and procedures to be 'necessary measures' to protect the marine environment from harmful effects from activities in the Area under Art. 145 UNCLOS. This is repeated in Art. 146 UNCLOS, according to which necessary measures to protect human life shall be taken and that the ISA shall adopt rules, regulations and procedures to this end.

Adoption of Rules and Regulations as Measures in Part XIII UNCLOS

The heading of Art. 255 UNCLOS stipulates *measures* to facilitate marine scientific research and to assist research vessels. The text of the regulation codifies that States shall endeavour to adopt reasonable rules, regulations and procedures to promote and facilitate marine scientific research conducted in accordance with the UNCLOS. Through this regulation, the UNCLOS parties show that they understand the adoption of rules and regulations as measures under the UNCLOS.

Historical Interpretation of Legislation Under the UNCLOS

The Drafting Committee of the UNCLOS has discussed the adoption of legislative measures. The Report of the Chairman of the Drafting Committee lists examples of legislative measures, including but not limited to Art. 21 (1), 194 (1), (2), 196 or 207 (1), (2) UNCLOS.[70] The Drafting Committee recommended that the wording 'legislative measures' should be replaced by 'laws and regulations', whereases it

[70] UN A/CONF.62/L.57/REV.1, pp. 116 f.

recommended that it was not necessary to qualify laws and regulations with the adjective 'national'.[71] Furthermore, while the word 'adopt' should be used in the context of 'laws and regulations', the word 'take' should be used in connection with measures, without, however, defining the content of measures.[72]

The evaluation of the list leads to two conclusions: Firstly, Art. 192 UNCLOS is not listed under the examples of provisions of 'legislative measures'. This does not contradict, however, that Art. 192 UNCLOS does entail the obligation to adopt national laws and regulations and international treaties to this end. This is because, firstly, the list of the Draft Committee of provisions that refer to the adoption of laws and regulations and the taking of measures is not conclusive. Further examples of the UNCLOS, which entail measures to be taken by the States that are not listed in the exemplary list, include but are not limited to Art. 61 (2)-(4), 62 (4), 63 (1), (2), 66 (2), 145, 146, 153 (4), (5), 194 (3)-(5), 195, 236, 255, 269 UNCLOS. Secondly, the wording of Art. 192 UNCLOS does not expressly contain the terms 'laws and regulations' or 'measures'. Naturally, it is therefore not included in the list concerning the wording of the UNCLOS with regard to laws, regulations and measures.

Secondly, the Report of the Draft Committee indicates that 'to take active measures' is the generic term for the 'adoption of national laws and regulations' as well as international treaties. This is because the report lists measures as examples of legislative acts. For the cooperation of States in the conservation and management of living resources on the High Sea, for instance, the Draft Committee lists Art. 118 (2nd sentence) UNCLOS as a legislative measure, which states that States 'shall enter into negotiations with a view to taking the measures necessary for the conservation of the living resources concerned.' The regulation of Art. 118 UNCLOS applies to the High Sea, which can only be governed by international law. The 'measure necessary for the conservation of living resources' under Art. 118 (2nd sentence) UNCLOS, which is an example of legislative measures according to the Report of the Draft Committee, can only connote to international legislation because no State may unilaterally adopt laws and regulations for any part of the High Sea (Art. 89 UNCLOS).

Concludingly, the list of 'legislative measure' of the Draft Committee is not an exclusive list of all legislative measures in the UNCLOS but provides examples of provisions with the aim of achieving linguistic uniformity throughout the UNCLOS. Furthermore, the clarification of the difference of 'laws and regulations', which refer only to 'national' laws and regulations on the one hand and 'measures' on the other hand, indicates that measure is the generic term of legislation that includes national laws and regulations and international treaties.

[71] UN A/CONF.62/L.57/REV.1, p. 117.

[72] UN A/CONF.62/L.57/REV.1, p. 117.

Soft Law as Measures

It is pointed out that measures under Art. 194 UNCLOS comprise the normative as well as executive implementations of the obligation to protect and preserve the marine environment for the implementation of the UNCLOS, which can also be soft law measures, such as recommendations and non-binding decisions.[73] Soft law measures are not eligible to comply with the obligation to protect and preserve the marine environment. On the Conference of Parties of the CBD in Japan 2010, for instance, 193 States have agreed to designate 10 per cent of the oceans as MPAs by 2020.[74] So far, only 7.65 per cent of the oceans and only 1.18 per cent of the High Seas are protected.[75] This shows that voluntary pledges are insufficient to comply with the obligation to protect and preserve the marine environment. Therefore, the only effective measure to fulfil the obligation to protect and preserve the marine environment by the States is the adoption of respective laws, regulations and international treaties.

Adoption of Rules and Regulations as Measures in the Jurisprudence

Lastly, the international jurisprudence clearly states that the UNCLOS imposes a duty on the States to adopt rules and regulations to protect and preserve the marine environment. In the *South China Sea Arbitration*, the PCA had to evaluate whether China's harvesting of endangered species breached its obligation under Art. 192, 194 (5) UNCLOS. The PCA expressly stated that 'where a State is aware that vessels flying its flag are engaged in the harvest of species recognized internationally as being threatened with extinction or are inflicting significant damage on rare or fragile ecosystems or the habitat of depleted, threatened or endangered species, its obligations under the Convention include a duty to adopt rules and measures to prevent such acts and to maintain a level of vigilance in enforcing those rules and measures.'[76] Thus, the obligation to protect and preserve the marine environment specifically entails the obligation to adopt rules and regulations to this end.

Conclusion: Obligation to Adopt Legislation

A comprehensive synthesis of all regulations of the UNCLOS proved that the adoption of national laws and regulations, as well as international treaties, are 'measures' in the sense of the UNCLOS. While not all 'measures' in the UNCLOS are the adoption of laws, regulations and international treaties, the adoption of the

[73] Proelss (2017), Art. 196, mn. 9.

[74] https://www.cbd.int/doc/strategic-plan/targets/T11-quick-guide-en.pdf; Grafton et al. (2011), p. 478.

[75] https://www.protectedplanet.net/en; https://www.protectedplanet.net/en/thematic-areas/marine-protected-areas.

[76] PCA, *South China Sea Arbitration*, Philippines v. China (Award), p. 382, para. 961.

latter are 'measures'. The PCA states in this regard that 'adopting appropriate rules and measures to prohibit a harmful practice is only one component of the due diligence required by States pursuant to the general obligation of Article 192, read in the context of Article 194 (5) and the international law applicable to endangered species.'[77] Those other measures, however, are not eligible to satisfy the obligation to protect and preserve the marine environment and only serve to promote, implement and enforce legislative acts. The duty of States to cooperate to adopt rules and regulations for protecting and preserving the marine environment is accepted as rule of customary international law. This duty is expressed in further, more specific regulations for the protection of the marine environment from pollution in Sections 5, 6 and 8 of Part XII UNCLOS. The relevant jurisprudence clearly States that the suitable means to fulfil the States' obligation to protect and preserve the marine environment is the adoption of administrative measures and the adoption of legislation to this end.[78] Active measures of States can take many forms. However, the only measure to implement a legally binding obligation of States to comply with their obligation to protect and preserve the marine environment is the obligation to adopt legally binding laws and regulations and international treaties to this end.

According to the PCA, the obligation to protect and preserve the marine environment does not only entail the obligation to maintain and improve the marine environment but also to protect it from future damages.[79] Consequently, States are obliged to adopt abstract and general legally binding legislation (rather than single administrative acts that only apply to a specific case and specific State) to regulate an indefinite number of cases for an indefinite number of States. It follows that the suitable measure to comply with the obligation to protect and preserve the marine environment in the understanding of the UNCLOS is the adoption of respective legislation.

6.3.5.3 Establishment of MPAs as Active Measures Under Art. 192 UNCLOS

The matter of adopting MPAs in the High Sea under the obligation of Art. 192 UNCLOS has been discussed in the fifth meeting of the United Nations Open-ended Informal Consultative Process on Oceans and the Law of the Sea. One delegation argued that establishing MPAs in the High Sea would be in keeping with the general obligation under Art. 192 UNCLOS as well as Art. 194 (5) UNCLOS. Several further delegations stated that the international community should consider specific ocean governance options under the existing legal

[77] PCA, *South China Sea Arbitration*, Philippines v. China (Award), p. 383, para. 964.

[78] ITLOS, *SRFC*, Advisory Opinion, ITLOS Reports 2015, pp. 14, 36, para. 119; PCA, *South China Sea Arbitration*, Philippines v. China (Award), p. 382, para. 961.

[79] PCA, *South China Sea Arbitration*, Philippines v. China (Award), p. 373, para. 941; Tanaka (2019), p. 333; Freestone (2009), p. 45.

framework. An international treaty about the establishment of MPAs in ABNJ should be adopted to this end. However, there has been no consensus on this topic.[80]

It has been established that the obligation to protect and preserve the marine environment obliges States to adopt legislation to this end. MPAs are geographically defined marine areas which are designated by legislation for a protection and conservation objective. Therefore, the establishment of MPAs is a suitable measure to fulfil the obligation to protect and preserve the marine environment, if and insofar as the adopted legislation applies to a geographical marine area.[81]

6.3.6 *The Obligation of Flag States*

The obligation to protect and preserve the marine environment, after examination, entails the obligation of States to adopt legislation to protect and preserve the marine environment on a national as well as international level. Ships are a source of various anthropogenic threats to the marine environment, such as pollution or harmful fishing techniques. The flag State's jurisdiction over vessels flying its flag is essential in the effective protection and preservation of the marine environment.

6.3.6.1 Legislative and Enforcement Competence of the Flag State

The jurisdiction in the law of the sea is primarily divided according to ocean spaces (*ratione loci*) with single jurisdictional rights concerning specific matters, such as the jurisdiction of the flag state for vessels flying its flag under Art. 92 (1), 94 UNCLOS.

Under the UNCLOS, all States are obliged to protect and preserve the marine environment in the different zones of the sea. In its *South China Sea Arbitration*, the PCA clarifies that their obligations as set forth in Art. 192, 194 UNCLOS, do not only apply in relation to activities directly taken by States and their organs, 'but also in relation to ensuring activities within their jurisdiction and control do not harm the marine environment.'[82] More specifically, according to the consistent jurisprudence of international courts and tribunals, the flag State is under the obligation to ensure that its fishing vessels are not involved in activities that undermine a flag State's responsibilities under the UNCLOS 'in respect of the conservation of living resources and the obligation to protect and preserve the marine environment.'[83] Pursuant to Art. 192, 193 UNCLOS, the 'flag State is under the "due diligence

[80]UNGA A/59/122, p. 23, para. 88.

[81]Franke (2007), p. 335.

[82]PCA, *South China Sea Arbitration*, Philippines v. China (Award), p. 375, para. 944.

[83]PCA, *South China Sea Arbitration*, Philippines v. China (Award), p. 375, para. 944; ITLOS, *SRFC*, Advisory Opinion, ITLOS Reports 2015, pp. 14, 36 ff., para. 119, 120, 124, 136; ICJ, *Pulp Mills on the River Uruguay* (Argentina v. Uruguay), Judgment, ICJ Reports 2010, pp. 14, 79, 197.

obligation" to take all necessary measures to ensure compliance and to prevent IUU fishing by fishing vessels flying its flag.'[84] This is an obligation of conduct and not of the result.[85] Because of the transzonal scope of Art. 192 UNCLOS, this obligation applies to all zones of the sea.[86] It follows that the flag State can exculpate itself if it has taken all necessary and appropriate measures to meet its due diligence obligation and to ensure that vessels flying its flag do not conduct activities that harm the marine environment.[87]

Summarizing, the obligation under Art. 192 UNCLOS provides for both the adoption of the necessary administrative measures as well as a due diligence obligation to ensure that activities by the States do not harm the marine environment.[88] This is confirmed by the ICJ in its *Pulp Mills on the River Uruguay* Case, in which it established that the obligation to 'preserve the aquatic environment, and in particular to prevent pollution by prescribing appropriate rules and measures [...] is an obligation which entails not only the adoption of appropriate rules and measures, but also a certain level of vigilance in their enforcement and the exercise of administrative control applicable to public and private operators [...].'[89] The obligation to protect and preserve the marine environment, therefore, imposes an obligation on the flag States to adopt appropriate laws and regulations and to ensure that vessels flying their flag adhere to relevant protecting and preservation measures.[90]

6.3.6.2 Enforcement Jurisdiction of the Flag State Under Art. 92, 94 UNCLOS

Under Art. 58, (2), 92 (1), 94 UNCLOS, the flag State has exclusive jurisdiction over vessels flying its flag in the EEZ and the High Sea. The exclusive flag State

---

[84] ITLOS, *SRFC*, Advisory Opinion, ITLOS Reports 2015, pp. 14, 40, para. 129 and pp. 14, 42, para. 136.

[85] PCA, South China Sea Arbitration, Philippines v. China (Award), p. 375, para. 944; ICJ, *Pulp Mills on the River Uruguay* (Argentina v. Uruguay), Judgment, ICJ Reports 2010, pp. 14, 69, para. 197; ITLOS, *SRFC*, Advisory Opinion, ITLOS Reports 2015, pp. 14, 59, para. 180; ITLOS, *Responsibilities and Obligations of States Sponsoring Persons and Entities with Respect to Activities in the Area*, Advisory Opinion, ITLOS Reports 2011, p. 10, p. 41, para. 110.

[86] ITLOS, *SRFC*, Advisory Opinion, ITLOS Reports 2015, pp. 14, 37, para. 120.

[87] ITLOS, *SRFC*, Advisory Opinion, ITLOS Reports 2015, pp. 14, 45, para. 148; Tanaka (2019), p. 312.

[88] PCA, *South China Sea Arbitration*, Philippines v. China (Award), p. 375, para. 944; ITLOS, *SRFC*, Advisory Opinion, ITLOS Reports 2015, pp. 14, 59, para. 180; ITLOS, *Responsibilities and Obligations of States Sponsoring Persons and Entities with Respect to Activities in the Area*, Advisory Opinion, ITLOS Reports 2011, p. 10, p. 41, para. 110.

[89] ICJ, *Pulp Mills on the River Uruguay* (Argentina v. Uruguay), Judgment, ICJ Reports 2010, pp. 14, 79, 197.

[90] PCA, *South China Sea Arbitration*, Philippines v. China (Award), pp. 383 f., para. 964–966; Caddell (2020), p. 264.

jurisdiction is broadly accepted as a rule of customary international law.[91] The exclusive jurisdiction of the flag State in Art. 92 (1), 94 UNCLOS only refers to enforcement jurisdiction and does not exclude the competent State, States or international organisations to adopt prescriptive legislation in the respective zones of the sea. The allocation of the exclusive enforcement jurisdiction to the flag State under Art. 92 (1), 94 UNCLOS ensures the freedom of navigation but does not exempt the vessels from conducting with the rules and regulations applicable in the respective zone of the sea.[92] In the EEZ, the coastal State, however, may take such measures, including boarding, inspection, arrest and judicial proceedings, as may be necessary to ensure compliance with the laws and regulations giving effect to its sovereign rights and jurisdiction in the EEZ under Art. 73 (1) UNCLOS.[93]

6.3.6.3 Flag State Jurisdiction and MPAs

The flag State is obliged to adopt legislation for the protection and preservation of the marine environment with regard to vessels flying its flag. Because of the lack of a spatial element, such laws and regulations for the protection and preservation of the marine environment do not meet the definition of MPAs. The obligation to protect and preserve the marine environment, thus, does not only entail the obligation of States to establish MPAs in a specific terrain but also to adopt legislation that applies to vessels flying their flags.

6.3.6.4 Conclusion: Flag State Jurisdiction

One of the major issues concerning the effectiveness of MPAs is the enforcement of preservation regulations in the wide High Sea due to the difficulty of monitoring the vast area of the High Sea. Illegal and unreported fishing is estimated to make up 15 per cent of the global fish catch, representing EUR 24 billion annually.[94] The flag State jurisdiction is a vital tool to ensure compliance with protection and preservation regulations. Would it be possible, for instance, to achieve a global ban on 'bottom otter trawling', the flag States could implement this prohibition by ensuring that none of their vessels carry respective bottom trawl equipment. Difficulties with monitoring activities and enforcing regulations on the vast High Seas would be alleviated by ensuring that vessels do not carry the respective gear in the first place. Another harm to the marine environment by fishing is the dumping of fishing gear. Dumped fishing gear makes up the most significant part of plastic pollution in the

[91] Proelss (2017), Art. 92, mn. 4.

[92] Proelss (2017), Art. 92, mn. 1 and 8.

[93] Proelss (2017), Art. 92, mn. 3.

[94] https://www.oecd.org/greengrowth/GGSD_2017_Issue%20Paper_New%20technologies%20in%20Fisheries_WEB.pdf, p. 5.

sea.[95] Flag State jurisdiction over their ships could require the States to adopt laws and regulations that oblige vessels to declare the length and number of their fishing nets before and after conducting fishing. Penalties can apply for negative discrepancies of fishing gear before and after, giving fishermen an incentive not to dump gear in the sea.

Under the *erga omnes* obligation to protect and preserve the marine environment, the flag State is obliged to adopt and enforce laws and regulations to protect and preserve the marine environment that applies to vessels flying its flag and ensure their conduct. As the obligation to protect and preserve the marine environment in this regard does not refer to geographically defined marine areas, the obligation to protect and preserve the marine environment does not only entail the obligation to establish MPAs but also to adopt laws and regulations to ensure that vessels flying their flag do not harm the marine environment.

6.3.7 Conclusion: Obligation of States to Establish MPAs

States have the freedom to conclude or not to conclude and to freely determine the content of a treaty as a consequence of Art. 2 Nr. 1 UN-Charter. States have limited their freedom by accepting the *erga omnes* obligation to protect and preserve the marine environment and to adopt active measures for this purpose. Their prerogative concerning if they adopt measures to protect and preserve the marine environment is thus reduced to zero. States are obliged to do so. Concerning their prerogative on how to protect and preserve the marine environment, the assessment has demonstrated that the only active measure capable of fulfilling the purpose of Art. 192 UNCLOS is the adoption of respective legislation. Furthermore, under the customary obligation of Art. 197 UNCLOS States are expressly obliged to cooperate on a global and regional basis directly or through competent international organisations, in formulating and elaborating international rules, standards, recommended practices and procedures consistent with the UNCLOS for the protection and preservation of the marine environment. Legislation is the adoption of treaties on an international level and laws and regulations on a national level. Legislation for the protection and preservation of the marine environment in specific marine terrains constitutes the establishment of MPAs. Furthermore, States are obliged to adopt laws and regulations to protect and preserve the marine environment from vessels flying their flag. Under the peremptory norm of Art. 192 UNCLOS, all States are obliged to establish MPAs in the marine environment and ensure that vessels flying their flags do not harm the marine environment.

---

[95] https://www.theguardian.com/environment/2019/nov/06/dumped-fishing-gear-is-biggest-plastic-polluter-in-ocean-finds-report.

6.4 Competence of International Courts to Oblige States to Adopt Legislation

After having established that States are obliged to establish MPAs in order to fulfil their obligation to protect and preserve the marine environment under the peremptory norm of Art. 192 UNCLOS, its enforceability in courts needs to be assessed. It has been pointed out in the literature that due to the general character of Art. 192 UNCLOS, judges would overstep their judicial role and stray into law-making when giving any substantive content to the obligation.[96] Furthermore, in German national law, due to the assessment prerogative of the legislature concerning the type and the content of a specific measure, the judicial review is limited to apparent violations. This is a consequence of the separation of powers between the legislative and judicial branches. To anticipate the result, it will be demonstrated that judges do not overstep their competence when obliging States to establish MPAs under the peremptory obligation to protect and preserve the marine environment.

6.4.1 Obligation to Establish MPAs

Firstly, it has been established that the obligation to protect and preserve the marine environment provides for the specific obligation of States to establish MPAs. A judge would therefore not exceed its judicial competence in obliging States to do so. Furthermore, an excess of judicial competence can be prevented by filing a precise submission. According to the *ne eat iudex ultra petita partium* principle (*non-ultra petita* principle) a judge may not decide on issues that have not been submitted to it.[97] This principle can be found in many domestic legal systems and is recognised in international law.[98] In international law, the arbitrary body is created by the parties. The *non-ultra petita* principle flows out of the mandate of the adjudicative body and is derived from the principle of consent.[99] A judicial award that goes beyond the applicant's request is *ultra vires*.[100] Accordingly, the tribunal in the *Boundary dispute between Argentina and Chile concerning the frontier line between boundary post 62 and Mount Fitzroy* Arbitration held that '[t]he competence of international judges is limited by the functions assigned to them by the parties in the case. Their powers are also limited by the extreme claims which the parties put forward in the hearings. To exceed these functions or powers means deciding *ultra vires* and rendering the decision null by reason of *excès de*

[96] Harrison (2017), p. 23.

[97] Tanzi (2019), para. 1.

[98] Tanzi (2019), para. 2.

[99] Tanzi (2019), para. 6.

[100] Kolb (2013), p. 1007.

pouvoir.'[101] According to the ICJ 'one must bear in mind the principle that it is the duty of the court not only to reply to the questions as stated in the final submissions of the parties, but also to abstain from deciding points not included in those submissions.'[102] Judges in finding their decision are bound by the submissions. To prevent *ultra vires* decision, the applicant must to specify its submission precisely.

6.4.2 Judicial Review of Legislations in Case of Obvious Violations

Secondly, the ICJ held in its *Tadić Case* that due to the lack of a law-making authority in public international law, the separation of powers of the executive, judicial and legislative branches does not apply to international law.[103] Therefore, the division of the competence of the judicial and legislative branches is not as clearly defined as in national law. Even with respect to the separation of powers and the prerogative of the legislature as in German law, a judicial review of the legislation is admissible in cases of apparent violations, that is, if the measure is objectively unsuitable or entirely inadequate. The abstention from taking any measures, that is, if States entirely disregard their obligation to establish MPAs, is the severest form of violation of their obligation to protect and preserve the marine environment. States have limited their sovereign immunity by subjecting themselves to the obligation to protect and preserve the marine environment, which entails the obligation to adopt legislative measures to this end. A judge, in this case, would not overstep its competence in obliging the State to establish MPAs, when the States failed to do so at all. With regard to the specific content of an MPA, States must comply with the obligations they have accepted under international law. A judge can decide whether an MPA by a State or States is sufficient to meet the protection obligations that States have subjected themselves to under international law.

---

[101] International Arbitral Tribunal, *Boundary dispute between Argentina and Chile concerning the frontier line between boundary post 62 and Mount Fitzroy*, Reports of International Arbitral Awards XII RIAA 3 (2006), pp. 3, 26, para. 77.

[102] ICJ, *Request for interpretation of the Judgment of 20th November 1950 in the Asylum Case*, Judgement, ICJ Reports 1950, pp. 395, 402.

[103] ICTY, *Prosecutor v. Dusko Tadić a/k/a 'Dule'*, Decision on the Defence Motion for Interlocutory Appeal on Jurisdiction of 2 October 1995, para. 43.

6.4.3 *Judicial Decisions as Subsidiary Means for the Determination of Rules of Law*

Under Art. 38 (1) (d) ICJ Statute, the Court shall apply judicial decisions as subsidiary means to determine rules of law. Hence, judicial decisions are not formal sources of international law but can confirm the existence and assist in the interpretation of laws that already exist.[104] Thus, judicial decisions cannot create the specific obligation of States to establish MPAs if there is no base for such an obligation in the formal sources of law itself. Art. 192 UNCLOS does provide the basis for the obligation of States to establish MPAs. A judge would therefore not stray into law-making but apply the existing law when confirming an obligation of the States to establish MPAs.

6.5 Competence to Establish MPAs in the Zones of the Sea

MPAs are geographically defined marine areas that are designated by legislation and require legislative competence. Sovereign rights of the States vary according to the zone of the sea.

6.5.1 *Territorial Sea*

In the Territorial Sea, the coastal State has comprehensive legislative and enforcement jurisdiction over its territory (*raione loci*) and over all matters (*ratione materiae*) and all people, regardless of their nationality (*ratione personae*).[105]

6.5.1.1 The Obligation of the Coastal State to Adopt National Laws

Due to its exclusive sovereignty under Art. 2 (1) UNCLOS, the coastal State is entitled to enact the measures resulting from the obligation to protect and preserve the marine environment with regard to prescriptive as well as enforcement jurisdiction in its Territorial Sea. According to Art. 2 (3) UNCLOS, exclusive sovereignty is to be exercised subject to the UNCLOS and other rules of international law, including the obligation to protect and preserve the marine environment. The coastal State is thus not only entitled but obliged to adopt the necessary measures to protect and preserve the marine environment as embodied under Art. 192 UNCLOS in its

[104] Scovazzi (2013), p. 299; see: Sources of International Law.

[105] Tanaka (2019), p. 9.

Territorial Sea. The obligation to protect and preserve the marine environment limits the exclusive sovereignty of the coastal State in its Territorial Sea under Art. 2 (1), (3) UNCLOS. The obligation to protect and preserve the marine environment plays an essential role for treaties that do not include AUNJ in their application.[106] Due to the exclusivity of the sovereignty of the coastal State, other States do not have sovereign rights to establish MPAs in the Territorial Sea of another State. Thus, the obligation to protect and preserve the marine environment through the establishment of MPAs exclusively obliges the coastal State in the Territorial Sea.

It is conceivable that a State establishes MPAs under the guise of the obligation to protect and preserve the marine environment to exclude navigation by foreign vessels in its Territorial Sea abusively. The exclusive sovereignty is not granted limitless and is balanced by the regulations on transit and innocent passage.

6.5.1.2 Straits Used for International Navigation (Transit Passage)

In order to equilibrate the interests of freedom of navigation of other States and the exclusive sovereignty of the coastal State in the Territorial Sea, the exclusive sovereignty is limited by the regulations on straits that are used for international navigation under Part III UNCLOS. The regime of transit passage regulates rights and duties of the State bordering the strait and ships using the strait for passage. The designation of a 12 NM Territorial Sea caused many international straits to fall within the Territorial Sea of a coastal State in the aftermaths of the UNCLOS.[107] The paramount importance of international straits for a functioning sea communication, however, necessitated the stipulation of exceptions to the States' sovereignty in AUNJ in favour of the freedom of navigation.[108] As the size of vessels is constantly rising and cargos potentially carry highly dangerous substances, the freedom of navigation for those vessels, has to be balanced with the coastal States' interest in the protection of its marine environment.

Use of International Straits

Under Art. 38 (1), 37 UNCLOS, all ships enjoy the right of transit passage in straits used for international navigation between one part of the High Sea or an EEZ and another part of the High Sea or an EEZ. This right is strictly limited to the activity of transit passage (Art. 39 (3) UNCLOS), which means the exercise of the freedom of navigation and overflight solely for continuous and expeditious transit of the strait.

---

[106] Harrison (2011), p. 24; PCA, *South China Sea Arbitration*, Philippines v. China (Award), p. 373, para. 940; Proelss (2017), Art. 192, mn. 5; Matz-Lück (2017), p. 411, mn. 38; McConnell and Gold (1991), p. 86.

[107] Tanaka (2019), pp. 94, 117.

[108] Tanaka (2019), pp. 94, 115; Proelss (2017), Art. 2, mn. 22.

The requirement of continuous and expeditious transit does not preclude passage through the strait for the purpose of entering, leaving or returning from a State bordering the strait, subject to the conditions of entry to that State under Art. 39 (2) UNCLOS.

Coastal State Jurisdiction

Under Art. 34 (1) UNCLOS, the regime of passage does not affect the legal status of the waters forming such straits. Generally, States have exclusive sovereignty in their Territorial Seas under Art. 2 (1) UNCLOS. According to Art. 2 (3) UNCLOS, this sovereignty is subjected to other rules of the UNCLOS and pursuant to Art. 34 (2) UNCLOS, the sovereignty and jurisdiction of bordering States is subject to Part III UNCLOS. The rights, rules and regulations on transit passage thus prevail in the Territorial Sea. Under Art. 38 (1), (2), 37 UNCLOS, the right of transit passage shall not be impeded. Therefore, national laws and regulations for protecting and preserving the marine environment do not apply to ships in transit passage if they impede this passage.

Internationally Accepted Regulations for Pollution

This is balanced by Art. 39 (2) (b) UNCLOS, according to which ships in transit passage shall comply with the generally accepted international regulations, procedures and practices to prevent, reduce and control pollution from ships. Internationally accepted rules and regulations, therefore, bind foreign vessels even in transit passage. The regime on transit passage does not lift the general obligation of all States to protect and preserve the marine environment in all zones of the sea. It follows that the State community is obliged to adopt internationally accepted rules and regulations for the protection and preservation of the marine environment that apply to ships in transit passage in the Territorial Sea of a State.

Traffic Separation Schemes and Pollution

Under Art. 41 (1) UNCLOS, States bordering straits may adopt Traffic Separation Schemes (TSS) to promote 'the safe passage of ships.' TSS have their origin in the customary practice among shipping companies.[109] The safe passage of ships refers to three elements, the safety of life at sea, safety and efficiency of navigation and the protection of the marine environment.[110] The bordering States has jurisdiction and sovereignty by virtue of Art. 42 (1) (b) and (c) UNCLOS, according to which it may

[109] Proelss (2017), Art. 41, mn. 1.

[110] Proelss (2017), Art. 41, mn. 1, f.

adopt laws and regulations concerning transit passage with respect to the prevention, reduction and control of pollution, by giving effect to applicable international regulations regarding the discharge of oil, oily wastes and other noxious substances in the strait and with respect to fishing vessels and the prevention of fishing, including the stowage of fishing gear. The bordering State thus has jurisdictional rights under Art. 34 (2), 41 (1), 42 (1) to adopt TSS for the protection of the marine environment and laws and regulations with respect to the prevention, reduction and control of pollution and fishing vessels, giving effect to applicable international regulations.

Art. 233 (1st sentence) UNCLOS reiterates that national laws and regulations may not impede transit passage under Art. 38 (1), (2), 37 UNCLOS, stipulating that even the prescriptive and enforcement jurisdiction under Section 5 and 6 of Part XII UNCLOS for the prevention, reduction and control of pollution shall not affect the legal regime of straits. Art. 233 (2nd sentence) UNCLOS, however, gives further effect to the TTS by prescribing enforcement jurisdiction to the bordering State in cases that a foreign ship (other than warships and ships named in Art. 236 UNCLOS) has violated laws and regulations that the coastal State adopted pursuant to Art. 42 (1) (a), (b) UNCLOS for the safety of navigation and the prevention, reduction and control of pollution to give effect to international regulations regarding the discharge of oil, oily waters and other noxious substances in the strait, which caused or threatened major damage to the marine environment of the straits.

Flag State Obligation

Furthermore, the obligation to protect and preserve the marine environment imposes an obligation on the flag States to adopt appropriate laws and regulations and to ensure that vessels flying their flag adhere to relevant protecting and preservation measures.[111]

6.5.1.3 Innocent Passage

The exclusive sovereignty of the coastal State is subjected to other rules of the UNCLOS under Art. 2 (3) UNCLOS. Subject to the UNCLOS, ships of all States enjoy the right of innocent passage in the Territorial Sea of another State under Art. 17 UNCLOS. Therefore, the specific rules of innocent passage apply in the Territorial Sea.

---

[111] See: The Obligation of Flag State.

Limitation by Innocent Passage

The rules and regulations on innocent passage only apply to activities by foreign States which fall under the definition of innocent passage. Pursuant to Art. 18 UNCLOS, passage means the continuous and expeditious navigation through the Territorial Sea for the purpose of traversing that sea without entering internal waters or calling at a roadstead or port facility outside internal waters or for the purpose of proceeding to or from internal waters or a call at such roadstead or port facility. Passage includes stopping and anchoring, but only in so far as the same are incidental to ordinary navigation or are rendered necessary by force majeure or distress or for the purpose of rendering assistance to persons, ships or aircraft in danger or distress. The passage is innocent according to Art. 19 (1) UNCLOS, so long as it is not prejudicial to the coastal State's peace, good order or security. Innocent passage shall take place in conformity with the UNCLOS and with other rules of international law. Passage shall not be considered innocent under Art. 19 (2) UNCLOS, *inter alia* if the ship engages in any act of wilful and serious pollution contrary to the UNCLOS (Art. 19 (2) (h) UNCLOS), any fishing activities (Art. 19 (2) (i) UNCLOS) or any other activity not having a direct bearing on passage (Art. 19 (2) (l) UNCLOS). All forms of passage that are not covered by this definition may be freely regulated by the national laws and regulations of the coastal State, especially with regard to its obligation to protect and preserve the marine environment under Art. 2 (1), 192 UNCLOS. Any fishing activity, serious pollution or activity not having a direct bearing in passage, are *per se* not covered by the regulations on innocent passage.

Laws and Regulations for Innocent Passage

The coastal State is expressly endowed with the right to adopt laws and regulations relating to innocent passage pursuant to Art. 21 UNCLOS in respect of the conservation of the living resources of the sea (Art. 21 (1) (c) UNCLOS), the preservation of the environment of the coastal State and the prevention, reduction and control of pollution thereof (Art. 21 (1) (f) UNCLOS). Therefore, the coastal State is even expressly obliged to adopt laws and regulations for the protection and preservation of the marine environment with regard to ships that exercise innocent passage. Pursuant to Art. 21 (2) UNCLOS, however, such laws and regulations shall not apply to the design, construction, manning or equipment of foreign ships unless they are giving effect to generally accepted international rules or standards.[112]

[112] Rothwell and Stephens (2016), p. 356.

6.5.1.4 Conclusion: Territorial Sea

Generally, the coastal State has exclusive sovereignty in the Territorial Sea over all persons and all matters. It is therefore exclusively obliged to adopt national laws and regulations to protect and preserve the marine environment in the Territorial Sea under the peremptory obligation to protect and preserve the marine environment in conjunction with Art. 2 (1), (3) UNCLOS. Furthermore, the flag States are obliged to adopt national laws and regulations to protect and preserve the marine environment from vessels flying their flag.

Pursuant to Art. 2 (3), 34 (2), 38 (1), (2), 37, 233 (1st sentence) UNCLOS, those laws and regulations may not impede transit passage through international straits, including the laws and regulations that are adopted to prevent, reduce and control pollution under Section 5-7 of Part XII UNCLOS. However, vessels in transit passage have to adhere to generally accepted international regulations, procedures and practices for the prevention, reduction and control of pollution from ships under Art. 39 (2) (b) UNCLOS. In conjunction with the obligation to protect and preserve the marine environment, this leads to the conclusion that States are obliged to adopt 'international' legislation for the protection and preservation of the marine environment in international straits. Furthermore, the bordering State may adopt laws and regulations (TSS) with regard to the prevention, reduction and control of pollution by giving effect to applicable international regulations regarding the discharge of oil, oily wastes and other noxious substances in the strait and with respect to fishing vessels, the prevention of fishing, including the stowage of fishing gear pursuant to Art. 42 (1) (b) and (c), 233 (2nd sentence) UNCLOS.

In the case of transit passage, the limitation of the sovereignty of the coastal State is covered by the international community's interest to use straits that are required for international navigation. Therefore, the regulations on transit passage serve the interest of freedom of navigation in international straits that often used to be the High Sea before the breadth of the Territorial Sea was extended from 3 to 12 NM. Innocent passage refers to the use of a foreign Territorial Sea only for the reason of traversing it. The interest of the respective coastal State to maintain its full sovereignty and regulate the use of its Territorial Sea, therefore, prevails for the regulation on innocent passage. While transit passage may generally not be impeded by national laws and regulations, the coastal State has more leeway to adopt rules and regulations to regulate innocent passage.

Under Art. 17 UNCLOS ships of all States have the right of innocent passage through the Territorial Sea of another State. However, the right of innocent passage is limited to activities that fall under its definition in Art. 18, 19 UNCLOS. The coastal State is entitled and obliged to adopt laws and regulations to protect and preserve the marine environment under Art. 192, 2 (1) UNCLOS, also with regard to innocent passage pursuant to Art. 21 (1) (f) UNCLOS. Those laws and regulations do not apply to the design, construction, manning or equipment of foreign ships unless they are giving effect to generally accepted international rules or standards.

Furthermore, the flag States are obliged to adopt laws and regulations for the protection and preservation of the marine environment that apply to their ships

6.5.2 *High Sea*

The establishment of MPAs requires legislative competence. With respect to the freedom of the High Sea and the no-sovereignty principle, it, therefore, needs to be assessed if States are competent to adopt relevant legislation in order to establish MPAs in the High Sea.

6.5.2.1 Art. 87 UNCLOS

Under Art. 87 (1) UNCLOS, the High Seas are open to all States, whether coastal or landlocked. The freedoms of the High Sea are not granted in an absolute manner. According to Art. 87 (1) (2nd sentence) UNCLOS, the freedoms of the High Sea have to be exercised under the conditions of the UNCLOS and other rules of international law. In exercising their freedoms of the High Sea, States have to pay due regard to the freedoms of other States and due regard for the rights with respect to activities in the Area under Art. 87 (2) UNCLOS. The High Sea is therefore not a zone without law (*vacuum juris*). The freedoms of the High Seas are subjected to other regulations of the UNCLOS pursuant to Art. 87 (1), (2) UNCLOS.[113] The regulation of activities in the High Sea is explicitly entailed in Art. 87 (1) UNCLOS. Because the obligation to protect and preserve the marine environment applies in all zones of the sea, the freedom of the High Sea is subjected to this obligation. Concludingly, States are obliged to protect and preserve the marine environment in the High Sea and adopt 'international' legislation to this end.

The no-sovereignty principle as codified in Art. 89 UNCLOS is granted limitless. States may not unilaterally assert any terrain of the High Sea to their exclusive territorial sovereignty. The establishment of MPAs in the High Sea does not interfere with this principle. States do not purport to subject terrains to their territorial sovereignty by establishing MPAs but exercise single sovereign rights to manage activities in the area.[114] The adoption of legislation to regulate activities in the sea for a protection and conservation objective falls within the scope of Art. 87 UNCLOS. Because of the obligation of all States to protect and preserve the marine environment, the adoption of legislation to this end is not only permissible, but States are obliged to do so. However, because the High Sea is generally free under Art. 87 (1) (1st sentence) UNCLOS only the State parties to High Sea treaties are bound by their provisions under Art. 34 VCLT. Single States may also adopt

[113] O'Connell (1988), p. 796; Tanaka (2019), p. 186; Proelss (2017), Art. 89, mn. 1, 3.

[114] See: Jus Cogens Status of Art. 89 UNCLOS.

national laws and legislations for the protection and preservation of the marine environment of the High Sea. However, other States are not bound by this legislation. The feasible means to protect and preserve the High Sea's marine environment is the adoption of international treaties, which is a universal obligation under international law under the peremptory norm of Art. 192 UNCLOS and Art. 197 UNCLOS.

6.5.2.2 Specific Regulations to Protect the Marine Environment in the High Sea

This result is reiterated in specific regulations of the UNCLOS, which provide for the obligation of States to adopt international treaties for the protection of the High Sea from specific issues. Under Art. 87 (1) (3rd sentence) (e), 118 UNCLOS, for instance, States shall cooperate in the conservation and management of living resources in the areas of the High Seas. Art. 207 (4), 213 UNCLOS expressly stipulates that States shall endeavour to adopt international rules and regulations in all zones of the Sea, including the High Sea, to prevent, reduce and control pollution and to enforce those rules. This regulatory approach is repeated in Art. 208 (5), 214 UNCLOS for pollution from seabed activities in AUNJ, 210 (4), 216 UNCLOS for pollution by dumping, 211 (1), 217 ff. UNCLOS for pollution from vessels, 212 (3), 222 UNCLOS for pollution from or through the atmosphere. For the seabed and ocean floor of ABNJ, namely the Area (Art. 1 (1) (1) UNCLOS), Art. 209, 215 UNCLOS refer to Part XI UNCLOS, which stipulate a whole regulatory regime for the Area itself. Therefore, the UNCLOS provides for the adoption of international rules and regulations in the High Sea, i.e. to prevent, reduce and control pollution. Thus, international rules and regulations may be adopted in the High Sea.

6.5.2.3 Exclusive Jurisdiction of the Flag State

Under Art. 92 (1) UNCLOS ships are under the exclusive jurisdiction of the flag State when sailing on the High Sea. Jurisdiction in the UNCLOS refers to legislative as well as enforcement jurisdiction. Art. 92 (1) UNCLOS limits the enforcement jurisdiction to the flag States, while with regard to the legislative or prescriptive jurisdiction, the international community is still obliged to adopt international treaties with regard to legal activities in the High Sea.[115] Under the peremptory obligation to protect and preserve the marine environment, States are obliged to adopt national laws and regulations as well as international treaties for the protection of the marine environment, particularly through the establishment of MPAs. With regard to ships, therefore, States are obliged to protect the marine environment by

[115] Proelss (2017), Art. 92, mn. 1.

adopting international treaties on the High Sea and passing national legislation to regulate the activities of ships flying their flag on the High Sea.

6.5.2.4 Conclusion: High Sea

To summarize, the UNCLOS distinguishes between sovereignty and single sovereign claims. Although there is no consensus on the legal status of the High Sea, there is a consensus that the High Sea is not a zone that is free from any law. This can evidently be seen in Art. 87 (1) (2nd sentence) UNCLOS, which subjects the freedom of the High Sea to a regulatory system that limits the exercise of the freedom of the High Sea to the conformity with other rules of international law. The interpretation of Art. 89 UNCLOS leads to the result that territorial sovereignty claims over the High Sea are not permissible. However, the invalidity of territorial sovereignty does not exclude the rights of the States to adopt treaties that apply to the High Sea. The adoption of international treaties to protect and preserve the marine environment is permissible.[116] The High Sea is generally free from any territorial sovereignty claims of the States and States may, therefore, not adopt national laws and regulations for the High Sea. However, the State community is obliged to adopt national laws and regulations for the protection and preservation of the marine environment.

6.5.3 Exclusive Economic Zone

The EEZ is a zone *sui generis*. Pursuant to Art. 58 (1), (2) UNCLOS specific freedoms of the High Sea as well as Art. 88-115 UNCLOS and other pertinent rules of international law apply in the EEZ in so far as they are not incompatible with Part V UNCLOS. The coastal State has single sovereign rights and jurisdiction over specific matters under Art. 56 UNCLOS. By virtue of Art. 56 (1) (b) (iii) UNCLOS, the coastal State has jurisdiction as provided for in the relevant provisions of the UNCLOS for the protection and preservation of the marine environment.

6.5.3.1 Application of Art. 89 UNCLOS in the EEZ

Via the cross-reference of Art. 58 (2) UNCLOS, the no-sovereignty principle of Art. 89 UNCLOS is applicable in the EEZ, in so far as it is not incompatible with Part V UNCLOS. Accordingly, no State may assert any part of the EEZ to its exclusive territorial sovereignty, except where permitted by Part V UNCLOS. It has been demonstrated that the exercise of single sovereign rights to establish MPAs does not

[116] Tanaka (2019), p. 189.

interfere with Art. 89 UNCLOS. The cross-reference of Art. 58 (2), 89 UNCLOS does not exclude the competence of the States to adopt legislation to establish MPAs in the EEZ. While in the High Sea, other States would not be bound by unilateral national laws and regulations of one State to establish MPAs because of a lack of sovereign rights to this end, in the EEZ, the coastal State has jurisdiction for the protection and preservation of the marine environment under Art. 56 (1) (b) (iii) UNCLOS.[117]

6.5.3.2 Jurisdiction

The coastal State has jurisdiction in the EEZ as provided for in the relevant provisions of the UNCLOS with regard to the protection and preservation of the marine environment pursuant to Art. 56 (1) (b) (iii) UNCLOS. It needs to be assessed if this jurisdiction provides for the adoption of national laws and regulations to protect and preserve the marine environment so that the coastal State may establish MPAs in its EEZ that are binding for other States.

Jurisdiction and Sovereign Rights Under Art. 56 (1) UNCLOS

Other than Art. 56 (1) (a) UNCLOS, which grants the coastal State ‘sovereign rights’ for the exploration and exploitation, conservation and management of the natural resources in the EEZ, Art. 56 (1) (b) UNCLOS provides ‘jurisdiction’ for protecting and preserving of the marine environment. The difference in the wording of both provisions leads to the question of a qualitative difference between the alternate terminology. Parts of the literature argue that the change of wording reflects a change of principles. The interpretation of Art. 56 UNCLOS, however, shows that there is no distinction between both terms.[118]

The ordinary meaning of ‘jurisdiction’ means the power to make legal decisions and judgements.[119] Sovereign rights are the supreme rights of the State, in most countries the government. Both provide for the right to establish branches to adopt and enforce rights.

A comparison with the French and Spanish versions is inconclusive as they use the same wording of ‘droits souvereains’ and ‘juridiction’ in French and ‘derechos de soberanía’ and ‘jurisdicción’ in Spanish.

Historically and teleologically, the terminology ‘jurisdiction’ has been agreed upon on the UNCLOS III Conference as a compromise in order to settle the dispute on States’ powers on matters as envisaged in Art. 56 (1) (b) UNCLOS, which does

[117] See: Art. 87 UNCLOS.

[118] Proelss (2017), Art. 56, mn. 20; Gavounelli (2007), p. 65.

[119] https://dictionary.cambridge.org/dictionary/english/jurisdiction.

not give further recourse in a difference between 'jurisdiction' and 'sovereign rights'.[120]

Contextually, the terminology in Part V UNCLOS varies from 'sovereign rights' in Art. 56 (1) (a) UNCLOS, 'jurisdiction' in Art. 56 (1) (b) UNCLOS, 'exclusive rights' in Art. 60 (1) UNCLOS to 'exclusive jurisdiction' under Art. 60 (2) UNCLOS. The varying terminology does not show any consistency: Art. 60 (1) (b) UNCLOS, for instance, stipulates the 'exclusive right' of the coastal State to construct installations and structures for the purpose provided for in Art. 56 UNCLOS, while Art. 56 UNCLOS stipulates 'sovereign rights' under Art. 56 (1) (a) UNCLOS and 'jurisdiction' under Art. 56 (1) (b) (i) UNCLOS.[121] Furthermore, under Art. 56 (2) UNCLOS the coastal State shall have due regard to the rights and duties of other States in exercising 'its rights and performing its duties' under the UNCLOS in the EEZ. This due regard rule merges both sovereign rights and jurisdiction in the exercise of its 'rights' and does not distinguish between those rights.[122] Lastly, while Art. 56 (1) (a) UNCLOS grants the sovereign rights for the stipulated purposes unlimitedly, Art. 56 (1) (b) UNCLOS limits the jurisdiction 'as provided for in the relevant provision of the UNCLOS'. This indicates that the distinction between the paragraphs is not due to a difference of the scope of 'sovereign rights' and 'jurisdiction' but to the extent to which they are granted.[123] A decision in the matter is not relevant to determine if coastal States have the competence to establish MPAs in their EEZ because both 'sovereign rights' and 'jurisdiction' provide the coastal State's competence to adopt relevant laws and legislation for the establishment of MPAs.

Exclusive Jurisdiction of the Coastal State

Art. 192 UNCLOS obliges States to adopt legislation for the protection and preservation of the marine environment. Art. 56 (1) (b) (iii) UNCLOS provides jurisdiction for the coastal State for the protection and preservation of the marine environment. In the EEZ, therefore, the coastal State has the competence to adopt national laws and regulations for the protection of the marine environment. This raises the question of whether other States are also obliged to adopt international treaties to protect and preserve the marine environment in the EEZ or if the jurisdiction under Art. 56 (1) (b) (iii) UNCLOS allocates this obligation to the coastal State exclusively.

For the Continental Shelf, Art. 77 (2) UNCLOS expressly stipulates that the sovereign right of the coastal State to explore and exploit their natural resources on the Continental Shelf under Art. 77 (1) UNCLOS is exclusive in the sense that if the coastal State does not explore the Continental Shelf or exploit its natural resources,

[120] Proelss (2017), Art. 56, mn. 20.
[121] Proelss (2017), Art. 56, mn. 20.
[122] Proelss (2017), Art. 56, mn. 20.
[123] Proelss (2017), Art. 56, mn. 20.

no other State may undertake these activities without the express consent of the coastal State. Art. 56 UNCLOS does not contain such a clause but only stipulates the jurisdiction as provided for in other regulations of the UNCLOS. Moreover, the coastal State is even obliged to make available the harvest of the surplus of the allowable catch of its living resources to other States under Art. 62 UNCLOS.

The systematic interpretation of the regulatory system of the EEZ shows that the coastal State's jurisdiction is exclusive: Generally, the no-sovereignty principle under Art. 58 (2), 89 UNCLOS does not exclude the rights of States to adopt international treaties in the High Sea or the EEZ, respectively. Under Art. 58 (1), 87 (1) (2nd sentence), 192 UNCLOS States are furthermore entitled and obliged to do so. Pursuant to Art. 58 (3) UNCLOS, in exercising their rights and performing their duties under the UNCLOS, other States must have due regard to the rights and duties of the coastal State and shall comply with the laws and regulations adopted by the coastal State in accordance with the UNCLOS and other rules of international law, in so far as they are not incompatible with this Part. Under Art. 56 (1) (b) (iii) UNCLOS, the coastal State has jurisdiction for the protection and preservation of the marine environment in the EEZ. Because of the limitation of the application of the no-sovereignty principle and the freedoms of the High Sea in favour of the jurisdiction clause in Art. 56 (1) (b) (iii) UNCLOS, the jurisdiction of the coastal State supersedes the right of other States to adopt international treaties for this purpose and assigns the legislative power to the coastal States. The coastal State is therefore exclusively mandated and obliged to protect and preserve the marine environment under Art. 56 (1) (b) (iii), 192 UNCLOS by designating MPAs through the adoption of national laws and regulations.

The interpretation of Art. 59 UNCLOS on the residual rights in the EEZ supports this result. Art. 59 UNCLOS regulates the residual rights if a conflict arises between the interests of the coastal State and any other State, in cases where the UNCLOS 'does not attribute rights or jurisdiction to the coastal State or to other States' within the EEZ. This wording shows that in cases in which the UNCLOS does attribute jurisdiction to the coastal State, this supersedes, it prevails the rights of other States.

This result is also not rebutted by Art. 62 UNCLOS, which obliges States to make available the surplus of the allowable catch of living resources to other States. On the contrary, it reiterates the right of the coastal State to manage fish stocks in its EEZ exclusively. Art. 62 UNCLOS does not provide that other States are allowed to freely access the surplus of the living resources of a coastal State in its EEZ but obliges the exclusively competent coastal State to enter into international treaties with other States for this purpose. Otherwise, other States would precisely not be allowed to harvest these resources because of the exclusive jurisdiction of the coastal State.

Therefore, the jurisdiction of the coastal State in its EEZ is exclusive. Because of the peremptory obligation to protect and preserve the marine environment the coastal State is not only competent but also obliged to adopt legislation for the protection and preservation of the marine environment by establishing MPAs in its EEZ.

Special Jurisdiction and Sovereign Rights in the EEZ

Specific expressions of the obligation to protect and preserve the marine environment are further codified as *lex specialis* in Art. 60 ff. UNCLOS. These regulations are important in the interpretation of the specific content of the general obligation to protect and preserve the marine environment, as the content of this obligation is informed by more specific rules of international law.[124] While the State parties to the UNCLOS have accepted these provisions as *lex specialis* to their obligation to protect and preserve the marine environment in their EEZ, non-State parties are not directly bound by the regulations of the UNCLOS. The specific content of the obligation to protect and preserve the marine environment must be established on a case-by-case basis. General accepted rules and standards, policies and expert opinions can help to interpret the content in each case.[125]

The coastal State has sovereign rights with regard to specific protection issues, such as the conservation of the living resources under Art. 61 UNCLOS, the coordination of conservation measures between States where the same stock or stocks of associated species occur within the EEZ of two or more coastal States pursuant to Art. 63 UNCLOS, or in the EEZ and ABNJ, the conservation of highly migratory species under Art. 64 UNCLOS, the protection of marine mammals under Art. 65 UNCLOS, conservation of anadromous species under Art. 66 UNCLOS and management of catadromous species under Art. 67 UNCLOS. With regard to the exploration, conservation and management of living resources, Art. 73 UNCLOS stipulated the legal basis for the enforcement of measures taken by the coastal State in its EEZ.

Jurisdiction to Prevent, Reduce and Control Pollution

Jurisdiction of the coastal State to protect and preserve the marine environment in its EEZ is specifically addressed with regard to pollution from dumping and its enforcement in Art. 210 (5), 216 UNCLOS, pollution from vessels and its enforcement in Art. 211 (5), (6), 218, 220 UNCLOS, as well as pollution from vessels in ice-covered areas within the EEZ under Art. 234 UNCLOS.[126] Under Art. 211 (5) UNCLOS, for instance, coastal States may, in respect of their EEZ, adopt laws and regulations for the prevention, reduction and control of pollution from vessels conforming to and giving effect to generally accepted international rules and standards for the purpose of the enforcement under Art. 211 (6) and Section 6, Part XII UNCLOS. Parts of the literature argue that the specific stipulation of those rights would be obsolete if Art. 56 (1) (b) (iii) UNCLOS already provided jurisdictional rights for this purpose.

[124] PCA, *South China Sea Arbitration*, Philippines v. China (Award), p. 373, para. 941.

[125] See: Specification of the Content.

[126] Proelss (2017), Art. 56, mn. 21.

Art. 210 (5), 211 (5), (6), 216, 218, 220 and 234 UNCLOS are more specific than the general regulations in Part V UNCLOS and are therefore *lex specialis*. Art. 211 (5) UNCLOS, for instance, prescribes specific regulations for the *enforcement* of the rules and regulations for the prevention of pollution from ships under Section 6 of Part XII UNCLOS. The investigation has furthermore already shown that the structure of the whole UNCLOS shows a certain lack of coherence and apparent duplications in general.[127] The argument that more specific rules would be obsolete if a general obligation was already entailed in previous regulations is not strong in the light of the UNCLOS.[128]

6.5.3.3 Art. 56 (1) (b) (iii) UNCLOS no Lex Specialis for Art. 192 UNCLOS

Lastly, it has been mentioned in the literature that the obligation in Art. 192 UNCLOS is not applicable to the EEZ because it is superseded by Art. 56 (1) (b) (iii) UNCLOS as its *lex specialis*. Furthermore, this notion cannot be supported legally.

Firstly, Art. 192 UNCLOS applies in all zones of the sea. Questions of sovereignty or jurisdictional zones are irrelevant to the applicability of Art. 192 ff. UNCLOS.[129] Secondly, Art. 192 UNCLOS stipulates the obligation of States to protect and preserve the marine environment, whereas Art. 56 (1) (b) (iii) UNCLOS stipulates 'jurisdiction' of the coastal States for the protection and preservation of the marine environment. The regulatory content of Art. 192 UNCLOS and Art. 56 (1) (b) (iii) UNCLOS therefore differs. While Art. 192 UNCLOS stipulates the general obligation of all States to protect and preserve the marine environment in all zones of the sea, Art. 56 (1) (b) (iii) UNCLOS specifically assigns jurisdiction to this end to the coastal States in the EEZ. Thirdly, as the formulation of Art. 56 (1) (b) (iii) UNCLOS shows, the jurisdiction of the coastal State to protect and preserve the marine environment is defined by the relevant provisions of the UNCLOS. Art. 56 (1) (b) (iii) UNCLOS, therefore, serves as a proxy for and is defined by the obligation under Art. 192 UNCLOS and does not supersede the general obligation in Part XII UNCLOS.[130]

6.5.3.4 Excurse: The Mediterranean Sea

Special regard needs to be paid to the Mediterranean. Especially the agreements concerning the Mediterranean Sea potentially play an important role, as the coastal

[127] Nordquist et al. (2013), XII.23.

[128] See: Obligation to Protect and Preserve the Marine Environment as Lex Generalis.

[129] PCA, *South China Sea Arbitration*, Philippines v. China (Award), p. 373, para. 941.

[130] Proelss (2017), Art. 56, mn. 20.

States of the Mediterranean Sea have not delimited their EEZs. Beyond the 12 NM border of the Territorial Sea, the Mediterranean Sea water is the High Sea. Had the coastal States established it, the whole Mediterranean, however, would fall in the EEZ of the respective States.[131] Therefore, it is argued that States potentially have the sovereign rights of the EEZ in the Mediterranean, which include measures such as the protection and preservation of the marine environment under Art. 56 (1) (b) (iii) UNCLOS or the prohibition, limitation or regulation of the exploitation of marine mammals within the EEZ of the coastal State under Art. 65 UNCLOS.[132]

The present author does not support this notion because the UNCLOS does not provide any base to make such a distinction. According to Art. 55, 57 UNCLOS States have the right to designate an EEZ up to 200 NM; any area beyond that is the High Sea (Art. 86 UNCLOS). According to the wording of Art. 86 UNCLOS, the High Sea expressly starts either beyond the Territorial Sea or the EEZ. Therefore, where a State does not choose to establish an EEZ, the waters adjacent to the Territorial Sea are the High Sea. There is no ground in the UNCLOS to distinguish between the High Sea in a broad and a strict sense. If a State wishes to utilize the single sovereign rights granted under Part V UNCLOS on the EEZ, it may establish an EEZ accordingly. Otherwise, this area is the High Sea. Therefore, the treaty system for the designation of MPAs in the Mediterranean faces the same impediments as other conservation treaties in ABNJ, namely the freedom of the High Seas and the *pacta tertiis non nocet* principle under Art. 34 VCLT, according to which its regulations bind only the parties to the treaties.[133]

6.5.4 *The Area*

Part XI UNCLOS regulates activities in the Area. The exploration of the scope of the regulations of the Area, its prevailing principle of the common heritage of mankind and the competence of the ISA and States in this terrain, will determine which States or international organisations are bound by the obligation to protect and preserve the marine environment and to establish MPAs in the Area.

---

[131] Scovazzi (2004), p. 18; Tanaka (2008), p. 198.

[132] Tanaka (2008), p. 206.

[133] See: Impediment for the Designation of MPAs – Zonal Division of the Sea and, Impediment for the Establishment of MPAs – Limited Binding Effect of Treaties.

6.5.4.1 Scope of Part XI UNCLOS

Pursuant to Art. 134 (2), (1) UNCLOS, Part XI UNCLOS governs activities in the Area. The specification to 'activities in the Area' already provides a limited scope of the application of Part XI UNCLOS.

Geographical Scope

The Area is defined in Art. 1 (1) (1) UNCLOS as the seabed, ocean floor and subsoil thereof beyond the limits of national jurisdiction. The Area begins either 200 NM off the baseline of the coast to measure the breadth of the Territorial Sea or at the outer edge of the continental margin (Art. 76 (1), 1 (1) (1) UNCLOS). The water column over the Area is, therefore, always the High Sea. MPAs in the High Sea and the Area are closely interrelated.[134]

Personal Scope

According to Art. 136 UNCLOS, the Area and its resources are the common heritage of mankind. Art. 311 (6) UNCLOS clarifies that State Parties agree that there shall be no amendments to the basic principle relating to the common heritage of mankind set forth in Art. 136 UNCLOS and that they shall not be a party to any agreement in derogation thereof. This regulation does not declare the status of the common heritage of mankind principle as *jus cogens* because *jus cogens* develops through customary law.[135] The cogent status of this principle, however, is widely acknowledged in the international community. The status as *jus cogens* only applies to the principle of common heritage of mankind. The regulations of Part XI UNCLOS on the exploration for and exploitation of resources in the Area were the reason why the USA has not signed the UNCLOS. The USA is neither bound by Part XI UNCLOS as treaty regulation nor by means of customs. This simultaneously prevents the general emergence of all rules of Part XI UNCLOS into *jus cogens*, as this would require a universal acceptance. Therefore, the regulations of Part XI UNCLOS generally only bind the State parties, except for where a rule has emerged into customary international law or even *jus cogens,* such as the common heritage of mankind principle.

---

[134]Tanaka (2008), p. 198.

[135]Treves (2011), p. 114.

Substantive Scope: Activities in the Area

Pursuant to Art. 1 (1) (3) UNCLOS, 'activities in the Area' mean any activity of exploration for and exploitation of the resources of the Area. 'Resources', under Art. 133 (a) UNCLOS are solid, liquid or gaseous mineral resources *in situ* in the Area or beneath the seabed, including polymetallic nodules. When recovered from the Area, resources are referred to as 'minerals' by virtue of Art. 133 (b) UNCLOS. Living resources, such as demersal fish species, are not comprised in the scope of Part XI UNCLOS.[136]

Conclusion: Scope of Application of Part XI

In summary, 'activities in the Area' and therefore the scope of Part XI UNCLOS is limited to the exploration for and exploitation of non-living mineral resources in the seabed and ocean floor and subsoil thereof, beyond the limits of national jurisdiction (Art. 134, (2), (1), 1 (1) (1) and (4), 133 UNCLOS).

6.5.4.2 Common Heritage of Mankind

The Area is governed by common heritage of mankind under Art. 136 UNCLOS. Common heritage of mankind is not legally defined in the UNCLOS. Its scope can be derived from its historical development and other regulations of Part XI UNCLOS.

Development of the Common Heritage of Mankind Principle

Before the codification of the common heritage of mankind principle, there were three possible classifications of the Area. The first one was to extend the coastal States' jurisdiction over the Continental Shelf to deeper regions of the ocean, making the whole ocean floor subject to the jurisdiction of coastal States. The second one was to subject the Area to the freedom of the High Seas, prohibiting the unilateral exercise of sovereignty. The third one classified the Area as *res nullis*, allowing States to conduct activities in the sea unrestrictedly and to subject the Area to their sovereignty.[137]

Despite a very different legal classification of the Area, the practical result, to date, would still be similar: States which can afford the necessary technology would be best placed in a race for space in the Area and rights to exploit its highly valuable

[136] Proelss (2017), Art. 133, mn. 1.

[137] Tanaka (2019), pp. 217 f.

resources.[138] As all three demonstrated options would not lead to a fair and equitable sharing of the resources of the Area, developing States called for a New International Economic Order.[139] In 1970, while expressly rejecting the possibility of States to assert sovereignty to any part of the Area, the General Assembly solemnly declared with 108 votes in favour, none against and 14 abstentions, that 'the sea-bed and ocean floor, and the subsoil thereof, beyond the limits of national jurisdiction [. . .], as well as the resources of the area, are the common heritage of mankind.'[140] The common heritage of mankind principle is a novum in the UNCLOS as it introduces mankind as an actor in international law.[141] The *ratio legis* of the abandonment of the traditional principles of sovereignty and freedom of the High Sea and the new declaration as common heritage of mankind was to not further exacerbate uneven developments of developed and rich countries and less developed countries, which do not possess the same means to engage in expensive activities to access highly valuable resources in ABNJ.[142]

Elements of the Principle

Although the common heritage of mankind principle is not defined in the UNCLOS, its content is commonly deduced by three principles that govern the Area: Firstly, under Art. 137 (1) UNCLOS, no State shall claim or exercise sovereignty or sovereign rights over any part of the Area or its resources, nor shall any State or natural or juridical person appropriate any part thereof. Secondly, pursuant to Art. 137 (2), 140 (1) UNCLOS, all rights in the resources of the Area are vested in mankind as a whole, on whose behalf the ISA shall act. In this regard, the ISA shall provide for the equitable sharing of financial and other economic benefits derived from activities in the Area through any appropriate mechanism on a non-discriminatory basis under Art. 140 (2) UNCLOS and in accordance with Art. 160 (2) (f) (i) UNCLOS. The principle of common heritage of mankind thus also provides for the equitable sharing of financial and other economic benefits. Lastly, by virtue of Art. 141 UNCLOS, the Area shall be open to use exclusively for peaceful purposes by all States, whether coastal or land-locked, without discrimination and without prejudice to the other provisions of the UNCLOS.[143]

---

[138]Tanaka (2019), p. 218.

[139]Tanaka (2019), p. 218.

[140]UNGA A/RES/2749 (XXV), para. 1.

[141]Tanaka (2019), p. 186.

[142]Tanaka (2019), p. 216, ff.

[143]Treves (2011), p. 114; Tanaka (2019), pp. 219 f.

6.5.4.3 Competences in the Area

Given the presented scope of application and prevailing principle in the Area, it needs to determined which international Organisation or States are bound by the obligation to protect and preserve the marine environment in this terrain?

Competence of the ISA

States have established the ISA under Art. 156 (1), 1 (1) (2) UNCLOS and conferred upon it the competence to organize, carry out and control activities in the Area under Art. 153 (1) UNCLOS. The regulations of the UNCLOS bind the ISA. Pursuant 1 (2) (2), 305 (f) UNCLOS in conjunction with Art. 1 Annex IX UNCLOS, the UNCLOS applies *mutatis mutanda* to the ISA. Therefore, the ISA is generally bound by the obligation to protect and preserve the marine environment in carrying out its competencies. Under Art. 157 (2) UNCLOS, the powers and functions of the ISA are limited to those expressly conferred upon it by the UNCLOS. The ISA is therefore obliged to adopt legislation and establish MPAs for the protection and preservation of the marine environment within its competencies, namely for the exploration for and exploitation of mineral resources in the seabed, ocean floor and subsoil thereof, beyond national jurisdiction.

Part XI UNCLOS, furthermore, explicitly codifies the competencies of the ISA to protect and preserve the marine environment under Art. 145 UNCLOS. Pursuant to Art. 145 (1st sentence) UNCLOS, the ISA shall, *inter alia,* take necessary measures in accordance with the UNCLOS with respect to activities in the Area to ensure effective protection for the marine environment from harmful effects, which may arise from such activities. Under Art. 145 (2nd sentence) (a) UNCLOS, the ISA is specifically obliged to adopt rules, regulations and procedures, *inter alia*, for the prevention, reduction and control of pollution and other hazards to the marine environment, including the coastline, and of interference with the ecological balance of the marine environment, particular attention being paid to the need for protection from harmful effects of such activities as drilling, dredging, excavation, disposal of waste, construction and operation or maintenance of installations, pipelines and other devices related to such activities. Pursuant to Art. 145 (b) UNCLOS the ISA shall, furthermore, adopt rules, regulations and procedures for the protection and conservation of the natural resources of the Area and the prevention of damage to flora and fauna of the marine environment under. Like the general competence, the special competence of the ISA under Art. 145 UNCLOS is limited to activities in the Area. Hence the ISA is only competent to establish MPAs in the Area with regard to the exploration for and exploitation of mineral resources.[144]

Concludingly, the ISA is an Authority with two faces: while it is the competent authority to regulate the exploration for and exploitation of the mineral resources in

[144] Proelss (2008), pp. 429 f.; Tanaka (2019), p. 224.

the Area, at the same time, it is obliged to take necessary measures to protect and preserve the marine environment from those activities. To date, the ISA has adopted three regulations to regulate activities in the area, known as the 'Mining Code', consisting of the Regulations on Prospecting and Exploration for Polymetallic Nodules in the Area, the Regulations on Prospecting and Exploration for Polymetallic Sulphides in the Area and the Regulations on Prospecting and Exploration for Cobalt-Rich Ferromanganese Crusts in the Area.[145]

Competence of the States

As the competence of the ISA is limited to activities in the Area, the question arises, which States are competent to manage and regulate activities on the Area that do not fall under the exploration for and exploitation of mineral resources, such as the exploration and exploitation of living organisms such as sedentary species?

Sovereign Rights for the Adoption Treaties in the Area

The *erga omnes* obligation to protect and preserve the marine environment applies to all terrains in the sea, including the Area. For the Area, however, Art. 137 (1) UNCLOS codifies that no State shall claim or exercise sovereignty or sovereign rights over any part of the Area or its resources, nor shall any State or natural or juridical person appropriate any part thereof. This indicates that the adoption of international treaties for the protection and preservation of the marine environment by States may be invalid in the Area. The undefined legal status of the Area as *res nullis, res communis or* resembling the one of the High Sea complicates the determination of sovereign rights in this terrain. At least there is a consensus that the introduction of the common heritage of mankind principle excludes the acquisition of territorial sovereignty in the sense of Art. 2 (1) UNCLOS and Art. 89 UNCLOS. At the same time, however, Art. 137 UNCLOS shall not lead to the result that the legal possibility of sovereign rights does not exist under general international law.[146] The regulation of Art. 137 UNCLOS, though, is balanced by Art. 138 UNCLOS, which stipulates that the general conduct of States in the Area shall be in accordance with the provisions of the UNCLOS and other international rules. Therefore, the *erga omnes* obligation to protect and preserve the marine environment through the adoption of legislation also applies in the Area.

[145] https://isa.org.jm/mining-code; ISBA/6/A/18, ISBA/19/C/17, ISBA/19/C/17; ISBA/16/A/21/Rev. 1; ISBA/18/A/11.

[146] Proelss (2017), Art. 137, mn. 8.

Regulations of Part XI UNCLOS Only Refer to Activities in the Area

Art. 134 (1), (2) UNCLOS stipulate that Part XI UNCLOS applies to the Area and that 'activities in the Area' shall be governed by the provisions of Part XI UNCLOS. This indicates that the regulations of Part XI UNCLOS do not even apply to activities in the Area other than those under Art. 1 (1) (1) (3) UNCLOS. The historical development of Part XI UNCLOS has shown that its *ratio legis* is the regulation of the exploration for and exploitation of mineral resources in the Area to prevent the exacerbation of the disadvantage of developing States that do not possess the same technical means as more affluent and developed States to accesses highly valuable resources in the seabed. From this perspective, the interpretation is more convincing that Part XI UNCLOS only applies to activities in the Area.

Application of the Regulations of the Water Column to the Seabed

Following the interpretation that Part XI UNCLOS only refers to 'activities in the Area', the question arises which regulations apply for other activities, i.e., exploitation of living resources.

General Regulation on Water Column and Special Regulations on the Seabed

The interpretation of the regulatory approach and the historical development of the UNCLOS shows that the regulations on the water column generally apply to its seabed and ocean floor, except for where special regulations are codified. This can be seen in the regulations on the Territorial Sea, which include the seabed and ocean floor of this area under Art. 2 (2) UNCLOS. For the EEZ, Art. 56 (3) UNCLOS stipulates that the rights set out in Art. 56 UNCLOS with respect to the seabed and subsoil shall be exercised in accordance with Part VI UNCLOS on the Continental Shelf. While Art. 56 UNCLOS, therefore, contains general regulations on the seabed, Part VI UNCLOS stipulates the prevailing *lex specialis*. In the High Seas, Art. 86 UNCLOS stipulates its general applicability to all parts of the sea that are not the Territorial Sea or EEZ, without distinguishing between water, seabed and ocean floor. This is further reiterated in Art. 112 UNCLOS, which regulates the laying of pipelines and submarine cables on the seabed of the High Sea and beyond the Continental Shelf, which is clearly an activity on the ocean floor. Part VII UNCLOS, therefore, evidently comprises regulations on the seabed, while Part XI UNCLOS on the Area provides for special regulations for the exploration for and exploitation of natural resources.[147]

[147] Proelss (2008), p. 430.

Legal Status of Superjacent Waters Affects Legal Status of Seabed

Moreover, pursuant to Art. 78 (1), 135 UNCLOS the regulations on the Continental Shelf and the Area respectively, shall not affect the legal status of the water column superjacent to these terrains. While these regulations were necessary to express that the regulations in Part VI and XI UNCLOS on the Continental Shelf and the Area are special regulations for these areas, the general regulations on the EEZ and the High Sea, vice versa, do not contain such a clarification. This shows, *e contrario,* that while the regulations on the seabed and ocean floor may not affect the legal status of the water column above, the regulations on the water column comprise the legal status of the seabed and ocean floor—except where special regulations are codified in Part VI, XI UNCLOS.

Freedom of the High Sea Prevails on Continental Shelf and Area

Furthermore, the regulations on the Continental Shelf and the Area themselves indicate that their prevailing general principle is the freedom of the High Sea. The Continental Shelf is the seabed and subsoil of the water *beyond* the Territorial Sea (Art. 76 (1) UNCLOS) and the Area the seabed, ocean floor and subsoil thereof *beyond* areas of national jurisdiction (Art. 1 (1) (1) UNCLOS). Because Part VI UNCLOS on the Continental Shelf and Part XI UNCLOS on the Area do not stipulate sovereign rights of the coastal State for these terrains (besides the exploration and exploitation of the natural resource of the coastal State in the Continental Shelf) and the Continental Shelf and the Area are the seabed and subsoil of the water *beyond* the Territorial Sea, the general principle in these terrains is the freedom from sovereign rights like in the High Sea. Only where and if the UNCLOS stipulates special rights of the coastal States, such as the right of the coastal States to explore and exploit the natural resources on the Continental Shelf under Art. 77 UNCLOS, the coastal States have sovereign rights for the regulated purposes.

Freedoms of the High Sea Traditionally Applicable to the Area

Lastly, this interpretation is supported by the historical development of the UNCLOS. Prior to the codification of Part XI UNCLOS on the UNCLOS III Conference, activities in ABNJ, no matter if in the water or on the seabed, were uniformly governed by the freedoms of the High Sea. The freedoms of the High Sea uniformly applied to both the water column and the seabed and ocean floor. A distinction was first made in order to regulate deep seabed mining in the Area on the UNCLOS III Conference, with a special mandate for the ISA in order to protect the interests of developing States (this is different for the legal regime on the EEZ and the Continental Shelf, which have developed independently).[148] Concludingly, any activity in the Area other than the exploration for and exploitation of mineral

[148] Proelss (2008), pp. 430 f.; Oude Elferink (2007), pp. 143 f.; Proelss (2017), Art. 56, mn. 34, Art. 55, mn. 3.

resources is governed by the principles of the High Sea. Accordingly, all States are obliged to adopt legislation for the protection and preservation of the marine environment in the Area, except for the exploration for and exploitation of natural mineral resources.

6.5.4.4 Conclusion: The Area

The ISA is competent and obliged to establish MPAs in the Area, however only with regard to the exploration for and exploitation of mineral resources.[149] Any other activity in the Area that is not directly linked to the exploration for and exploitation of mineral resource falls within the competence of States and is governed by the principles on the High Sea. Therefore, States are obliged to adopt legislation to protect and preserve the marine environment in the water column of the High Sea and its seabed, ocean floor and subsoil thereof.

6.5.5 Continental Shelf

Under Art. 76 (1) UNCLOS, the Continental Shelf of the coastal State measures at least 200 NM from the baseline and is congruent with the breadth of the EEZ where it is established, or, if the outer edge of the continental margin extends beyond this border, to the outer edge of the continental margin. Especially seamounts, hydrothermal vents and cold-water corals are rich marine ecosystems that mainly appear on the continental margin of States. These maritime features provide a vibrant ecosystem with large numbers of fish and diverse flora and fauna. In the following, the sovereign rights of the coastal State in the Continental Shelf as well as the general rights of all States in this terrain will be explored to establish which State or States are bound by the obligation to protect and preserve the marine environment in this area.

6.5.5.1 Specific Sovereign Rights on the Continental Shelf

Art. 77 (1), (2), (4) UNCLOS stipulates exclusive sovereign rights of the coastal State for the purpose of exploring and exploiting the natural resources of the Continental Shelf. The natural resources of the Continental Shelf, by virtue of Art. 77 (4) UNCLOS consist of mineral and other non-living resources of the seabed and subsoil together with living organisms belonging to sedentary species. Pursuant to Art. 77 (2) UNCLOS, the sovereign right of the coastal State is exclusive, meaning that no other State may exploit them without permission by the coastal States.

[149] Proelss (2008), pp. 429 f.

Under Art. 79 (1) UNCLOS, all States are entitled to lay submarine cables and pipelines in the Continental Shelf. The coastal State may not impede the laying or maintenance of such pipelines; however, this is subject to the coastal State's right to take reasonable measures for the exploration of the Continental Shelf, the exploitation of its natural resources and the prevention, reduction and control of pollution from pipelines under Art. 79 (2) UNCLOS. Furthermore, the coastal State has the exclusive right to construct and authorize and regulate the construction and use of artificial islands, installations and structures on the Continental Shelf under Art. 80 UNCLOS in conjunction with Art. 60 UNCLOS. Under Art. 81 UNCLOS, the coastal State has the exclusive right to authorize and regulate drilling on the Continental Shelf for all purposes.

6.5.5.2 Specific Obligation to Protect and Preserve the Marine Environment on the Continental Shelf

For the Exploration and Exploitation of the Natural Resources

Other than in the EEZ or High Sea, for which Art. 61 ff., 117 ff. UNCLOS stipulate specific obligations to conserve the living resources, Art. 77 UNCLOS only stipulates sovereign rights for the purpose of exploring and exploiting the natural resources of the Continental Shelf. A narrow read of Art. 77 UNCLOS may, therefore, indicate that States do not have an obligation to conserve the natural resources. This is supported by the comparison of the wording of Art. 77 UNCLOS and the regulations on the EEZ, for which Art. 56 (1) (a) UNCLOS stipulates sovereign rights for the coastal State for 'exploring and exploiting, *conserving and managing* the natural resources [. . .]'. Because the regulations on the Continental Shelf do not contain such a reference, it may be argued that the sovereign rights do not comprise the protection and preservation or conservation of the marine environment.

This view is not convincing. The reference to 'managing and conserving natural resources' in Art. 56 (1) (a) UNCLOS refers to the duties imposed by Art. 61 ff. UNCLOS. Other than Art. 61 ff, 117 ff. UNCLOS for the EEZ and High Sea, the regulations on the Continental Shelf do not contain specific provisions for the conservation and management of living resources. Because there is no such duty in Part VI UNCLOS, by logical implication, there is no such reference in Art. 77 UNCLOS.

Furthermore, although Part VI UNCLOS does not expressly codify sovereign rights of the coastal States to this end, all States are obliged to respect the *erga omnes* obligation to protect and preserve the marine environment in all zones of the sea. Moreover, like Art. 192 UNCLOS, Art. 193 UNCLOS applies to all zones of the sea. Art. 193 UNCLOS generally subordinates and links the sovereign rights of the States to exploit their resources to their obligation to protect and preserve the marine environment.[150] In exploring and exploiting the specified resources on the Continental Shelf, States are obliged to respect their obligation to protect and preserve the marine environment and to take active measures to this end.[151]

Lastly, the corollary of a right to do something is always the right not to do something. The right to exploit the resources in the Continental Shelf is, therefore, complemented by the right not to exploit those resources.[152] Other than in the EEZ, in which other States have the right to access the surplus of the allowable catch that the coastal State does not harvest (Art. 62 (2) UNCLOS), pursuant to Art. 77 (2) UNCLOS, the rights referred to in Art. 77 (1) UNCLOS are exclusive in the sense that if the coastal State does not explore the Continental Shelf or exploit its natural resources, no one may undertake these activities without the express consent of the coastal State. The coastal State necessarily must have the right to manage the exploration and exploitation in order to manage its resources on the Continental Shelf effectively.[153] In conjunction with the erga omnes obligation to protect and preserve the marine environment, the coastal States are therefore obliged to adopt national laws and regulations for the protection and preservation of the marine environment from activities its sovereign rights on the Continental Shelf.

Protection and Preservation from Pollution

Art. 208 (1) UNCLOS expressly stipulates the specific obligation of States to adopt laws and regulations to prevent, reduce and control pollution of the marine environment arising from or in connection with seabed activities subject to their jurisdiction and from artificial islands, installations and structures under their jurisdiction, pursuant to Art. 80, 60 UNCLOS. As to the minimum scope of this obligation, Art. 208 (3) UNCLOS stipulates that such laws, regulations and measures shall be no less effective than international rules, standards and recommended practices and procedures. States, acting especially through competent international organizations or diplomatic conferences, are obliged to establish global and regional rules, standards and recommended practices and procedures to prevent, reduce and control pollution of the marine environment referred to in paragraph one under Art. 208 (5) UNCLOS. The coastal State thus has the sovereign right and the corresponding obligation to adopt national laws and regulations to prevent, reduce and control pollution of the marine environment arising from or in connection with seabed activities subject to their jurisdiction and from artificial islands, installations and structures under their jurisdiction, pursuant to Art. 80, 60 UNCLOS.

[150] Rothwell and Stephens (2016), p. 342; Mossop (2017), p. 97.

[151] Molenaar (2004), p. 223; Mossop (2007), p. 289.

[152] Mossop (2007), p. 289.

[153] Mossop (2007), p. 290.

6.5.5.3 Obligation to Protect and Preserve the Marine Environment from Other Activities on the Extended Continental Shelf

The sovereign rights of the coastal State on the Continental Shelf under Art. 77 (1), (4) UNCLOS and the corresponding obligation to protect and preserve the marine environment are limited to exploring and exploiting the natural resources and living organisms belonging to sedentary species. This raises the question of which State or States are competent to adopt legislation to protect and preserve the marine environment regarding other activities in the sea, such as carbon sinking or fishing.

Varying Legal Regimes for Continental Shelf, EEZ and High Sea

The issue arises for the extended Continental Shelf. According to Art. 78 (1) UNCLOS, the coastal States' rights over the Continental Shelf do not affect the legal status of the superjacent waters. The water column above the Continental Shelf can therefore be the EEZ if and to the extent that it has been established or the High Sea, where no EEZ is established or where the continental margin reaches beyond 200 NM (extended Continental Shelf). Due to the varying legal regimes of the seabed and ocean floor of the Continental Shelf and the superjacent water, discrepancies arise for the regulation of activities in the respective terrains. Activities such as bottom trawling, for instance, affect both sedentary species on the Continental Shelf and fish swimming in the water column.[154]

Within the 200 NM zone of the EEZ, the coastal State has more sovereign rights to regulate activities by other States, such as jurisdiction for the protection and preservation of the marine environment under Art. 56 (1) (b) (iii) UNCLOS. In the case and to the extent that an EEZ has been established, the coastal State has sovereign rights and the respective obligation to protect and preserve the marine environment for both the activities in the water column and on the ocean floor in so far as the sovereign rights cover the activity on the Continental Shelf.[155] The sovereign rights of the coastal State decrease the further away from the land. Beyond the 200 NM border, activities of other States in the water column are covered by the freedom of the High Sea, while the coastal State has exclusive sovereign rights on the Continental Shelf for the purposes stipulated in Art. 77 ff. UNCLOS. The coastal State, however, may have an interest to regulate activities in the water column over the Continental Shelf that have harmful effects on the seabed on the ocean floor.[156] It will be investigated which State or States are bound by the obligation to protect and preserve the marine environment for specific activities that take place on the Continental Shelf but also affect the water column, such as carbon sinking and

[154]Mossop (2017), p. 119.

[155]Mossop (2017), p. 174.

[156]Mossop (2017), p. 119; Mossop (2007), p. 296.

activities that affect both, the water column and the Continental Shelf, such as bottom trawl fishing.

Activities on the Continental Shelf That Affect the Water Column (Carbon Sinking)

The development of new technologies led to activities in the sea that did not exist in the times of the adoption of the UNCLOS. The capture and storage of carbon in the Continental Shelf (carbon sinking), for instance, is a technique that is currently being explored to reduce the carbon dioxide that has been released into the atmosphere. From a legal perspective, carbon sinking could be categorised as marine pollution under Art. 1 (1) (4) UNCLOS, exploration and exploitation of the marine environment under Art. 56 (1), (3) UNCLOS in conjunction with Art. 77 (1), (4) UNCLOS and drilling and tunnelling on the Continental Shelf under Arts. 60, 80, 81 and 85 UNCLOS.[157] Because carbon sinking directly affects the Continental Shelf, the coastal State is competent and obliged to regulate this activity, including the right to exclude others. Other States do not have a right to use the Continental Shelf in a way that interferes with the sovereign rights of the coastal State in this terrain; a discrepancy between the rights of the coastal State and other States does not arise.

Activities That Affect the Water Column and Continental Shelf (Bottom Trawl Fishing)

Other activities can affect both the water column and the Continental Shelf, such as bottom trawling. Bottom trawl fishing targets the living organisms in the water column and is covered by the freedom of fishing. The dragging of the heavy trawl gear across the ocean floor, however, naturally affects the resources on the Continental Shelf significantly, which are covered by the exclusive sovereign rights of the coastal States under Art. 77 UNCLOS. Therefore, the coastal State may be interested in establishing MPAs that exclude bottom trawling on its extended Continental Shelf.

Another difficulty arises due to the specification as sedentary or non-sedentary species. The sovereign rights of the coastal State on the Continental Shelf regarding living organisms are limited by Art. 77 (1), (4) UNCLOS to the exploration and exploitation of sedentary species, organisms which, at the harvestable stage, are either immobile on or under the seabed or are unable to move except in constant physical contact with the seabed or the subsoil. The emphasis of the regulation on the Continental Shelf, thus, is put on species that live in connection with the seafloor, comparable to crops in a field. The idea that the sovereign rights under Art. 77 UNCLOS should be extended to all bottom-dwelling fishes was rejected in the

[157] Proelss (2017), Art. 81, mn. 13 and Art. 56, mn. 35.

UNCLOS III Conference.[158] Art. 77 UNCLOS demonstrates that the regime on the Continental Shelf only applies to the seabed and ocean floor and not to the water column above.[159]

Species that populate hydrothermal vents and seamounts include but are not limited to tubeworms, clams, mussels, barnacles, snails, lobsters, clams, anemones, limpets, shrimps, benthic fish species and microbes.[160] In practice, the distinction between sedentary species that are regulated by the coastal State and other living organisms in the water column of the extended Continental Shelf that are free to all States has led to international disputes: In 1994, an American vessel was arrested over harvesting scallops on the Canadian Continental Shelf. The dispute ended when the USA ultimately accepted the status of scallops as sedentary species. In 1963, a 'lobster war' arose when French fishermen harvested lobster on the Continental Shelf of Brazil, with France claiming that lobsters are non-sedentary species because of their capability to swim. The dispute was settled by a compromise that granted France limited access to the lobsters.[161] While a line must be drawn in order to make a distinction between sedentary and non-sedentary species, in practice this is difficult and can seem artificial. As the following statement derived from parliamentary debates in the UK shows, what it comes down to is that '[...] lobsters swim and crabs do not. Therefore, crabs are within the Convention and lobsters are not.'[162]

The competence to adopt regulations for living organisms on the Continental Shelf thus depends on their classification as sedentary species, which fall within the exclusive sovereign right of the coastal State, and other living organisms that are covered by the regulations on the water column, which can be the EEZ or High Sea.[163] While the coastal State has sovereign rights for the exploitation of fish in the EEZ under Art. 56 (1) (a) (i), 61 ff. UNCLOS with a corresponding obligation to protect the marine environment under Art. 56 (1) (b) (iii) UNCLOS, in conjunction with the *erga omnes* obligation to protect and preserve the marine environment, the exploration of fish in the High Sea is covered by the freedom of fishing of all States under Art. 87 (1) (e), 116 ff. UNCLOS. All States are obliged to protect and preserve the marine environment in this terrain. On the extended Continental Shelf, a discrepancy thus arises between the competencies and obligation of the coastal State on the Continental Shelf and the competencies and corresponding obligations of the State community in the water column of the High Sea.

158 Mossop (2007), pp. 291 f.

159 Proelss (2017), Art. 77, mn. 24.

160 Freestone (2012), p. 193; Rogers (2019), p. 44; Mossop (2017), p. 114.

161 Mossop (2007), p. 292.

162 Hansard, HC Vol. 688, CS 277 (1964).

163 Mossop (2017), p. 106.

Involvement of RFMOs

Under the customary regulation of Art. 197 UNCLOS (and Art. Art. 61 (2) (2nd sentence) UNCLOS specifically for the EEZ), States are obliged to cooperate and coordinate to protect and preserve the marine environment. Under Art. 116 (b) UNCLOS in conjunction with Art. 64 (1), 65 UNCLOS States are specifically obliged to establish international organisations for the conservation of highly migratory fish stock and marine mammals in the High Sea and the EEZ.

The extant literature points out that the most effective way for a coastal State to implement an MPA on the extended Continental Shelf that restricts activities in the High Sea is in cooperation with an RFMO, because where and if mandated, RFMOs can adopt legally binding rules for the water column.[164] The OSPAR Commission, for instance, is one of the first organisations that successfully implemented a cross-regional MPA that applies to ABNJ and the Continental Shelf in Portugal and harmonises international regulations for the ABNJ and Portuguese legalisations to this end.[165] The Altair Seamount and Antialtair Seamount on the extended Continental Shelf of Portugal are protected by Portuguese measures relating to the seabed and ocean floor and measures by OSPAR for the water column. The jurisdiction of OSPAR, however, is limited to its mandate and cannot enact measures regarding fisheries, mining or navigation. Other organisations with competencies in this area include but are not limited to the IMO, the IWC or the NEAFC.[166] Memoranda of understanding for the cooperation between these organisations have been pursued by the OSPAR and been signed *inter alia* with the International Council for the Exploration of the Seas, the NEAFC and the ISA.

The success of OSPAR and NEAFC MPAs is due to the mandate and participation of the States, which is supported by the fact that the relevant States are members of the EU. Through the Natura 2000 Directives and the Marine Strategy Directive, the member States of the EU are obliged to adopt national laws and regulations to protect the marine environment. The legal pressure on the States through a binding obligation to protect the marine environment evidently enhances the protection efforts by the States. The recognition of the international, legally binding obligation to adopt national and international legislation to protect and preserve the marine environment through, therefore advances the cooperation of the States with regional and international organisations for the protection and preservation of the marine environment and the enhanced establishment of MPAs to this end.

The problem with RFMOs, however, is their limited regional and substantive competence. RFMOs either apply only to a specific region such as the North-East Atlantic (OSPAR and NEAFC) and activity such as fishing (NEAFC) or pollution (OSPAR). Furthermore, and most critically, regulations by RFMOs meet the same restrictions as other international agreements and only bind their parties. Third States

164 Mossop (2017), p. 108.

165 O'Leary et al. (2012), p. 598; https://www.ospar.org/documents?v=7279; Mossop (2017), p. 109.

166 Mossop (2017), pp. 218 f.

are not bound by their regulations. Moreover, regional and international organisations do not exist for all parts of the oceans, so that there is no comprehensive coverage for all parts of the sea. Where established, RFMOs provide a suitable forum for discussions and, therefore, can be a tool to fulfil the obligation to cooperate and enhance the establishment of comprehensive MPAs.

Limitation of Art. 78 (2) UNCLOS

If the activity directly impacts the exclusive sovereign right of the coastal State on its resources under Art. 77 UNCLOS, the coastal State has the sovereign right to establish an MPA in this terrain that regulates this activity. This is the case, for instance, if other States conduct bottom trawling for sedentary species on the Continental Shelf of another State. This is different if the trawling activity does not primarily target sedentary species but other living resources in the water column. While the targeted species does not fall within the exclusive resources of the coastal State, the impact of the heavy trawl gear that is being dragged across the ocean floor significantly harms the resources of the coastal State on its Continental Shelf. In this case, the right of the coastal State to establish an MPA competes with the High Sea freedoms of the other State. The right of the coastal State to regulate the respective activity has to be established on a case-by-case basis and with respect to its impact on the resources of the coastal State.[167]

Pursuant to Art. 78 (2) UNCLOS, the exercise of the rights of the coastal State over the Continental Shelf must not infringe or result in any unjustifiable interference with navigation and other rights and freedoms of other States as provided for in the UNCLOS. The freedoms of other States under (Art. 58 (2) UNCLOS in conjunction with) Art. 87 UNCLOS, therefore, must be respected by the coastal State when implementing national laws and regulations for the protection and preservation of the marine environment. Vice versa, the freedoms of the States in the High Sea must be exercised with due regard for the interests of other States in their exercise of the freedom of the High Seas and with respect to activities in the Area under Art. 87 (2) UNCLOS and are conditioned by other regulations of the UNCLOS under Art. 87 (1) (2nd sentence) UNCLOS. States exercising activities in the High Sea are therefore obliged to adopt international legislation for the protection and preservation of the marine environment. Other regulations inform the interpretation of justifiable and unjustifiable interferences of the coastal State of the UNCLOS and general international law. Generally, as long as a regulation for the protection and preservation of the marine environment by the coastal State that restricts the freedom of the High Sea is demonstrably connected to exercising its sovereign rights under Art. 77 UNCLOS, the restrictions by the coastal State are justified. The regime on the Continental Shelf, therefore, may give leverage to the coastal State to control activities of other States in the High Sea.[168]

[167] Mossop (2017), p. 188.

[168] Mossop (2007), pp. 297 and 299.

Although the coastal State is not competent to exclude all activities in the High Sea that potentially impact its resources on the Continental Shelf, also the other State that exercises the activity is under the obligation to protect and preserve the marine environment due to the *erga ones* status and the conditioning of the freedoms of the High Sea by Art. 87 (1) (2nd sentence) UNCLOS.[169] All States are obliged to protect and preserve the marine environment and the freedoms of the High Sea are subordinated under this obligation. For this reason, the unjustifiable interference clause in Art. 78 (2) UNCLOS does not invalidly interfere with the cogent status of the obligation to protect and preserve the marine environment in the light of Art. 53 VCLT.

General Obligation to Protect and Preserve the Marine Environment

Other than, for instance, Art. 59 UNCLOS for the EEZ, Part VI UNCLOS does not contain a clause on residual rights in the Continental Shelf. The question arises, which States are generally obliged to adopt legislative measures to protect and preserve the marine environment for activities on the Continental Shelf that do not fall within the exploration and exploitation of the natural resources on the Continental Shelf in the sense of Art. 77 (1), (4) UNCLOS and that are not covered by other regulations of the UNCLOS. Although not particularly codified, such as in Art. 58 (2) UNCLOS, the extant literature suggests that other activities are free to all States.[170] Consequently, all States would be obliged to protect and preserve the marine environment from activities that do not fall within the sovereign right of the coastal State on the Continental Shelf.

Freedoms of the High Sea Generally Apply to Continental Shelf

Other than Art. 58 (1) and (2) UNCLOS, which expressly declare the freedoms on the High Sea as applicable in the EEZ with some limitations, the regulations on the Continental Shelf do not specifically refer to the applicability of the freedoms. However, Art. 79 (1) UNCLOS confirms the freedom of all States to lay submarine cables and pipelines on the Continental Shelf and stipulates specific requirements to do so in Art. 79 (2)-(5) UNCLOS. Both the Continental Shelf as well as the EEZ 'are intended to be exercised far beyond the traditionally recognised extent of the Territorial Seas, in areas where the régime of the High Seas used undoubtedly to hold sway. In this sense, both of these régimes should be considered as derogation from traditional international law.'[171] The general principle that applies on the Continental Shelf and in the EEZ, therefore, is the freedom of the High Sea, with

[169] Mossop (2017), p. 107.

[170] Mossop (2017), pp. 107 and 120.

[171] ICJ, *Continental Shelf* (Tunisia v. Libyan Arab Jamahiriya), Judgment, Dissenting Opinion Judge Oda, ICJ Reports 1982, pp. 18, 231, para 126.

specific regulations for each terrain. The regime on the Continental Shelf and the EEZ are extensions of the rights of the coastal State but beyond the limits of its Territorial Sea to an area, that was free of sovereign rights. The basic principle in these areas, therefore, is the freedoms of the High Sea, with limitations in the respective provisions of the EEZ and the Continental Shelf.[172] Thus, the freedoms of the High Sea generally apply in the Continental Shelf, where the regulations of the Continental Shelf do not stipulate sovereign rights to the coastal State. All States are therefore obliged to adopt international legislation by adopting international treaties for the protection and preservation of the marine environment under Art. 87 (1) (2nd sentence) UNCLOS in conjunction with the cogent obligation to protect and preserve the marine environment on the extended Continental Shelf.

No Application of the Sovereign Rights of the EEZ to the Continental Shelf

If and to the extent that an EEZ has been established, the application of the freedoms of the High Sea to the Continental Shelf leads varying degrees of sovereign rights of the coastal State on the Continental Shelf and the overlying body of water. Pursuant to Art. 78 (1) UNCLOS, the rights of the coastal State over the Continental Shelf do not affect the legal status of the superjacent waters. The question arises if reversely the legal status of the superjacent water is capable of influencing the legal status of the Continental Shelf, in favour of the harmonisation of the regimes of the water column and its underlying seabed and ocean floor. Specifically, do the sovereign and jurisdiction rights of the coastal State in the EEZ apply to the Continental Shelf within the 200 NM zone (where and to the extent an EEZ is established), so that the legal status of this inner Continental Shelf corresponds to the legal status of its water column? This would lead to stringent results in practice because activities in the superjacent water and the underlying seabed and subsoil are often hard to distinguish. However, a distinction of the legal regimes that apply to the Continental Shelf within 200 NM where an EEZ is established and outside this area would lead to a split 'inner' and 'outer' Continental Shelf.

No Distinction Between Inner and Outer Continental Shelf

It needs to be assessed if a distinction of the Continental Shelf within the 200 NM off the relevant baselines ('Inner Continental Shelf') and beyond this limit ('Outer Continental Shelf') is permissible. This is supported by Art. 82 (1) UNCLOS, which distinguished between inner and outer Continental Shelf. Accordingly, the coastal State shall make payments or contributions in kind in respect of the exploitation of the non-living resources of the Continental Shelf beyond 200 NM from the relevant baselines.

[172] Proelss (2017), Art. 79, mn. 2.

However, this does not apply to the general legal regime of the Continental Shelf. The EEZ and the Continental Shelf were developed separately.[173] While the Continental Shelf was already entailed in the 1958 CCS, the EEZ was first introduced in the 1982 UNCLOS. In the 1958 Geneva Conventions, the water column beyond the Territorial Sea was the free High Sea under Art. 1, 2 CHS. Under Art. 1 CCS, the Continental Shelf was defined as the seabed and subsoil of the submarine areas adjacent to the coast but outside the Territorial Sea, to a depth of 200 m or, beyond that limit, to where the depth of the superjacent waters admits of the exploitation of the natural resources of the said areas. Art. 2 (1), (2) CCS granted the coastal State the exclusive sovereign right for the exploration and exploitation of the natural resources of the Continental Shelf. When introducing the regime of the EEZ in the 1982 UNCLOS, the State parties to the UNCLOS made the separateness of the EEZ and the Continental Shelf clear in the regulations of the UNCLOS, by stipulating that the rights with respect to the seabed and ocean floor must be governed by Part VI UNCLOS and not Part V UNCLOS (Art. 56 (3) UNCLOS).[174] The legal regimes of the EEZ and the Continental Shelf are, therefore, related but independent and the legal rights of the Continental Shelf are essentially the same, inside and outside the 200 NM limit.[175] The sovereign rights of the coastal State in the EEZ and the Continental Shelf can therefore differ.

This result is congruent with the consistent jurisprudence of international courts and tribunals. In the *Barbados v. Trinidad and Tobago Arbitration*, the PCA rejected the idea of a split Continental Shelf and confirmed the consistent jurisprudence by stating that 'the continental shelf and the EEZ coexist as separate institutions, as the latter has not absorbed the former [. . .].'[176] According to the PCA, 'there is in law only a single "Continental Shelf" rather than an inner Continental Shelf and a separate extended or outer Continental Shelf.'[177] As judge Oda put it in its dissenting opinion of the *Continental Shelf (Tunisia v. Libyan Arab Jamahiriya) Case,* the consequence is 'the relation of the [EEZ] to the Continental Shelf remains profoundly ambiguous, particularly where such "interface" issues as the exploitation of ocean-floor minerals are concerned.'[178]

---

[173] ICJ, *Continental Shelf* (Tunisia v. Libyan Arab Jamahiriya), Judgment, Dissenting Opinion Judge Oda, ICJ Reports 1982, pp. 18, 231, para 126.

[174] Mossop (2017), p. 9.

[175] Mossop (2017), p. 9.

[176] PCA, *Barbados v. The Republic of Trinidad and Tobago*, Award of the Arbitral Tribunal of 11.04.2006, p. 71, para. 234; ICJ, *Continental Shelf*, Libyan Arab Jamahiriya/Malta, Judgment, ICJ Reports 1985, pp. 13, 24, para. 33.

[177] PCA, *Barbados v. The Republic of Trinidad and Tobago*, Award of the Arbitral Tribunal of 11.04.2006, p. 65, para. 213; Mossop (2007), p. 288.

[178] ICJ, *Continental Shelf* (Tunisia v. Libyan Arab Jamahiriya), Judgment, Dissenting Opinion Judge Oda, ICJ Reports 1982, pp. 18, 229, para 120.

6.5.5.4 Conclusion: Continental Shelf

The coastal State has exclusive sovereign rights for exploring and exploiting the natural resources and living organisms belonging to sedentary species under Art. 77 UNCLOS. The right to manage its resources comprises the right of the coastal State to exclude others from accessing them, especially because the sovereign rights are exclusive under Art. 77 (2) UNCLOS and Part VI UNCLOS do not oblige the State to allow access to the surplus of its resources, such as in the EEZ under Art. 62 (2) UNCLOS. To the extent of its sovereign rights in Art. 77 UNCLOS, the *erga omnes* obligation to protect and preserve the marine environment, therefore, applies to the coastal State. The coastal State is obliged to adopt national legislation to protect and preserve the marine environment from the exploration and exploitation of the natural resources and living organisms belonging to sedentary species.

The coastal State can regulate activities in the superjacent water column in so far as they directly affect those sovereign rights. Activities of other States in the superjacent water or on the Continental Shelf that do not directly affect the exclusive sovereign right of the coastal State are free to all States and need to be regulated similarly to the regime on the High Sea. Thus the international community as a whole is obliged to adopt international legislation for the protection and preservation of the marine environment from those activities.

Pursuant to Art. 208 (1) UNCLOS coastal States are furthermore obliged to adopt national laws and regulations to prevent, reduce and control pollution of the marine environment from activities on the seabed and artificial islands, installations and structures. Other States, acting especially through competent international organizations or diplomatic conferences, are obliged to establish global and regional rules, standards and recommended practices and procedures to prevent, reduce and control pollution of the marine environment referred to in paragraph one under Art. 208 (5) UNCLOS.

Pursuant to Art. 78 (2) UNCLOS, the exercise of the rights of the coastal State over the Continental Shelf must not infringe or result in any unjustifiable interference with navigation and other rights and freedoms of other States as provided for in the UNCLOS. Other rights and freedoms of the other States, vice versa, must be exercised with due regard for the interests of other States in their exercise of the freedom of the High Seas and are conditioned by other regulations of the UNCLOS under Art. 87 (1) (2nd sentence) UNCLOS. The obligation to protect and preserve the marine environment applies to both the coastal State as well as other States in exercising their activities. The limitation of activities on the Continental Shelf by the coastal State, therefore, does not unjustifiably interfere with other rights and freedoms of the coastal State if and to the extent that it is in complying with its obligation to protect and preserve the marine environment because other States, likewise, are bound by this obligation.

6.5.6 Conclusion: Competence to Establish MPAs in the Zones of the Sea

The obligation to protect and preserve the marine environment applies to all areas of the sea, irrespective of sovereignty, sovereign or jurisdictional zones.[179] The obligation to protect and preserve the marine environment entails the obligation to adopt legislation to this end. In so far as this legislation applies to a specific terrain in the ocean, this definition meets the definition of the establishment of MPAs. Legislation is the adoption of national laws and regulations and international treaties.

In the Territorial Sea the coastal States have exclusive sovereignty over the water column as well as the seabed and subsoil under Art. 2 (1), (2) UNCLOS. The obligation to protect and preserve the marine environment in this area obliges the coastal State to adopt national legislation to this end. The sovereign rights of the coastal States wane the further away from land.

Prior to the UNCLOS, all areas adjacent and beyond the Territorial Sea used to be the High Sea under Art. 2, 1 CHS. The freedoms of the High Sea, therefore, generally apply to all areas beyond the Territorial Sea. Pursuant to Art. 87 (1) (2nd sentence) UNCLOS, the freedoms of the High Sea are not granted limitless but are conditioned by other regulations of the UNCLOS and general international law. The *erga omnes* obligation to protect and preserve the marine environment thus applies in this terrain; States are obliged to adopt international legislation for the protection and preservation of the marine environment for activities in the High Sea.

In the EEZ, the Continental Shelf and the Area the freedoms of the High Sea generally apply except where other competencies are regulated. In the EEZ, the coastal State has jurisdiction for protecting and preserving the marine environment under Art. 56 (1) (b) (iii) UNCLOS and is therefore obliged to adopt national legislation to this end in the EEZ. On the Continental Shelf, the coastal State has exclusive sovereign rights for exploring and exploiting the natural resources and the living organisms belonging to sedentary species pursuant to Art. 77 UNCLOS and is obliged to adopt national legislation for the protection and preservation of the marine environment from activities in this connection. In the Area, the ISA is the competent authority for exploring and exploiting non-living mineral resources and adopting international legislation to ensure effective protection for the marine environment under the obligation to protect and preserve the marine environment in conjunction with Art. 145, 134, (2), (1), 1 (1) (1) and (4), 133 UNCLOS.

[179] PCA, *South China Sea Arbitration*, Philippines v. China (Award), p. 373, para. 940.

6.5.7 International Organisations

International organisations play an essential role in promoting conservation objectives and enhancing the cooperation of States to conclude agreements and treaties to this end.[180]

6.5.7.1 International Organisations General

The UNCLOS is binding for international organisations under Art. 1 (2), 305 (1) (f) UNCLOS that become party to it. The obligation to protect and preserve the marine environment, therefore, also applies to international organisations that are party to the UNCLOS.[181]

One major impediment to the progressive protection and preservation of the marine environment is that there is (generally) no authority in international law, which is mandated to adopt laws. International organisations are limited to their competence. The parties to the UNCLOS did not establish one single Organisation, which is mandated for all aspects concerning the Sea.[182] Rather, various international bodies are involved in managing the law of the sea. Pursuant Art. 197 UNCLOS States shall cooperate on a global basis and, as appropriate, on a regional basis, directly or through competent international organisations, in formulating and elaborating international rules, standards and recommended practices and procedures consistent with the UNCLOS for the protection and preservation of the marine environment. The formulation of 'competent international organization' shows that States can address a range of international bodies for this purpose.[183] The obligation to cooperate is expressed in further specific regulations such as Art. 118 UNCLOS for the conservation of and management of living resources in the High Sea. Under Art. 118 (3rd sentence), States are obliged to cooperate to establish subregional or regional fisheries organizations for the conservation and management of living resources in the areas of the High Seas.

Through the adoption of universal international treaties or the creation of rules of customary international law, States may create a legal basis to mandate States or international organisations to adopt legally binding laws. On a global level, for instance, the ISA has been provided with the competence to adopt appropriate rules, regulations and procedures for, *inter alia,* the protection and conservation of the natural resources of the Area and the prevention of damage to flora and fauna of the marine environment under Art. 145 (b) UNCLOS. However, the mandate of the ISA is limited to the exploration for and exploitation of mineral resources on the seabed, ocean floor and subsoil of ABNJ. Within this scope, the ISA is obliged to

---

[180] See: Involvement of RFMOs.

[181] Nordquist et al. (2013), 192.2.

[182] Scott (2019), p. 162; Wolfrum (1990), pp. 324 f.

[183] Harrison (2017), p. 31.

protect and preserve the marine environment and adopt respective legislation under Art. 145 UNCLOS. The IMO is the United Nations agency responsible for developing and adopting measures to improve the safety and security of international shipping and to prevent pollution from ships. The IMO serves as an umbrella organisation for many specific conventions that require the establishment of an according organisation, such as for the 1973/78 MARPOL, 1974 SOLAS or the 1972 London Convention.[184] The IMO has adopted mandatory rules as well as guidelines to protect the marine environment to this end. Examples are Particularly Sensitive Sea Areas that have been designated under the IMO Guidelines or Special Areas under the 1973/78 MARPOL Convention.[185] Further global organisations with mandates for issues relating to the sea include but are not limited to the Food and Agriculture Organization to promote the 'conservation of natural resources and the adoption of improved methods of agricultural production' (Art. I (2) Constitution of the United Nations Food and Agriculture Organization),[186] the UNEP, the IWC, the EU or the Committee of the World Heritage Convention.[187]

The obligation to cooperate in Art. 197, 118 UNCLOS is also given effect through the establishment of a variety of RFMOs to this end.[188] Examples of RFMOs include but are not limited to the Association of Southeast Asian Nations (ASEAN), the OSPAR Commission, the NEAFC, the CCAMLR or the UNEP Regional Seas Programme and Convention.[189] Regional institutions may bear the advantage to have special knowledge of the legal, political and ecological needs of certain regions, which can make cooperation easier.[190] However, regional and international organisations do not yet exist for all parts of the oceans and their competence is limited to their mandate.[191] In total, there is no specialized authority with a comprehensive mandate to regulate all activities in all areas in the sea. Special organisations in the law of the sea either have a general mandate but are limited to a specific region or are global organisations but only have a mandate regarding specific issues.[192]

---

184 https://www.imo.org/en/About/Conventions/Pages/ListOfConventions.aspx; https://www.imo.org/en/About/Pages/Default.aspx; Freestone (2012), p. 196.

185 https://www.imo.org/en/OurWork/Environment/Pages/PSSAs.aspx.

186 FAO (2017), p. 3.

187 Sands (2012), p. 95; Harrison (2017), p. 31; https://www.cbd.int/cop/.

188 Mossop (2007), p. 297.

189 Sands (2012), pp. 108 ff.

190 Harrison (2017), p. 31; Tanaka (2019), pp. 427 f.

191 See: Involvement of RFMOs.

192 Freestone (2012), p. 195.

6.5.7.2 Security Council

'We must save the ocean if we are to save ourselves' is the credo of the famous marine biologist and so-called mother of the ocean Elisabeth Mann Borgese.[193] One of the major impediments for effective marine protection, is the lack of legally binding laws adopted by a universally mandated authority. International law is governed by the sovereign equality of States under Art. 2 Nr. 1 UN-Charter. States can determine the extent and if they bestow sovereign rights on international organisations. The members of the UN conferred on the Security Council primary responsibility for the maintenance of international peace and security under Art. 24 (1) UN Charter and agreed that in carrying out its duties under this responsibility, the Security Council acts on their behalf. Pursuant to Art. 25 UN Charter, the Members of the UN agreed to accept and carry out the decisions of the Security Council in accordance with Chapter V UN Charter. The Security Council of the UN thus is mandated to adopt decisions to maintain international peace and security that are legally binding for the UN member States.

Problems with increasing pressure on the terrestrial and marine environment from human activities are reflected in contemporary legal issues such as climate litigation or developments in legal personhood of natural features. Has marine protection grown into an issue of international peace and security because 'we must save the oceans if we are to save ourselves', so that the Security Council is mandated to adopt legally binding decisions for this purpose?[194]

Environmental Protection in Armed Conflicts

The mandate of the UN Security Council comprises the deliberate and non-deliberate destruction of marine environment in armed conflict. As the destructive capacity of weapons can 'have effects extremely harmful to human welfare' and these effects increased with new technology, international law reacted with limiting the extent to which the destruction of the environment in times of armed conflict is justifiable or even maybe deliberately used as a weapon.[195] When Iraq deliberately bombed Kuwaiti oil fields in the Gulf War, the Security Council declared in its Resolution 687 that Iraq is 'liable under international law for any loss, damage, including environmental damage and the depletion of natural resources, or injury to foreign Governments, nationals and corporations as a result of Iraq's unlawful

---

[193] 'Wir müssen die Ozeane retten, wenn wir uns selbst retten wollen!' (Elisabeth Mann-Borgese, translated by author); https://www.ardaudiothek.de/lesungen/elisabeth-mann-borgese-die-meer-frau/78862666; https://www.deutscher-meerespreis.de/2006-2009_en.html.

[194] Elisabeth Mann-Borgese, https://www.ardaudiothek.de/lesungen/elisabeth-mann-borgese-die-meer-frau/78862666; https://www.deutscher-meerespreis.de/2006-2009_en.html.

[195] Preamble 1976 UN Convention on the Prohibition of Military or Any Other Hostile Use of Environmental Modification Techniques (ENMOD, UNTS, Vol. 1108, p. 151); Reilly (1995–1996), p. 780.

invasion and occupation of Kuwait [. . .].'[196] Also, the non-deliberate destruction of the environment as the consequence of warfare is generally condemned by the international community.[197] 'States must take environmental considerations into account when assessing what is necessary and proportionate in the pursuit of legitimate military objectives.'[198]

Human Rights as Issues of International Peace and Security

While the traditional understanding of issues regarding international peace and security was limited to armed conflict, the Security Council has interpreted its powers as not debarred from taking measures such as for the protection of Human Rights in armed conflict for many years.[199] In response to the Libyan civil war, for instance, the Security Council demanded an immediate cease-fire and authorized the international community to *inter alia* establish a no-flight zone and freeze Libyan assets.[200] Moreover, the Security Council's mandate to adopt binding resolutions is accepted for the protection of Human Rights in times of peace because, as the president of the Security Council noted in 1992, '[t]he absence of war and military conflicts amongst States does not in itself ensure international peace and security. The non-military sources of instability in the economic, social, humanitarian and ecological fields have become threats to peace and security. The United Nations membership as a whole, working through the appropriate bodies, needs to give the highest priority to the solution of these matters.'[201]

Human Right to (Marine) Environment

If there is a Human Right to (marine) environment, the mandate of the Security Council to adopt legally binding decisions could be extended in this regard.

Human Right to Environment in International Law

The question if there is a Human Right to a safe, healthy, clean or sustainable environment is controverse. In the extant literature, there is no unanimous notion to this end. In a 2011 study, the High Commissioner for Human Rights stated that the

[196] UNSC S/RES/687, p. 7, para. 16.

[197] Art. 1 ENMOD; Art. 35 (3) 1977 Protocol I 1948 Geneva Convention (UNTS, Vol. 1125, No. I-17512); https://www.icrc.org/en/doc/resources/documents/article/other/57jn38.htm; https://archive.unu.edu/inter-linkages/docs/IEG/Elliot.pdf.

[198] ICJ, *Nuclear Weapons*, Advisory Opinion, ICJ Reports 1996, pp. 226, 242, para. 30.

[199] UNGA A/RES/60/1, p. 30, para. 139; Tomuschat (2019), p. 596.

[200] UNSC S/RES/1973 (2011), p. 2, para. 1, p. 3, para. 6, p. 5, para. 19.

[201] UN Docs S/23500, p. 3.

recognition of a Human Right to a healthy environment poses challenging questions; however, it confirms that 'environmental degradation has the potential to affect the realization of human rights.'[202] 'Hard' international Human Rights Law does not explicitly codify a Human Right to Environment. Under Art. 25 (1) of the 1948 Universal Declaration of Human Rights, everyone has the right to a standard of living adequate for the health and well-being of himself and of his family. The 1986 African Charter on Human and Peoples' Rights stipulates in Art. 24 that all peoples shall have the right to a general satisfactory environment favourable to their development.[203]

Several soft law regulations and other international agreements and treaties outside Human Rights Law do accept the right to environment as a basic Human Right.[204] Although proposals for an environmental Human Right were rejected at the Stockholm Conference in 1972, Principle 1 of the 1972 Stockholm Declaration declares that 'both aspects of man's environment, the natural and the man-made, are essential to his well-being and to the enjoyment of basic human rights the right to life itself.'[205] Principle 1 of the 1992 Rio Declaration states that 'human beings are at the centre of concerns for sustainable development. They are entitled to a healthy and productive life in harmony with nature.' Whether these principles constitute a Human Right to Nature is debated.[206] The 1982 UN World Charter for Nature stipulates that '[m]ankind is a part of nature and life depends on the uninterrupted functioning of natural systems which ensure the supply of energy and nutrients [. . .]. Nature shall be respected, and its essential processes shall not be impaired.'[207]

The adoption of Human Rights marked a paradigm shift in the history of international law by transferring sovereign powers of single States over individuals to the State community as a whole due to their fundamental value for mankind. Similarly, in Art. 25, 24 (1) UNCLOS, States have abdicated sovereign powers for the maintenance of peace and security to the Security Council by mandating it to adopt legally binding decisions to this end. The sovereign equality of States under Art. 2 Nr. 1 UN Charter comprises the positive freedom to create rights and the negative freedom to renounce them. By codifying Art. 192 UNCLOS and letting this obligation evolve into an *erga omnes* rule of customary international law, States have abdicated their sovereign rights for the protection and preservation of the marine environment by entering a legally binding obligation to this end. This is particularly the case where an obligation has evolved into *jus cogens,* which debars the freedom of States to dispose freely of this right under Art. 2 Nr. 1 UN-Charter, Art. 53 (1st sentence) VCLT entirely. By letting a regulation evolve into *jus* cogens,

[202] UNGA A/HRC/19/34, pp. 4 f. para. 11 and p. 5, para. 15.

[203] CAB/LEG/67/3 rev. 5, 21 ILM. 58 (1982).

[204] Handl (2020), p. 137; https://legal.un.org/avl/ha/dunche/dunche.html.

[205] https://legal.un.org/avl/ha/dunche/dunche.html.

[206] https://legal.un.org/avl/ha/dunche/dunche.html.

[207] UNGA A/RES/37/7, Preamble (a) and General Principle 1.

States, therefore, waive their freedom of treaties and sovereign powers to this end.[208]

At the same time, peremptory norms of international law are 'fundamental values of international community.'[209] It is for this essential status that the sovereign rights of States are limited in favour of *jus cogens* regulations.[210] States have accepted this fundamental value of the marine environment for mankind and limited their sovereign rights in favour of its protection, by stipulating Art. 192 UNCLOS and letting this regulation develop into customary international law that grew into a peremptory norm of international law. The limitation of sovereign powers of the State for fundamental values of mankind is the core appliance of Human Rights. This core principle is reflected in the obligation to protect and preserve the marine environment, where States have irreversibly limited their sovereign powers to dispose of this right under Art. 53 VCLT because of its fundamental value for mankind. Therefore, the protection and preservation of the marine environment resembles the case in which the Security Council is mandated to adopt legally binding regulations for the protection of Human Rights. The Security Council is thus mandated to adopt decisions for the protection and preservation of the marine environment that are legally binding for all UN members.

Human Right to Environment Accepted by Relevant Organisations

Atmospheric related environmental impacts such as air pollution, climate change and ozone layer depletion, land-based environmental threats such as desertification, deforestations and freshwater scarcity, threats to the marine environment through stress on the ocean, depletion of species and pollution cause hunger, deprivation of livelihoods, environmental refugees, disruption of political relationships between States, natural disasters such as hurricanes, tropical cyclones, tsunamis, droughts and floods.[211] Hazardous waste such as nuclear waste, chemical contamination and pollution as well as the loss of biodiversity are threats to the environment that impact Human Rights.[212]

International organisations such as the Office of the High Commissioner for Human Rights and the Council of Europe accept the existence of a Human Right to Environment. In a 2011 study, the High Commissioner for Human Rights stated that the recognition of a Human Right to a healthy environment poses difficult questions; however he confirms that 'environmental degradation has the potential to affect the realization of human rights.'[213] As the High Commissioner of Human Rights put it in its report: 'In summary, a number of environmental threats have, or

---

[208] Caflish (1992), p. 78; Wiegandt (2001), p. 72.

[209] Charlesworth and Chinkin (1993), p. 65.

[210] Reilly (1995–1996), p. 767.

[211] UNSC S/RES/1973 (2011), p. 5, para. 16 ff.; https://archive.unu.edu/inter-linkages/docs/IEG/Elliot.pdf.

[212] UNSC S/RES/1973 (2011), p. 5, para. 19.

[213] UNGA A/HRC/19/34, pp. 4 f. para. 11 and p. 5, para. 15.

will have, an adverse impact on all aspects of human rights and well-being, and environmental protection must be ensured to protect human rights and sustain and improve human well-being. [. . .] human rights and the environment are interrelated, [. . .] the environment plays a critical part in protecting and promoting human rights. [. . .] the need to protect and promote a healthy environment is indispensable not only for the sake of human rights, but also to protect the Common Heritage of Mankind.'[214] Likewise, the Council of Europe confirms that '[c]lean environment is a precondition to the enjoyment of human rights: the full enjoyment of everyone's rights to life, health, quality private and family life or home, depends on healthy ecosystems and their benefits to people.'[215]

Human Right to Environment in National Jurisprudence

There is a rising number of successful cases in climate litigation in national law that confirm the interconnectedness of the right to life and environmental protection. The Dutch Supreme Court confirmed that the risks of climate change fall within the scope of Art. 2 (right to life) and Art. 8 (private and family life) of the ECHR and acknowledged that climate change is a human rights issue. The Supreme Court recognised that each State is obliged to prevent climate change and affirmed the Netherlands' obligation to reduce its greenhouse gas emissions by at least 25 per cent by the end of 2020 (as compared to 1990 levels).[216] The Federal Court of Australia ruled in 2021 that the environment minister has a duty of care to younger people, which obliges it not to act in a way that causes harm from climate change to younger people.[217] Other national cases confirmed the obligation of States to take efficient climate action, such as the Friends of the Irish Environment Case, in which the Irish Supreme Court found that Irish climate change mitigation plans lacked important details.[218] In Germany, the Federal Constitution Court ruled in 2021 that the climate action legislation was not sufficient to meet the goal of limiting global warming to 2 or 1,5 degrees Celsius, because it lacks regulations for emission reduction targets for the time after 2030. The ruling forces the legislature to improve the legislative act.[219]

---

214 UNGA A/HRC/19/34, p. 6, para. 22 f.

215 https://www.coe.int/en/web/portal/human-rights-for-the-planet.

216 https://www.herbertsmithfreehills.com/latest-thinking/the-new-environment-for-climate-change-litigation; https://www.lexology.com/library/detail.aspx?g=9b6564bd-6ca2-437c-bc64-03293ded2928.

217 https://theconversation.com/in-a-landmark-judgment-the-federal-court-found-the-environment-minister-has-a-duty-of-care-to-young-people-161650.

218 https://www.bailii.org/ie/cases/IESC/2020/2020IESC49.html; https://www.ejiltalk.org/the-european-convention-of-human-rights-and-climate-change-finally/.

219 BVerfG, 1 BvR 2656/18; https://www.bundesverfassungsgericht.de/SharedDocs/Pressemitteilungen/DE/2021/bvg21-031.html; https://www.tagesschau.de/inland/klimaschutzgesetz-bundesverfassungsgericht-101.html.

Human Right to Environment in International Jurisprudence

The ECtHR has ruled in approximately 300 cases related to the environment. In the first application concerning Human Rights and Climate Change, eight Portuguese young people (between eight and 21 years) applied to the ECtHR, arguing that the increased forest fires in Portugal are the direct result of global warming.[220] In the Senior Women for Climate Protection Switzerland, a group of senior women is taking the Swiss Government to the ECtHR because they see their health threatened by heatwaves, landslides and floods, which are enhanced due to the climate crisis.[221]

Further issues concerning Human Rights and environmental claims arise with regard to sea-level rise due to climate warming, which poses potential harms to people living on threatened coastlines. A group of eight inhabitants of the Torres Strait Islands submitted a petition to the United Nations Human Rights Committee, alleging the failure of the Australian Government to take action to reduce greenhouse gas emissions.[222] The UN Special Rapporteur for Human Rights and the Environment Mr. David R. Boyd laid down an independent legal brief to the Human Rights Committee that '[h]uman rights depend on a healthy environment, which includes a safe climate. The effects of the climate crisis are being felt right now by those on the climate frontline, such as residents of small islands, but they don't have a seat at the table. By failing to accept that climate change is affecting the Torres Strait Islander people, failing to substantially reduce emissions and failing to facilitate adaptation to the changes, the Australian Government isn't meeting their human rights obligations.'[223]

A further historic case concerns the threatened deportation of Mr. Ioane Teitiota and his family to their home country Kiribati by New Zealand. Mr. Teitiota applied to the UN Human Rights Committee, arguing that the deportation is unlawful because the sea level rise had rendered Kiribati uninhabitable. The Committee accepted the claim; however, it determined that enough protection measures were put in place. Although the claim was unsuccessful, the Committee confirmed that harm induced by climate change can occur through sudden onsets such as flooding and storms and slow onsets processes such as sea-level rise. Both can be a reason for individuals to prompt individuals to cross borders and to seek protection from harms related to climate change.[224]

---

[220] https://www.coe.int/en/web/portal/human-rights-environment.

[221] https://klimaseniorinnen.ch/english/; https://www.greenpeace.org/international/press-release/45545/climate-seniors-to-sue-switzerland-before-the-european-court-of-human-rights/.

[222] UNHCHR (2021), p. 52; UNGA, A775/298 Annex, p. 9, para. 30; http://climatecasechart.com/climate-change-litigation/non-us-case/petition-of-torres-strait-islanders-to-the-united-nations-human-rights-committee-alleging-violations-stemming-from-australias-inaction-on-climate-change/.

[223] https://www.clientearth.org/latest/press-office/press/un-experts-lend-weight-to-torres-strait-human-rights-climate-complaint/; https://nit.com.au/torres-strait-eight-backed-by-un-human-rights-experts/.

[224] https://www.ohchr.org/EN/NewsEvents/Pages/DisplayNews.aspx?NewsID=25482&LangID=E.

An overall assessment of the latest developments in diplomacy, international organisations and national as well as international jurisprudence shows a trend toward the acceptance that the wellbeing of humans and the environment are interconnected. Although there is no 'hard' Human Right to Environment in international Human Rights Law yet, its acceptance in the international community is growing. Activities in the sea that evidently have destructive effects on the marine environment, such as bottom trawling could be prohibited by the Security Council through by adopting legally binding decisions.

Conclusion: Security Council

All UN member States have abdicated sovereign rights to the Security Council, which adopts some form of ultimate global authority that may offer hope for a more effective environmental protection.[225] It may adopt legally binding decisions for the purpose of the maintenance of international peace and security under Art. 25, 24 (1) UN-Charter, which comprise the protection of the environment and the protection of Human Rights.

Although a Human Right to Environment is not yet expressly contained in any 'hard' international Human Rights Declaration, the trend obviously marches in the direction of the recognition of the interconnectedness of human wellbeing and the wellbeing of the environment and the acknowledgement of a Human Right to Environment. The emergence of the obligation to protect and preserve the marine environment into *jus cogens* procures its status as Human Right. Peremptory norms of international law are universally accepted because of their fundamental value to the international community as a whole and States have already limited their sovereign right to derogate this obligation under Art. 53 VCLT.

Under Art. 34 UN-Charter, the Security Council may investigate any situation which might lead to international friction or give rise to a dispute. Any Member State of the UN may bring any such situation to the attention of the Security Council under Art. 35 (1) UN-Charter. One of the significant impediments to securing the effectiveness of MPAs is their enforcement on the wide High Sea. Therefore, a further significant advantage of the involvement of the Security Council is its possibility to adopt measures to give effect to its decisions under Art. 39 ff. UNCLOS, such as sanctions under Art. 41 UN-Charter and actions under Art. 42 (1st sentence) UN-Charter.[226] Decisions and measures by the Security Council would be particularly effective in areas in which the adoption and enforcement of multilateral treaties is difficult because of the manifold diverging interests of States, for instance, to limit sovereign rights to fish in the High Sea for the protection of the marine environment.[227] A summary of the trend in national and international courts and

[225] Reilly (1995–1996), p. 765.
[226] Reilly (1995–1996), p. 777.
[227] Reilly (1995–1996), p. 769.

organisations, as well as the emergence of the obligation to protect and preserve the marine environment into a peremptory norm of international law, prove the status of this obligation as a Human Right, which mandates the Security Council to adopt legally binding decisions for this purpose.

6.6 Specific Content, Minimum and Maximum Scope

> It is not self-evident anymore that human beings live and can continue to live on this globe.[228]

The obligation to protect and preserve the marine environment is broad. Like the diverse activities in the sea, its content can take many forms. In order to protect and preserve a specific terrain from pollution from vessels, for instance, it is not necessary to implement an absolute ban on navigation in all ocean terrains but to implement sufficient guidelines to protect and preserve the marine environment from adverse impacts of navigation, such as routing systems. In the following, the specific content of this obligation, including its minimum and maximum scope, will be determined. The scope of application of a regulation is primarily determined by the interpretation and application of the regulation itself and can be further limited by competing regulations.

6.6.1 Specification of the Content

According to the PCA in its *South China Sea Arbitration*, the specific content of the obligation to protect and preserve the marine environment under Art. 192 UNCLOS is specified in other regulations of the UNCLOS, as well as other rules of international law.[229] However, not all States are parties to the UNCLOS or have adopted all regulations of international law. Because of the peremptory status of the obligation to protect and preserve the marine environment with *erga omnes* effect, the direct application of regulations that are not universally accepted is problematic. It would derogate the States' freedom to conclude and not to conclude a treaty because, in fact, all States would be bound by the derogative regulations via the cogent obligation to protect and preserve the marine environment, even if they did not consent to them.

The specific content of the obligation to protect and preserve the marine environment depends on the substantiation of its elements. The substantive content must be demonstrated and proven on a case-by-case basis by scientific reports, expert

[228] Tomuschat (2019), p. 580.

[229] UNGA A/44/461, p. 5; PCA, *South China Sea Arbitration*, Philippines v. China (Award), pp. 373 f., para. 941.

opinions and witnesses. Many of the regulations for the protection and preservation of the marine environment are, of course, based on expert reports and scientific opinions. Therefore, other (non-universal) provisions of the UNCLOS and international law do not bind non-parties through the obligation to protect and preserve the marine environment directly; however, they inform the interpretation of the content of the obligation.

For the example of the prevention of pollution of the marine environment from vessels, for instance, Art. 211 (1), (2) UNCLOS, provide that States are obliged to establish international rules and standards and national laws and regulations to this end and promote the adoption wherever appropriate of routing systems designed to minimise the threat of accidents that might cause pollution of the marine environment. The 168 UNCLOS parties are bound by this regulation directly. Its broad acceptance also provides sway for the interpretation of the content of the obligation to protect and preserve the marine environment for non-State parties. Further widely accepted guidelines for the safety of ships and protection and preservation of the marine environment from pollution from vessels are particularly the ones adopted by the IMO, which is the UN specialised agency with responsibility for the safety of shipping and the prevention of marine environment from pollution by ships.[230] Key IMO Conventions include but are not limited to the 1974 International Convention for the Safety of Life at Sea, the 1973/78 MARPOL and its Annexes and the 1996 London Protocol.

The relevant legal framework to inform the content of the obligation to protect and preserve the marine environment is very broad, including customary and conventional global, regional and national rules for the protection of the marine environment in general or regarding specific issues, species or regions.[231] The stronger a regulation is recognised by the international community, the greater its binding effect for the interpretation of the content of the obligation to protect and preserve the marine environment. In the *South China Sea Arbitration*, for instance, the PCA used the Appendixes for CITES and the CBD to identify threatened and endangered species and ecosystems. CITES is almost universally accepted by 183 parties and, therefore, has a significant weight in the interpretation of the obligation to protect and preserve the marine environment.[232] Likewise, the CBD Convention is accepted by 196 parties and weighs strongly in the interpretation of its content.[233] Some regulations are universally accepted and are therefore eligible to inform the content of the obligation to protect and preserve the marine environment directly. Under the obligation to cooperate in Art. 197 UNCLOS, States are obliged to formulate international rules for the protection and preservation of the marine

[230] https://www.imo.org/en/About/Pages/Default.aspx.

[231] See: Overview of the International Legal Framework of MPAs and see: States' Practice to Adopt International Treaties.

[232] https://cites.org/eng/disc/parties/index.php; PCA, *South China Sea Arbitration*, Philippines v. China (Award), p. 380, para. 956; Kojima (2015), p. 173.

[233] https://www.cbd.int/information/parties.shtml; Mossop (2017), p. 99.

environment. The customary obligation under Art. 197 UNCLOS is universally accepted and directly informs the content of the obligation to protect and preserve the marine environment. To this end, it expressly reiterates the States obligation to protect and preserve the marine environment through the adoption of international treaties.[234]

Regulations of the UNCLOS and other international laws contain specifications regarding the minimum and maximum scope of the obligation to protect and preserve the marine environment. Those regulations can help interpret the specific content of the obligation to protect and preserve the marine environment. Concerning the minimum scope of protection regulations, Section 5 of Part XII UNCLOS generally requires that national laws and regulations concerning marine pollution shall be at least as effective as internationally accepted rules and standards. Acknowledged rules to interpret Section 5 of Part XII UNCLOS are, for instance, the IMO Guidelines, which provide for Particularly Sensitive Sea Areas and the 1973/78 MARPOL Convention with its Special Areas.[235]

6.6.2 General Predominance of International Rules and Standards Over National Laws and Regulations

The harmonisation of national laws and regulations with international rules, standards and recommended policies is a crucial feature of Part XII UNCLOS to reconcile diverging interests of States. Some developing States, for instance, argued that they should enjoy a more lenient regime with respect to land-based and vessel sourced pollution and that environmental policies should be subordinated to economic and technological interests. Other States insisted on the possibility to adopt more stringent national laws than international treaties with regard to issues, such as the design and construction of foreign vessels to prevent pollution of the marine environment in AUNJ.[236]

In general, the UNCLOS adopted a comprehensive approach that entails the predominance of international rules and standards over national rules and regulations. Laws and regulations of the coastal State in their Territorial Sea, for instance, shall not apply to the design, construction, manning or equipment of ships unless they are giving effect to generally accepted international rules or standards under Art. 21 (2) UNCLOS. National laws and regulations of the coastal State to prevent, reduce and control pollution from vessels under Art. 211 (2) UNCLOS shall have at

[234]Preamble of the OSPAR Convention; Proelss (2017), Art. 197, mn. 1 and 10, f.; Kojima (2015), p. 173; PCA, *South China Sea Arbitration*, Philippines v. China (Award), pp. 376 f., para. 945; ITLOS, *MOX Plant*, Ireland v. United Kingdom, Provisional Measures (3 December 2001), ITLOS Reports 2001, pp. 95, 110, para. 82; McConnell and Gold (1991), p. 91.

[235]https://www.imo.org/en/OurWork/Environment/Pages/PSSAs.aspx.

[236]Nordquist et al. (2013), XII.14.

least the same effect as that of generally accepted international rules and standards. This regime is repeated for the other sources of pollution in Section 2 of Part XII UNCLOS, namely pollution from land-based sources, seabed activities subject to national jurisdiction, activities in the Area, dumping and from or through the atmosphere under Art. 207 (1), 208 (3), Art. 209 (2) (2nd sentence), 210 (6), 212 (1) UNCLOS. Under the UNCLOS, international rules and standards generally dominate and give guidelines on the content of national rules and regulations regarding their minimum and maximum content.

6.6.3 Competing Regulations

The UNCLOS aims to strike a balance between the desire to protect the ocean on the one hand and the use of ocean spaces on the other.[237] The need to reconcile competing interests in the law of the sea is recognised in the preamble of the UNCLOS, which states 'the desirability of establishing through this Convention [. . .] a legal order for the seas and oceans which will facilitate [. . .] the conservation of their living resources, and the study, protection and preservation of the marine environment, [. . .], with due regard for the sovereignty of all States [. . .].' MPAs are designated marine areas where activities are managed and regulated through legislation for a conservation and protection objective and directly address this conflict of interest.

It has been established that the scope of a regulation is firstly deduced from the scope of the regulation itself, which is determined by interpretation using expert opinions and other rules and regulations of international law. Secondly, the interpretation and application of one regulation can interfere with the application of another regulation and *vice* versa, so that the regulations limit each other. The capping of the scope of the cogent obligation to protect and preserve the marine environment by other regulations is subject to the limitations of Art. 53 VCLT because peremptory norms of international law may not be derogated and only modified by subsequent norms having the same character. In order to establish the scope of the obligation to protect and preserve the marine environment, the commensuration of conflicting norms in international law will be introduced generally and subsequently with specific regard to *jus cogens* regulations before applying the results to the obligation under Art. 192 UNCLOS in a third step.

6.6.3.1 Commensuration of Norms in International Law

A conflict of norms in public international law arises, when after their harmonious interpretation in good faith, the obedience or application of one norm necessarily or

[237] UNGA A/44/461, pp. 5 f., para. 9.

potentially violates the other norm. A conflict is resolved by balancing both norms by means of proportionality.[238] The commensuration of two norms in international law, thus, follows two steps: the harmonious interpretation of the norms in good faith under Art. 31 ff. VCLT and the equilibration by means of proportionality.

Harmonious Interpretation in Good Faith

The UNCLOS does not contain any regulations on the interpretation of its provisions. The customary provisions on the interpterion of treaties under Art. 31 ff. VCLT must be applied.[239] Accordingly, a treaty shall be interpreted in good faith in accordance with the ordinary meaning to be given to the terms of the treaty in their context and the light of its object and purpose under Art. 31 (1) VCLT. If, after the harmonious interpretation in good faith, the obeying or applying of one norm necessarily or potentially violates the other norm, a conflict exists between the norms, which must be solved by means of proportionality in a second step.[240] The relevant collision of both regulations, therefore, needs to be of a normative character.[241]

General Proportionality in Public International Law

There is no general rule in public international law on how to balance conflicting norms. The principle of proportionality was introduced by the German jurist Carl Gottlieb Svarez in 1794 and is now acknowledged in the legislation and jurisprudence of many States.[242] In EU law, for instance, the collision of freedoms must be balanced by means of proportionality. The proportionality is further codified in the ECHR, according to which any limitation of human rights must be *absolutely necessary* (Art. 2 (2) ECHR).

Although the principle of proportionality is not generally codified in general public international law, it can be derived from the wording of different regulations such as 'necessary', 'commensurate' or 'reasonable'. Under Art. 51 UN-Charta, for instance, '[n]othing in the present Charter shall impair the inherent right of individual or collective self-defence if an armed attack occurs against a Member of the United Nations, until the Security Council has taken measures necessary to maintain

[238] Vranes (2006), p. 418; Dörr and Schmalenbach (2018), p. 990, Art. 53, mn. 54; Villiger (2009), p. 674, Art. 53, mn. 20; Linderfalk (2009), pp. 965 f.

[239] Schladebach (2020), pp. 25 f., mn. 3; Linderfalk (2007), p. 7; Bernhardt (1984), p. 321; PCA, *Chagos Marine Protected Area Arbitration*, Mauritius v. UK (Award) 2015, p. 197, para. 501.

[240] UNGA A/74/10, p. 146 and pp. 198 f.; Vranes (2006), p. 418; Dörr and Schmalenbach (2018), p. 990, Art. 53, mn. 54; Villiger (2009), p. 674, Art. 53, mn. 20.

[241] Linderfalk (2009), p. 965.

[242] Peters (2016), p. 1.

international peace and security.' The *necessity* of an act is defined under Art. 25 ARS if it is the only way for the State to safeguard an essential interest against a grave and imminent peril and if it does not seriously impair an essential interest of the State or States towards which the obligation exists or of the international community as a whole. Under Art. 51, 49 ARS, countermeasures of an injured State against a State responsible for an internationally wrongful act must be *commensurate* with the injury suffered, taking into account the gravity of the internationally wrongful act and the rights in question.

The application of a proportionality test can also be seen in the jurisprudence of international courts and tribunals. In the *Whaling in the Antarctic* Case, the ICJ had to decide whether a special permit granted by Japan to kill whales for the purpose of scientific research was *reasonable* in relation to achieving the objective of the allowance of this special permit under Art. VIII IWC.[243] The ICJ held that the use of lethal weapons is only permissible if it is feasible to obtain the objective, if the use of lethal weapons is necessary to achieve this objective or if there is no less harmful measure. Lethal weapons may only be used if they are essential to the stated objectives and if they are the last resort and no other means are available.[244] In the *Arctic Sunrise Arbitration*, the tribunal found that measures taken by coastal States had to be reasonable, necessary, and proportionate.'[245]

The review demonstrates that there are many regulations that indicate the existence of a general principle of proportionality in public international law. Even if the notion that the principle of proportionality has grown into a rule of customary international law in public international law is disputed, the necessity to commensurate norms at least follows from specific regulations of international law itself.

Specific Proportionality in the UNCLOS

The UNCLOS shows the need to balance different interests by subjecting or conditioning rights to other rights and by stipulating *due regard, unjustifiable interferences* or *in accordance with* rules.

Under Art. 2 (3) UNCLOS, sovereignty over the Territorial Sea is exercised *subject to* the UNCLOS and other rules of international law. Under Art. 56 (2) UNCLOS, the coastal State shall have *due regard* to the rights and duties of other States when exercising its rights under Art. 56 UNCLOS. Other States shall have *due regard* to the interests of the coastal State in exercising its duties in the EEZ and shall comply with the laws and regulations adopted by the coastal State in accordance with the provisions of the UNCLOS and other rules of international law

[243] ICJ, *Whaling in the Antarctic*, Australia v. Japan: New Zealand intervening, Judgment, ICJ Reports 2014, pp. 226, 254, para. 67, p. 258, para. 88, p. 260, para. 97 and p. 267, para. 127.

[244] ICJ, *Whaling in the Antarctic*, Australia v. Japan: New Zealand intervening, Judgment, ICJ Reports 2014, pp. 226, 268, para. 129–133.

[245] Mossop (2017), p. 189.

under Art. 58 (3) UNCLOS. Pursuant to Art. 78 (2) UNCLOS, the exercise of the rights of the coastal State over the Continental Shelf must not infringe or result in any *unjustifiable interference* with navigation and other rights and freedoms of other States as provided for in the UNCLOS. The freedoms of the High Sea shall be exercised by all States with *due regard* for the interests of other States in their exercise of the freedom of the High Sea under Art. 87 (2) UNCLOS and are *conditioned by* other rules of the UNCLOS and general international law under Art. 87 (1) (2nd sentence) UNCLOS. Subject to Art. 193 UNCLOS, States shall exercise their sovereign right to exploit resources *in accordance* with their duty to protect and preserve the marine environment. Pursuant to Art. 194 (4) UNCLOS, in taking measures to prevent, reduce or control pollution of the marine environment, States shall refrain from *unjustifiable interference* with activities carried out by other States in the exercise of their rights and in pursuance of their duties in conformity with the UNCLOS. According to Art. 234 (2nd sentence) UNCLOS, laws and regulations of the coastal State to prevent, reduce and control pollution of the marine environment from vessels in ice-covered areas within their EEZ shall have *due regard* to navigation and the protection and preservation of the marine environment.

Subject to, Condition by and in Accordance with Regulation

The content of the *subject to* and *conditioned by* regulations was at issue in the *Chagos Marine Protected Area Arbitration*. The wording of Art. 2 (3) UNCLOS differs from other regulations because it stipulates that sovereignty 'is' exercised subject to other rights rather than 'shall be' exercised. The PCA first established that Art. 2 (3) UNCLOS nonetheless poses a legally binding obligation.[246] Secondly, with regard to its content, the PCA found that Art. 2 (3) UNCLOS has a similar wording to Art. 1 (2) CTSCZ, from which it was derived.[247] Art. 1 (2) CTSCZ was the subject of discussion during the preparations of the ILC Draft Articles, which adopted the regulation from the League of Nations Codification Acts in The Hague in 1930.[248] The Act described the purpose of Art. 1 (2) CTSCZ by establishing its difference to sovereignty over land as follows: 'Obviously sovereignty over the territorial sea, like sovereignty over the domain on land, can only be exercised subject to the conditions laid down by international law. As the limitations which international law imposes on the power of the State in respect of the latter's sovereignty over the territorial sea are greater than those it imposes in respect of the domain on land, it has not been thought superfluous to make special mention of

[246] PCA, *Chagos Marine Protected Area Arbitration*, Mauritius v. UK (Award) 2015, p. 196, para. 500 ff.

[247] PCA, *Chagos Marine Protected Area Arbitration*, Mauritius v. UK (Award) 2015, p. 198, para. 506.

[248] ILC, A/CN.4/SR.165, p. 150, para. 25.

these limitations in the text of the article itself.'[249] After several discussions in the preparations, the view prevailed that '[i]t was vital that specific reference should be made to the limitations imposed by international law on sovereignty over the territorial sea, particularly in view of the recent tendency to increase the breadth of that sea.'[250] In the UNCLOS I Conference, which led to the adoption of the CTSCZ, Art. 1 (2) CTSCZ had not been a main issue.[251]

However, pursuant to Art. 87 (1) (2nd sentence) UNCLOS, formerly stipulated in Art. 2 CHS, the freedom of the High Seas is exercised under the conditions laid down by these articles and by the other rules of international law. This limitation was included because '[a]ny freedom that was to be exercised in the interests of all entitled to enjoy it must be regulated'[252] Therefore, the 'freedom of the high seas should be made subject to the articles of the convention and the other rules of international law.'[253] In the *Chagos Marine Protected Area Arbitration*, the PCA found that these comments uniformly expressed that Art. 2 CHS poses a restriction on the freedom of the High Sea and because Art. 1 (2) CTSCZ poses a comparable provision, also the *subject to* regulation poses a restriction of the exclusive sovereignty of the coastal State in the Territorial Sea.[254]

In general, the subjecting of the sovereignty of the coastal State in the Territorial Sea, thus, limits the power of the coastal State to other rights in the UNCLOS and international law. Likewise, the conditioning of the freedoms of the High Sea under Art. 87 (1) (2nd sentence) UNCLOS stipulates a limitation of the freedoms to other rights of the UNCLOS.

Specifically, the ordinary meaning of the limitation of the *subject to, in accordance with and conditioned by* regulations, stipulate a hierarchy by which these rights are subordinated to other rights and obligations under the UNCLOS and rules of international law. Other rights of the UNCLOS and general international law, including the obligation to protect and preserve the marine environment, prevail over the limited right. The obligation to protect and preserve the marine environment is, therefore, elevated above the relevant *subject to, conditioned by and in accordance with* regulations of the UNCLOS.[255]

[249] League of Nations (1930), p. 202, Art. 1; ILC, A/CN.4/SR.165, p. 150, para. 25; PCA, *Chagos Marine Protected Area Arbitration*, Mauritius v. UK (Award) 2015, p. 198, para. 506–509.

[250] ILC, A/CN.4/SR.165, p. 150, para. 34; PCA, *Chagos Marine Protected Area Arbitration*, Mauritius v. UK (Award) 2015, pp. 199 f., para. 511.

[251] PCA, *Chagos Marine Protected Area Arbitration*, Mauritius v. UK (Award) 2015, p. 200, para. 513.

[252] UN A/CONF.13/40, p. 39, para. 42.

[253] UN A/CONF.13/40, p. 39, para. 26.

[254] PCA, *Chagos Marine Protected Area Arbitration*, Mauritius v. UK (Award) 2015, p. 200, para. 513 f.

[255] Rothwell and Stephens (2016), p. 342.

Due Regard, Good Faith and Unjustifiable Interference Regulations

Due regard, good faith and *unjustifiable interference* regulations are general principles of international law that address the relationship of States carrying out activities in the sea.[256]

The ILC points out that *unjustifiable interference* is 'determined by the relative importance of the needs and the interest involved.'[257] According to the ILC, interference due to the exploration and exploitation of natural resources on the Continental Shelf (now codified under Art. 78 (2) UNCLOS), 'even if substantial, with navigation and fishing might, in some cases, be justified. On the other hand, interference even on an insignificant scale would be unjustified if unrelated to reasonably conceived requirements of exploration and exploitation of the continental shelf.'[258]

In its *Chagos Marine Protected Area* Arbitration, the PCA had to decide on the lawfulness of an MPA established by the UK in the 200 NM zone off the baselines of the Chagos Archipelago in Mauritius, which was administered by the UK as British Indian Ocean Territory.[259] Mauritius contested the lawfulness of the MPA and claimed that the UK did not have due regard, unjustifiably interfered and did not act in good faith with respect to Mauritian fishing rights. According to the PCA, *unjustifiable interference* is functionally equivalent to *due regard* and good faith obligations. However, there is no general definition or universal rule of conduct; each case must be dealt with individually.[260] Like the *due regard* and *good faith* obligation, the *unjustifiable interference* clause 'requires a balancing act between competing rights, based upon an evaluation of the extent of the interference, the availability of alternatives, and the importance of the rights and policies at issue.'[261] In its *South China Sea Arbitration*, the PCA confirmed this view and restated that 'the extent of the regard required by the Convention will depend upon the nature of the rights held by Mauritius, their importance, the extent of the anticipated impairment, the nature and importance of the activities contemplated by the United Kingdom and the availability of alternative approaches. In the majority of cases, this assessment will necessarily involve at least some consultation with the rights-holding State.'[262] In the *Chagos Marine Protected Area Arbitration*, the PCA did, therefore, 'not exclude the possibility that environmental considerations could

[256] Oude Elferink (2018), p. 449.

[257] ILC, A/CN.4/SER.A/1956/ADD.L, p. 299, Art. 71.

[258] ILC, A/CN.4/SER.A/1956/ADD.L, p. 299, Art. 71; the ILC commentary on the 1956 Draft Articles on the Law of the Sea concerned Art. 71, which procured Art. 78 UNCLOS.

[259] PCA, *Chagos Marine Protected Area Arbitration*, Mauritius v. UK (Award) 2015, p. 1, para. 5.

[260] PCA, *Chagos Marine Protected Area Arbitration*, Mauritius v. UK (Award) 2015, p. 202, para. 519; Mossop (2017), p. 183.

[261] PCA, *Chagos Marine Protected Area Arbitration*, Mauritius v. UK (Award) 2015, p. 211, para. 540.

[262] PCA, *Chagos Marine Protected Area Arbitration*, Mauritius v. UK (Award) 2015, p. 202, para. 519; PCA, *South China Sea Arbitration*, Philippines v. China (Award), p. 293, para. 742.

potentially justify, for the purposes of Article 194(4), the infringement of Mauritian fishing rights in the territorial sea. Such justification, however, would require significant engagement with Mauritius to explain the need for the measure and to explore less restrictive alternatives.'[263] The PCA established that the UK's obligation to act in good faith and to have due regard to Mauritius' rights and interests, entailed the consultation and a balancing exercise with the rights and interests at hand.[264]

Concludingly, *due regard, good faith* and *unjustifiable interference* obligations require that competing rights have to be balanced by evaluating the nature and importance of the rights and policies held by both States, the extent of interference and anticipated impairment and the availability of alternatives, which involves the consultation of the States whose rights are stake.[265] The exact content of those rules depends on the circumstances in each individual case and the nature of the right.[266]

No Abuse of Rights Under Art. 300 UNCLOS

Pursuant to Art. 300 UNCLOS, the States Parties shall fulfil in good faith the obligations assumed under the UNCLOS and shall exercise the rights, jurisdiction and freedoms recognised in the UNCLOS in a manner which would not constitute an abuse of right. The good faith obligation applies to all regulations of the UNCLOS. The subordination of the *subject to, in accordance with, conditioned by, due regard* and *unjustifiable interference* regulations to other regulations may not lead to an abuse of rights pursuant to Art. 300 UNCLOS. Therefore, although the regulations of *subject to, in accordance with* and *conditioned by* regulations generally stipulate a hierarchy by which those rights are subordinated under other rights of international law, this subordination may not lead to an abuse of rights under Art. 300 UNCLOS. Balancing evaluations such as for the *due regard* and *unjustifiable interference* rules must be considered when interpreting their content.[267]

6.6.3.2 Commensuration and Jus Cogens Regulations

With regard to the commensuration of the obligation to protect and preserve the marine environment with other regulations, its *jus cogens* character needs to be taken

---

[263] PCA, *Chagos Marine Protected Area Arbitration*, Mauritius v. UK (Award) 2015, pp. 211 f., para. 541.

[264] PCA, *Chagos Marine Protected Area Arbitration*, Mauritius v. UK (Award) 2015, p. 210, para. 534.

[265] PCA, *Chagos Marine Protected Area Arbitration*, Mauritius v. UK (Award) 2015, p. 211, para. 540; PCA, *South China Sea Arbitration*, Philippines v. China (Award), p. 293, para. 742.

[266] PCA, *Chagos Marine Protected Area Arbitration*, Mauritius v. UK (Award) 2015, p. 211, para. 541.

[267] PCA, *Chagos Marine Protected Area Arbitration*, Mauritius v. UK (Award) 2015, p. 203, para. 520.

into account. As a peremptory norm of international law, the obligation to protect and preserve the marine environment may not be derogated by derivative norms of international law and may only be modified by subsequent norms having the same character (Art. 53 (2nd sentence) VCLT). A regulation that conflicts with a peremptory norm of international law is void (Art. 53 (1st sentence) VCLT); rules of customary international law that conflict with a peremptory norm of international law do not emerge or cease to exist.[268] The prohibition to derivate *jus cogens* regulations is the core of their imperative character due to the fundamental value of their content for humankind. At the same time, an uncapped provision of the obligation to protect and preserve the marine environment can lead to an abuse of rights because any restriction by a State or States to regulate activities in the sea would always be justified as long as they are connected to the objective of protecting and preserving the marine environment. In practice, the way how other rules must be applied and interpreted in light of the obligation to protect and preserve the marine environment is essential in order to determine which activities in the sea are permissible. How can the content and the maximum scope of this obligation be determined if *due regard* or *unjustifiable rules* are not applicable?

Harmonious Interpretation in Good Faith

Firstly, regulations that *prima facie* collide need to be interpreted harmoniously in good faith. Art. 53 VCLT does not prohibit the interpretation of *jus cogens* regulations. The obligation to protect and preserve the marine environment and colliding regulations thus have to be interpreted in good faith in a way that leads to the broadest possible application of both norms.[269] Only where after the harmonious interpretation of a norm, its obeying or applying necessarily or potentially violates the other norm, a conflict exists between the norms.[270] A collision in the sense of Art. 53 (1st sentence) VCLT, thus, must be of normative character. The investigation will demonstrate that a collision between the obligation to protect and preserve the marine environment and other regulations can exist *prima facie*; however, an interpretation of the scope of the respective regulations under Art. 31 ff. VCLT leads to the result that a relevant *normative collision* of the obligation to protect and preserve the marine environment and other derivative regulations of the UNCLOS cannot exist.[271]

---

[268] UNGA A/74/10, pp. 144 f.

[269] UNGA A/74/10, p. 146, p. 199.

[270] UNGA A/74/10, p. 146 and pp. 198 f.; Vranes (2006), p. 418; Dörr and Schmalenbach (2018), p. 990, Art. 53, mn. 54; Villiger (2009), p. 674, Art. 53, mn. 20.

[271] Linderfalk (2009), p. 965.

Normative Collision and Proportionality

If there is a regulation that imposes a normative conflict with the obligation to protect and preserve the marine environment, the second step would be to balance both norms proportionately. However, a balancing of *jus cogens* regulations is only permissible with subsequent norms of international law having the same character (Art. 53 (2nd sentence) VCLT). A collision of a derivative norm with a *jus cogens* regulations leads to the voidness of the former (Art. 53 (1st sentence) VCLT).

This result is reflected in the jurisprudence of the PCA in its *South China Sea Arbitration*. In this case, the PCA had to evaluate several activities by China, which allegedly violated its obligation to protect the marine environment, namely the harvesting of endangered species and harmful construction activities.[272] The PCA examined whether the respective activity impairs the obligation to protect and preserve the marine environment and, subsequently, China's responsibility for the breach.[273] After having established the breach of the obligation to protect and preserve the marine environment for the respective activity by China, the PCA did not put the violation of Art. 192 UNCLOS in proportion to any other rights of China but stated the unlawfulness of these activities.[274] This indicates that the PCA refrained from applying a proportionality examination for the activities with regard to the obligation to protect and preserve the marine environment, which is granted unlimitedly.

Concludingly, in cases of *jus cogens* regulations, both norms have to be interpreted harmoniously in good faith in a way that leads to the broadest possible extent of both regulations. Therefore, the *jus cogens* obligation also has to be interpreted and applied in a way that leaves the maximum possible scope of the other regulation. To determine a conflict of the norms, only a normative collision of both regulations after their harmonious interpretation is relevant. Secondly, balancing a *jus cogens* regulation with another regulation is only permissible if the other regulations, likewise, is a *jus cogens* regulation. In cases of colliding derivative and *jus cogens* regulations, the derivative regulation is subjected to the fate of Art. 53 (1st sentence) VCLT. Activities that violate the obligation to protect and preserve the marine environment are unlawful.

[272] PCA, *South China Sea Arbitration*, Philippines v. China (Award), p. 378, para. 950, p. 388, para. 976 ff.

[273] PCA, *South China Sea Arbitration*, Philippines v. China (Award), p. 381, para. 959 f., p. 382, para. 961 ff.

[274] PCA, *South China Sea Arbitration*, Philippines v. China (Award), p. 384, para. 366, p. 397, para. 991, p. 397, para. 992 f.

6.6.3.3 Application to the Obligation to Protect and Preserve the Marine Environment

These findings will be applied to the obligation to protect and preserve the marine environment in the following. The investigation will show, firstly, that there is no other peremptory norm of general international law that modifies this obligation. Secondly, a harmonious interpretation of other regulations of the UNCLOS and the obligation to protect and preserve the marine environment shows that a normative collision of derogative norms of the UNCLOS with the obligation to protect and preserve the marine environment is not possible.

No Modification by the No-Sovereignty Principle

Pursuant to Art. 53 (2nd sentence) VCLT, cogent regulations may be modified only by subsequent norms of international law having the same character. A *jus cogens* regulation that potentially conflicts with the obligation to protect and preserve the marine environment is the no-sovereignty principle under Art. 89 UNCLOS. On the Informal Consultative Process on Oceans and the Law of the Sea held by the UN in 2013, one of the main issues was the need for the protection of vulnerable marine ecosystems beyond national jurisdiction.[275] Discussed means included *inter alia* the designation of High Seas MPAs, which was supported, for instance, by the Netherlands, who recommended to take 'immediate action'.[276] Norway instead contested that MPAs conflict with the freedom of the High Sea under Art. 89 UNCLOS, as well as the prohibition of the acquisition or exercise of any rights with respect to minerals recovered from the Area under Art. 137 (3) UNCLOS.[277]

While Art. 89 UNCLOS prohibits the assertion of territorial sovereignty over any ocean space of the High Sea, the exercise of sovereign rights in the High Sea is regulated under Art. 87 UNCLOS. The obligation to establish MPAs does not provide for the unilateral right of one State to claim territorial sovereignty over an ocean territory beyond its national jurisdiction and thus does not interfere with Art. 89 UNCLOS.[278] Because the obligation to protect and preserve the marine environment does not provide for the assertion of territorial sovereignty in the High Seas, the no-sovereignty principle and the obligation as entailed under Art. 192 UNCLOS, therefore, do not collide or modify each other.

[275] UNGA A/58/95, pp. 6 ff., para. 13 ff.

[276] UNGA A/AC.295/8, p. 6, para. 24.

[277] UNGA A/AC.295/10, p. 2., para. 3; Oral (2006), p. 102.

[278] See: Art. 89 UNCLOS.

Harmonious Interpretation in Good Faith

The obligation to protect and preserve the marine environment and other activities in the sea must be interpreted and applied harmoniously in good faith in a way that provides the broadest possible scope of both regulations.[279] Relevant means of interpretation are the ordinary meaning, context and objective and purpose of the regulation under Art. 31 ff. VCLT. The following interpretation of the obligation to protect and preserve the marine environment and other regulations of the UNCLOS, as well as the exemplary application of the findings to the freedom of fishing and deep seabed mining, will disclose that although the activities in the sea *prima facie* seem to collide with the obligation to protect and preserve the marine environment in the same terrain, no relevant normative collision exists.

No Ban of All Activities in the Sea

The harmonious interpretation of both rights requires an interpretation that provides the broadest possible application of both regulations. Therefore, the obligation to protect and preserve the marine environment needs to be interpreted in a way that serves its purpose but also provides scope for the other regulation to be applied. An interpretation in a way that prohibits any activity in the sea, for instance, would provide the broadest possible scope of the protection and preservation of the marine environment but did not leave any scope of application of other rights, such as Art. 87 UNCLOS.

The wording of the obligation to protect and preserve the marine environment does not stipulate a ban of all activities in the sea but obliges States to protect and preserve the marine environment. The teleological interpretation of the obligation to protect and preserve the marine environment also does not lead to the result that all activities in the sea need to be banned entirely. On the contrary, as the wording of other provisions of the UNCLOS, such as Art. 193 UNCLOS show, States are required to take active measures to protect and preserve the marine environment *in exercising their activities* in the sea.

This is furthermore expressed in the preamble of the UNCLOS, which states the purpose of the UNCLOS is to establish a legal order for the seas and oceans which will promote the peaceful uses of the seas and oceans, the equitable and efficient utilisation of their resources, the conservation of their living resources and the study, protection and preservation of the marine environment, with due regard for the sovereignty of all States. The interpretation that the obligation to protect and preserve the marine environment does not require an absolute ban of all activities in the sea is further reiterated in Section 5 of Part XII UNCLOS concerning marine pollution. The regulations oblige States to prevent, reduce and control pollution from the respective source; however, they do not stipulate a ban on those activities. To prevent, reduce and control pollution much more shows some flexibility as to the

[279] UNGA A/74/10, p. 146, p. 199.

content and outcome of the international rules and regulations that need to be adopted for the protection of the marine environment and can be understood as imposing a due diligence obligation on the States.[280] This shows that the exercise of activities in the sea is clearly entailed in the UNCLOS, however in doing so, States must adopt active measures to protect and preserve the marine environment.

Specific Content of the Obligation to Protect and Preserve the Martine Environment

The interpretation of the specific content of the obligation to protect and preserve the marine environment is informed by other rules and regulations of the UNCLOS and general international law.[281] Because not all other regulations are universally binding, they cannot be applied to the obligation to protect and preserve the marine environment directly but only help to interpret its content on a case-by-case basis. The specific content of the obligation to protect and preserve the marine environment depends on the substantiation of the elements of the obligation to protect and preserve the marine environment, by experts opinions and scientific reports in the individual case.[282]

General Subordination of Other Rights Under the Obligation to Protect and Preserve the Marine Environment

A normative conflict between two regulations under Art. 53 VCLT arises if, after their harmonious interpretation in good faith, the application of one regulation collides with the other. The interpretation of the obligation to protect and preserve the marine environment and other regulations of the UNCLOS discloses that a normative conflict cannot arise.

Hierarchy Subordinates Other Rights Under the Obligation to Protect and Preserve the Marine Environment

According to their ordinary meaning, other regulations of the UNCLOS are provided limitedly, while the obligation to protect and preserve the marine environment is provided absolutely. Especially the wording of the *subject to*, in *accordance with* and *conditioned by* regulations stipulate a hierarchy, by which the obligation to protect and preserve the marine environment is elevated above them. Due to the hierarchy, a normative conflict cannot arise.[283]

[280] Harrison (2017), p. 28.

[281] UNGA A/44/461, p. 5; PCA, *South China Sea Arbitration*, Philippines v. China (Award), pp. 373 f., para. 941.

[282] See: Specification of the Content.

[283] See: Specific Proportionality in the UNCLOS.

Erga Omens Obligation to Protect and Preserve the Marine Environment Applies to State Exercising Activities in the Sea

Furthermore, even if a regulation does not contain a *conditioned by*, *subject to* or *in accordance with* regulation, such as the *due regard* and *unjustifiable interference* rules, the interpretation in their context still shows that the obligation to protect and preserve the marine environment cannot conflict with any other (non-peremptory) norm in the law of the sea because the obligation to protect and preserve the marine environment applies to all States in exercising activities in all zones of the sea. Therefore, also the State exercising activities in the sea is bound by this obligation, which applies to all States, irrespective of their adoption of the UNCLOS as *erga omnes* cogent or at least customary rule. In invoking an infringement of its rights, a State is bound by the obligation to protect and preserve the marine environment itself. Hence, other rights and regulations must be interpreted in light of the obligation to protect and preserve the marine environment. A normative conflict is not possible.

No Abuse of Rights Under Art. 300 UNCLOS

Because all States shall fulfil in good faith the obligations assumed under the UNCLOS and shall exercise the rights, jurisdiction and freedoms recognised in the UNCLOS in a manner which would not constitute an abuse of right pursuant to Art. 300 UNCLOS, Art. 26 VCLT, the subordination of the *subject to*, *due regard, in accordance with*, *unjustifiable interference* and *conditioned by* regulations to other regulations may not lead to an abuse of rights pursuant to Art. 300 UNCLOS. Balancing evaluations such as for the *due regard* and *unjustifiable interference* rules must be considered when interpreting the content *subject to*, *in accordance with* and *conditioned by* regulations.[284]

Less Restrictive Measure to Comply with the Obligation Under Art. 192 UNCLOS

Although the obligation to protect and preserve the marine environment does not require an absolute ban on all activities in the sea, the harmonious interpretation requires that both regulations maintain their applicability while leaving scope for the other regulation to be applied. This necessitates that although subordinated, the other regulation is restricted by the obligation to protect and preserve the marine environment as little as possible. This requires that the measure to regulate the other regulations is the least restrictive measure while still posing sufficient protection and preservation of the marine environment, whereby when in doubt, more value has to be given to the obligation to protect and preserve the marine environment due to its general superiority over other regulations in the UNCLOS. On the one hand, it needs to be considered which measures need to be taken in order to fulfil the

[284] PCA, *Chagos Marine Protected Area Arbitration*, Mauritius v. UK (Award) 2015, p. 203, para. 520.

obligation to protect and preserve the marine environment. On the other hand, those measures need to provide the maximum possible scope of other regulations of the UNCLOS, such as the freedom of fishing. MPAs vary from slightly protected areas with some tourist regulation to fully protected areas, in which no human activity is allowed.[285] It needs to be assessed on a case-by-case basis, which specific measures must be adopted to protect and preserve the marine environment in a specific terrain based on scientific research and expert opinions. The following exemplary application to the freedom of fishing and deep seabed mining will demonstrate how to determine regulations for the protection and preservation of the marine environment from fishing and mining while providing the broadest possible scope of the freedom of fishing.

Application to Large-Scale Fishing Techniques

Commercial or industrial fishing techniques allow a large amount of catch in a short time, such as bottom trawling, pelagic trawling, driftnet fishing or longlining. Large-scale fishing techniques harm the marine environment due to overfishing of targeted species and the uncontrollable amount of bycatch of other fish species and corals.

Global Moratorium on Bottom Trawling

Bottom trawling has been proven to have a significant harmful effect on flora and fauna of the ocean floor, such as coral reefs and sponges and has led to the depletion of many fish stock such as orange roughy.[286] The devastative effect of bottom trawling on vulnerable marine ecosystems is recognised almost universally in the State community. Today, only a limited number of States, which are estimated to include but are not limited to New Zealand, Japan, Cook Islands, Spain, Korea and the Faroe Islands, still engage in this activity in ABNJ.[287] Due to the monitoring difficulties of the High Sea, the exact number is difficult to establish.

The ban of bottom trawling in areas of vulnerable marine ecosystems has been strongly endorsed by the UN General Assembly and the work of the FAO. A global ban on bottom trawling endorsed by the UN Generally Assembly, however, was blocked by single fishing States such as Iceland and Russia.[288] Vulnerable ecosystems are marked by high biodiversity that is susceptible to human activities in the sea and require stricter protection regulations than other areas in the sea.[289] However, the

[285] See: Level of Protection and Categories.

[286] Mossop (2017), p. 120; see: Bottom Trawling.

[287] https://www.un.org/press/en/2004/deepseapc.doc.htm.

[288] UNGA A/RES/59/25, UNGA A/RES/61/105, UNGA A/RES/64/72, UNGA A/RES/66/68, UNGA A/RES/71/123, UNGA A/RES/74/18, UNGA A/RES/75/89, UNGA A/RES/75/157; Mossop (2017), p. 230; Caddell (2020), p. 269; https://www.seattletimes.com/nation-world/fishing-nations-block-un-trawling-ban/.

[289] Mossop (2017), p. 190.

latest scientific findings and reports have repeatedly evidenced that, in fact, the whole ocean is one ecosystem as a whole. Even deeper areas in the ocean that were previously thought to be scarce of any life, such as the bathypelagic and abyssalpelagic zones, show a vast array of species that have adapted to living in the dark, such as crabs, worms, octopuses, sea cucumbers, frilled sharks, bioluminescent fish or the giant squid.[290] The fangtooth fish (*anoplogaster cornuta*), for instance, has been discovered to swim at depths as low as 5.000 m.[291] Six-gill sharks (*hexanchus griseus*), whose descendants are believed to date back to the Jurassic era, belong to the oldest living species on Earth and live in depths of 2.500 m.[292] The bycatch of coral in bottom trawling can amount to almost one-third of the whole catch.[293] The regulation of fishing only in vulnerable marine ecosystems, therefore, may be a less restrictive measure to a global ban on bottom trawling; however, it does not yield sufficient protection for the marine environment in all marine zones in the light of marine research such as the Census on Marine Life.[294] The obligation to protect and preserve the marine environment, therefore, requires a global ban on bottom trawling.

Impact of Other Large-Scale Fishing Techniques

Another less restrictive measure than banning all large-scale fishing techniques in all zones of the sea could be the prohibition of bottom trawling on the seafloor that still allows large-scale fishing activities in the water column above. However, also other large-scale fishing techniques in the water column, including driftnet fishing, pelagic trawling and longlining, have caused the depletion and extinction of many species. Drift netting is a type of gillnet fishing by which the nets hang vertically in the water column without being anchored to the bottom.[295] Drift net fishing has proven to be the most harmful pelagic fishing technique due to its impact on vulnerable species.[296] Pelagic trawls do not touch the seafloor but are generally much larger than bottom trawls with net sizes of up to 200 m width and 150 m in depth.[297] The average length of long fishing lines in the US is 45 km with thousands of baited

---

[290] https://ocean.si.edu/ecosystems/deep-sea/deep-sea; see: Marine Life in the Water (Pelagic Zones).

[291] https://www.nationalgeographic.com/environment/article/deep-sea-creatures.

[292] https://www.seattleaquarium.org/blog/what-are-sixgill-sharks.

[293] https://news.mongabay.com/2021/08/trawling-bycatch-increases-risk-of-marine-life-extinction-in-brazil/; https://portals.iucn.org/library/sites/library/files/documents/Rep-2004-001, p. ii.

[294] http://www.coml.org/.

[295] https://www.seafish.org/responsible-sourcing/fishing-gear-database/gear/gill-nets/; https://www.seafish.org/responsible-sourcing/fishing-gear-database/gear/drift-nets/.

[296] https://www.pewtrusts.org/-/media/post-launch-images/2014/oceans/oceans-2012/assets/moving_towards_low_impact_fisheries.pdf, p. 7.

[297] https://www.msc.org/what-we-are-doing/our-approach/fishing-methods-and-gear-types/pelagic-trawls; https://www.seafish.org/responsible-sourcing/fishing-gear-database/gear/pelagic-trawl/.

hooks.[298] Even fisheries organisations that promote fishing, such as NOAA, acknowledge the vast and extensive amount of bycatch caught in large scale fishing due to the large size of the nets, length of lines and the number of hooks that catch any species indifferently.[299] Large-scale fishing techniques, such as pelagic trawling, driftnet fishing and longlining, account for half of the world's bycatch while only contributing to less than 20 per cent of fish production. Bycatch includes but is not limited to endangered species listed under Appendix I CITES, such as dolphins, sharks, whales, sea turtles and the Albatross. Animals caught as bycatch usually get discarded overboard, which most of the animals do not survive or at least get injured severely. The quantity and composition of bycatch vary significantly according to the respective fishing techniques, net types and sizes, as well as target species and the fishing zone.[300] Furthermore, lost drift nets, traps and fish aggregating devices are the most commonly lost debris in the oceans and pose most of the risks to marine life, which causes 2.9 to 6.7 times higher deaths of marine animals and makes up about 10 per cent of the plastic pollution in the sea.[301]

A series of UN Resolutions called on all members of the international community to 'ensure that a global moratorium on all large-scale pelagic driftnet fishing is fully implemented on the high seas'.[302] Although resolutions by the UN General Assembly are not legally binding, they can help to inform the content of the obligation to protect and preserve the marine environment and also draw attention to the current threats to the marine environment.[303] In particular with regard to large-scale fishing techniques, such as bottom trawling and driftnet fishing, the standards requested by the UN General Assembly enhanced the adoption of respective regulations by States and RFMOs, even to the extent that some of the drift net resolutions are regarded as rules of customary international law.[304]

To summarise, all techniques of large-scale fishing have detrimental and uncontrollable effects on marine ecosystems. Bottom trawling not only leads to the extinction of species before they have even been identified, such as the pacific armourhead but also erodes the marine flora with its heavy fishing gear that weighs several tonnes and is being dragged across the ocean floor. Scientific evidence, reports and the growing number of overfished, depleted and endangered fish stock suggest that also other large-scale fishing techniques that do not primarily affect the ocean floor have disastrous impacts on the marine ecosystems because of the large

[298] https://www.fisheries.noaa.gov/national/bycatch/fishing-gear-pelagic-longlines.

[299] https://www.fisheries.noaa.gov/national/bycatch/fishing-gear-gillnets; https://www.fisheries.noaa.gov/national/bycatch/fishing-gear-pelagic-longlines.

[300] https://www.bfn.de/en/activities/marine-nature-conservation/pressures-on-the-marine-environment/fisheries-and-fish-stocks/impacts-of-bottom-trawling.html.

[301] https://www.greenpeace.de/sites/www.greenpeace.de/files/publications/20190611-greenpeace-report-ghost-fishing-ghost-gear-deutsch.pdf, p. 4.

[302] UNGA RES/46/215, para. 1 (c); UNGA RES/44/225, UNGA RES 45/197; Sands (2012), p. 589.

[303] Harrison (2011), p. 204.

[304] UNGA A/RES/46/215, UNGA A/RES/44/225, UNGA A/RES 45/197; Caddell (2020), p. 266; Sands (2012), p. 589.

number of fish that is being caught per second and that empty the ocean, along with a large amount and wide composition of uncontrollable bycatch. Although targeted fish can be controlled very limitedly through varying mesh and net sizes, large fishing nets of hundreds of square metres and longlines with several thousands of baited hooks do not allow to target specific species individually and inevitably causes large amounts of bycatch as well as overfishing and extinction of species. Concludingly, large-scale fishing techniques are not reconcilable with the obligation to protect and preserve the marine environment.

Less Restrictive Alternative

The investigation has shown that large-scale fishing techniques are that detrimental that the obligation to protect and preserve the marine environment requires a global ban of those techniques. Less restrictive alternatives such as the limitation to vulnerable marine ecosystems are not sufficient to protect targeted species from overfishing and control the high number of bycatch because scientific evidence shows that the whole ocean is an ecosystem rich in species and biodiversity. At the same time, a global ban on all fishing techniques would reduce the content of the freedom of fishing to zero. The availability of alternative (small-scale) fishing techniques and their impact on the marine environment has to be investigated by experts. A less restrictive measure than an absolute ban of fishing activities would be the ban of large-scale fishing techniques, including but not limited to bottom trawling, pelagic trawling, driftnet fishing and long lining that only permits low impact fishing techniques. Rod-and-reel fishing, for instance, is a much less harmful technique because fish is not harvested from the sea at an unsustainable level, and bycatch can be released immediately. Studies such as 'Moving Towards Low Impact Fisheries In Europe – Policy Hurdles & Actions' by Seas at Risk help identify the most damaging fishing techniques and the impediments in changing to more sustainable techniques. The three main obstacles to reducing the harmful impact of fishing techniques are technical and financial issues as well as a lack of knowledge.[305] The obligation to protect and preserve the marine environment is an obligation of conduct. It requires States to mitigate obstacles for sustainable fishing. This can include the provisions of technical and financial means as well as the education of the community and affected industry in less harmful fishing techniques.

Determination of Allowable Techniques Through Other Regulations

The specific content of the obligation to protect and preserve the marine environment needs to be established with regard to other regulations of the UNCLOS and international agreements, which provide information of less restrictive measures than an absolute ban of shining.

305 https://www.pewtrusts.org/-/media/post-launch-images/2014/oceans/oceans-2012/assets/moving_towards_low_impact_fisheries.pdf, p. 8.

For instance, in the EEZ, the coastal State is expressly under the obligation to ensure through the adoption of national laws and regulations that the maintenance of the living resources in its EEZ is not endangered by over-exploitation by virtue of Art. 61 UNCLOS, taking into account the best scientific evidence. Pursuant to Art. 119 (1) (a) UNCLOS, in the High Sea, States shall determine the allowable catch and establish conservation measures based on the best scientific evidence to maintain or restore populations of harvested species at levels that can produce the maximum sustainable yield, as qualified by relevant environmental and economic factors, taking into account fishing patterns, the interdependence of stocks and any generally recommended international minimum standards, whether subregional, regional or global. Under Art. 119 (1) (b) UNCLOS, States shall take into consideration the effects on species associated with or dependent upon harvested species with a view to maintaining or restoring populations of such associated or dependent species above levels at which their reproduction may become seriously threatened. The right of the States to conduct fishing in the High Sea is furthermore explicitly subjected to the obligations of the State under the UNCLOS as well as their obligations under other treaties by virtue of Art. 116 UNCLOS.

Global Ban Necessary for Enforcement

One of the major problems with regard to the implementation of existing fisheries guidelines is the lack of their enforcement. For once, the area of the High Sea is too vast to be effectively controlled and monitored. Even modern technologies such as satellite and radar do not allow effective control of fishing vessels that can switch off their radar systems and fish in the cover of darkness at night. A total ban of the respective equipment could help to implement those restrictions. However, a second major impediment to the enforcement of fishing guidelines is the influential fishing lobby in the States. The total value of the sale of fish is estimated to have reached USD 401 billion in 2018.[306] It is not surprising that there is resistance from the States to effectively enforce protection measures and control and regulate fishing in this light. Therefore, the only effective implementation of protection guidelines is the establishment of a legally binding obligation to protect and preserve the marine environment. Ultimately, however, there is only as much supply as there is demand. Therefore, the most critical factor in efficiently protecting the seas is every individual's demand for seafood.

Application to Deep-Sea Mining

When new terrains are being discovered, the ordinary sequence is to explore the area before exploiting it. In the ocean, though, humankind took another approach and

[306] FAO, SOFIA Report 2020, p. 2; Oral (2006), pp. 102–106.

started exploiting its resources before exploring the marine spaces exhaustively.[307] Looking at deep-sea mining, its consequences on the ecosystem of the seabed and water column above are still largely unknown. Neither the terrain of the marine environment in the depths relevant for deep-sea mining nor the consequences of the activity have been explored exhaustively. The only consensus is that the impact of deep-sea mining on the marine environment will be significant.[308] Nonetheless, in June 2021, the island State Nauru has given notice to the ISA pursuant to Art. 162 (2) (o) (ii) UNCLOS in conjunction with Art. 15 (b) Annex to the 1994 Agreement relating to the Implementation of Part XI of the UNCLOS of 10 December 1982, setting in motion a two year deadline for the ISA to complete rules, regulations and procedures necessary to facilitate the approval of plans of work for exploration or exploitation of the resources in the Area.

Deep-sea mining interferes with the obligation to protect and preserve the marine environment and has to be interpreted with this obligation harmoniously. The regulations on the deep seabed specifically determine the sequence of exploring the Area before exploiting, such as under Art. 1 (1) (3), 77, 153 UNCLOS. The exploitation of resources before the completion of the exploration poses unforeseeable threats to the marine environment. Furthermore, the obligation to protect and preserve the marine environment is an obligation of conduct that obliges States and international organisations in all zones of the sea. Art. 153 UNCLOS, in conjunction with the obligation to protect and preserve the marine environment, and Art. 145 UNCLOS pose a legal obligation on the ISA to only grant permissions when the exploration of the seabed has been finalised. This will have to be respected with regard to the recent application of Nauru for deep-sea mining.[309] The interpretation of both regulations, the obligation to protect and preserve the marine environment as well as the regulations on deep-sea mining, require that the exploration of the seabed must be completed before the exploitation of resources may commence. Before the exhaustive exploration of the deep seabed has been finalised, exploitation activities violate the obligation to protect and preserve the marine environment and are illegal.

Obligation to Cooperate: Engagement of the States Concerned

The interpretation of the obligation to protect and preserve the marine environment in its context shows that States are under the general principle of Art. 197 UNCLOS to cooperate in formulating and elaborating international rules, standards and recommended practices and procedures consistent with the UNCLOS for the

[307] https://www.abc.net.au/radio/programs/conversations/edith-widder-oceans-bioluminescence-submersibles-giant-squid/13502994.

[308] https://www.bmbf.de/bmbf/en/research/environment-and-climate/pollution-of-the-oceans/deep-sea-mining-ecological-impacts/deep-sea-mining-ecological-impacts.html; Schladebach and Esau (2012), p. 479; see: The Deep Seabed.

[309] https://www.reuters.com/business/environment/exclusive-deep-sea-mining-rules-be-fast-tracked-push-nauru-source-2021-06-25/.

protection and preservation of the marine environment.[310] This obligation is explicitly stipulated with regard to specific activities in the sea, including but not limited to Art. 117, 118 UNCLOS for the conservation of living resources in the High Sea or Art. 61 (2) UNCLOS for the coastal State to ensure that the living resources in the EEZ are not endangered by over-exploitation. The obligation to cooperate requires both the adoption of international treaties to protect and preserve the marine environment and the engagement of the States concerned.

The engagement of affected States is a vital element in enhancing compliance with and promotion of regulatory guidelines for the establishment of effective MPAs. Evidence has shown that a key element for compliance with protection measures is that the community understands the scope of the measures.[311] The efficacy of protection measures is therefore conditioned by the engagement of the relevant actors to create an understanding of the measure with regard to its content as well as benefits.

For instance, in the fishing industry, the engagement and education of the State and community can lead to the understanding that a decline in the fisheries sector can be overcompensated through the development of long-lasting and sustainable economic branches, such as ecotourism. Regulation of fisheries and rehabilitation of coral reefs can lead to the establishment of eco-resorts as attractive tourist destinations. This is certainly linked to the management and regulation of the sustainable use of the reef by tourists. Otherwise, the destruction of the marine environment will only be shifted from fisheries to other harmful human activities in the sea. The success of shifting from the exploitation of the environment to other branches is evident in the Cabo Pulmo coral reef in Mexico. The reef was highly threatened by overfishing and irresponsible tourism. The designation as Natural Protected Area with the regulation of fishing and education of the local community has led to an increase of fish by more than 400 per cent. Key factors in the success of the implementation of the regulation were legally binding laws on the one hand and the involvement of the local community on the other, which stopped fishing activities on the reef voluntarily to support the environmental protection of the reef. The lack of income from the fisheries sector was compensated by an expanding tourism branch, which provides jobs for the local community that offers more sustainable tourist activities, such as diving for small groups.[312] The engagement of affected States, therefore, is not only a requirement to justify interferences but also a decisive element in designating longlisting, sustainable and effective marine protection regulations.

---

[310] ITLOS, *Land Reclamation in and around the Straits of Johor* (Malaysia v. Singapore), Provisional Measures, Order of 8 October 2003, ITLOS Reports 2003, pp. 10, 25, para. 92; ITLOS, *MOX Plant*, Ireland v. United Kingdom, Provisional Measures (3. December 2001), ITLOS Reports 2001, pp. 95, 110, para. 82; Roach (2014), pp. 240 and 250.

[311] Kellerher (1999), p. 2.

[312] https://www.greenpeace.org/aotearoa/story/cabo-pulmo-an-ocean-sanctuary-success-story-for-people-and-wildlife/.

Conclusion: Harmonious Interpretation

There is no normative conflict of the obligation to protect and preserve the marine environment and other activities in the sea. The wording as well as the objective and purpose of the UNCLOS, as evident through the preamble and Art. 193 UNCLOS show that the obligation to protect and preserve the marine environment does not require an absolute ban of all activities in the sea.

However, due to the *subject to*, *conditioned by* and *in accordance with* regulation, the obligation to protect and preserve the marine environment generally prevails over other regulations. Furthermore, in conducting activities in the sea, the other States are bound by the obligation to protect and preserve the marine environment as *erga omnes* regulation, too. Although the obligation to protect and preserve the marine environment generally prevails, this may not lead to an abuse of rights under Art. 300 UNCLOS. Evaluations such as for the *due regard* and *unjustifiable interference* regulations have to be considered in interpreting rights and obligations under the UNCLOS.

A harmonious interpretation of activities in the sea and the obligation to protect and preserve the marine environment requires that both regulations maintain their broadest possible application while leaving scope for the other regulation to be applied. This requires that the other activity is interfered with as little as possible, namely that the measure adopted under the obligation to protect and preserve the marine environment is the least restrictive measure for the other activity and *vice versa*.

The specific content of the obligation to protect and preserve the marine environment and the other activities is informed by other rules and regulations. Specific conventions, guidelines and expert opinions help inform the content of this obligation, whereby the specific content must be established on a case-by-case basis. The obligation to cooperate is universally accepted and informs the content of the obligation to protect and preserve the marine environment directly. It requires States to cooperate in adopting international treaties to protect and preserve the marine environment, which reiterates the obligation to protect and preserve the marine environment and the engagement of the States concerned.

The application of the interpretation on fishing has shown that large-scale fishing techniques to catch fish at an unsustainable rate and yield an uncontrolled number of bycatches cannot be interpreted in a way that is harmonious with the obligation to protect and preserve the marine environment. Less restrictive alternatives, such as the limitation of a ban on large-scale fishing only to vulnerable marine ecosystems, are not effective enough in light of the latest scientific findings that prove that the whole ocean is one marine ecosystem and that marine life exists in the deepest parts of the ocean. However, an absolute ban of all fishing techniques in the sea would eliminate the content of the freedom of fishing entirely. A less restrictive alternative is the allowance of low-impact fishing techniques that respects catch limits, such as imposed by Art. 61, 119 UNCLOS, and reduces the amount of bycatch. Lastly, a global ban on large-scale fishing techniques is necessary for the enforcement of regulations. The lack of effective monitoring and control of fishing on the High Sea is one of the most significant impediments to realising protection guidelines. The obligation to protect and preserve the marine environment imposes a due diligence obligation on the State to ensure that no vessel carries respective large-scale fishing equipment. Fishing gear is one of the main contributors to plastic pollution in the ocean. The restriction of respective gear is, therefore, mandatory under the obligation to protect and preserve the marine environment.

With regard to deep seabed mining, a harmonious interpretation with the obligation to protect and preserve the marine environment requires that the exploration of the Area is completed before permissions for the exploitation of its resources are granted. The exploitation of the Area before completing its exploration cannot be interpreted harmoniously with the obligation to protect and preserve the marine environment and is illegal.

Application of Art. 194 (4) UNCLOS to the Obligation to Protect and Preserve the Marine Environment

Pursuant to Art. 194 (4) UNCLOS, in taking measures to prevent, reduce or control pollution of the marine environment, States shall refrain from unjustifiable interference with activities carried out by other States in the exercise of their rights and in pursuance of their duties in conformity with the UNCLOS. It is problematic whether this regulation applies to the obligation to protect and preserve the marine environment. As a *jus cogens* regulation, the obligation to protect and preserve the marine environment may not be derogated by derivative regulations of international law, such as the freedoms of the High Sea. Regulations that require balancing the two rights, such as *due regard* and *unjustifiable interference* regulations, may therefore not be applied to the obligation to protect and preserve the marine environment directly.

The *unjustifiable interference* regulation in Art. 194 (4) UNCLOS, however, does not stipulate the unjustifiable interference with rights of other States but with their activities. For this reason, it could be argued on the one hand that Art. 194 (4) UNCLOS (besides the issue of its applicability to other measures than those aimed at preventing, reducing or controlling pollution of the marine environment) does not require the balancing of rights but of the obligation to protect and preserve the marine environment with activities in the sea.

Because Art. 194 (4) UNCLOS refers to activities rather than rights, it does not derogate the obligation to protect and preserve the marine environment on a normative level. A normative collision in the sense of Art. 53 VCLT cannot occur. On the other hand, activities in the sea under Art. 194 (4) UNCLOS are being carried out *in the exercise of their rights*, as the wording of this paragraph explicitly states. Activities in the sea are governed by corresponding rights. A balance of the obligation to protect and preserve the marine environment with activities of States in the sea, therefore, would be a balancing of the obligation to protect and preserve the marine environment with the right that provides for the activity. Art.

194 (4) UNCLOS, therefore, is not applicable to the obligation to protect and preserve the marine environment.

References

Bernhardt R (1984) Interpretation in international law. In: Bernhardt R (ed) Encyclopedia of Public International Law (EPIL) 7, History of international law, foundations and principles of international law, sources of international law, law of treaties. North Holland, pp 318–327

Boyle A (2005) Further development of the law of the sea convention: mechanisms for change. Int Comp Law Q 54(3):563–584

Brunée J, International legislation, Max Planck Encyclopedia of Public International Law (MPEPIL) 1429

Caddell R (2020) Chapter 12: deep-sea bottom fisheries and the protection of seabed ecosystems: problems, progress and prospects. In: Banet C (ed) The law of the seabed – access, uses, and protection of seabed resources, vol 90. Publications on Ocean Development, Leiden, pp 255–284

Caflish L (1992) Unequal treaties. German Yearb Int Law (GYIL) 52:52–80

Charlesworth H, Chinkin C (1993) The gender of Jus Cogens. Hum Rights Q 15:63–76

Dahm G, Delbrück J, Wolfrum R (2002) Völkerrecht Band I/3, Formen des völkerrechtlichen Handelns - Die inhaltliche Ordnung der internationalen Gemeinschaft, 2nd edn. Berlin

Dalaker Kraabel K (2019) The BBNJ PrepCom and institutional arrangements: the hype about the hybrid approach. In: Nordquist MH, Norton Moore J, Long R (eds) The marine environment and United Nations Sustainable Development Goal 14, vol 22. Center for Oceans Law and Policy, Leiden, pp 137–172

Dörr O, Schmalenbach K (2018) Vienna Convention on the law of treaties – a commentary, 2nd edn. Berlin

Druel E (2011) Marine protected areas in areas beyond national jurisdiction: the state of play. Institut du Développement Durable et des relations Internationales (IDDRI) Working Paper Number 7/11 (Paris, 11.09.2011)

Food and Agriculture Organization of the United Nations (FAO) (2017) Basic texts of the Food and Agriculture Organization, volumes I and II. Rome

Franke V (2007) The European Community and marine environmental protection in the international law of the sea - implementing global obligations at the regional level, vol 58. Publications on Ocean Development, Leiden

Freestone D (2009) Modern principles of high seas governance – the legal underpinnings. Environ Policy Law 39(1):44–49

Freestone D (2012) International governance, responsibility and management of areas beyond national jurisdiction. Int J Mar Coast Law (IJMCL) 27(2):191–204

Gavounelli M (2007) Functional jurisdiction in the law of the sea, vol 62. Publications on Ocean Development, Leiden

Grafton RQ, Akter S, Kompas T (2011) A policy-enabling framework for the ex-ante evaluation of marine protected areas. Ocean Coast Manag 54(6):478–487

Guo J (2020) The developments of marine environmental protection obligation in article 192 of UNCLOS and the operational impact on China's marine policy – a south China sea fisheries perspective. Mar Policy - Int J Ocean Aff (Mar Policy) 120(104140):1–7

Hafner G (2006) Schutz der Meeresumwelt. In: Vitzthum W (ed) Handbuch des Seerechts. Munich, pp 355–421

Handl G (2020) The human right to a clean environment and rights of nature. In: von Arnauld A, von der Decken K, Susi M (eds) The Cambridge handbook of new human rights. Cambridge, pp 137–153

Hansard, HC 1803-2005, Fifth Series, Vol. 688, Commons Sitting of 28. January 1964 (277)
Harrison J (2011) Making the law of the sea - a study in the development of international law. Cambridge
Harrison J (2017) Saving the oceans through law – the international legal framework for the protection of the marine environment. Oxford
Jowett B, Aristotle: politics, Book 2, Part 1, http://classics.mit.edu/Aristotle/politics.2.two.html
Kellerher G (1999) Guideline for marine protected areas. World Commission on Protected Areas of IUCN – The World Conservation Union, Gland
Kingsbury B, Krisch N, Stewart RB, Wiener JB (2005) Global governance as administration - national and transnational approaches to global administrative law. Law Contemp Probl 68-(1, Numbers 3 and 4):1–14
Kojima C (2015) South China Sea Arbitration and the protection of the marine environment: evolution of UNCLOS Part XII through interpretation and the duty to cooperate. Asian Yearb Int Law (AYIL) 21:166–180
Kolb R (2013) The International Court of Justice. Oxford
League of Nations, Acts of the Conference for the Codification of International Law, The Hague, March 13th to April 12th, 1930, Meeting of the Committees, Volume III, Minutes of the Second Committee, Territorial Waters, Series of League of Nations Publications V. Legal 1930. V. 16., Annex III
Lee S, Bautista LB (2018) Part XII of the United Nations Convention on the law of the sea and the duty to mitigate against climate change: making out a claim, causation, and related issues. Ecol Law Q 45:129–156
Linderfalk U (2007) On the interpretation of treaties - the modern international law as expressed in the 1969 Vienna Convention on the law of treaties, law and philosophy library, vol 83. Dordrecht
Linderfalk U (2009) Normative conflict and the fuzziness of the international ius cogens regime. Zeitschrift für auslöndisches öffentliches Recht und Völkerrecht (ZaöRV) 69:961–977
Matz-Lück N (2017) Meeresschutz. In: Proelss A (ed) Internationales Umweltrecht. Berlin, pp 393–453
McConnell ML, Gold E (1991) The modern law of the sea: framework for the protection and preservation of the marine environment. Case West Reserve J Int Law 23(1):83–106
Molenaar EJ (2004) Unregulated deep-sea fisheries: a need for a multi-level approach. Int J Mar Coast Law (IJMCL) 19(3):223–246
Mossop J (2007) Protecting marine biodiversity on the continental shelf beyond 200 nautical miles. Ocean Dev Int Law 38(3):283–304
Mossop J (2017) The continental shelf beyond 200 nautical miles: rights and responsibilities. Oxford
Nordquist MH, Nandan S, Rosenne S (2013) UN Convention on the Law of the Sea Commentary 1982 Online. Center for Oceans Law and Policy, Leiden
O'Connell D (1988) Patrick, the international law of the sea, vol II, 1st edn. Oxford
O'Leary BC, Brown RL, Johnson DE, von Nordheim H, Ardron J, Packeiser T, Roberts CM (2012) The first network of marine protected areas (MPAs) in the high seas: the process, the challenges and where next. Mar Policy - Int J Ocean Aff (Mar Policy) 36(3):598–605
Oral N (2006) Protection of vulnerable marine ecosystems in areas beyond national jurisdiction: can international law meet the challenge? In: Strati A, Gavouneli M, Skourtos N (eds) Unresolved issues and new challenges to the law of the sea, time before and time after, vol 54. Publications on Ocean Development, Leiden, pp 85–108
Oude Elferink AG (2007) The regime of the area: delineating the scope of application of the common heritage principle and freedom of the high seas. Int J Mar Coast Law (IJMCL) 22:143–176
Oude Elferink AG (2012) Governance principles for areas beyond national jurisdiction. Int J Mar Coast Law (IJMCL) 27(2):205–260

Oude Elferink AG (2018) Coastal states and MPAs in ABNJ: ensuring consistency with the LOSC. Int J Mar Coast Law (IJMCL) 33:437–466

Peters A (2016) Verhältnismäßigkeit als globales Verfassungsprinzip. In: Baade B, Ehricht S, Fink M, Frau R, Möldner M, Risini I, Stirner T (eds) Verhältnismäßigkeit im Völkerrecht, in: Marauhn, Thilo/Walter, Christian, Jus Internationale et Europaeum. Tübingen, pp 1–19

Proelss A (2008) Marine genetic resources under the UNCLOS and CBD. German Yearb Int Law (GYIL) 51:417–446

Proelss A (2017) United Nations Convention on the Law of the Sea – a commentary. Munich

Reilly B (1995–1996) 'Clear and present danger': a role for the United Nations Security Council in protecting the global environment. Melb Univ Law Rev 20:763–804

Roach JA (2014) Today's customary international law of the sea. Ocean Dev Int Law 45(3): 239–259

Rogers A (2019) The deep – the hidden wonders of our oceans and how we can protect them. London

Rothwell DR, Stephens T (2016) The international law of the sea, 2nd edn. Oxford

Sands P (2012) Principles of international environmental law, 3rd edn. Cambridge

Schladebach M, Esau C (2012) Aktuelle Herausforderungen im Seerecht. Deutsches Verwaltungsblatt (DVBl), Köln, pp 475–483

Schladebach M (2020) Weltraumrecht. Tübingen

Schmidt-Aßmann E, Molnár-Gábor F (2019) European Administrative Law, Max Planck Encyclopedia of Public International Law (MPEPIL) 1819

Scott K (2019) Area-based protection beyond national jurisdiction: opportunities and obstacles. Asia-Pac J Ocean Law Policy 4:158–180

Scovazzi T (2004) Marine protected areas on the high seas: some legal and policy considerations. Int J Mar Coast Law (IJMCL) 19(1):1–17

Scovazzi T (2013) Where the judge approaches the legislator: some cases relating to law of the sea. In: Boschiero N, Scovazzi T, Pitea C, Ragni C (eds) International courts and the development of international law - essays in honour of Tullio Treves. The Hague, pp 299–310

Tanaka Y (2008) A dual approach to ocean governance - the cases of zonal and integrated management in international law of the sea. Surrey

Tanaka Y (2019) The international law of the sea, 3rd edn. Cambridge

Tanzi A (2019) Ultra Petita, Max Planck Encyclopedia of International Procedural Law 2239. MPEiPro

Tomuschat C (2019) Enforcement of international law. Zeitschrift für ausländisches öffentliches Recht und Völkerrecht (ZaöRV) 79:579–631

Treves T (2011) Judicial action for the common heritage. In: Hestermeyer H, Matz-Lück N, Seibert Fohr A, Vöneky S (eds) Law of the sea in dialogue, Beiträge zum ausländischen öffentlichen Recht und Völkerrecht, Band 221. Heidelberg, pp 113–136

United Nations High Commissioner for Human Rights (UNHCHR), Frequently Asked Questions on Human Rights and Climate Change Fact Sheet No. 38 (New York, 2021)

Villiger ME (2009) Commentary on the 1969 Vienna Convention on the Law of Treaties. Leiden

Vranes E (2006) The definition of 'norm conflict' in international law and legal theory. Eur J Int Law (EJIL) 17(2):395–418

Wiegandt J (2001) Internationale Rechtsordnung oder Machtordnung? Eine Anmerkung zum Verhältnis von Macht und Recht im Völkerrecht. Zeitschrift für ausländisches öffentliches Recht und Völkerrecht (ZaöRV) 71:31–76

Wolfrum R (1990) Purposes and principles of international environmental law. German Yearb Int Law (GYIL) 33:308–330

Chapter 7
Special Regulations

International legal instruments on marine protection include more than 300 binding or non-binding treaties, policies and guidelines regarding specific activities, regions or species. On a global level, two instruments stand out beside the *erga omnes* obligation to protect and preserve the marine environment as embodied under At. 192 UNCLOS: Art. 194 (5) UNCLOS, which is the most commonly acknowledged basis for the establishment of MPAs, as well as the BBNJ, which is recently discussed in the UN.

7.1 Art. 194 (5) UNCLOS

Under Art. 194 (5) UNCLOS, measures taken in accordance with Part XII UNCLOS shall include those necessary to protect and preserve rare or fragile ecosystems as well as the habitat of depleted, threatened or endangered species and other forms of marine life.

7.1.1 Scope of Art. 194 (5) UNCLOS

7.1.1.1 Geographical Scope

Art. 194 (5) UNCLOS is a special expression of the obligation to protect and preserve the marine environment in the context of fragile ecosystems and habitats.[1] Like Art. 192 UNCLOS, it is stipulated separately from the zones of the sea and applies to all marine areas. Due to its spatial approach of protecting ecosystems and

[1] Proelss (2017), Art. 194, mn. 31.

A. von Rebay, *The Designation of Marine Protected Areas*,
https://doi.org/10.1007/978-3-031-29175-3_7

the habitat of certain species, it meets the criteria of 'geographically defined marine area' of MPAs. It is, therefore, the most commonly acknowledged basis for the establishment of MPAs in the UNCLOS.[2]

7.1.1.2 Substantive Scope

The substantive scope of Art. 194 (5) UNCLOS encompasses the protection of ecosystems and biodiversity as a whole.

Not Limited to Pollution

Although the heading of Art. 194 UNCLOS refers to measures to prevent, reduce and control pollution of the marine environment, the wording of its last paragraph, Art. 194 (5) UNCLOS refers to all measures and is not limited to a specific threat.[3] It is generally accepted that Art. 194 (5) UNCLOS 'extends to measures focused primarily on conservation and preservation of ecosystems.'[4]

Ecosystems and Habitats

Art. 194 (5) UNCLOS protects rare and fragile ecosystems and the habitat of depleted, threatened or endangered species. There is no definition in the UNCLOS of rare or fragile ecosystems and habitats or a conclusive list to this end. Indicators that help identify ecosystems and habitats of depleted, endangered or threatened species need to be established on a case-by-case basis, whereby other conventions, such as the almost universally accepted CBD or CITES, can help inform the content of Art. 194 UNCLOS.[5]

Ecosystems

An internationally acknowledged definition of ecosystem is provided in Art. 2 CBD, which defines ecosystem as a dynamic complex of plant, animal and micro-organism

---

[2]PCA, *Chagos Marine Protected Area Arbitration*, Mauritius v. UK (Award) 2015, p. 211, para. 538 and pp. 128 f., para. 320; Proelss (2017), Art. 194, mn. 35; Oude Elferink (2018), p. 445.

[3]See: Application of Art. 194 (5) UNCLOS to Art. 194 (1)-(4) UNCLOS.

[4]PCA, *Chagos Marine Protected Area Arbitration*, Mauritius v. UK (Award) 2015, p. 211, para. 538 and pp. 128 f., para. 320; PCA, *South China Sea Arbitration*, Philippines v. China (Award), p. 376, para. 945; ITLOS, *Southern Bluefin Tuna Cases*, New Zealand v. Japan; Australia v. Japan, Provisional Measures, ITLOS Reports 1999, pp. 280, 295, para. 70; Proelss (2017), Art. 194, mn. 30, 35.

[5]Proelss (2017), Art. 194, mn. 33; PCA, *South China Sea Arbitration*, Philippines v. China (Award), pp. 388 ff., para. 977 ff. and p. 380, para. 983.

communities and their non-living environment interacting as a functional unit.[6] The ILC Commentary provides another widely acknowledged definition in the 1994 Draft Articles on the Law of the Non-Navigational Uses of International Watercourses, which defines ecosystems as 'an ecological unit consisting of living and non-living components which are interdependent and function as a community.'[7] Art. 194 (5) UNCLOS hence comprises both the protection of the living as well as non-living resources.[8]

In order to be rare or fragile, the ecosystem does not have to be pristine. In the *South China Sea Arbitration*, the PCA categorized all seven reefs and their surroundings of the Spratly Islands as rare and fragile ecosystems, although they have been heavily affected before by human impacts, such as construction activities, human habitation, overfishing and other destructive fishing practices. The determination of rare and fragile ecosystems has to be evaluated in each individual case.[9]

Habitats

The second alternative of Art. 194 (5) UNCLOS includes the habitat of depleted, threatened or endangered species. Those habitats do not have to be rare or fragile and may even be pre-damaged. The need for protection arises because they are home to threatened, endangered or depleted species.[10] Appendix I of the CITES lists the most endangered species threatened from extinction, including hundreds of species such as sea turtles and a long list of cetaceans, including almost all species of whales. Appendix II lists thousands of species that are not necessarily endangered now but threatened to become so if the trade is not closely controlled. The list includes *inter alia* all dolphins not listed in Appendix I, all stony coral species, the great white shark, whale shark and devil ray. Appendix III has been included at the request of a party to regulate trade in the species and the cooperation of other countries to prevent unsustainable or illegal exploitation.[11] Especially Appendix I and II CITES, therefore, can give information on endangered, threatened and depleted species.

Adoption of Legislation

Art. 194 (5) UNCLOS provides the right of States to take active measures to protect and preserve the marine environment. It is well acknowledged and has been

[6]PCA, *South China Sea Arbitration*, Philippines v. China (Award), p. 376, para. 945; Proelss (2017), Art. 194, mn. 33.

[7]UN Doc A/45/10, p. 57.

[8]Proelss (2017), Art. 194, mn. 30.

[9]PCA, *South China Sea Arbitration*, Philippines v. China (Award), pp. 388 ff., para. 977 ff. and p. 394, para. 983; Proelss (2017), Art. 194, mn. 33.

[10]Proelss (2017), Art. 194, mn. 33.

[11]https://cites.org/eng/app/index.php.

established in this study that active measures in the sense of Art. 194 (5) UNCLOS mean the adoption of legislation.[12] Legislation is the adoption of laws and regulations on a national level and the conclusion of agreements on an international plane.[13]

7.1.1.3 Personal Scope

Art. 194 (5) UNCLOS has been repeatedly accepted as customary international law. Many of the States' statements as investigated regarding the obligation to protect and preserve the marine environment previously in this study are not limited to the customary status of Art. 192 UNCLOS but refer to the customary status of Part XII UNCLOS in general.

The consistent States' practice and corresponding *opino juris* to protect and preserve the marine environment through the adoption of respective treaties and the establishment of MPAs also include the protection and preservation of rare and fragile ecosystems or the habitat of depleted, threatened or endangered species.[14] Because there are no persistent objectors to this regulation, like Art. 192 UNCLOS, Art. 194 (5) UNCLOS is a rule of customary international law with *erga omnes* effect, which binds the whole State community.

7.1.1.4 Obligation to Adopt Measures

Art. 194 (5) UNCLOS generally stipulates that measures taken in accordance with Part XII UNCLOS shall include those that are necessary to protect and preserve the relevant areas. Art. 194 (5) UNCLOS only provides a right but not a legally binding obligation to adopt measures. It needs to be read in accordance with other provisions of the UNCLOS, which fill the content of Art. 194 (5) UNCLOS. Therefore, under Art. 194 (5) UNCLOS, in conjunction with the obligation to protect and preserve the marine environment, States are obliged to adopt the relevant measures under this provision.

7.1.1.5 Establishment of MPAs Under Art. 194 (5) UNCLOS

National and international legislation for the protection and preservation of the marine environment in a specific geographical terrain constitute the establishment MPAs as per their definition. Because of its spatial approach, Art. 194 (5) UNCLOS

[12] PCA, *Chagos Marine Protected Area Arbitration*, Mauritius v. UK (Award) 2015, p. 211, para. 538 and pp. 128 f., para. 320; Proelss (2017), Art. 194, mn. 35; Oude Elferink (2018), p. 445.

[13] See: Obligation to Adopt Active Measures – Establishment of MPAs.

[14] See: Art. 192 UNCLOS as Customary International Law.

stipulates the basis for the obligation of States to establish MPAs in rare or fragile ecosystems as well as the habitat of depleted, threatened or endangered species.

7.1.2 Unjustifiable Interference Art. 194 (4) UNCLOS

According to Art. 194 (4) UNCLOS, in taking measures to prevent, reduce or control pollution of the marine environment, States shall refrain from unjustifiable interference with activities carried out by other States in the exercise of their rights and pursuance of their duties in conformity with the UNCLOS.

7.1.2.1 Application to Art. 194 (5) UNCLOS

The unjustifiable interference clause is stipulated in Art. 194 (4) UNCLOS, which raises the question if it applies to Art. 194 (5) UNCLOS. While the PCA in its *Chagos Marine Protected Area Arbitration* applied Art. 194 (4) to (5) UNCLOS, systematic evaluations could indicate that the stipulation of Art. 194 (5) UNCLOS after the unjustifiable interference clause shows that it does not apply to Art. 194 (5) UNCLOS. The unjustifiable interference clause in Art. 194 (4) UNCLOS reflects a general rule of international law. Regardless of systematic evaluations, it, therefore, applies to Art. 194 (5) UNCLOS in any case.[15]

7.1.2.2 Interference with Activities

The unjustifiable interference rule requires the interference with activities.[16] While *due regard* rules such as Art. 56 (2) UNCLOS codify that the coastal State shall have due regard to the *rights and duties* of other States, Art. 194 (4) UNCLOS stipulates that States shall not unjustifiably interfere in *activities* by other States. It thus only applies to the interference with activities and not to future or prospective rights. Therefore, the specific activity has to be evaluated in a case-by-case study rather than an evaluation of the right for future cases.[17]

[15] Proelss (2017), Art. 194, mn. 1; Nordquist et al. (2013), 194.10(n).

[16] Mossop (2017), p. 202.

[17] PCA, *Chagos Marine Protected Area Arbitration*, Mauritius v. UK (Award) 2015, p. 211, para. 540; PCA, *South China Sea Arbitration*, Philippines v. China (Award), p. 293, para. 742; Proelss (2017), Art. 194, mn. 28.

7.1.2.3 Unjustifiable Interference

There is no general definition or rule of conduct for the *due regard* and *unjustifiable interference* rules; each case has to be dealt with individually.[18] *Due regard rules* and *unjustifiable interference* are functionally equivalent and require a 'balancing act between competing rights, based upon an evaluation of the extent of the interference, the availability of alternatives and the importance of the rights and policies at issue.'[19] The following examinations will exemplify the application of the unjustifiable interference clause by demonstrating the establishment of an MPA by the Coastal State to regulate its resources on the Continental Shelf under Art. 77 UNCLOS by restricting large-scale fishing techniques including bottom trawling, pelagic trawling, drift net fishing and long lining. Art. 194 (5), (4) UNCLOS apply to all zones of the sea, including the Continental Shelf and its water column, which can either be the EEZ or High Sea. For the Continental Shelf, Art. 78 (2) UNCLOS stipulates a special *unjustifiable interference* clause, according to which the exercise of the coastal State's rights over the Continental Shelf must not infringe or result in any unjustifiable interference with navigation and other rights and freedoms of other States as provided for in the UNCLOS. The balancing criteria of the extent of the interference are to be applied under both the unjustifiable interference clause in Art. 194 (4) and 78 (2) UNCLOS.

Extent of Interference

Competence to Protect the Marine Environment in Different Zones

The extent of an interference differs according to the varying competencies of the States in the zones of the sea. Interferences can occur in any part of the sea, whereby the competencies and powers of States vary in the different zones. Measures to protect and preserve the marine environment by States are likely to interfere with the rights of other States stronger the more rights and competencies the other States possess in the respective zone of the sea. Whereases the coastal State has exclusive sovereignty and respective competencies in the Territorial Sea, the sovereign rights of the States decrease further away from land. The EEZ and High Sea are governed by the freedoms under Art. 58 (1) UNCLOS in conjunction with Art. 87 UNCLOS, with jurisdiction rights for the protection and preservation of the marine environment of the coastal State in the EEZ under Art. 56 (1) (b) (iii) UNCLOS. Where a coastal State adopts measures to protect and preserve the marine environment in areas under exclusive sovereignty or in areas in which it possesses jurisdiction rights to this end, those measures are less likely to interfere with the activities of other States in the same terrain. Exercising its sovereignty and sovereign right cannot be regarded as

[18] Mossop (2017), p. 183.

[19] PCA, *Chagos Marine Protected Area Arbitration*, Mauritius v. UK (Award) 2015, p. 211, para. 540; PCA, *South China Sea Arbitration*, Philippines v. China (Award), p. 293, para. 742.

interference, and in cases of conflicting claims, the sovereignty and sovereign rights of the coastal State (rebuttably) presumes the competency of the coastal State to take active measures under Art. 194 (5) UNCLOS. On the High Sea, the coastal State does not have any competence to adopt unilateral measures under Art. 89 UNCLOS. However, the State community is obliged to protect and preserve the marine environment and rare or fragile ecosystems as well as the habitat of depleted, threatened or endangered species and other forms of marine life through the adoption of international treaties (international legislation).

Applying these evaluations to the example of an MPA to regulate fishing activities on the Continental Shelf, the coastal State has more competence to interfere with the rights of other States the more they interfere with its exclusive severing rights. Therefore, where, i.e., fishing activities of other States directly interfere with the resources on the Continental Shelf of the coastal State, the stronger they interfere with the coastal State's rights under Art. 77 UNCLOS. Bottom trawling directly impacts and harms the non-living resources and sedentary species on the Continental Shelf. Therefore, the coastal State has an elevated interest in regulating activities that affect its resources, which is legally supported by its right under Art. 77 UNCLOS.

In the water column above, the coastal State does not have exclusive sovereign rights under Art. 77 UNCLOS. Pursuant to (Art. 58 (1) UNCLOS in conjunction with) Art. 87 UNCLOS, it is free to all States. The interests of the coastal State weigh less. However, activities in the water column may indirectly harm resources on the Continental Shelf, in which case the interests of the coastal States is interfered with. Furthermore, in the EEZ, the coastal State has jurisdiction and corresponding competencies for the protection and preservation of the marine environment under Art. 56 (1) (b) (iii) UNCLOS. In the High Sea, both States equally enjoy the freedom of the High Sea under Art. 87 UNCLOS. However, both States are equally bound by the obligation to protect and preserve rare and fragile ecosystems and the habitat of depleted, endangered and threatened species under Art. 194 (5) UNCLOS, which applies to all States in all zones of the sea.[20]

Concludingly, the competencies of the coastal State to protect and preserve the marine environment outweigh the interests of other States in cases in which the sovereign rights of the coastal State under Art. 77 UNCLOS are either interfered with directly, i.e., through bottom trawling or indirectly through fishing activities that do not take place on the ocean floor but harmfully affect the resources on the ground. Furthermore, the coastal State's jurisdiction for the protection and preservation of the marine environment in the water column in the EEZ outweighs the interests of other States in this terrain. In the High Sea, however, the freedom of the High Sea and the obligation to protect and preserve the marine environment bind all States equally. The extent of the interference with the competencies of the States is only a step in balancing competing rights. Further evaluations need to be taken into

[20] See: Erga Omens Obligation to Protect and Preserve the Marine Environment Applies to State Exercising Activities in the Sea.

account to evaluate the admissibility of bottom trawling and fishing in the water column.

Measuring the Extent of Interference

Another factor in measuring the extent of interference is to value its economic impact. A standard of measurement (metric) can be used to represent and provide a measure of the overall biodiversity. Biodiversity metrics are used in biodiversity-related Conventions, such as the CBD, to monitor, plan and implement biodiversity strategies. A common tool to measure marine biodiversity, for instance, is the richness of species.[21] In practice, a holistic measurement of ecological biodiversity in economic values is difficult, which is impeded by the vastness of the sea that has not even been discovered in its totality. Significant work has been put into establishing a value on ecosystems and biodiversity.[22] 'The Economics of Ecosystems and Biodiversity', for instance, is a global initiative that has been established to assess the cost of loss of biodiversity and the associated decline in ecosystem services in order to inject the value of ecosystem services and biodiversity into global decision-making.[23] In the example provided, the economic value of fishing for specific species, on the one hand, has to be evaluated in light of the value to maintain their biodiversity on the other. This has to be established on a case-by-case basis.

Less Restrictive Alternatives and Engagement of Affected States

Competing norms must be interpreted and applied in a way that mutually provides the maximum scope of each norm. By implication, this means that the interpretation and application of one norm must interfere as little as possible with the other norm. If several measures are available to implement a norm, the measure that interferes the least with the scope of the other norm must be chosen and *vice versa*.[24] Correspondingly, in the *Chagos Marine Protected Area Arbitration,* the PCA did not exclude the possibility that environmental considerations could potentially justify an infringement of Mauritian fishing rights in the Territorial Sea of the UK due to the *unjustifiable interference* clause in Art. 194 (4) UNCLOS. 'Such justification, however, would require significant engagement with Mauritians to explain the

---

[21] https://www.biodiversitya-z.org/content/biodiversity-metric-marine.pdf, p. 1, f.

[22] Mossop (2017), pp. 190, 202.

[23] https://ec.europa.eu/environment/nature/biodiversity/economics/#:~:text=The%20Economics%20of%20Ecosystems%20and%20Biodiversity%20(TEEB)%20is%20a%20global,of%20ecosystem%20services%20and%20biodiversity; https://www.mckinsey.com/~/media/McKinsey/Business%20Functions/Sustainability/Our%20Insights/Valuing%20nature%20conservation/Valuing-nature-conservation.pdf.

[24] Mossop (2017), p. 202.

need for the measure and to explore less restrictive alternatives.'[25] Therefore, the unjustifiable interference clauses require both exploring less restrictive alternatives and the engagement of specially affected States.

Less Restrictive Alternatives: Low Impact Fishing Techniques

MPAs vary from slightly protected areas with some tourist regulation to fully protected areas, in which no human activity is allowed.[26] It needs to be established if a less restrictive alternative than an absolute ban of large-scale fishing is available that, at the same time, respects the obligation to protect and preserve the marine environment.

The impact of large-scale fishing techniques, such as bottom trawling, driftnet fishing, pelagic trawling and longlining, are not compatible with the obligation to adopt measures necessary to protect and preserve rare or fragile ecosystems as well as the habitat of depleted, threatened or endangered species and other forms of marine life.[27] The unsustainable number of fish caught in a short period of time leads to overexploitation and extinction of marine species; the limited means of targeting specific species in large-scale fishing leads to a large amount of bycatch, including threatened species and corals. The weight of the heavy bottom trawl gear erodes flora and fauna on the ocean floor and destroys reservoirs of CO2 that gets released into the atmosphere. Lost fishing gear makes up the main component of marine plastic debris. The obligation to adopt measures necessary to protect and preserve rare or fragile ecosystems as well as the habitat of depleted, threatened or endangered species and other forms of marine life requires a global ban of these fishing techniques in all zones of the sea.

A global ban of all fishing activities, however, would exclude the right under Art. 87 (1) (3rd sentence) (e) UNCLOS entirely. A less restrictive measure than banning all fishing techniques allows low-impact fishing techniques, such as rod and reel fishing. Specific techniques that are reconcilable with the obligation to adopt measures necessary to protect and preserve rare or fragile ecosystems as well as the habitat of depleted, threatened or endangered species and other forms of marine life need to be scientifically investigated. Indicators to provide information, such as on allowable catch limits, can be deduced from international regulations, such as Art. 61, 119 UNCLOS.

Engagement of Specifically Affected States

The restriction of fishing activities for the protection and preservation of rare and fragile ecosystems and the habitat of depleted, endangered and threatened species

[25] PCA, *Chagos Marine Protected Area Arbitration*, Mauritius v. UK (Award) 2015, pp. 211 f., para. 541; Mossop (2017), p. 191.

[26] See: Level of Protection and Categories.

[27] See: Less Restrictive Measure to Comply with the Obligation under Art. 192 UNCLOS.

requires the engagement of the States whose rights are infringed and the explanation of the measures. The customary obligation of States to cooperate *inter alia* in formulating rules and regulations for the protection and preservation of the marine environment is stipulated in Art. 197 UNCLOS and in specific regulations, such as for specific for the conservation of fish stock under Art. 87 (1) (3rd sentence) (e), 116 (b), 63 (2), 64 UNCLOS. The engagement of the local communities and States has led to the establishment of effective and efficient MPAs, which allow the compensation of the restriction of activities in the water through the establishment of new economic branches.[28] In the *Chagos Marine Protected Area* Arbitration, the lack of the engagement of Mauritius by the UK was not evident and the reason why the PCA concluded 'unanimously, that in establishing the MPA surrounding the Chagos Archipelago, the United Kingdom breached its obligations under Articles 2 (3), 56 (2) and 194(4) of the Convention.'[29]

Nature of the Rights

In consistent jurisprudence, the PCA sets out that 'the extent of the regard required by the Convention will depend upon the nature of the rights held by [one State], their importance, the extent of the anticipated impairment, the nature and importance of the activities contemplated by the [the other State] and the availability of alternative approaches.'[30]

On the one hand, the obligation to protect and preserve the marine environment is a *jus cogens* regulation and represents the most valuable rights of humankind. The obligation to adopt active measures to protect and preserve rare and fragile ecosystems and the habitat of depleted, endangered and threatened species is a specification of this obligation. It is, therefore, an expression of the fundamental value of humankind. Moreover, the regulation itself is a rule of customary international law that is universally accepted and, thus, has a broad binding scope. The nature of other rights in relation to this obligation needs to be assessed.

General Subordination of Other Rights Under Art. 194 (5) UNCLOS

The wording of *subject to*, *conditioned by* and *in accordance* with regulations infer a hierarchy of regulations, which generally subordinates these rights under other regulations of the UNCLOS and general international law, including Art. 194 (5) UNCLOS.[31] The freedoms of the High Sea, for instance, are *conditioned*

---

[28] See: Obligation to Cooperate – Engagement of the States Concerned.

[29] PCA, *Chagos Marine Protected Area Arbitration*, Mauritius v. UK (Award) 2015, p. 215, para. 547.

[30] PCA, *Chagos Marine Protected Area Arbitration*, Mauritius v. UK (Award) 2015, p. 202, para. 519; PCA, *South China Sea Arbitration*, Philippines v. China (Award), p. 293, para. 742.

[31] See: Subject To, Condition By and In Accordance With Regulation.

by other regulations of the UNCLOS under Art. 87 (1) (2nd sentence) UNCLOS, which generally subordinates the freedoms of the High Sea under the obligation of Art. 194 (5) UNCLOS. The obligation of the State to adopt measures necessary to protect and preserve rare or fragile ecosystems as well as the habitat of depleted, threatened or endangered species and other forms of marine life is thus generally elevated over the other State's freedom of the High Sea. This subordination, however, may not lead to an abuse of rights pursuant to Art. 300 UNCLOS, and balancing evaluations as required under *due regard* and *unjustifiable interference* regulations still need to be applied.[32]

Nature and Importance of the Rights Infringed

With specific regard to the nature of the right, it needs to be respected that the freedoms of the High Seas are universally accepted rules of public international law and therefore have the same status as Art. 194 (5) UNCLOS.

The freedoms of the High Sea belong to the most traditional rights in the law of the sea. The dispute of an open or closed High Sea has already been settled in the fifteenth century in favour of a free High Sea. The obligation to protect and preserve the marine environment, on the other hand, only arose in the twentieth century with the discovery and increasing knowledge of the nature of the ocean. While the bounty of the sea was thought to be inexhaustible and immune to any pollution for a long time, the harmful effects of human influences in the sea can now be seen and measured by new technologies. Today it is known that the ocean is vital for life on Earth and the protection and preservation of the marine environment arose to a fundamental value for humankind.[33]

The development of new technologies and knowledge advances the evolution of society. Industrialisation, for instance, has brought upon new possibilities and technical development that significantly influence the life of every individual with a boom in industry and economy. It reorganised and transformed an agrarian society into an industrial society.[34] Today, it is known that greenhouse gases and pollution of the atmosphere lead to global warming, requiring the restriction on CO2 emissions and the development of less emissive alternatives. Correspondingly, the invention of commercial fishing has brought about the possibility of catching a massive number of fish in a relatively short time. Today, the knowledge that fish stocks are not inexhaustible and that commercial fishing leads to the depletion and extinction of entire species requires the restriction of commercial fishing and the development of less harmful alternatives.

As the ICJ stated in the *Case concerning the Gabčíkovo-Nagymaros Project,*

---

[32] See: No Abuse of Rights under Art. 300 UNCLOS.

[33] https://oceanservice.noaa.gov/facts/why-care-about-ocean.html; https://www.un.org/depts/los/global_reporting/WOA_RPROC/Chapter_55.pdf; see: Fundamental Value, p. 100.

[34] https://cleartax.in/g/terms/industrialisation#:~:text=Industrialisation%20is%20the%20period%20of,grow%20on%20a%20significant%20scale.

> [t]he Court is mindful that, in the field of environmental protection, vigilance and prevention are required on account of the often irreversible character of damage to the environment and of the limitations inherent in the very mechanism of reparation of this type of damage. Throughout the ages, mankind has, for economic and other reasons, constantly interfered with nature. In the past, this was often done without consideration of the effects upon the environment. Owing to new scientific insights and to a growing awareness of the risks for mankind - for present and future generations - of pursuit of such interventions at an unconsidered and unabated pace, new norms and standards have been developed, set forth in a great number of instruments during the last two decades. Such new norms have to be taken into consideration, and such new standards given proper weight, not only when States contemplate new activities but also when continuing with activities begun in the past. This need to reconcile economic development with protection of the environment is aptly expressed in the concept of sustainable development.[35]

The limitation of sovereign rights, once before, has brought upon a fundamental shift for humankind, with the recognition of basic human rights. The paradigm shift was the transfer of the power of single States over individuals and national minorities to the State community as a whole. The restriction of State sovereignty and acceptance of the States' responsibility led to the recognition of basic values of Human Rights, which bind the international community as a whole. Likewise, the obligation to protect and preserve the marine environment is a fundamental value of humankind and brings upon the possibility of such change.[36] Because of its immeasurable value to the survival of species on planet Earth, the obligation to protect and preserve the marine environment has thus grown into a peremptory norm of international law, which is non-derogatory and which can only be modified by a subsequent norm having the same character. At the same time, the freedoms of the High Sea, such as fishing, are weakened by the growing awareness and evidence of the destructive influence of human activities on the marine environment and the environment of the whole planet. Commercial fishing techniques, such as bottom trawling, pelagic trawling, driftnet fishing or longlining, empty the ocean at an unmaintainable rate, yield a large number of bycatches and are thus irreconcilable with the sustainable use of the ocean. While the importance and value of the obligation to protect and preserve the marine environment thus constantly rises, the value of the free and unrestricted activities in the sea constantly decreases. This supremacy of the obligation to protect and preserve the marine environment over other activities in the sea is reflected in its cogent status, as opposed to the derivative freedoms of the High Sea.

Application of Art. 194 (5) UNCLOS to All States

The obligation under Art. 194 (5) UNCLOS, in conjunction with the obligation to protect and preserve the marine environment, also applies to the State that is exercising its freedoms of the High Sea. The States exercising activities in the sea,

---

[35] ICJ, *Case concerning the Gabčíkovo-Nagymaros Project*, Judgement (Merits), ICJ Reports 1997, pp. 7, 77 f, para. 140.

[36] Wolfrum (1990), p. 308.

thus, must adopt national laws and regulations and international treaties and ensure that their vessels protect and preserve the marine environment when engaging in fishing on the High Sea, which amplifies the superiority of Art. 194 (5) UNCLOS above Art. 87 UNCLOS. The State thus is not limited only by the rights of the other State to protect and preserve the marine environment; it is obliged to do so in exercising its freedoms itself.

Conditions by Specific Regulations of the UNCLOS

The UNCLOS stipulates special regulations that inform the content of the specific rights in the sea. Regulations include but are not limited to the following examples of fishing, pollution from vessels or the regulation of access to the EEZ.

Fishing in the High Sea According to Section 2 of Part VII UNCLOS

The freedom of fishing, for instance, is specifically subjected to the conditions of the special regulations under Art. 87 (1) (3rd sentence) (e) UNCLOS in conjunction with Art. 116 ff. UNCLOS. Pursuant to Art. 116 UNCLOS, the right of fishing of the States is subjected to their treaty obligations (Art. 116 (a) UNCLOS), the rights and duties as well as the interests of coastal States provided for, *inter alia*, in Art. 63 (2) UNCLOS and Art. 64 to 67 UNCLOS (Art. 116 (b) UNCLOS) and the provisions of Section 2, Part VII UNCLOS (Art. 116 (c) UNCLOS).

The treaty obligations of the States under Art. 116 (a) UNCLOS comprise all bilateral and multilateral treaties and the UNCLOS itself. The regulation of Art. 116 (a) UNCLOS clarifies that the adoption of treaties as envisaged in Art. 118 UNCLOS to regulate the freedom of fishing is valid and ensures that other agreements are not invalidated by the UNCLOS.[37] Significant treaties with regard to the regulation of fisheries are the 1993 FAO Compliance Agreement, which aims to enhance the role of the flag State and strengthens its control over vessels, or the 1995 UNFSA, which promotes the long-term conservation and sustainable use of straddling and highly migratory fish stocks on the High Seas.[38] The reference in Art. 116 (a) UNCLOS is not limited to fisheries conservation and management treaties but includes all treaties by the States.[39]

Art. 116 (b), 63 (2), 64–67, 117 and 118 UNCLOS specifically restate the obligation of States to adopt necessary measures and to cooperate to conserve and protect the respective fish stock of each provision. Regarding fish stock that occurs in the EEZ and the High Sea as well as highly migratory fish stock, the *due regard* rule of Art. 87 (2) UNCLOS, to take into account the interests of other States in their

[37] Proelss (2017), Art. 116, mn. 17.

[38] http://www.fao.org/iuu-fishing/international-framework/fao-compliance-agreement/en/; http://www.fao.org/fileadmin/userupload/legal/docs/012s-e.pdf; Proelss (2017), Art. 116, mn. 18.

[39] Proelss (2017), Art. 116, mn. 18.

exercise of the freedoms of the High Sea, is regulated even stricter in Art. 116 (b), 63 (2), 64 UNCLOS, which expressly require the relevant States to agree upon measures necessary to coordinate and conserve these stocks. Under Art. 116 (b), 65–67 UNCLOS, States shall expressly adopt measures to protect marine mammals, anadromous species and catadromous species, whereby Art. 65 (1st sentence) UNCLOS clarifies that nothing in Part VII UNCLOS restricts the right of a coastal State or the competence of an international organisation, as appropriate, to prohibit, limit or regulate the exploitation of marine mammals more strictly than provided for in Part VII UNCLOS. Under Art. 117 UNCLOS, furthermore, States have the duty to cooperate with other States in taking measures for their respective nationals as may be necessary for the conservation of the living resources of the High Sea. Under Art. 118 UNCLOS, States shall, furthermore, cooperate with each other in the conservation and management of living resources in the High Seas.[40]

Examples of measures that must be adopted when conducting High Sea fishing are listed in Art. 119 UNCLOS. Accordingly, States have to take measures which are designed, on the best scientific evidence available to the States concerned, to maintain or restore populations of harvested species at levels that can produce the maximum sustainable yield as qualified by relevant environmental and economic factors, including the special requirements of developing States, and taking into account fishing patterns, the interdependence of stocks and any generally recommended international minimum standards, whether subregional, regional or global (Art. 119 (1) (a) UNCLOS). Under Art. 119 (1) (b) UNCLOS States shall take into consideration the effects on species associated with or dependent upon harvested species with a view to maintaining or restoring populations of such associated or dependent species above levels at which their reproduction may become seriously threatened.

While regional fisheries management and conservation treaties lack in their global binding effect, the regulations on fishing in the UNCLOS are universally accepted. Oppositions against the general binding effect of the UNCLOS, such as from the USA or Turkey, are limited to the regulations on deep seabed mining and the Territorial Sea, respectively. The regulations on fishing, however, are universally accepted. Therefore Section 2 of Part VII UNCLOS may fully inform the content of the measures that have to be taken into account to protect and preserve rare or fragile ecosystems as well as the habitat of depleted, threatened or endangered species and other forms of marine life.

Concludingly, States are obliged to cooperate and adopt measures to protect living resources from the effects of fishing. In particular, States have to adopt measures based on the best scientific evidence available to maintain or restore populations of harvested species at levels that can produce the maximum sustainable yield, as qualified by relevant environmental and economic factors and taking into account fishing patterns, the interdependence of stocks and any generally recommended international minimum standards, whether subregional, regional or

[40] Freestone (2012), p. 200; Tanaka (2019), p. 288.

global. States are furthermore obliged to take into consideration the effects on species associated with or dependent upon harvested species with a view to maintaining or restoring populations of such associated or dependent species above levels at which their reproduction may become seriously threatened. Therefore, States are prohibited under the UNCLOS to fish stock at an unsustainable level, which means that level of fish stock cannot be maintained. This does not only follow from the general obligation to protect and preserve the marine environment as well as rare or fragile ecosystems and the habitat of depleted, threatened or endangered species and other forms of marine life but from the regulations of the freedom of fishing themselves. The freedom of fishing is universally binding and prohibits all States from engaging in fishing on an unsustainable level.

Pollution from Vessels

Specific interpretation guidelines for the obligation to protect and preserve the marine environment regarding pollution are stipulated in Section 2 of Part XII UNCLOS.

Art. 211 (5) UNCLOS, for instance, regulates the restriction of shipping in the EEZ. Under Art 211 (5) UNCLOS, coastal States may legislate to implement international rules and standards in the EEZ for the prevention, reduction and control of pollution from vessels, conforming to and giving effect to generally accepted international rules and standards established through the competent international organisation or general diplomatic conference. According to one view in the literature, this shows that coastal States do not have unfettered power to adopt any laws and regulations for the protection and preservation of the marine environment in their EEZ, but this right is restricted by Art. 211 (5) UNCLOS.[41]

Art. 211 UNCLOS confers the right of States to adopt even more stringent rules and regulations to prevent, reduce and control the pollution of the marine environment than the generally accepted international rules and standards to this end, as, i.e., stipulated under Art. 211 (2) (2nd sentence) UNCLOS. Accordingly, laws and regulations adopted by the States for the prevention, reduction and control of the pollution of the marine environment shall *at least* have the same effect as that of generally accepted international rules and standards. Art. 211 (5) UNCLOS codifies the obligation to adopt laws and regulations for the prevention, reduction and control of pollution from vessels conforming to and giving effect to generally accepted international rules and standards only for the purpose of enforcement. For prescriptive measures, however, Art. 211 UNCLOS obliges States to give effect to international standards in adopting rules and regulations in their own territories, which may be more stringent than international rules.[42]

[41] Rothwell and Stephens (2016), p. 356.

[42] UNGA A/58/65, p. 22, para. 61; Rothwell and Stephens (2016), p. 357.

Freedom in the EEZ and the Obligation to Protect and Preserve the Marine Environment

The freedoms of the High Sea apply to the EEZ under the conditions of Art. 58 (1), (2) UNCLOS. Pursuant to Art. 58 (3) UNCLOS, States shall have due regard to the rights and duties of the coastal State and shall comply with the laws and regulations adopted by the coastal State in accordance with the provisions of the UNCLOS and other rules of international law in so far as they are not incompatible with Part V UNCLOS. The coastal States have jurisdiction in the EEZ with regard to the protection preservation of the marine environment under Art. 56 (1) (b) (iii) UNCLOS.

In 2002, the oil tanker *MV Prestige* sank off the northern coast of Spain, spilling 50.000 tonnes of oil into the sea. In response to this, France, Portugal and Spain took unilateral measures to ban single-hull tankers that are 15 years or older carrying heavy fuel oils in their respective EEZs. In a report, the UN Secretary General pointed out that these measures do not conform to the freedom of navigation as granted under Art. 58 UNCLOS.[43] The report continues, however, by pointing out that Belgium, France, Ireland, Portugal, Spain and the UK are intending to designate a Western European particular sensitive sea area in this regard and that also the General Assembly of the UN in its resolution 57/141 expressed its concern as to the severe harm brought about by oil spills and calls upon all States to adopt necessary and appropriate measures to prevent catastrophes of this kind in the future.[44]

It is not clear from the report which part of the measures adopted by France, Portugal and Spain in response to the *MV Prestige* accident is considered to be inconsistent with Art. 58 UNCLOS by the Secretary General. As the Secretary General seems to accept the designation of an MPA through an international treaty to this end, it seems to reprimand the unilaterality of the measures or the missing harmonisation with the freedom of navigation by the ban of the respective tankers. In the light of the jurisdiction granted to the coastal State under Art. 56 (1) (b) (iii) UNCLOS, the first view does not seem convincing. Art. 56 (1) (b) (iii) UNCLOS specifically grants the coastal State jurisdiction with regard to the protection and preservation of the marine environment. As to the latter, Art. 56 (2) UNCLOS states that in exercising its rights and performing its duties under the UNCLOS in the EEZ, the coastal State shall have *due regard* to the rights and duties of other States and shall act in a manner compatible with the provisions of the UNCLOS. While a blatant ban of all foreign navigation in the EEZ would restrict the freedom of navigation in a way that it would render the freedom obsolete, the ban of tankers by Portugal, France and Spain did not apply indifferently to all tankers but was specified on single-hull tankers that are 15 years or older carrying heavy fuel oils. Considering the evidence of the hazardous harm from oil spills due to tanker accidents and the restriction only to specific tankers that pose an enhanced danger

---

[43] https://www.bbc.com/news/world-europe-24930976; UNGA, A/58/65, p. 21, para. 57; Rothwell and Stephens (2016), p. 356.

[44] UN A/58/65, p. 21, para. 57 ff.

to hazardous oil spills, the measures by Portugal, Spain and France do not interfere with the freedom of navigation.

Burden of Proof

There is no general definition or rule of conduct for *due regard* and *unjustifiable interference* rules.[45] The factors that need to be taken into account are therefore not limited to the evaluation of the extent of the interference, the availability of alternatives and the importance of the rights and policies at issue but comprise other factors too.

The wording of Art. 194 (4) UNCLOS indicates that interferences are *per se* permissible under the UNCLOS, as long as they are not unjustified.[46] This has consequences for the burden of proof. The burden of proof determines which party in a lawsuit needs to raise a claim or defence and to produce evidence to this end. The *actori incumbit onus probandi* rule is a general principle of international law and literally means 'he who asserts must proof'. Generally speaking, the burden of proof is on the party that asserts a claim, while the defence is on the respondent.[47] If a case has been brought to an international court or tribunal by means of a special agreement between States, there is no applicant and respondent. Nonetheless, it can still generally be said that the party who asserts facts in its favour bears the burden of proof.

The burden of proof can be a decisive factor in a lawsuit, although it has not been a major issue in international courts and tribunals rather than the merits of the case.[48] The wording of Art. 194 (4) UNCLOS establishes a *prima facie* presumption that the interference is justified as long as it is not unjustified. The party seeking to assert that the interference is not justified thus, bears the burden of proof. Accordingly, there is a *prima facie* presumption that measures taken to protect and preserve the marine environment under Part XII UNCLOS are justified even when they interfere with activities by other States. The party who wants to assert the contrary bears the burden of proof.

Conclusion: Unjustifiable Interference with Fishing

> Today the time-honoured concept of freedom of the sea is to be understood in the context of the present range of marine activities and in relation to all the potentially conflicting uses and

---

[45] Mossop (2017), p. 183.

[46] Proelss (2017), Art. 194, mn. 28.

[47] WTO Doc WT/DS246/AB/R, para. 88; WTO Doc WT/DS26/AB/R, WT/DS48/AB/R, para. 104; WTO Doc WT/DS46/ AB/R, 2, para. 139–141; WTO Doc WT/DS231/AB/R, 26, para. 275; Crawford (2012), p. 564.

[48] Foster (2010), p. 27; ICJ, *Corfu Channel Case*, Judgment, ICJ Reports 1949, pp. 4, 18.

interests, such as the protection of the marine environment and the sound exploitation of marine living resources.[49]

Concludingly, in the example of the ban of commercial fishing techniques by a coastal State on the Continental Shelf and EEZ, the investigation has shown that the coastal State has the competence to establish the relevant MPA on the Continental Shelf, the Territorial Sea and the EEZ under Art. 77, 2 (1), 56 (1) (b) (iii) UNCLOS. On the High Sea, the State community is obliged to adopt the relevant legislation to regulate fishing. To this end, the UNCLOS obliges the States to cooperate in formulating and elaborating international rules, standards and recommended practices and procedures consistent with the UNCLOS for the protection and preservation of the marine environment under Art. 197 UNCLOS and specific regulations such as Art. 116 (b), 63 (2), 64 UNCLOS.

Because the freedom of fishing is generally conditioned by the obligation to protect and preserve the marine environment and to adopt necessary measures to protect and preserve rare or fragile ecosystems as well as the habitat of depleted, threatened or endangered species and other forms of marine life, the hierarchy subordinates the freedom under this obligation. However, under Art. 300 UNCLOS, this subordination may not lead to an abuse of rights. The extent of the regulation on fishing needs to be equilibrated, taking into account economic and ecological factors. Art. 194 (5) UNCLOS does not require the ban of any activity in the sea; a harmonious interpretation requires that the regulation of the activity needs to be the least restrictive measure while still maintaining the objective of the protection and preservation of rare or fragile ecosystems as well as the habitat of depleted, threatened or endangered species and other forms of marine life. Because of the evidence of the extinction and depletion of fish stock due to commercial fishing techniques as well as the extent of uncontrollable bycatch that harms already threatened species, the least restrictive alternative is a ban of large-scale fishing that only allows low impact fishing techniques. Because of the scientific evidence of the vulnerability of the entire ocean, which is one ecosystem as a whole and full of marine life, this restriction applies to all zones of the sea.

Regarding the hierarchy of the regulations, it needs to be noted that, although not a *jus cogens* regulation, the freedom of fishing is universally accepted. However, rules and regulations must develop in accordance with society. While the necessity to protect and preserve the marine environment was largely unknown in the first half of the twentieth century, it developed into a fundamental value of humankind today. At the same time, rising evidence on the depletion and extinction of species and the pollution of the marine environment necessitate a stricter regulation of activities in the sea. The adoption of MPAs that exclude commercial fishing techniques, which evidently lead to the overexploitation of fish stock and produce a large amount of bycatch, including depleted, endangered and threatened species, therefore, does not unjustifiably interfere with the freedom of fishing in any zone of the sea. The State

---

[49] Scovazzi (2004), p. 1.

contesting the lawfulness of an MPA established under Art. 194 (5) UNCLOS bears the burden of proof that the interference with its fishing activities is unjustified.

This result is in harmony with the result of the interpretation of the obligation to protect and preserve the marine environment and the restriction of commercial fishing, which, likewise, concluded that commercial fishing techniques including but not limited to bottom trawling, drift net fishing, pelagic trawling and longlining, cannot be interpreted in a way that is harmonious with the cogent obligation to protect and preserve the marine environment and are therefore not lawful under the regulations of the UNCLOS.

7.2 International Legally Binding Instrument for Biodiversity Beyond National Jurisdiction

The objective of the BBNJ is the development of an international legally binding instrument under the UNCLOS on the conservation and sustainable use of marine biological diversity of areas beyond national jurisdiction. The BBNJ focuses on four areas: marine genetic resources, including the sharing of benefits, area-based management tools, including MPAs, environmental impact assessments and capacity-building and the transfer of marine technology.[50]

The adoption of an international treaty for the conservation and sustainable use of marine biological diversity in ABNJ poses the known obstacles of treaties:[51] the conclusion of an international, legally binding treaty requires the consent of the States. Non-State parties are not bound by its regulations (Art. 34 VCLT). The adoption of the UNCLOS, for instance, took three UNCLOS Conferences from 1958 until 1982, and it is still not signed and ratified by the whole State community.[52] A legally binding obligation to this end is, therefore, essential in adopting a global instrument for the protection of conservation and sustainable use of marine biodiversity in ABNJ.

Furthermore, the limitation of the freedoms of the sea through the establishment of MPAs interferes with the economic and political interests of States. The conclusion of a respective treaty ought to encounter severe opposition. The result of this study, the legally binding, *erga omnes* obligation of States to adopt international treaties to protect and preserve the marine environment, therefore, provides essential leverage for the adoption of the BBNJ.

---

[50] UNGA A/CONF.232/2020/3, p. 1, para. 2; Gjerde et al. (2019), p. 6; UNGA A/RES/72/249; https://www.un.org/depts/los/biodiversity/prepcom_files/Chairs_streamlined_non-paper_to_delegations.pdf; https://www.un.org/bbnj/content/background.

[51] See: Impediment for the Designation of MPAs – Zonal Division of the Sea; Impediment for the Establishment of MPAs – Limited Binding Effect of Treaties; Tiller et al. (2019), p. 240.

[52] See: Historical Development.

With regard to MPAs, the BBNJ shall include guiding principles and approaches on issues including but not limited to the process for the establishment of MPAs, identification of areas, the designation process and their implementation.[53] Although the BBNJ itself does not entail a legal obligation of States to establish MPAs in the ABNJ, it promotes the cooperation of States to this end. In conjunction with the obligation to protect and preserve the marine environment, the BBNJ provides valuable guiding principles that can be used to establish MPAs in ABNJ effectively.

References

Crawford JR (2012) Brownlie's principles of public international law, 8th edn. Oxford

Foster CE (2010) Burden of proof in international courts and tribunals. Aust Year Book Int Law (Aus. YBIL) 29:27–86

Freestone D (2012) International governance, responsibility and management of areas beyond national jurisdiction. Int J Mar Coast Law (IJMCL) 27(2):191–204

Gjerde KM, Clark NA, Harden-Davies HR (2019) Building a platform for the future - the relationship of the expected new agreement for marine biodiversity in areas beyond national jurisdiction and the UN Convention on the Law of the Sea. In: Chircop A, Coffen-Smout S, McConnel ML (eds) Ocean yearbook online (Ocean Y.B. Onl.), vol 33, issue 1, pp 1–44

Mossop J (2017) The continental shelf beyond 200 nautical miles: rights and responsibilities. Oxford

Nordquist MH, Nandan S, Rosenne S (2013) UN Convention on the Law of the Sea Commentary 1982 Online. Center for Oceans Law and Policy, Leiden

Oude Elferink AG (2018) Coastal states and MPAs in ABNJ: ensuring consistency with the LOSC. Int J Mar Coast Law (IJMCL) 33:437–466

Proelss A (2017) United Nations Convention on the Law of the Sea – a commentary. Munich

Rothwell DR, Stephens T (2016) The international law of the sea, 2nd edn. Oxford

Scovazzi T (2004) Marine protected areas on the high seas: some legal and policy considerations. Int J Mar Coast Law (IJMCL) 19(1):1–17

Tanaka Y (2019) The international law of the sea, 3rd edn. Cambridge

Tiller R, De Santo E, Mendenhall E, Nyman E (2019) The once and future treaty: towards a new regime for biodiversity in areas beyond national jurisdiction. Mar Policy - Int J Ocean Aff (Mar Policy) 99:239–242

Wolfrum R (1990) Purposes and principles of international environmental law. German Yearb Int Law (GYIL) 33:308–330

[53] https://www.un.org/Depts/los/biodiversity/prepcom_files/Chairs_streamlined_non-paper_to_delegations.pdf, pp. 20 ff.; UNGA A/CONF.232/2020/3, pp. 13 ff.

Chapter 8
Conclusion and Summary in Theses

8.1 Conclusion

8.1.1 Connection of Society and the Ocean

'I must go down to the seas again, to the lonely sea and the sky, And all I ask is a tall ship and a star to steer her by'[1] is the opening of John Masefield's poem 'Sea-Fever'. This reflects that for centuries, the ocean has played a fundamental role in the life and development of humankind, from the saturation of fundamental needs to the provision of the most intimate and intangible spiritual relationships: it is a source for livelihood for billions of people through trade, fisheries, shipping and tourism. It provides for life on Earth by supplying oxygen, minerals, energy and food. It impacts weather and freshwater through rain. Travel, sports, activities and discoveries around and in the sea serve the connection of individuals with nature and of groups, families and friends amongst each other. The ocean is the heritage of many cultures. It is the junction of the realm of Poseidon, Neptune and Varuna; it connects spirituality, inspiration, recreation and rejuvenation.[2] The reasons why people 'must down the seas again' are as manifold as individuals on Earth. The variety of anthropogenic threats to the sea is equally broad—as are rising attempts to protect the ocean. Activism and the provision of knowledge through science are crucial means to create understanding, mitigating the harmful influence of humans on the sea and enhancing compliance with protection regulations. However, experience has shown that the effectiveness of protection measures necessitates the codification of legally binding commitments.[3] The establishment of a legally binding obligation for the protection of the marine environment is the scaffold that provides the framework

[1] Untermeyer (1920), V. 1–2.

[2] https://www.un.org/depts/los/global_reporting/WOA_RegProcess.htm.

[3] https://www.cbd.int/doc/press/2017/pr-2017-06-05-mpa-pub-en.pdf.

A. von Rebay, *The Designation of Marine Protected Areas*,
https://doi.org/10.1007/978-3-031-29175-3_8

for the creation, implementation and enforcement of a sustainable human relationship with the sea through comprehensive and effective marine protection.

8.1.2 *Necessity of Law to Adapt to the Needs of Society*

Laws and regulations emerge as tools to manage the life of people amongst each other and as part of society. Change and evolution of society simultaneously require the adaptation of its laws and regulations. The law of the sea has developed over centuries. In the fifteenth century, the beginning of the Age of Discovery, the establishment of trade routes across the oceans made the distribution of jurisdictional rights the focal point of interest in the law of the sea.[4] In the twentieth century, hazardous influences of human activities in the sea sparked the awareness of the sensitivity and need for protection of the marine environment. However, when the UNCLOS was negotiated, the notion that the resources of the sea were inexhaustible was still widely accepted.[5] It was not yet known that humankind would create an epoch, which, due to the devastating influences of human activities on the planet, unprecedently would not be named after geological specifics of that time, but that puts the human in the centre of the geochronological timekeeping: the Anthropocene (Greek: 'anthropo' for man, and 'cene' for new).[6] In the 'New Era of Man', the influence of humans on the global biosphere and geosphere grew to such an extent that it altered the Earth's surface and geological compositions; 'humanity has become the dominant force of global environmental change.'[7] Thus, while 500 years ago, the expansion and maintenance of sovereign rights in the sea were the centre of politics and society, dire oil spills, scarcity of fish stock and maintaining Earth as an habitable planet has moved in the centre of concern in the twenty-first century. Activities such as deep seabed mining, carbon sinking and overexploitation of fish stock simply did not exist and did not have to be considered in times when Hugo Grotius pleaded for the free usage of the sea.[8] The central challenge of the Anthropocene era is to regulate human activities and to stop their destructive influence on the Earth's sphere.[9] But has the law adapted to this need?

The establishment of MPAs touches on one of the oldest conflicts of the law of the sea: *mare clausum* vs *mare liberum*. MPAs pose islands of protection in an otherwise free High Sea. Shortcomings in the progressive designation of MPAs are

---

[4] See Sect. 2.1.1.

[5] Harrison (2017), p. 1; Hafner (2006), p. 355, mn. 1.

[6] https://www.nationalgeographic.org/encyclopedia/anthropocene/.

[7] Stephens (2018), pp. 121 f.; https://www.britannica.com/science/Anthropocene-Epoch; Rothwell et al. (2015), p. 898; https://www.nationalgeographic.org/encyclopedia/anthropocene/.

[8] Scovazzi (2004), p. 6.

[9] https://www.sydney.edu.au/environment-institute/opinion/international-law-and-the-anthropocene/.

therefore still due to the spatial distribution of sovereign rights in the sea and the concept of the freedom of the High Sea; legal systems that were invented more than 400 years ago.[10] In the light of the concerns of the population of the twenty-first century, it is thus the governing principles of the law of the sea that must be shifted from an economic-centred to a conservation-centred approach: instead of allowing a free sea with some closed protection areas, the sea must be generally closed, with human activities permitted only within specifically designated areas. Instead of implementing no-take and no-trawl zones in an otherwise free sea, fishing, navigation, mining and any other activity must be generally prohibited, except for special areas in which activities are permitted.

Keeping in mind the difficulties of treaty negotiations on an international level and the UNCLOS in particular, changing the direction of the wheels of such old-established basic principles of international law like the freedom of the High Sea certainly is a paradigm shift. However, once before, the adaption and development of international protection standards have brought about a turning point in the history of modern international law: the introduction of Human Rights.[11] The fundamental shift was the transfer of the power of single States over individuals and national minorities to the State community as a whole. Today we have the opportunity to experience a similar turning point, says Rüdiger Wolfrum, former judge and president of the ITLOS. In order to protect the marine environment from the detrimental effects of activities in the sea, the sovereignty of individual States to manage their activities in the sea must be restricted and transferred to the international community as a whole.[12]

Instead of resigning to the idea that the destruction of the Earth's environment has passed a point of no return, knowledge of the devastative effects of human activities in the sea provides the 'Anthropos' of this era the tool to stop detrimental influences by shaping a multilateral treaty regime to effectively protect and preserve the marine and terrestrial environment.[13] Science has proven the destructive influences of human activities on the marine environment and the limits of the bounty of the marine resources, which are not immune to depletion by humans. Knowledge provides responsibility and the power to take appropriate measures to maintain a habitable planet; ignorance bears the risk of waking up as victims, literally gasping for air when the ocean, as the source of more than half of the world's oxygen, has been destroyed.[14]

If the law of the sea and international environmental law are to maintain their relevance, States must accept their responsibility by using the knowledge of Earth system science and respective governance literature to formulate a comprehensive

---

[10] See Sect. 2.2.1.4.

[11] Wolfrum (1990), p. 308.

[12] Wolfrum (1990), p. 308.

[13] Stephens (2018), p. 124.

[14] https://oceanservice.noaa.gov/facts/ocean-oxygen.html.

framework of environmental governance.[15] In the twenty-first century, States must accept their obligation to protect and preserve the marine environment by designating global MPAs. The *jus cogens* obligation of all States to establish MPAs in all zones of the sea is a starting point.

8.1.3 Necessity of the Individual to Adapt to the Needs of Planet Earth

The magnitude of the task to stop global warming and the overexploitation of the Earth's resources can lead to a sense of powerlessness on the part of the individual. However, it is a misconception to think that only global politics can bring about the necessary change, for irrespective of the assessment of the legal permissibility of activities in the sea, one fact has been proven by decades of market economy: the supply is determined by the demand. Unsustainable fishing techniques, pollution of the marine environment and exploitation of resources only occur because there is still enough demand for fish, oil and other resources. The only reason that led to the emergence of unsustainable fishing techniques was the demand and consumption of humans. In the end, the most important factor for safeguarding the environment is changing the habits of each individual, whereby 'changing' means *Change*. It means *changing* the habits; it means to compromise one's favourite food and finding more sustainable sources of nutrients than heavily overfished fish stocks. There is only as much supply as there is demand. Without the change by each individual, politics cannot save the environment. The most important factor in protecting the seas efficiently is every single individual and its demand for resources.[16]

8.2 Summary in Theses

This study has empirically proven that Art. 192 UNCLOS provides a cogent, legal obligation of the whole international community of States to adopt national and international legislation to designate MPAs in all zones of the sea, irrespective of sovereign rights. The following 15 points corroborate this result:

1. Definition

   MPAs are geographically defined marine areas (geographical element), designated by legislation (legislative element) for a protection or conservation objective (protective element).

[15] Stephens (2018), p. 121.

[16] See the section 'Global Ban Necessary for Enforcement' in Chap. 6.

2. *Erga Omnes* Effect

   The universal conduct and discourse of States, including UNCLOS non-member States, prove that the obligation under Art. 192 UNCLOS has emerged into a customary international law with *erga omnes* effect. It protects a universally accepted fundamental value of humankind from which no derogation is permitted and which may only be modified by subsequent norms of international law having the same character. It is *jus cogens*.
3. Legal Standing

   Procedurally, any State is entitled to invoke a violation of the obligation to protect and preserve the marine environment by another State, even if the State has not suffered individual harm.
4. Legislative Element

   States have a prerogative in assessing if and how to implement their obligation to protect and preserve the marine environment in international law (Art. 2 Nr. 1 UN-Charter). States have derogated their freedom to consent or to oppose the obligation to protect and preserve the marine environment by subjecting themselves to this cogent obligation. They no longer have a prerogative if they adopt active measures to this end; they are obliged to do so. The only active measure suitable to protect and preserve the marine environment is the adoption of national laws and regulations and international treaties (legislation).
5. Geographical Element

   Legislative measures for the protection of the marine environment are MPAs if they apply to geographically defined marine areas. The jurisdiction in the law of the sea to adopt legislative measures is primarily divided spatially according to ocean areas (*ratione loci*) with only single jurisdictional rights concerning specific matters (*ratione materiea*). Legal measures of States to protect and preserve the marine environment that apply spatially to a specific marine area meet the definition of MPAs.
6. Marine Environment

   The marine environment comprises the seabed, water column and airspace above. Scientific research has shown that marine life and biodiversity in the ocean is abundant further than the eye can see. The long-prevailing notion that there is no life in the deeper regions of the sea has been proven incorrect. The marine environment in deeper parts of the ocean is now known to be rich in biodiversity and endemic species. The entire ocean is one ecosystem as a whole.
7. Competencies

   The obligation to protect and preserve the marine environment applies to all areas of the sea, irrespective of sovereignty or sovereign and jurisdictional zones. States are obliged to adopt national laws and regulations and international treaties for the designation of MPAs.
8. Security Council

   The Security Council is authorised to adopt legally binding decisions for the protection and preservation of the marine environment. The recognition of the interconnectedness of human wellbeing and the wellbeing of the environment is increasing. The evolution of a Human Right to Environment is procured through the developments in national and international jurisprudence and diplomacy and through the evolution of this obligation into a *jus cogens* obligation, which limits the sovereign right of States to dispose of this obligation freely.

9. Specific Content

   The specific content of the obligation to protect and preserve the marine environment under Art. 192 UNCLOS is specified in and limited by other regulations of the UNCLOS and rules of international law. The elements of the legal obligation must be substantiated by experts on a case-by-case basis. Many of the regulations for the protection and preservation of the marine environment in specific terrains are based on expert reports and scientific opinions. They help to interpret and inform the content of the obligation in each case. The wider an international rule is accepted in the State community, the stronger its binding effect to determine the specific content of the obligation to protect and preserve the marine environment.

10. Obligation to Protect and Preserve the Marine Environment Prevails

   The investigation of potentially colliding freedoms of the sea proved that they must be interpreted harmoniously with the cogent obligation to protect and preserve the marine environment, bearing in mind the necessity not to undermine the freedoms in spite of the cogent obligation of Art. 192 UNCLOS (Art. 300 UNCLOS). The cogent obligation to protect and preserve the marine environment applies to all States in exercising their activities in all zones of the sea; 'in exercising their activities' States must take active measures to protect and preserve the marine environment (Art. 193 UNCLOS). The wording of the *subject to*, in *accordance with* and *conditioned by* regulations stipulate a hierarchy by which the obligation to protect and preserve the marine environment is elevated above those regulations; the cogent obligation generally prevails over other derivative regulations of the UNCLOS.

   There is no other cogent regulation that modifies the obligation to protect and preserve the marine environment. Art. 89 UNCLOS prohibits the exercise of territorial sovereignty; the designation of MPAs constitutes the exercise of single sovereign rights. The regulations do not interfere.

11. Application to Large-Scale Fishing Techniques

   The application of the results and harmonious interpretation with large-scale fishing activities reveals that techniques such as bottom trawling, pelagic trawling, driftnet fishing and longlining are not compatible with the obligation to protect and preserve the marine environment and are unlawful. A less restrictive measure than an absolute ban of fishing is the permission of low impact fishing techniques. The main impediments to switching from large-scale to low impact fishing techniques are due to technical and financial means as well as a lack of knowledge. The obligation to protect and preserve the marine environment is an obligation of conduct, which poses a due diligence obligation on the States. It requires States to mitigate obstacles for sustainable fishing. This includes the provision of technical and financial means as well as the education of the community and affected industry in less harmful fishing techniques.

12. Application to Deep Sea Mining

    A harmonious interpretation of the regulations on deep seabed mining and the obligation to protect and preserve the marine environment reveals that the normative content of the UNCLOS stipulates a sequence by which the exploration of the terrain must be finalised before its exploitation may commence. This sequence of exploring before exploiting must be respected in light of the application by Nauru to the ISA to commence deep seabed mining.

13. Obligation to Cooperate—Engagement of Affected States

    The obligation of States to adopt legislation for the protection and preservation of the marine environment is reiterated in the general principle of Art. 197 UNCLOS and special regulations of the UNCLOS that oblige States to cooperate in formulating and elaborating international rules, standards and recommended practices and procedures for the protection and preservation of the marine environment. The engagement of affected States and communities is not only a requirement to justify interferences but also a decisive element in designating long lasting, sustainable marine protection regulations.

14. Art. 194 (5), (4) UNCLOS

    In conjunction with the obligation to protect and preserve the marine environment, Art. 194 (5) UNCLOS poses an *erga omnes* obligation to establish MPAs to protect and preserve rare or fragile ecosystems as well as the habitat of depleted, threatened or endangered species and other forms of marine life. The unjustifiable interference clause in Art. 194 (4) UNCLOS reflects a general principle of international law and applies to Art. 194 (5) UNCLOS.[17] There is no general definition or rule of conduct for the due regard and unjustifiable interference rules; each case has to be dealt with individually. *Due regard* rules and *unjustifiable interference* are functionally equivalent and require that competing rights have to be balanced by evaluating the nature and importance of the rights and policies held by both States, the extent of interference and anticipated impairment, the availability of alternatives and the consultation of the States that's rights are at stake. The wording of Art. 194 (4) UNCLOS indicates that interferences are *per se* permissible under the UNCLOS, as long as they are not unjustified. This wording establishes a *prima facie* presumption that an interference with activities in the sea is justified as long as it is not unjustified. The party seeking to assert that it is not justified, thus, bears the burden of proof to refute the *prima facie* presumption that interferences of measures taken to protect and preserve the marine environment under Part XII UNCLOS with other activities are justified.

15. Biodiversity Beyond National Jurisdiction

    The BBNJ is one of the most widely discussed instruments in the contemporary law of the sea. It is touted as a potential milestone to promote ocean governance and effective measures for marine protection in ABNJ—yet its adoption will face considerable obstacles due to the consent principle and the

[17] See Sect. 7.1.2.1.

interests of the States at stake. The recognition of the legally binding obligation of all States to adopt international treaties for the protection and preservation of the marine environment, therefore, significantly enhances the successful adoption of the BBNJ.

References

Hafner G (2006) Schutz der Meeresumwelt. In: Vitzthum W (ed) Handbuch des Seerechts. C.H. Beck, Munich, pp 355–421

Harrison J (2017) Saving the oceans through law – the international legal framework for the protection of the marine environment. Oxford University Press, Oxford

Rothwell DR, Oude Elferink AG, Scott KN, Stephens T (2015) Charting the future for the law of the sea. In: Rothwell D, Oude Elferink AG, Scott KN, Stephens T (eds) The Oxford handbook of the law of the sea. Oxford University Press, Oxford, pp 888–912

Scovazzi T (2004) Marine protected areas on the high seas: some legal and policy considerations. Int J Mar Coast Law 19(1):1–17

Stephens T (2018) What is the point of international environmental law scholarship in the Anthropocene? In: Pedersen OW (ed) Perspectives on environmental law scholarship – essays on purpose, shape and direction. Cambridge University Press, Cambridge, pp 121–139

Untermeyer L (1920) Modern British Poetry, 98. John Masefield – Sea Fever, V. 1–2

Wolfrum R (1990) Purposes and principles of international environmental law. Ger Yearb Int Law 33:308–330